Washington's Heir

Washington's Heir

The Life of Justice Bushrod Washington

GERARD N. MAGLIOCCA

OXFORD
UNIVERSITY PRESS

OXFORD
UNIVERSITY PRESS

Oxford University Press is a department of the University of Oxford. It furthers the University's objective of excellence in research, scholarship, and education by publishing worldwide. Oxford is a registered trade mark of Oxford University Press in the UK and certain other countries.

Published in the United States of America by Oxford University Press
198 Madison Avenue, New York, NY 10016, United States of America.

Library of Congress Control Number: 2021919428

ISBN 978–0–19–094704–0

DOI: 10.1093/oso/9780190947040.001.0001

Pod

For Carlo Andreani, from his nephew

I am conscious of the purity of my motives, and I trust that those at least who know me, will in this respect do me justice.

—Bushrod Washington, 1821

Contents

Acknowledgments		ix
	Introduction: The Keeper of the Flame	1
1.	Privilege and Courage	3
2.	An Apprentice and a Slave	9
3.	A Young Gentleman of Talents	19
4.	A Lawyer's Lawyer	28
5.	An Imperfect War	37
6.	The Marshall Court Begins	52
7.	Master of Mount Vernon	66
8.	Riding Circuit	78
9.	The Supreme Court's Balance Wheel	96
10.	Southern Gentlemen Understand	118
11.	*Corfield v. Coryell*	130
12.	A Long Judicial Life	143
	Epilogue: Half-Blind Justice	157
Notes		161
Bibliography		259
Index		275

Acknowledgments

After finishing my book on John Bingham, the lead drafter of Section One of the Fourteenth Amendment to the Constitution, I was certain that I would never write another biography. But one night I was in a hotel unable to sleep and suddenly thought: "What about Bushrod Washington?" I do not know where this question came from, but I knew at once that I wanted to give an answer. Two happy results of that decision were the opportunity to spend time at Mount Vernon and be a Fellow at the Fred W. Smith National Library for the Study of George Washington, where every day is December 1799 and America's future is bright. Even during the pandemic, the dedicated professionals there continued to respond to my requests and to correct my errors. Kevin Butterfield, Mark Santangelo, Samantha Snyder, Mary Thompson, Jason Boroughs, and Dawn Bonner were especially helpful, and I am delighted that this book will contribute to our understanding of Mount Vernon and the Washington family.

Let me next thank David McBride, Emily Benitez, Jubilee James and everyone else at Oxford University Press who worked on the book for their support. Even with that support, my research would have failed without the generosity of the other libraries and archives that hold Justice Washington's papers. So I want to salute the librarians at the American Bible Society, American Philosophical Society, Chicago History Museum, Cincinnati History Library and Archives, Connecticut Historical Society, Duke University, Harvard Law School, Huntington Library, Indiana University Ruth M. Lilly Library, J. P. Morgan Library, Library of Congress, Library of Virginia, Massachusetts Historical Society, Morristown National Historical Park, New-York Historical Society, New York Public Library, University of Michigan William L. Clements Library, and University of Virginia who helped me access those materials. Jennifer Stetzer at the Papers of Bushrod Washington project provided invaluable assistance by giving me early access to this important work in progress. Other special shout-outs go to David Haugaard of the Historical Society of Pennsylvania, who spent countless hours searching that collection for Washington items, and Lee Little, who obtained vital microfilm reels for me through Indiana University. I also could not have completed the book without the *Notre Dame Law Review*, which published my article "Rediscovering *Corfield v. Coryell*" in 2019 and graciously gave me permission to use that article in a chapter of this book.

When I was first thinking about how to write this book, Bill Nelson was particularly helpful by inviting me to present my rough ideas at his Legal History

Colloquium at NYU Law School. Then he invited me back again after I finished my draft, which was icing on the cake. My colleague Liz Monroe in the IUPUI History Department, who knows more about the legal elite of nineteenth-century Virginia than almost anyone, was a wonderful guide early on. And I got valuable feedback during the drafting process from a workshop at the University of Wisconsin Law School organized by my friend Anuj Desai. Once the draft was complete, I received many thoughtful comments from Bruce Ackerman, Carlo Andreani, Scott Casper, Nicholas Georgakopoulos, Brian Kalt, Carlton Larson, David Lynch, Richard Primus, Florence Roisman, Kim Roosevelt, Rena Seidler, Tom Shakow, David O. Stewart, Mary Thompson, and Tom Wilson. The willingness of others to take time from their busy lives to read an entire unfinished draft never ceases to amaze.

As always, my final thanks go to my colleagues at the Indiana University Robert H. McKinney School of Law, who have provided a wonderful professional home for two decades, and to my wife, Preeti, and our daughter, Avika, who bring joy and perspective when I need them most. I am a lucky man.

Introduction

The Keeper of the Flame

In March 1821, a United States Supreme Court justice gathered his slaves and told them that they would never be free.[1] This declaration came from no ordinary justice at no ordinary place. The justice was Bushrod Washington, George Washington's nephew and Chief Justice John Marshall's right-hand man on the Supreme Court.[2] The place was Mount Vernon, which Bushrod had inherited after Martha Washington died. George Washington's will, which made the justice his principal heir, provided that all the former president's enslaved people would be free upon Martha's death.[3] Bushrod Washington honored that pledge but restored slavery to Mount Vernon by bringing his own slaves there. One of those enslaved people was West Ford, who was probably Bushrod's half-brother or nephew and was the only slave that the justice ever freed. When a journalist criticized Bushrod for his moral wrong of owning and selling people, he issued a public defense that laid bare the contradictions that would split the Union.[4] Yet when the Civil War was over and Congress sought to make Blacks equal citizens through a civil rights law and a constitutional amendment, many Republicans relied on one of Washington's judicial opinions as the best explanation of the liberties that all citizens should enjoy, including the right to vote.[5]

Bushrod Washington was George Washington's literal and figurative heir. While he inherited his family's legacy as enslavers, he also carried forward his uncle's ideals as a soldier during the Revolution, a delegate to Virginia's convention that ratified the Constitution, and a Supreme Court justice for over thirty years.[6] In each of those roles, he worked to strengthen the national government and the rule of law. He was widely viewed as a model judge who mastered the art of instructing juries, wrote opinions that fleshed out the Constitution's meaning, laid the foundation for many legal concepts now taken for granted, and built up the fragile authority of the federal courts. Bushrod also brought George's balanced temperament to the Supreme Court. The Founders agreed that George Washington was not the most brilliant among them, but that he possessed an uncanny ability to make the right decision. His unerring judgment came, Thomas Jefferson said, from never acting "until every circumstance, every consideration, was maturely weighed; refraining if he saw a doubt but, when once decided, going through with his purpose."[7] Bushrod Washington was described in almost the

Washington's Heir. Gerard N. Magliocca, Oxford University Press. © Oxford University Press 2022.
DOI: 10.1093/oso/9780190947040.003.0001

same terms by his colleagues, and their trust in his wisdom stabilized the Court in challenging times. Despite Justice Washington's contributions to the law, his relationships with George Washington and John Marshall, and his fascinating life at Mount Vernon, there has been no published biography of him until now.[8]

Bushrod Washington is overlooked because he stood in the shadows of two great men, but also because on the Supreme Court he did his best work in the shadows. Like many leaders who come to power after a revolution, the justice was an institutionalist. He wanted to enhance the legitimacy of the Supreme Court as the third coequal branch of government. Much of the time, the best way of accomplishing that goal was by saying nothing in public and letting Chief Justice Marshall speak for the Court. Justice Washington was well suited for that role because he bore America's most famous name and lived in the country's most famous house; he did not crave attention. But behind the scenes, Bushrod was so influential that one of the justices told Jefferson that Washington and Marshall "are commonly estimated as one Judge."[9] While much of their partnership is shrouded in mystery, a careful review of Washington's and Marshall's letters and other untapped sources reveals how these lifelong friends collaborated to enhance the Court's prestige. Other documents, such as one of Justice Washington's secret journals, disclose how he approached difficult cases and sometimes changed his mind as he weighed competing arguments. My conclusion from this research is that the Marshall Court was more of a team effort than the product of Chief Justice Marshall's individual genius, although some members of the team (most notably Justice Washington and Justice Joseph Story) did more than others.

George Washington left his nephew many gifts and many unanswered questions. Some were personal. What should be done with the former president's papers? How should Mount Vernon be run once the estate became a shrine to America's greatest hero? Others were philosophical. What is the appropriate balance between federal and state power under the Constitution? What are the limits of party partisanship? When should courts exercise judicial review in a republic? And how could the founding creed that "all men are created equal" be reconciled with slavery? Bushrod Washington spent much of his life grappling with these fundamental questions that flowed from the American Revolution. We still do.

1
Privilege and Courage

George Washington explained in his will that he made Bushrod his heir "partly in consideration of an intimation to his deceased father while we were Bachelors."[1] John Augustine "Jack" Washington was the caretaker of "my Estate during my Military Services in the former War between Great Britain and France" and was promised that if George died "Mount Vernon (then less extensive in domain than at present), should become his property."[2] Late in life, George described Jack as his "much loved Brother who was the intimate companion of my youth and the most affectionate friend of my ripened age."[3] Jack was born in 1736 at what later became Mount Vernon, though in a cottage far more modest than the now-iconic mansion. When Jack was two and George was six, the Washington family moved to a home along the Rappahannock River near Fredericksburg, Virginia, named Ferry Farm. The family patriarch, Augustine Washington, owned about fifty enslaved people and 10,000 acres when he died in 1743. But some of Augustine's property, including the Mount Vernon land, went to his sons by his first marriage, which left Jack, George, and their siblings without the money for a formal education. After Augustine's death, Jack was raised at Ferry Farm by his mother, Mary Ball Washington, who until recently was described by family biographies as a strict and sour person.[4]

When George joined the colonial militia and was sent off to the frontier, he started corresponding with Jack and using him as his eyes and ears back home. Their first surviving letter from May 1754 described a skirmish between Washington's troops and a French squadron that precipitated the French and Indian War.[5] In that letter, George bragged to Jack: "I can with truth assure you, I heard Bullets whistle and believe me there was something charming in the sound."[6] After Lieutenant Colonel Washington returned home on leave a year later, he agreed to rent Mount Vernon's 2,216 acres and eighteen enslaved people from his half-brother Lawrence's widow, Anne.[7] (George inherited Mount Vernon after Anne's death.) With another tour of duty about to begin, George needed someone trustworthy to run the plantation in his absence. He asked Jack. Mary was dismayed by this request and traveled to Mount Vernon to demand that George abandon his military career so that she would not lose Jack's help at Ferry Farm. She did not win that argument, and Jack took charge of Mount Vernon, though he continued to oversee Ferry Farm to smooth over any ruffled feelings. Once George was back at the front, he also asked Jack to run personal

Washington's Heir. Gerard N. Magliocca, Oxford University Press. © Oxford University Press 2022.
DOI: 10.1093/oso/9780190947040.003.0002

errands such as sending along a new pair of boots and delivering a letter to a female friend.[8] A more sensitive request involved sounding out the leading men of Fairfax County (where Mount Vernon was located) about a campaign for a seat in the House of Burgesses, Virginia's colonial legislature. Jack was told to gather their views "with[ou]t disclosing much of mine; as I know your own good sense can furnish you with means enough without letting it proceed immediately from me."[9] If they seemed enthusiastic, "you then may declare my intentions and beg their assistance. If, on the contrary, you find them more inclined to favour some other, I w[oul]d have the affair entirely subside."[10] Four decades later, George's reliance on Jack's discretion for delicate tasks would be repeated with Jack's eldest son.

In 1756, Jack Washington married Hannah Bushrod, whose maiden name would give Bushrod his unusual first name.[11] Hannah was from one of Virginia's elite families, and her father, John, was a longtime member of the House of Burgesses. The family seat was Bushfield, a tobacco and hemp plantation of 1,200 acres on Nomini Creek, which feeds into the Potomac about ninety-five miles downstream from Mount Vernon. How Jack and Hannah met is unclear, although John Bushrod and Jack's half-brother, Augustine Washington Jr., did serve together in the House of Burgesses representing Westmoreland County.[12] Hannah was eighteen when the couple wed and moved to Mount Vernon. Over the next year or two, they lived there while Jack supervised the estate during the first expansion of the mansion and the gardens. When George returned home following his resignation from the military and married Martha Custis, Jack and Hannah moved to Bushfield.[13] Hannah inherited the estate and its thirty-five enslaved people when her father died in 1760.[14] A visitor in 1774 described Bushfield as presenting "the most agreeable Situation, of any I have yet seen in Maryland or Virginia."[15] The Potomac "washes [its] Garden on the North, the River Nomini is within a stone's throw on the West, [there is] a level open Country on the East; a lane of a mile and three quarters accurately measured lies from the House South-East . . . [and] has from the House the whole distance a uniform Descent." Bushfield was destroyed during the War of 1812 and there is no clear description of the home's interior.[16]

Bushrod Washington was born at Bushfield on June 5, 1762. His personal slave as an adult, Oliver Smith, was born there two years earlier and was owned by Jack.[17] While Bushrod and Oliver were just boys, the first protests heralding the American Revolution reached Virginia. Following Parliament's passage of the Stamp Act in 1765, Jack and twenty-four other prominent white men in Westmoreland County signed the Leedstown Resolves, which said that they were "roused by danger and alarmed by attempts, foreign and domestic, to reduce the people of this country to a state of abject and detestable slavery by destroying that free and happy condition of government under which they have hitherto lived."[18] In protesting these taxes, they said: "We know it to be the Birthright privilege of every British subject (and of the people of Virginia as being such), founded on Reason, Law, and Compact; that he cannot be legally tried, but by his peers; and that he cannot be taxed, but by consent of a Parliament, in which he is represented by persons chosen by the people, and who themselves pay a part of the tax they impose on others."[19] "If therefore," the Resolves went on, "any person or persons shall attempt by any action or proceeding, to deprive this Colony of those fundamental rights, we will immediately regard him or them, as the most dangerous enemy of the community; and we will go to any extremity, not only to prevent the success of such attempts, but to stigmatize and punish the accuser." The Stamp Act was soon repealed, but the rift between Britain and her colonies would not be healed.

Bushrod's youth is largely a mystery. He was one of five children, but was destined to outlive his siblings by decades and care for many of their children.[20] There were no schools of note near Bushfield, and thus he was taught at home or at neighboring homes by private tutors.[21] When he was sixteen, he moved to Fredericksburg to study at a school run by John Lowe, a Scottish immigrant, "and finished my greek, latin & Mathematical Studies."[22] One letter to his mother makes clear that Jack and Hannah Washington believed that all their children, including their daughters, should receive the best possible education.[23] But their view that girls should learn about matters outside the home was uncommon, which meant that there were, in Bushrod's opinion, "few proper tutors to be found in Virginia—what a pity! Good Heavens! What an idea must those have of your sex, who think that nature formed you to move in a sphere subservient to Man, or in any respect inferior."

While Bushrod was immersed in the classics, the conflict between Britain and the colonies became violent. When Parliament closed Boston Harbor in response to the Tea Party, Jack became the chairman of a local relief committee that sent grain to Boston, and George was elected to the First Continental Congress. A few days after shots were fired at Lexington and Concord, Jack was at Mount Vernon visiting his brother.[24] Jack promptly joined Westmoreland County's Committee for Safety, which served as the local de facto government as royal power ebbed. In June 1775, George wrote Jack to say "adieu . . . I have been called upon by the unanimous Voice of the Colonies to take Command of the Continental Army."[25] Concerned about how his prolonged absence would affect Martha, he hoped that Jack and Hannah "will find as much leisure this Summer as to spend a little time at Mount Vernon." General Washington proceeded to write Jack from the outskirts of Boston describing the siege of the city until the British withdrew in March 1776.[26] Meanwhile, Jack was selected as a member of the Fifth Virginia Convention along with Founding Fathers such as George Mason, James Madison, and Patrick Henry.[27] This illegal assembly, which met in May and June

1776, ratified the Virginia Declaration of Rights, wrote a new state constitution, and instructed its delegates to the Second Continental Congress to declare independence.[28] Over the next few trying years, George kept Jack up to date on his military operations and sometimes vented his frustrations to his brother.[29]

As a teenager, Bushrod appeared more concerned about rumors of his social life than about the Revolution. In his first surviving letter, written in March 1778 from his school in Fredericksburg, he told his mother: "The uneasiness I have suffered since the reception of yours can scarcely be express[ed] . . . I cannot conjecture by what means you could possibly be informed of a report which never had any other foundation than the busy tongues of those who seem to wish for strife."[30] Her letter is lost, but she was asking about his possible relationship with a young woman. Bushrod replied: "It has always been my choice since I came to town rather to expend any small portion of an Evening I had to spare from my stud[ies] amongst the Ladies . . . and I will be bold and say that I pas[sed] my time with more innocence and heartfelt satisfaction in that way than many of my acquaintances in pursuit of their wild inclinations." "The Lady you refer to was often present," and "was often my partner at several Balls and other amusement[s]." But "when I was every day under your immediate inspection you never denied me the like amusements." Bushrod asked Hannah to "inform Papa (if the report has come his Ears) that I have wrote and shall be miserable 'till I hear from you again that I may know you are satisfied."

In 1780, Bushrod moved to Williamsburg to study law at William and Mary, the second-oldest college in the colonies. A year earlier, Governor Thomas Jefferson had named his mentor, George Wythe, as a professor of law there.[31] Wythe was the first law professor in the United States and was well suited for this unique position. One of Virginia's leading lawyers, Wythe signed the Declaration of Independence, served in the Fifth Virginia Convention with Jack Washington, was a state court judge, and taught many of the nation's early leaders.[32] The heart of Wythe's course was a series of lectures, modeled on William Blackstone's *Commentaries on the Law of England*, that attempted to identify general principles from decided cases.[33] Wythe introduced the idea that students should participate in mock appellate arguments, now known as "moot courts," once or twice every month. One of Bushrod's classmates explained this oral exercise: "Mr. Wythe and the other professors sit as Judges. Our Audience consists of the most respectable of the Citizens, before whom we plead Causes given out by Mr. Wythe. Lawyerlike, I assure you."[34] Wythe insisted that his students also participate in mock legislatures, held every Saturday in the old state capitol building, so that they could get practical experience by debating bills from the real legislature. And he tried to broaden their minds by assigning them political philosophy and classical poetry from Horace and Virgil.

Figure 1.1 George Wythe, one of the Founding Fathers and Bushrod's law professor at William and Mary. Drawing by James Barton Longacre. National Portrait Gallery

When Bushrod looked around the room at the forty or so men who were listening to Professor Wythe's lectures every Tuesday and Thursday, he may have wondered but could not have known how some of them would shape his future. In one chair sat a lanky veteran fresh from a long tour of duty in the Continental Army, John Marshall.[35] Marshall attended William and Mary for less than three months before moving to Richmond to start his legal practice, but he and Washington did became acquainted and took part in debates held by Phi Beta Kappa.[36] In another chair sat Spencer Roane, who would become one of the Marshall Court's sharpest critics as a judge on the Virginia Court of Appeals.[37] Bushrod gave Hannah an upbeat report in July 1780: "As to my situation here it is, I confess, as agreeable as I could wish, having my choice in the society of Gentlemen whose characters are good and examples edifying, Here, then, when free from scholastic employment, we either entertain ourselves with innocent diversions or recapitulate what we have read through the day and delivered without reserve those observations we have made on different objects."[38] He also took the opportunity to study French and attend philosophy lectures by Bishop James Madison, the cousin of the future president.[39]

The World Turned Upside Down

Then war came to Virginia. In December 1780, Benedict Arnold made the most of his treason by invading the state with 1,700 British troops.[40] Arnold sacked Richmond, the state capital, and forced Governor Jefferson to flee.[41] William and Mary shut down, with Phi Beta Kappa noting at its final meeting "the Confusion of the times, and the present Dissolution which threatens the University."[42] In April 1781, veterans led by Lord Charles Cornwallis entered the state after some victories in Georgia and North Carolina.[43] George Washington put the Marquis de Lafayette in charge of defending Virginia, but Lafayette was outnumbered.[44] When the call went out for more volunteers, Bushrod enlisted in a cavalry brigade outfitted by Colonel John Mercer.[45] Though Bushrod said virtually nothing about his military service, he did receive a letter from one comrade reminiscing on their life "under the command of Colonel Mercer" and observing that they were now "the only survivors of that gallant band of youths."[46] Bushrod was more modest, recalling that he "did nothing worthy of Notice" during the campaign.[47]

Colonel Mercer's cavalry received their baptism under fire on July 6, 1781, at the Battle of Green Spring.[48] The British left Williamsburg on the Fourth of July and moved along the James River with Lafayette in pursuit. Cornwallis pretended to put his army across the James on the sixth, but he actually sent only a token force with orders to light many campfires to give the appearance that a large battalion was there. He was hoping to goad the Americans into an attack, and they fell into the trap.[49] Lafayette's troops were cornered at Green Spring Farm, a village bordered by marshes and by the James. Only a brave stand, including a bayonet charge by infantry from Pennsylvania, prevented a catastrophe, although more than a hundred Americans were killed. Bushrod's fellow soldier recalled in his 1825 letter "you nearby me or near me when my horse fell at the battle of Greenspring."[50] Washington told a similar story, stating that in "the action at Greenspring we lost some of our horses & amongst them Colo. Mercers was shot under him, in a successful attempt to dislodge some of the enemy who in the Commencement of the action had taken possession of a small house in front."[51]

After the Battle of Green Spring, Bushrod went back to Bushfield. He explained that he left Mercer's cavalry because "my father's anxiety about my education induced him to recall me home." Thus, he did not participate in the Yorktown battle or in Cornwallis's defeat in October 1781.[52] But independence was on the horizon.

2

An Apprentice and a Slave

After the triumph at Yorktown, George Washington took a more active interest in his nephew's education. A traditional path for an aspiring lawyer during this era was to serve as an apprentice to an attorney. In March 1782, the General wrote James Wilson, one of the leading lawyers in Philadelphia and a signer of the Declaration of Independence.[1] He said that Bushrod, "a nephew of mine—is sent at his own desire to this City to study the Law—His Father having requested me to get him properly fixed, it would give me much pleasure to see him placed under your care, if it is convenient to you to take another student." "The young Gentleman, I am told," he added, "has had a good Classical education, but the Invasions of Virginia under the direction of . . . Arnold & Cornwallis were very injurious to the schools of that Country—obliging the youth of it to resort to Arms in the place of prosecuting their studies—this was the case of my nephew whose study of other branches of Literature was much interrupted by the movements of the enemy." Wilson demanded a princely sum—one hundred guineas—to serve as Bushrod's teacher, but George agreed: "Permit me to recommend my Nephew to you—not only as a student requiring your instruction—but to your attentions as a friend. His youth and inexperience may require it, and I persuade myself his sensibility & gratitude will make you every return which may be in his power."[2] Bushrod would spend the next two years in Philadelphia and begin his lifelong love affair with the city.

Why did George Washington take Bushrod under his wing? They hardly knew each other. George did visit Bushfield a few times when Bushrod was a child, and Jack brought Bushrod to Mount Vernon before the Revolution, but that was the extent of their relationship.[3] The answer is probably that George was doing Jack a favor. Jack was still George's go-to person for touchy personal problems. For instance, when their mother, Mary, discovered that the overseer at Ferry Farm was embezzling funds, George informed Jack and said, "I must therefore desire the favor of you to take it under your care—I know of none in whose hands it can be better placed."[4] He also complained to Jack in the same letter regarding Mary's concerns about money: "The reason of my mentioning these matters to you is, that you may enquire into her real wants and see what is necessary to make her comfortable. . . . At the same time I wish you to represent to her in delicate terms

Washington's Heir. Gerard N. Magliocca, Oxford University Press. © Oxford University Press 2022.
DOI: 10.1093/oso/9780190947040.003.0003

the impropriety of her complaints. . . . It will not do to touch upon this subject in a letter to her—and therefore I have avoided it."

Thankless as these tasks were, George may have expressed his gratitude by placing Bushrod with James Wilson and by paying Wilson's apprenticeship fee at a time when Jack could not afford a hundred guineas.[5] As Jack explained to Bushrod shortly after his arrival in Philadelphia, his uncle's generosity was "the means of lessening your immediate expenses to me at a time . . . that I must labour under some degree of distress," probably due to the damage that the British invasion inflicted on Virginia's economy.[6] At one point in Philadelphia, Bushrod was short of cash and wrote a friend asking for a $35 loan.[7] He explained that he had moved from rented accommodations, but the "brutish people whose house I have left mean to detain the articles I have there until payment is made, and I have reason from their threats last night to apprehend the worst which my situation and this advantage it has given them over me can warrant. . . . I had no way left me to appease them for a moment but by promising to pay them today, even if I should be obliged to sell my clothes for that purpose." In a postscript that reflects his lack of sophistication in handling money, Bushrod said: "I forgot to mention that I should be obliged to ask [for] about 6 dollars more . . . for I have not a single shilling at present."

The emergency loan probably came through, but some whisper of Bushrod's troubles may have reached General Washington. In January 1783, George wrote his nephew and began by saying: "You will be surprised perhaps at receiving a letter from me—but if the end is answered for which it is written, I shall not think my time misspent. Your Father, who seems to entertain a very favorable opinion of your prudence, and I hope, you merit it; in one or two letters of his letters to me, speaks of the difficulty he is under to make you remittances. Whether this arises from the scantiness of his funds, or the extensiveness of your demands is a matter of conjecture, with me—I hope it is not the latter," he said. "Yet when I take the view of the inexperience of youth, the temptation and vices of Cities; and the distresses to which our Virginia Gentlemen are driven by an accumulation of Taxes and the want of a market, I am almost inclined to ascribe it in part to both. Therefore, as a friend, I give you the following advice."[8] This sounds like a tactful way of saying that George knew or strongly suspected that Bushrod was mismanaging his funds, though the fact that this letter followed Bushrod's request for a loan might be a coincidence.

The advice that followed is revealing about George's views. "Let the object, which carried you to Philadelphia be always before your Eyes," he explained, for "remember, that it is not the mere study of the Law, but to become eminent

Figure 2.1 George Washington. Painting by Adolf Ulrik Wertmuller. Mount Vernon Ladies' Association.

in the profession of it which is to yield honor and profit." "It is easy to make acquaintances," he said, "but very difficult to shake them off, however irksome and unprofitable they are found after we have once committed ourselves to them—the indiscretions and scrapes which very often they involuntarily lead one onto, proves equally distressing and disgraceful. Be courteous to all, but intimate with few, and let those few be well tried before you give them your confidence." "Do not conceive that fine Clothes make fine Men, any more than fine feathers make fine Birds," he added. But "the last thing I shall mention is first of importance, and that is to avoid Gaming—This is a vice which is productive of every possible evil. . . . It is the child of Avarice—the brother of inequity—and father of Mischief—It has been the ruin of many worthy families—the loss of many a man's honor—and the cause of Suicide." A day after writing this letter, George told Jack: "I have heard a favorable account of Bushrod and doubt not this prudence will direct him to a proper line of Conduct. I have given him my sentiments of this head; and persuade myself that, with the advice of Mr. Wilson, to whose friendship as well as instruction in his profession I recommend him . . . he will stand as good a chance of most youth of his age to avoid the Vices of large Cities, which have their advantages and disadvantages in fitting a man for the great theater of public life."[9]

The High Life in Philadelphia

With his uncle's backing, Bushrod moved freely in the leading legal and social circles of the nation's capital. His new teacher, James Wilson, is perhaps the most underrated Founding Father.[10] Born in Scotland, he moved to Pennsylvania in the mid-1760s and shot to fame after publishing a pamphlet in 1774 arguing that Parliament lacked the authority to regulate the colonies.[11] Service in the Continental Congress followed, but Wilson's bravest act was to defend Americans accused of treason by Pennsylvania during the Revolution. Anger over that representation became so intense that an armed mob attacked Wilson's house and drove him into hiding.[12] At the Constitutional Convention and at Pennsylvania's ratifying convention for the Constitution, Wilson proved one of the most influential delegates in articulating the need for a strong federal government.[13] President Washington then named Wilson to the Supreme Court in 1789. When Wilson died in 1798, his successor was his former student Bushrod Washington.[14]

Neither Wilson's nor Bushrod's papers shed any light on what he did as an apprentice. No standard method existed for mentoring lawyers during this era—each attorney decided for himself. One account gave Wilson a dismal review on how he interacted with his trainees: "Mr. Wilson devoted little of his time to his students in his office. . . . [H]is intercourse with them was rare, distant, and reserved. As an instructor he was almost useless to those who were under his direction. He would never engage with them in professional discussions; to a direct question he gave the shortest possible answer and a general request for information was always evaded."[15] At one point, Jack suggested to Bushrod that he move back to Virginia and serve as an apprentice to George Wythe because Wilson was a member of Congress and thus "you must in all probability study by yourself."[16] Washington's political and judicial philosophy later in life was similar to Wilson's, but there is no evidence to suggest that this can be attributed to the apprenticeship.

Bushrod never criticized Wilson but also never said anything positive about him. Decades later, Wilson's son wrote the justice asking for his opinion about an allegation that Wilson had been part of a cabal in Congress that sought to replace

George Washington as the leader of the Continental Army.[17] Bushrod replied that "neither from the papers of General Washington, nor from any conversation with him during his life, had I cause to suspect that he considered your father as having been unfriendly to him at any period."[18] The justice then wrote: "When my father sent me to Philadelphia in the winter of [17]81–2 with a view to the study of the law, the General happened to be in this city, and kindly undertook to superintend the necessary arrangements for my establishment. Although your father required from his students a much higher fee than was usually paid to the other gentlemen of the law, the General unhesitatingly overruled the intention I expressed to him of entering some other office on account of that difference, by arguments strongly indicating the high opinion he entertained of your father." Notably absent was any statement by Bushrod that he entertained a high opinion of Wilson.

The most important relationship that Bushrod formed in Philadelphia was with Elizabeth "Eliza" Willing Powel. She was the mayor's daughter and married Samuel Powel, who himself became the mayor.[19] Her brilliance and dazzling charm won the respect of George Washington. One of his biographers described their friendship as "his only deep, direct one with a woman who qualified as an intellectual peer and treated him as such."[20] When he was mulling retirement after his first term as president, Eliza wrote him a letter making a convincing case against stepping down.[21] During the Constitutional Convention, the delegates socialized at the Powels' home, an elegant three-story mansion on Third Street that stands today.[22] After George introduced his nephew to the Powels, Bushrod became a frequent houseguest.[23] The Powels had no surviving children of their own and took a special interest in Bushrod.[24] He reveled in their company and once referred to them in a letter to his mother as his "Guardian Angels."[25] That same letter described Eliza Powel this way: "From a natural refinement of Genius, cultivated by education, tempered by prudence and polished by the best company, you may now form an idea of a character which—[w]hen I have added to the sweetest disposition needs nothing more to render it complete." "Do not Imagine," he went on, "that I have drawn a partial portrait of this Lady; she is what I have said of her, I only wish I may have done her Justice." Eliza, in turn, adored Bushrod, writing Hannah that "any Instances of Mention, or Affection, that he may receive from us are more than compensated by his Company and Manner of Receiving them."[26]

To celebrate his twenty-first birthday, Bushrod sat for a portrait by Henry Benbridge, a favorite of Benjamin Franklin who was suggested by Samuel Powel.[27] The portrait makes plain a fact that disappointed people throughout Bushrod's life: he did not look like his uncle. A visitor to Mount Vernon

Figure 2.2 Bushrod Washington. Painting by Henry Benbridge. Oil on canvas. Mount Vernon Ladies' Association.

during the 1820s said that the justice's "features possess but little expression, and his, as unlike the late General, as any man in the United States."[28] George Washington was over six feet tall, was one of the most talented horsemen of the age, and had an oversized head made for marble busts.[29] Bushrod, by contrast, was a short, cerebral man with delicate features and is depicted in the painting with a book. Bushrod wrote Hannah to say that she would soon receive the portrait and that "I shall be anxious to hear your opinion."[30] He was worried that Benbridge portrayed him in "a thoughtful posture which in my opinion rather borders on austerity than intense meditation."[31] But, he added, Eliza and Samuel had reassured him "that the countenance is not an ill-natured one, nor entirely thoughtful, but rather a mixture of thought with pensiveness, and that they have sometimes seen me in that situation." Eliza joked that Bushrod had "a very good opinion of Yourself and vainly suppose yourself a perfect Adonis," and he recalled that "I could not help blushing . . . [but] soon recovered and we had a hearty laugh at my expense."[32]

Figure 2.3 Elizabeth Willing Powel, Bushrod's "guardian angel" in Philadelphia and an influential political voice. Painting attributed to Matthew Pratt. Philadelphia Academy of Arts.

The affection, albeit platonic, between Bushrod and Eliza Powel would endure for their entire lives. Shortly after he moved back to Virginia, she sent a delightful letter chastising him for not writing to her. Referring to herself in the third person, Eliza said: "She is unwilling to ascribe the Neglects of her Friends to any Cause derogatory of them, but so every Effect must have its Cause, she thinks it possible that the severity of the last Winter may have operated so violently on his Herculean Hands, as to have numbed his Fingers, she has therefore taken the Liberty to send him, with ye Compliments of the Season, a pair of furred gloves."[33] Bushrod could be equally playful with her. Her niece recalled that when Washington was in Philadelphia holding trials and hearing appeals (which he did almost every year between 1803 and 1829), he regularly dined on Sundays with Eliza, who was by then a widow and lived on Chestnut Street.[34] "I was always taken there to dine on Sunday too as a child," her niece said. "Thus, I remember my father delighted to tease my Aunt by saying . . . [that her portrait] of

General Washington was badly painted, when she invariably appealed to Judge Washington who always sustained her . . . [by saying it] was an admirable likeness." In her will, Eliza left Bushrod "twenty Guineas to purchase a piece of plate as an evidence of my friendship and respect for his Virtues."[35]

Another female friendship was with Anne Nancy Shippen, the married daughter of a leading Philadelphia doctor. Her journal described Bushrod as having a "handsome face, with sparkling black eyes, and good complexion—a small person—his Manners particularly agreeable and engaging—Strong sense and an improved understanding for he spends most of his time in study. His conversation is interesting and agreeable, and he never fails to please, and makes his friends all those who have the happiness of knowing him."[36] Anne's social life with Bushrod revolved around teas, formal dances (the minuet was all the rage), chess, and singalongs with friends.[37] Her marriage was unhappy and she may have developed feelings for Bushrod, as she confided in her diary that she "cried like a Child" when he moved back to Virginia.[38] Whether Bushrod felt as deeply about their separation is unclear, but in a final letter to Anne he practically sighed at the prospect of giving up his carefree life as an apprentice: "I have often wished that Philadelphia had fewer charms for me, or that Fortune had fixed me there for Life."[39]

A family tragedy in February 1784 hastened Bushrod's departure. Word arrived that his teenage brother Augustine was dead, killed in a gun accident at boarding school.[40] Jack wrote George that Augustine's sudden death "affected me a good deal, as I had entertained very high expectations from him. He had nearly finished his Education, was bless[ed] with abilities, to qualify him for any of the Learned Professions—and possessed as sweet a disposition as ever a Youth did, I intended this fall or at the farthest next spring to have sent him to Edinburgh to study."[41] He added: "I wish to God Mrs. Washington could have borne this loss as well as myself, but the shock was too great for her. . . . I thought that the most likely way to quiet her mind was to get her Children about her." Jack told George that he had asked Bushrod to travel as soon as possible to Baltimore, where a fresh horse would be waiting for him to ride to Bushfield. Anne Shippen wrote that "Mr. Washington is much afflicted at the loss of his favorite brother, who was killed in a very sad accident, a school fellow of his was playing with a loaded gun, and by accident shot [him] through the body."[42] Though Bushrod was probably near the end of his studies in any event, he hurried back to comfort his grieving parents and did not return to Philadelphia until he was a Supreme Court justice.[43]

Bushrod was promptly admitted to the Virginia bar, but before he even started practicing law his uncle wrote Jack with a special request. Back at Mount Vernon after the Treaty of Paris formally recognized American independence, George wanted to tour his frontier landholdings.[44] "If Bushrod's health will permit, and it does not interfere with his studies, or plan of Settlement for the practice of Law," George told Jack, "I would take him with me with pleasure. . . . He would require only a Servant and a Blanket or two—everything else I shall provide unless he should choose to carry a Gun for his amusement as we would more than probably—see [an] abundance of Game."[45] Jack replied that he thought this was a wonderful idea, as "he I hope will never be more at leisure than at present, that he is waiting for the arrival of his Law Library, nor can he ever see that Country under greater advantages than by accompanying . . . you."[46] In a follow-up letter, Jack added: "I want much to establish some lands there if it can be done to advantage by exchanging Negroes for Land—I have desired Bushrod to make the fullest inquiries as to the Soil, produce, Climate &c. &c. of the different parts of the western Country together with their advantages and disadvantages respecting the future prospects of trade, & also the likeliest way to obtain lands upon a certainty as to title."[47] That autumn, Bushrod traveled for over a month with his uncle, a family friend, and three enslaved people in a taxing expedition across the Appalachians that covered approximately 680 miles.[48] This was the longest and most intimate time that George and Bushrod Washington would ever spend together.

West Ford Washington

Sometime between March 1783 and November 1785, a slave named West Ford was born at Bushfield.[49] During that period, Jack Washington owned about 130 enslaved people.[50] When Hannah died in 1801, she referred in her will to "a lad called West, son of Venus, who was born before my husband's will was made and not therein mentioned[;] I offered to buy him of my dear sons Bushrod and Corbin Washington, but they generously refused to sell him but presented the boy to me as a gift. [I]t is my earnest wish and desire [that] this lad West may be as soon as possible inoculated for the small pox, after which to be bound to a good tradesman until the age of twenty-one years, after which he is to be free the rest of his life."[51] West Ford was the only enslaved person freed in Hannah or Jack's will. He was also the only one given as a gift to anyone by her surviving sons. Ford lived at Mount Vernon after gaining his freedom and worked there as a master carpenter when Bushrod owned the plantation.[52] An alleged pencil sketch of Ford when he was in his twenties shows that he resembled Bushrod.[53] And when Bushrod died in 1829, he gave Ford 160 acres next to Mount Vernon.[54] Ford was the only Black person who was a beneficiary of Bushrod's will. All this evidence leads Washington family and Mount Vernon scholars to the conclusion that West Ford was, in fact, a Washington.[55]

West Ford was a remarkable man and is a name to remember. Self-taught, he was entrusted by Bushrod and his family to manage Mount Vernon and was described by Bushrod's nephew as "my venerable lieutenant."[56] With the proceeds from selling the land that the justice gave him in his will, Ford founded the free Black community of Gum Springs, Virginia.[57] When he brought two of his children to Alexandria in 1831 for their official registration as free Blacks, the clerk described Ford as "a yellow man about forty seven years of age, five feet

Figure 2.4 Bushrod Washington and West Ford. Purported pencil sketch of Ford by unknown artist. Mount Vernon Ladies' Association.

eight and a half inches[,] high pleasant countenance, wrinkle resembling a scar on the left cheek, a scar on the left corner of the upper lip."[58] In 1858, a journalist for *Harper's New Monthly Magazine* interviewed Ford at Mount Vernon and described him as "an old mulatto" (in other words, someone of mixed race) and as "a very intelligent man."[59] By this time, Ford was the second-richest free Black person in Fairfax County, though of course he was not equal with whites under the law.[60] An oral tradition among West Ford's descendants said that George Washington was his father.[61] But there is no evidence for this claim. By contrast, Ford was given special treatment by Hannah and Bushrod and did look like the men in that branch of the Washington family. Thus, the more logical view is that one of the four Washington men at Bushfield was Ford's father.

Which one of these four—Augustine, Corbin, Jack, or Bushrod—was the most likely man? Alas, there is no way to know. Information about Augustine is scanty, other than the fact that he died in 1784 and thus could have fathered a child during the time range for West Ford's birth. Not that much more is known about Bushrod's younger brother Corbin, who predeceased Hannah.[62] Jack Washington is obviously a possibility given that he was the master of Bushfield. Could Bushrod have been West Ford's father? It's not impossible.[63] Even if he was not, though, he surely knew that Ford was his blood relative. This knowledge made his tolerance of slavery even more horrible, as he saw nearly every day that he lived at Mount Vernon with West Ford how fine the line was between freedom and bondage.

3
A Young Gentleman of Talents

In 1785, Bushrod began his personal and professional life in earnest. He turned down an invitation from his old commander, the Marquis de Lafayette, to visit France.[1] Instead, the new lawyer found work where he could, sometimes on behalf of his uncle.[2] He became involved in Virginia politics, culminating in his election to the state ratifying convention for the Constitution. He drew closer to George, especially after Jack Washington's death in 1787. Most important of all, he married Julia Ann "Nancy" Blackburn, who would be his partner until they died within a few days of each other in 1829.[3]

Nancy Blackburn

Writing to Hannah in 1783, Bushrod described his ideal wife. "When I marry," he explained, "I shall look for one whose disposition can please, and whose conversation can improve me—neither would I be blind to domestic accomplishments. . . . If possible I am a greater Enthusiast than ever for music and think that it is one of the most necessary amongst fine accomplishments."[4] He may have had Eliza Powel in mind when he wrote this from Philadelphia. But after returning to Virginia, Bushrod was introduced to Julia Blackburn, who lived at Rippon Lodge, a plantation in Prince William County between Mount Vernon and Bushfield.[5] She was the daughter of Colonel Thomas Blackburn, who had served in the House of Burgesses and in the Continental Army under General Washington, where he was badly wounded at the Battle of Germantown.[6] Nancy, as her husband called her, was sixteen when she married Bushrod, and by all accounts she was a vivacious woman who was well-read, played the piano, and loved music.[7] Her passion for music and literature lasted for life, as Bushrod's will referred to her "organ and pianos, and books of music and her Library of books kept separate from mine."[8] George and Martha could not attend the wedding on October 13, 1785, but they invited the newlyweds to visit.[9] Six days later, Nancy and Bushrod arrived at Mount Vernon with Hannah, Jack, Colonel Blackburn, and other family members in tow.[10]

A veil of privacy hangs over the marriage of Nancy and Bushrod. Almost none of their correspondence to each other survives.[11] This was consistent with the practice in the Washington family, as Martha destroyed virtually all the letters

Washington's Heir. Gerard N. Magliocca, Oxford University Press. © Oxford University Press 2022.
DOI: 10.1093/oso/9780190947040.003.0004

Figure 3.1 Julia Ann "Nancy" Blackburn Washington. Painting by an unknown artist. On loan from Peter H. Brady. Collection of the Supreme Court of the United States.

between herself and George after his death and hardly any letters remain between Jack and Hannah.[12] The only candid account of Bushrod and Nancy's early relationship comes from a letter that Bushrod sent from Philadelphia to a male friend not long after the wedding.[13] "I am married," Bushrod explained, "and in one of my letters, I informed you of it, in the language of a new made Husband. All that I can add at this time is that I feel an increasing admiration for the state and am more than ever convinced that Nature has rendered this connection of the sexes so necessary to our existence that it becomes a point of Duty, as well as a matter of solid happiness." He then gave a description familiar to anyone who remembers the excitement of new love: "I am scarcely yet entitled to the appellation of husband as the ardor of a lover has not left me: but I have hopes of keeping the two forever united, nor can I conceive of any reason why they should be separated, where love was the principal motive for the union. Having said this, I suppose it will be unnecessary to add that I have not yet been *surfeited* [in other words, sexually satiated]. I take it," he added, "that this must be a very humiliating situation for a man to be in, and therefore my maxim is, *Moderation* and *Uniformity*." Despite their passion, Bushrod and Nancy had no children. Like George and Martha, who also had no children together, Bushrod and Nancy raised many of their orphaned relatives as their own.[14]

Sadly, Nancy suffered from chronic ill health for most of her married life.[15] Martin Van Buren, the future president, said in his memoir that he visited Mount Vernon at Christmas in the early 1820s and that by then Nancy "had been a long time bed-ridden."[16] Another visitor in 1818 called her a "rather queer" person.[17] While Nancy usually came to Philadelphia when Bushrod held circuit court there, a lawyer who often appeared before that court said that the justice adjourned for the day precisely at three o'clock.[18] When asked why, Bushrod said that the sound of the clock chiming three "is as distinctly heard by Mrs. Washington at our lodgings, as it is heard by us in the courtroom; and if I am not in her parlor within five minutes afterwards, she imagines that some evil has happened to me, and her nerves are disordered for the rest of the day. Their condition is at all times bad, but then it becomes much worse. In general, I give the whole of the evening to reading aloud to her such books as will amuse and interest her, until drowsiness comes on. I look at neither book nor paper in the cause until the next morning, and then, by early hours, I endeavor to redeem the time."[19] Nancy's condition is unclear. Medical science was, of course, far more limited then for diagnosing, let alone treating, an illness. One account called Nancy "valetudinary," which meant frail but could also refer to a hypochondriac.[20] Bushrod's account of Nancy's nerves being in disarray, however, suggests that she had something like acute anxiety.

What is strange is that John Marshall's wife, Polly Ambler, suffered from a similar set of symptoms. The Marshalls did have children, but they also lost four babies.[21] Perhaps as a result, Polly was afflicted with severe anxiety and depression.[22] She spent most of her days in bed and rarely left their home in Richmond.[23] Marshall told his brother in 1816: "My wife continues in wretched health. Her nervous system is so affected that she cannot sit in a room while a person walks across the floor."[24] Indeed, the chief justice of the United States was sometimes forced to chase away noisy animals in the street that disturbed Polly's sleep or reassure her that nobody was hiding under their bed.[25] The fact that their wives struggled with mental health issues may have deepened the bond between Washington and Marshall, as few men then could relate to the emotional toll of being a caretaker for an invalid wife.

A link between Nancy Washington and Polly Marshall is harder to establish. Their common ailment could be a coincidence. On the other hand, their depression could have been a consequence of the limited opportunities for bright women in this era. Eliza Powel was in this respect the exception rather than the rule, and even she could voice her political opinions only in private. Bright women might have felt their disadvantages all the more as their husbands soared into the highest offices of state. Still, Nancy gave Bushrod essential love and support throughout his life, and he did the same for her. When Van Buren made his Christmas visit to Mount Vernon, he observed that the singing of her nephews brought her out of bed "to the head of the staircase and it was delightful to see how much this circumstance excited the Judge's sensibilities and added to the general hilarity."[26]

The Road to the Constitution

Like many young lawyers then and now, Bushrod also got involved in local politics. The mid-1780s were a time of great dissatisfaction with government. The Articles of Confederation—America's first constitution—worked poorly.[27] The national government was very weak, with no executive branch, no courts, and no power to tax. The states erected trade barriers against one another and did not, in the view of many, respect property rights or contracts. In a letter to a friend in 1786, Bushrod said: "We are all . . . politicians in Virginia—Men, women, and children have learned to discuss some particular subjects of State importance—Paper Money—British Debts and the increase of congressional power are the principal topics."[28] Paper money that was not adequately backed by gold or silver created inflation that helped debtors, but Bushrod was more inclined to support creditors, even if they were British. The Treaty of Paris provided that debts owed by Americans to British lenders should be paid, but Bushrod said: "I am afraid that little is to be hoped either from the honesty or wisdom of our assembly in fulfilling this part of a sacred treaty. . . . [T]hey say that Great Britain has first broken the treaty by carrying off our slaves and further that if we give up this advantage, we shall have lost every opportunity of either compelling Great Britain to deliver the western forts [as promised in the treaty] or to recompense ourselves if they refuse." Finally, he opined that "there cannot be a more important object than giving more power to Congress," which would be the main issue that would drive the delegates to the Philadelphia Convention in 1787.

In September 1786, Bushrod wrote his uncle to let him know what he was doing to change elite opinion in Virginia. "We have lately instituted a society in these lower counties, called the *Patriotic Society*," he said.[29] "As it is something new, and there are a few men both good and sensible who disapprove of it, it will be of high gratification to me to know your sentiments of it, if you will be so kind to communicate them," he went on. "The object of the institution is to inquire into the state of public affairs; to consider in what the true happiness of the people consists . . . to inquire into the conduct of those, who represent us, and to give them our sentiments upon those laws, which ought to be or are already made." Moreover, "if any real good should result from such a society, we hope similar ones will be generally instituted through the State; and, if so, they may establish a very formidable check upon evil-disposed men, who clothed with power, make interested motives, and not public good, the rule of their conduct."

Three days later, George Washington wrote back skeptically. "Generally speaking," he said, "I have seen as much evil as good result from such societies as you describe the constitution of yours to be . . . and as often clog, as facilitate public measures."[30] "To me, it appears a much wiser and more politic conduct, to choose able and honest representatives and leave them in all national questions to determine from the evidence of reason, and the facts which shall be adduced, when internal and external information is given to them in a collective state." After all: "What certainty is there that societies in a corner, or remote part of a state, can possess all that knowledge which is necessary for them to decide on many important questions which may come before an Assembly? What reason is there to expect that the Society itself may be accordant in opinion on such subjects? May not a few members of this society (more sagacious and designing than the rest) direct the measures of it to private views of their own? May not this embarrass an honest, able delegate who hears the voice of his country from all quarters and thwart public measures?"

A month passed before Bushrod replied with a spirited defense. "In a government where the voice and sentiments of the people are delivered by representation," he began, "the few who are elected to speak these sentiments are the servants of the electors. . . . [I]n grand points of national concern, the people are the best judges of their wants, their own interests, and can more sensibly feel those evils, which they wish to be corrected. . . . [S]ilence at a time when they had reason to apprehend a conduct in these servants contrary to their wishes would be highly criminal."[31] "I am fully convinced that nothing could be more effective of the prosperity of this country, than the method you have pointed out of electing able representatives. To recommend this to the attention of the people," Bushrod continued, "is a principal object with this Society." "Thus you will perceive," he ended, "that this institution assumes no other power, than that of recommending to the people an attention to their own interests, and of furnishing them with the sentiments and opinions of a few, which they may either reject or adopt."

George's final reply shifted the conversation from political philosophy to the practical issue of constitutional reform. He wrote that it "was not the intention of my former letter either to condemn, or give my voice in favor of the Patriotic Society of which you are a member."[32] "I offered observations, under the information you gave of it, the weight of which were to be considered. As first thoughts they were undigested and might be very erroneous." Then he asked his nephew a pointed question: "Among the great objects which you took into consideration at your meeting in Richmond, how came it to pass that you never turned your eyes towards the inefficiency of the Federal government, so as to instruct your Delegates to accede to the propositions of the Commissioners lately convened at Annapolis—or to devise some other mode to give it that energy which is necessary to support a national character?"[33] "Every man who considers the present Constitution of it, and sees to what it is verging," he said, "trembles and deprecates the event. The fabric which took nine years (at the expense of much blood and treasure) to enact, now totters to the foundation, and without support must fall soon."

This exchange of letters was telling for both men. Bushrod expressed confidence in his views and was not intimidated by his uncle, but he also tried to persuade him by conceding the elder Washington's central point about the need to choose wise representatives. George took his nephew's position seriously and acknowledged that he might be wrong, even as he presented his own view forcefully. In the end, nothing much came of the Patriotic Society. Bushrod decided that he would rather be an elected representative than instruct them. He stood for the House of Delegates (the new name for the House of Burgesses) and was elected in 1787.[34] In that assembly, where Bushrod served with John Marshall, Patrick Henry, George Mason, and James Monroe, the most critical task was the one foreshadowed by George's most recent letter—organizing the elections to the state ratifying convention for the new proposed Constitution.[35] Washington was cautiously bullish on Bushrod, telling a friend: "With great pleasure I received the information respecting the commencement of my Nephew's political course. I hope he will not be so buoyed up the favorable impression it has made as to become a babbler."[36] George Washington was many things, but he was no babbler.

Amid these exciting events, both uncle and nephew received shocking news. Jack Washington died suddenly in January 1787 from what his brother described as "a fit of Gout in the head."[37] Jack's letters later in life do complain of gout, but it is not clear that gout was the cause of death.[38] George was heartbroken, writing to his nephew: "I condole most sincerely with you, my Sister and family, on the death of my Brother. I feel most sensibly for this event; but resignation being our duty, to attempt an expression of my sorrow on this occasion would be feebly described, as it would be unavailing when related."[39] Bushrod's reaction is unknown, but Jack's untimely death (at age forty-nine) shaped his son's future in at least two ways. First, his inheritance came sooner than expected. More than 1,500 acres of land and many enslaved people (including Oliver Smith and his wife, Doll, who took care of Bushrod's personal needs) made his life easier.[40] Second, Jack's death probably furthered, and could even have inspired, Bushrod's political career. If Jack had lived, he might have been the local delegate to Virginia's ratifying convention for the Constitution, given his political service during the Revolution. Instead, the torch passed to Jack's eldest son.

Two weeks after George returned from the Constitutional Convention, Bushrod arrived at Mount Vernon for a three-day visit.[41] He was probably eager to learn as much as his uncle was willing to share about what had been said behind closed doors at Independence Hall. A month later, George wrote his nephew about the criticisms of the Constitution by the House of Delegates and by others in the state.[42] "I am sorry," he said, "that Virginians entertain too high an opinion of the importance of their own Country [in other words, Virginia]." "The warmest friends and the best supporters of the Constitution," he wrote, "do not contend that it is free from imperfections; but these were not to be avoided, and they are convinced if evils are likely to flow from them, that the remedy must come thereafter; because, in the *present moment* it is not to be obtained." Besides, "I think the people (for it is with them to judge) can, as they will have the aid of experience on their side, decide with as much propriety on the alterations and amendments which shall be found necessary, as ourselves; for I do not conceive that we are more inspired—have more wisdom—or possess more virtue than those who will come after us." "The power under the Constitution," he explained, "will always be with the people. It is entrusted for certain defined purposes and for a certain limited period to representatives of their own choosing; and whenever it is exercised contrary to their interests, or not according to their wishes, their Servants can, and undoubtedly will be, recalled." George wrapped up with this wise thought: "No man is a warmer advocate for *proper* restraints and *wholesome* checks in every department of government than I am; but neither my reasoning, nor my experience, has yet been able to discover the propriety of preventing men from doing good, because there is a possibility of their doing evil."

Bushrod was a steadfast supporter of the Constitution's ratification. In late 1787, he told a friend: "I have no doubt that you will discover some imperfections in it, but when it is considered that it is the child of mutual concessions between States different in Situation and Interest, and that without some Efficient Government we must shortly be involved in Anarchy that certain road to Despotism. I think that we should not hesitate concerning its adoption."[43] He acted on that opinion by running for and being elected as a delegate to Virginia's ratifying convention.[44] James Madison gave Thomas Jefferson a rundown of the election results and listed among the Constitution's supporters, who were called Federalists, "Bushrod Washington, considered as a young Gentleman of talents."[45] To help Bushrod prepare for the convention, Eliza Powel sent him a transcript of the Pennsylvania convention, which voted in favor of the Constitution, so that he could study James Wilson's defense of the proposal.[46] Why did Bushrod support the Constitution? He never spelled this out, but his time in Philadelphia observing the inept national government in action may have been a factor. The most obvious explanation, though, is that his uncle's favorable view carried considerable weight.

Virginia's ratifying convention met in Richmond in June 1788 at the New Academy Theatre, a "spacious and airy building" that could accommodate hundreds of spectators.[47] This was a grand state occasion, but for Bushrod the convention was also something of a law school reunion. George Wythe, his old professor, sometimes presided over the deliberations, and John Marshall spoke frequently in support of the Constitution.[48] The Federalists in the conclave were led by Madison, Edmund Pendleton, who was president of the Virginia Court of Appeals, and Edmund Randolph, the governor.[49] The Anti-Federalists, who opposed the Constitution's ratification, followed Patrick Henry, the most powerful orator in the land, and George Mason, who had attended the Constitutional Convention but refused to sign the proposal.[50] Nobody was sure of the outcome. And without Virginia's support, any new national government would be crippled.

Five days into the proceedings, Bushrod wrote his uncle a detailed report. "The convention has hitherto made a very slow progress towards finishing the business before them," he explained, "and leads me to apprehend, that we shall be detained here much longer than I at first expected."[51] "We have determined to go through the constitution clause by clause, before any question shall be put," he said. "This regulation, if attended to, would expedite the business, by confining us to the particular parts objected to. But the debates have hitherto been general and desultory, although we have proceeded no farther than the third section of the first clause. The defects of the old confederation, and the necessity of framing an entirely new one, seem to have claimed the principal share of our attention." He then gave this blow-by-blow account:

> Mr. Henry on Thursday called upon the friends to the proposed plan to point out the objections to the present federal constitution. This challenge, which was given with an appearance of great confidence, drew from the governor yesterday a very able and elegant harangue for two hours and a half; for I suppose you have been informed of Mr. Randolph's determination to vote for the proposed government with previous amendments. He pointed out those defects, and painted in a masterly and affecting manner the necessity of a more solid union of the States. Mr. Henry's confidence in the power and greatness of Virginia, which said she might rest though dismembered from her sister States, was very well exposed by the above speaker. Mr. Madison followed, and with such force of reasoning, and a display of such irresistible truths, that opposition seemed to have quitted the field. However, I am not so sanguine as to trust appearances, or even to flatter myself that he made many converts. A few

I have been confidently informed he did influence, who were decidedly in the opposition.

"Were I to attempt to predict the fate of the constitution," Bushrod concluded, "it must be founded on conjecture."[52]

One curious aspect of the convention was that Bushrod never spoke on the floor even though he attended every session and voted on every motion. His reticence may have been due to his relative youth and inexperience. Or he may just have been cautious. When Bushrod was elected to the House of Delegates, George's advice was to exercise restraint in public. "Except in local matters which respect your Constituents and to which you are obliged, by duty, to speak," he said, "rise but seldom—let this be on important matters—then make yourself thoroughly acquainted with the subject. . . . [O]ffer your sentiments with modest diffidence—opinions thus given, are listened to with more attention than when delivered in a dictatorial style. The latter, if attended to at all, although they may *force* conviction, is sure to convey disgust."[53] Bushrod's silence also reflected a dilemma that he faced as George Washington's nephew: anything that he said in public could be attributed to his uncle. While George's support for the Constitution was clear given that he chaired the Philadelphia Convention, Bushrod may well have hesitated to say something that the presumptive president of the United States did not believe. The wisest course was probably for Bushrod to say nothing on the record. As he would later show on the Supreme Court, keeping quiet in public and working behind the scenes was more effective on a team.

In the end, the Virginia convention voted 89–79 (with Bushrod in the majority) to ratify the Constitution.[54] The Federalist and Anti-Federalist leaders that Bushrod encountered in Richmond would soon become his friends and rivals in the state's legal profession.

4
A Lawyer's Lawyer

Following the ratification convention, Bushrod withdrew from politics to concentrate on his legal practice. He moved from Bushfield to Alexandria, telling his uncle that "the cares of a plantation and the attention due to a professional life are altogether incompatible. It is necessary to relinquish my farm or my profession . . . The life as well as the capacity of man is insufficient to attain even a competent degree of perfection in more than one Study, and as my inclination is attached to that of Law, I wish not be to diverted from it by any other pursuit."[1] George agreed with his nephew's plan to focus on the law and offered his house in Alexandria to him rent-free, responding that "to manage a Virginia estate well there cannot be a divided attention."[2] (Their back-and-forth here is ironic, as the concerns that each expressed anticipated the dilemma that Bushrod would face once he was tasked with running Mount Vernon while he was a justice.) In January 1789, Bushrod and Nancy visited Mount Vernon for four days in what would be their last visit before George left for the presidential inauguration in New York.[3]

About six months later, Bushrod made the first great unforced error in his life. He wrote the president asking if he might be considered for an appointment as a United States attorney for Virginia. A United States attorney (then and now) leads all federal prosecutions and government civil suits in a district. The office requires presidential nomination and Senate confirmation.[4] The letter making this request is lost.[5] What followed was this frosty reply from the president:

> You cannot doubt my wishes to see you appointed to any office or honor or emolument in the new government, to the duties to which you are competent—but however deserving you may be of the one you have suggested, your standing at the bar would not justify my nomination of you as attorney to the Federal district Court in preference of some of the oldest and most esteemed General Court Lawyers in your own State, who are desirous of this appointment. My political conduct in nominations, even if I was uninfluenced by principle, must be exceedingly circumspect and proof against just criticism, for the eyes of Argus are upon me, and no slip will pass unnoticed that can be improved into a supposed partiality for friends and relatives.[6]

Washington's Heir. Gerard N. Magliocca, Oxford University Press. © Oxford University Press 2022.
DOI: 10.1093/oso/9780190947040.003.0005

When Bushrod made his request, the statute creating the office of United States attorney was still being drafted and discussed by Congress.[7] As a result, the request could have been more hypothetical than real. Nonetheless, he exercised poor judgment by making any suggestion of family patronage and should have known his uncle well enough to realize that he would be scrupulous on that subject.

Five months passed before Bushrod offered an apology.[8] He said that his response was delayed because he had been busy with cases and then hurt his hand, which made it impossible to write letters.[9] Perhaps this was true, though Bushrod may have simply needed time to craft an appropriate response. "Permit me to approve and admire the principles upon which you had founded your choice," he said. "In Justice to myself I must assure you," he added, "that had I supposed that you were to make the nomination, I should have never hinted to you my wishes on that, or any similar subject, well knowing your character, and sensible of the indelicacy of such an application." "But I was informed," he concluded, "that the nomination and appointment of those inferior officers were vested in the Judges of the Several Courts agreeable to that article of the Constitution which permits this to be done."[10] This explanation makes little sense. First, a lawyer should do more than rely on what someone else says about how an appointment is made before writing the president asking for one. Second, if federal judges were making the choice, then why write the president? Bushrod's clumsy correspondence suggests that he was dissatisfied with private practice in Alexandria and looking for some other opportunity.[11]

The Richmond Bar and John Marshall

In 1792, Bushrod and Nancy moved to Richmond.[12] The state capital was a more promising place for young attorneys. More important, the lawyers working there in the 1790s were truly exceptional. Patrick Henry and John Marshall teamed up for high-profile trials, with Henry handling the witnesses and making the speeches while Marshall took care of the legal questions.[13] Edmund Randolph, once he was done serving as President Washington's first attorney general and then as secretary of state, returned home and became Bushrod's frequent jousting opponent in the Virginia Court of Appeals.[14] The arguments in that highest state court were presided over by President Edmund Pendleton, whom Jefferson called "the ablest man in debate I have ever met."[15] Last but not least, George Wythe ran the Court of Chancery, which handled equity cases.[16] Despite the stiff competition and formidable bench, Washington in just a few years became one of the best attorneys in Virginia.[17] Bushrod's friend Benjamin Latrobe, the future architect of the Capitol, said that "the public voice" rated Washington and John Marshall among the top three lawyers in the state in the 1790s.[18] By 1794, Bushrod was able to tell the president that "my prospects here in business, are equal to my expectations."[19] And George replied a year later: "It gives me much pleasure to hear, through a variety of Channels, that you are becoming eminent and respectable in the Law. In this, and every transaction of your life, let honor and probity be your polar star."[20]

What made Bushrod so persuasive? Part of the answer can be found in a tribute written after his death by Horace Binney, a distinguished Philadelphia attorney who tried many cases before Justice Washington in circuit court. Binney thought that Washington "was by no means as good a writer as he was an extempore speaker in the law. His pen was never so expressive as his tongue."[21] Oral communication skills were vital for a lawyer at that time, as courts relied less on written briefs than they do now. Binney also said that Washington "had a great quickness and accuracy of apprehension" and "a most ready command of precise and expressive language, to narrate facts or to communicate thoughts, and a power of logical arrangement in his statements and reasonings." These traits suggest how the justice may have played his critical part within the Supreme Court: convincing his colleagues in face-to-face deliberations about the cases before the opinions were issued.

Bushrod was also successful because he worked hard. Proof of that comes from his published reports of cases decided by the Virginia Court of Appeals from 1790 to 1796. Washington's reports were the most sophisticated set of reports written in the United States up until that time and an important step forward for the orderly development of the common law.[22] Courts cannot decide cases based on precedents if they do not know the precedents. The solution, first developed in England, was to publish summaries of these decisions, known as law reports.[23] America was slow to adopt the practice, and the reports from early cases were often haphazard. Bushrod wrote in the preface to his reports that "the notes were taken for my own use, without any view to a publication of them."[24] But he decided to publish because such a collection was essential for the bench and bar even though he had "not had time to polish" the work. Washington included notes from cases he argued as well as from ones in which he was an observer. Taking all these notes was a laborious task, and Bushrod must have become a familiar face at the Court of Appeals.

Washington dedicated his reports to President Pendleton, due to "the very high opinion the author holds of his distinguished character and talents."[25] Pendleton led five judges on the Court of Appeals that (starting in 1795) included Judge Spencer Roane, Bushrod's classmate from law school.[26] Pendleton was by then in his seventies and needed crutches, but his mind was as sharp as ever.[27] Jefferson once described Pendleton's rhetoric as "cool, smooth, and persuasive;

his language flowing, chaste and embellished; his conceptions quick, acute and full of resource . . . Add to this, that he was one of the most virtuous and benevolent of men, the kindest friend, the most amiable and pleasant of companions, which ensured a favorable reception to whatever came to him."[28] Pendleton's great innovation was to get the Court of Appeals to announce its judgments through a single opinion when possible.[29] In England and in other states, the typical practice was that each judge gave an opinion in each case.[30] Pendleton's method was an improvement because lawyers and other judges could more easily understand the rationale for the Court's decision. A single opinion also gave those opinions more authority by concealing any disagreements among the judges and by presenting a united front. When John Marshall became the chief justice, the Supreme Court adopted Pendleton's practice most of the time, almost certainly with Justice Washington's support.

Most of Bushrod's cases in the Court of Appeals involved disputed estates, deeds, or contracts where significant sums of money were at stake.[31] For example, *Shermer v. Shermer's Executors* was about an estate valued at over £11,000, with 2,600 acres and 120 enslaved people, where the owner died without a will.[32] In another case, Bushrod represented the beneficiary of a will against a challenge that the will's author (the beneficiary's father) was not of sound mind when the will was signed.[33] Bushrod gamely argued that the evidence was insufficient to show incompetence, even though one witness to the will testified that the son told him on the way to witnessing the signature that his father had "lost his reason."[34] (Worse still, another witness testified that the father said after signing the will that "he must have been drunk" when the will was written.)[35] The court ruled against Bushrod in that case, but he remained a persistent and resourceful advocate.[36] As Edmund Randolph told the Court of Appeals after Washington ascended to the Supreme Court, Bushrod "scarcely ever used a weak argument" in his presentations.[37]

In many cases, Bushrod worked with, but more often went up against, John Marshall. They were involved in over a dozen appeals together or as rivals.[38] Each man took the measure of the other; sometimes winning, sometimes losing.[39] While they competed for clients, this was the period when the two men began forging the close personal and professional bond that would last for the rest of their lives.[40] Until 1795, they were practically neighbors, as the Marshalls lived between Eighth and Ninth Streets and the Washingtons lived between Seventh and Eighth Streets.[41] Bushrod and Marshall were active members of Richmond's civic life. They served on the Common Hall (that is, the City Council) from 1794 to 1795 and worked on committees dedicated to police and fiscal reform.[42] Sometimes they worked together on ad hoc committees named by the state legislature, including one led by George Wythe that was tasked with gathering all the laws in Virginia related to real property for publication.[43]

Figure 4.1 John Marshall. Painting by Cephas Thompson. National Portrait Gallery.

Bushrod and Marshall also litigated cases involving human property. In one letter, Washington stated that "Mr. Marshall and myself have brought a very important case in the Court of Chancery" on the "use nature of Negro property."[44] And in *Shelton v. Barbour*, a case before the Court of Appeals, Marshall and Washington combined forces to defeat a claim of freedom.[45] An enslaved man seeking liberty sued his owner for false imprisonment. His owner answered by producing a judgment in a case between the man's mother and another owner that concluded that the mother was an enslaved person. This verdict, the owner argued, proved as a matter of law that her son was also enslaved. The trial court disagreed and instructed the jury that the judgment was only some evidence of slave status, whereupon the (presumably all-white) jury found for the Black man. On appeal, Marshall contended that the general rule was that a prior judgment so closely related to the facts of another case must govern, pointing out that if the mother had been ruled free then her son would also be deemed free under the same rule. Bushrod added that such a general rule was necessary "so that there may be an end put to lawsuits; for it would be inconvenient if men's titles once decided, should be always at sea."[46] A lawyer for the Black man countered that "since the law, as well as the best feelings of the human heart favor liberty, the rule contended for ought rather to be moderated than extended in the present case."[47] His plea fell on deaf ears, as President Pendleton wrote an opinion reversing the jury's verdict, stating: "It has been contended in this case that liberty is to be favored. This is true, but the court cannot do that, or on any favored subject infringe the settled rules of law."[48]

Shelton was a harbinger for how Marshall would handle slavery cases as a judge. One scholar of slavery notes that the chief justice never "wrote an opinion supporting a claim to liberty brought by a slave."[49] The extent of Marshall's slave ownership was not known until recently, but by the 1830s he was enslaving hundreds of people throughout Virginia.[50] Bushrod also owned many people and told the Court of Appeals that slaves "form a great deal of the wealth of the people," emphasizing "the high value set upon that kind of property by the people and Legislature of this country."[51] Nevertheless, as Chapter 10 will explain, Justice Washington wrote two opinions giving enslaved men freedom and others that decided fugitive slave cases in ways that he disliked as a slaveowner but were in his mind required by the law fairly applied.

Bushrod's practice outside the Court of Appeals is less well documented, but his most famous client (other than George Washington) was Thomas Jefferson.[52] Jefferson wrote that due to Washington's "natural abilities [and] greater reading in the law, he has the reputation of being all attention to business and that of his client."[53] He hired Bushrod in 1795 to get an injunction against a neighbor who was raising a dam that would (if built) ruin one of Jefferson's water mills.[54] "There are two difficulties to be foreseen," Jefferson explained. "The one is that [any injunction] will be disobeyed, and he will go on raising his dam. What is to be done most speedy and effectual in that case?" The other was that his neighbor, "being absolutely penniless," would not have the money to tear down anything that he built.[55] "What is to be done here again? . . . [I]f I am to furnish the expense of pulling down what they have built up and are building, it will be considerable. I pray you to send me the writ without a moment's delay which may be avoided." Bushrod replied: "I can say only that I shall use diligence in pushing it forward and shall try by a motion out of turn to get it sooner decided." He apologized for writing on "this small piece of paper. I never discovered until I had set down to write, that I had no more, and have not time now to send for a supply as your messenger is very impatient."[56] Jefferson was satisfied with Washington's work, as he retained him in other matters afterward.[57]

The most important question upon which Bushrod gave legal advice as an attorney concerned a bill pending in the state legislature to take property (or "glebes") from the Episcopal Church. Before the Revolution, Virginia had a state church—the Anglican Church, led by King George III.[58] Following independence, the church (renamed Episcopal) lost its legal monopoly but was allowed to keep its lands and property. Laws enacted in 1776 and thereafter confirmed this compromise, but by 1797 there was momentum in the legislature to repeal these statutes and confiscate the church's property. The church's wealth was a tempting target, but there was also a principled argument that the church's privileges violated Section 16 of the Virginia Declaration of Rights, which said: "All men are equally entitled to the free exercise of religion, according to the dictates of conscience."[59] As adherents of other religions were forced to pay taxes to the Anglican Church before 1776, one claim was that they were entitled to some of the church's property and denying them those benefits violated their free exercise of religion.

In a memo analyzing the proposed legislation, Bushrod concluded that Virginia could not constitutionally repeal the previous legislative grants to the church.[60] First, he stated that "the legislature cannot divest such a right without establishing a precedent, by which they may revoke every grant the Commonwealth has ever made."[61] "If the rights of the church can be decided upon in the legislature," he said, "what is to prevent that body from dissolving every corporation in the state, and seizing upon their possessions for public uses . . . And how will the most ingenious man be able to get rid of the precedent by distinguishing it from the other cases?"[62] Second, he said the proposal would leave the church's members with nothing and constitute unlawful "intermeddl[ing] where the judiciary may properly exercise the power of deciding."[63] Third, on the free exercise claim he wrote: "If it be contended that by depriving the dissenters [non-Episcopalians] of their proportion of that property, their religious sentiments may be thereby influenced, [t]he argument will cut both ways. For by depriving the members of the church of the means of supporting their clergy, they will be interrupted in the free exercise of their religion."[64] He thought that any doubts about the meaning of the free exercise provision were resolved by the fact that the legislature in 1776, comprising many of the same men who ratified the Declaration of Rights in that same year, passed the first statute guaranteeing the church its property: they must have thought that the statute was valid.[65] Lastly, citing the Magna Carta and Blackstone, Bushrod said that property rights could not be taken away without a jury trial.[66] The reason that Bushrod's legal advice was consequential is that Virginia did end up repealing the Episcopal Church's grants, the Virginia Court of Appeals upheld that repeal, and in 1815 part of that dispute reached the United States Supreme Court.[67] And the Court's opinion in that case, written by Justice Joseph Story and discussed in Chapter 9, would include phrases and arguments similar to the ones in Washington's 1797 memo.

The proposal to strip the Episcopal Church of its assets also hit close to home because this was Bushrod's church. Like almost all elite Virginians, he had been brought up in the Anglican Church and remained an Episcopalian following the Revolution. Washington's faith was deep and sincere. Justice Joseph Story once said that Washington "was a Christian, full of religious sensibility, and religious humility. Attached to the Episcopal Church by education and choice, he was one of its most sincere, but unostentatious, friends."[68] In a letter to Hannah in 1789, Bushrod gave his thoughts on the "all-important subject of religion."[69] "Complaints against Providence," he wrote, "are the result of weak minds. I verily believe that Religion founded on the purest principles has supported you in trials which would have shaken the most resolute minds. I trust that the same divine cause will never cease to inspire you with contentment and resignation in any future event which it may please Heaven to bring about." Consistent with that view, he served as the vice president of the American Bible Society from its inception in 1816 until his death.[70] The Society, which is still active around the world, makes Bibles available to every person who wants to learn God's word in a language that they can understand.[71] While his faith may have shaped his reasoning in the Episcopal Church case, the memo also bristles with a devotion to property rights and to the common law that Washington would later articulate from the bench.

* * *

In January 1797, Bushrod fell ill and was confined to bed. Writing to his uncle, he said that he was suffering from "a severe attack of the pleuresy [*sic*]," which was a catch-all word in that era for a lung infection that caused pain while breathing.[72] A few weeks later, Hannah wrote: "Be careful my love of your dear eye—use it as little as possible. Oh my dear Bushrod you can't be too careful."[73] Her note indicates that he was having trouble seeing from one eye or could not see from an eye at all, though it is unclear if his eyesight was deteriorating before his illness or worsened only once the pleurisy began. His vision in that eye never returned. When Secretary of State Timothy Pickering recommended Washington for the Supreme Court in 1798, he told President John Adams: "His indefatigable pursuit of knowledge and the business of his profession has deprived him of the sight of one eye—It will be happy [in other words, apt] if the loss of the other does not make him perfectly the emblem of [blind] Justice."[74] Pickering's explanation for Bushrod's condition does not make sense, for if hard work as an attorney caused sightlessness the condition would be widespread. While there is insufficient proof that Bushrod's illness alone cost him his vision, the 1797 sickness was certainly a factor.

Washington's visual impairment changed his appearance and some of his work habits. For example, a visitor to the Supreme Court in 1815 described the justice as "a little, sharp-faced gentleman, with only one eye, and a profusion of snuff distributed over his face."[75] He stopped keeping publication notes of the cases heard by the Virginia Court of Appeals in 1797, probably because the strain of that effort was too great.[76] Likewise, he would decline the opportunity to write a biography of George Washington (and gave the job to John Marshall) out of concern that his sight was too weak for such a large project. Bushrod's work as a judge is remarkable given that he was half-blind for the rest of his life.

5
An Imperfect War

George Washington's retirement from the presidency in March 1797 drew Bushrod back into politics. The divisions in the president's cabinet between Alexander Hamilton and Thomas Jefferson over domestic and foreign affairs became embodied in two parties—the Federalists and the Democratic-Republicans—that fought the presidential election of 1796.[1] Vice President John Adams prevailed and the Federalists secured control of Congress, with Jefferson elected as vice president under the original Electoral College, which gave the vice presidency to the runner-up in the presidential campaign.[2] Although Bushrod played no role in the 1796 election, he was a Federalist and would remain so throughout his life. Indeed, Justice Story later called him "a good old-fashioned federalist, of the school of the days of [George] Washington."[3]

What did it mean to be a Federalist in the 1790s? A Federalist then was not identical to a Federalist in 1787, who supported the Constitution's ratification. By 1796, being a Federalist meant backing closer ties with Great Britain, though France was America's ally during the Revolution.[4] A Federalist was more supportive of national power and read the Constitution in that spirit rather than in favor of states' rights.[5] He championed the Bank of the United States, a central bank modeled on the Bank of England, and financial policies that favored creditors over debtors and industry over agriculture.[6] And there was also a personal dimension to being a Federalist. George Washington, at least after his presidency, considered himself one, and so did those close to him such as John Marshall and Bushrod.[7] Likewise, the men closest to Jefferson, most notably James Madison and James Monroe, adopted many of his Republican positions and attitudes.

The most divisive issue during the Adams administration was America's relationship with France in the wake of the French Revolution. President Washington declared the United States neutral in the war that broke out in 1793 between Britain and France, and subsequently he signed the Jay Treaty with Britain to resolve outstanding issues from the Revolutionary War.[8] The French were outraged by these moves given our prior alliance and responded by attacking American ships trading with Britain.[9] In 1796, Hamilton put Marshall and "Young Washington the Lawyer" on his short list to be the next ambassador to France to help resolve the crisis.[10] President Adams ended up sending three envoys to Paris, including Marshall, in June 1797.[11] They spent nearly a year in France, but the negotiations were unsuccessful, in large part because

Washington's Heir. Gerard N. Magliocca, Oxford University Press. © Oxford University Press 2022.
DOI: 10.1093/oso/9780190947040.003.0006

Foreign Minister Talleyrand demanded a large bribe as a precondition for the talks.[12] When Marshall returned home in June 1798, he received a hero's welcome for rejecting Talleyrand's demand and for refusing to tolerate corruption in what became known as the "XYZ Affair."[13] In Alexandria, a banquet was held in Marshall's honor, with Bushrod telling the assembled guests: "When future generations peruse the history of America, they will find the name of Marshall on its sacred page as one of the brightest ornaments of the age in which he lived."[14]

Candidate for Congress

At first, George Washington's retirement meant that Bushrod was forced to spend more time on family errands. In August 1797, he dined with his uncle at Mount Vernon for the first time in eight years.[15] They swapped letters often, mainly about legal problems that George wanted solved.[16] Bushrod did most of that work for free, leading George to say: "You may think me an unprofitable applicant in asking opinions and requiring services of you without dousing my money; but pay day may come. If the cause should go to the higher Courts, I shall expect you will appear for me, and Mr. Marshall also."[17] Bushrod was also tasked with helping Martha Washington, "who was exceedingly fatigued and distressed for want of a good housekeeper."[18] When he found someone, George peppered his nephew with questions: "Widow or wife? If the latter, where her husband is? What family she has? What her age is? Of what temper? Whether active and spirited in the execution of her business? Whether sober and honest? Whether much knowledge in Cookery and understands ordering, and setting out a Table?"[19] In scrambling to fulfill these requests, Bushrod was repeating the role once filled by Jack Washington.

But as tensions with France mounted and war loomed, their conversations took on a more sober tone. In July 1798, following the XYZ Affair, President Adams appointed his predecessor as the lieutenant general of a new national army that would, if necessary, see action against the French.[20] Bushrod wrote his uncle to "sincerely lament the necessity which calls you again from your retirement to the busy scenes of public life."[21] George responded: "I little thought when I retired to the Shades of Private life, last year, that any event would happen, in my day, that could bring me again on the Public theatre; but so it is; and the remnant of a life which required ease and tranquility, will end more than probably in toil and responsibility."[22] He asked Bushrod for advice about applicants for officer commissions.[23] Then, in August, George wrote: "The Crisis is important. The temper of the People of this State in many (at least in some) places, are so violent and outrageous, that I wish to converse with General Marshall and yourself on the Elections which must soon come on."[24] (Washington referred to

Marshall as a general because he was a brigadier general in the state militia.)[25] The ex-president was convinced that Jefferson, whom he now referred to only as "that man," and his party were dangerous to the Republic and that the Federalists must maintain control of Congress in the midterm elections.[26] George's plan was to recruit two heavyweight candidates for the House of Representatives—John Marshall and Bushrod Washington.

More than two decades later, Bushrod told Martin Van Buren the story of that visit to Mount Vernon as they walked the grounds of the estate.[27] In his memoir, Van Buren recalled that scene and what Bushrod told him: " 'I received,' said he, 'a letter from the General,' (his invariable synonym for his uncle) . . . 'requesting Mr. Marshall,' as he always called the future Chief Justice, 'and myself to come to Mount Vernon. The court was sitting and a compliance with his request of course inconvenient, but it never occurred to either of us to postpone his business to our own.' " "On our arrival in the evening," Bushrod continued, "the General took me into the library and informed me that he wished Mr. Marshall and myself to offer for Congress at the approaching election—Mr. Marshall for Henrico district and myself for Westmoreland." He was handed the thankless task of giving Marshall the request. "Having explained his wishes and briefly assigned his reasons he desired me to break the matter to Mr. Marshall so that he could have our answer at supper. I called Mr. Marshall out, and on this walk we had our consultation. We had of course the strongest possible desire to conform to the General's wishes but could not bring our minds to any other conclusion than that to do so in this instance would be destructive of our prospects in the pursuit we preferred, and injurious to our families. Although it was not so with Marshall, I was myself deeply conscious of an unfitness for political life."

Marshall then convinced Bushrod to go back and tell Uncle George no for them both. "It was made my duty to state our objections to the General which I did very earnestly," he said. "He heard me through without interruption, and then answered in his usual grave and emphatic way—'Bushrod, it must be done!' " (One wonders how many other times Bushrod heard this command.) "With this I returned to my friend," he stated, "still lingering in this grove in painful suspense. We resumed our walk and finally agreed that we must comply with the General's wishes at all hazards. We returned to him and informed him of our assent to his proposition. He expressed his satisfaction in very kind terms and said that he was sensible of the inconvenience to which a compliance with his views might subject us but was certain that he had asked nothing from us which he would not have done himself if our situations had been reversed."[28]

Why were Marshall and Bushrod lukewarm about George's request? First, there was the issue of money. Marshall had lost a year from his practice while in France, was not independently wealthy, and had a wife and children to support. Serving in Congress would mean more financial sacrifice. Bushrod had just sold his house and moved into a new home in Richmond, which probably left him strapped for cash.[29] Earlier in the year, he had declined a nomination by President Adams to represent the United States in negotiations with the Cherokee tribe, a decision that may have been motivated by financial concerns.[30] Second, their prospects for victory were not promising, as they would be running for seats held by incumbents from the other party.[31] Indeed, when Jefferson heard about their candidacy he told a friend that Marshall's "election is doubtful" and that Bushrod "stands little chance."[32]

Then there is Bushrod's comment that he was "deeply conscious of an unfitness for political life." Why was that? One possibility is that his partial blindness made him reluctant to enter the arena, although his withdrawal from politics after the Virginia ratifying convention suggests that he felt this unease before his eye was injured. Another thought is that Bushrod sensed that any political career would be in the shadow of his uncle and that his freedom of action in office would be limited. Perhaps the answer is that he was more introverted and did not like the social demands of politics. (By contrast, Marshall was outgoing and gregarious, which may explain why he enjoyed politics.)[33] Yet despite all these reasons to say no, there was little doubt that Marshall and Bushrod would, in the end, acquiesce to the General's request. Marshall deeply admired his old commander, under whom he had served during the darkest days at Valley Forge.[34] And when push came to shove, Bushrod followed his uncle's lead.

The Supreme Court Appointment

Shortly before Washington strong-armed his protegés into running for Congress, Justice James Wilson died at the home of Justice James Iredell.[35] The news reached President Adams in September, and he immediately wrote Secretary of State Pickering: "I have received your letter of the 6th, with Judge Iredell's Letter enclosed, informing of the Death of Judge Wilson. The Reasons urged by Judge Iredell for an early Appointment of a successor, are important. I am ready to appoint either General Marshall or Bushrod Washington. The former I suppose ought to have the Preference."[36] Adams independently reached the same conclusion as George Washington, which was that Marshall and Bushrod were the two best Federalists available for public service.[37] One factor that influenced the president's thinking was that none of the justices was from Virginia, which was the nation's largest state and deserved some representation on the Supreme Court.[38] In a separate letter, Adams told Pickering that "Marshall is first in age, rank and public services, [and] probably not second in talents." His nomination would also be a political triumph for the president, given Marshall's popularity due to the XYZ Affair. Pickering replied that he would ask Marshall, but said, "I am sorry to think there is little chance of his gratifying the public wish as well as yours; in a word, there is little hope that an eminent lawyer, in the full tide of practice at the bar, and receiving eight or ten thousand dollars a year, will relinquish it for the meagre reward of thirty-five hundred dollars."[39] (Pickering did not know that Marshall had decided to run for Congress.) The secretary of state was enthusiastic about Bushrod, as his was "a name that I have never heard mentioned but with respect, for his talents, virtues, and genuine patriotism: But he is young, not more I believe than three or four and thirty." "It would seem," he concluded, "that Virginia should fill the vacant seat; and if General Marshall should decline. Mr. Washington has decidedly a superior claim to any other gentleman there of the profession."

John Marshall chose not to accept this seat on the Supreme Court. Why he made this decision is unclear. Marshall may have thought that his commitment to run for Congress could not be broken. Or he could have been unwilling to give up his legal practice entirely. In that era, members of Congress were permitted to

Figure 5.1 John Adams, who appointed Washington to the Supreme Court. Painting by John Trumbull. National Portrait Gallery.

represent clients and make money, but as a justice he could not do that and would be limited to his government salary.[40] There is also a chance that Marshall was interested in the Court only if he could be the chief justice. Whatever his reasons, Marshall told Pickering that he was not interested, but he thought Bushrod would say yes and that "I am equally confident that a more proper person could not be named."[41] His view that Bushrod would accept the nomination was correct, but whether that was based on a talk they had after Marshall received Pickering's letter or was simply an astute judgment of his friend's mentality is unknown. Upon receiving the letter from the secretary of state asking him to join the Court, Bushrod promptly accepted a recess appointment and withdrew as a candidate for the House of Representatives. He was unanimously confirmed by the Senate shortly thereafter.[42]

The first delicate task that Justice Washington faced was letting President Washington know that he would not be running for Congress.[43] In October 1798, Bushrod broke the news:

> Upon my return to this place I met with a Commission from the President of the United States appointing me one of the Judges of the Supreme Court. This appointment I have accepted and was induced thereto by the strongest motives. I was very unwilling to abandon a profession, to which I was much attached, and to the study of which I had devoted the greatest part of my life. A situation which permits me to pursue it, and to improve the knowledge which I have acquired in this science, without endangering my sight (already considerably injured) could not fail to be agreeable to me. Independent of this consideration, I could not upon a small piece of poor land in Westmoreland have paid debts which I owe and supported my family. Knowing the wish you had, that I should be a Candidate for Congress, I have felt much uneasiness lest my acceptance of this appointment should be disagreeable to you. The desire of attempting to serve my country in that line had also created in myself an anxiety for success in the election, although I foresaw the extreme inconvenience which would result from it, in my private affairs; I was however willing to make the sacrifice. I trust that this candid statement of my situation will be an apology with you for having relinquished my first intention, and I flatter myself that my services will not be less useful to my Country in the office which I now hold, than they would have been in the legislative counsels.[44]

There is an anxiousness to Bushrod's letter, as if he was anticipating George's disapproval. By now he must have understood that he could become his uncle's heir and may have wanted to take pains to placate him. Still, Bushrod's explanation for choosing the Supreme Court over a race for the House of Representatives rings true, even if he did tug on the heartstrings a bit by invoking his damaged eyesight and family dependents. Indeed, the nomination probably came as a great relief to Bushrod, for he now had a perfect excuse to leave a political campaign that he was not excited about and might well have lost. In any event, George promptly wrote back: "I think you were perfectly right in accepting the appointment of Associate Judge—Not only for the reasons you have mentioned, but on every other account."[45]

Bushrod Washington's first duty as a Supreme Court justice involved traveling to Georgia in what was known as "circuit riding."[46] The federal courts were organized differently in the 1790s than they are now. Each Supreme Court justice was required to spend months each year away from the capital in a designated section of the country (a circuit) holding trials and hearing appeals alongside a federal district judge.[47] There were no federal appellate judges. The circuit system, which dated back to the Judiciary Act of 1789, had several problems.[48] First, the absence of a justice because of death or illness meant that a circuit court could not be held unless some other justice could substitute.[49] Second, appeals taken from the circuit courts meant that a justice was hearing an appeal of his own decision, which presented a conflict of interest. Third, traveling long distances by coach was dangerous. When George wrote to congratulate Bushrod on his appointment, he said: "I wish your Circuit may be pleasant and honorable to you, and that you may return safe to your family and friends."[50] His wish for Bushrod's safe return was not idle chitchat, as many justices were hurt in carriage accidents while on circuit duty.[51] Indeed, during the War of 1812, Justice Story told Bushrod to stay "safe from the Enemy and what I deem more perilous, the danger of the roads to and from Philadelphia."[52] No records exist from Bushrod's first circuit, so what he did there is mostly unknown.[53] But he did return safe and sound to Virginia in December and began preparing for his first session on the Supreme Court.[54]

At the end of January 1799, Bushrod returned to Philadelphia for the first time since his apprenticeship.[55] Philadelphia was still the nation's capital and the Supreme Court heard its cases at City Hall, which was next to Independence Hall.[56] When Horace Binney entered his boarding house on North Third Street one day, "I perceived sitting in the parlor a newcomer, of about the common height, of slight figure, sallow complexion, and straight brown hair, the features of his face generally small, one of his eyes apparently sightless, and the other having more than the fire of an ordinary pair. His chin was nearly or quite beardless," and this gave Bushrod the appearance "of being an old young man, or a young old man—it was difficult at first to tell which—an expression that to some degree continued till his death."[57] "Judge Washington," Binney wrote, "had just arrived and taken lodgings at the same house. I soon found that he was easy in his manners, and affable, unaffected, unpretending, and as far as possible from stateliness. I could hardly believe that he was a Judge of the highest Court in the land.

Though I was many years younger than he was, and but a law-student at the time, he permitted me to become acquainted with him, and very soon to be without restraint in my intercourse with him."[58] Bushrod also renewed his friendship with Eliza Powel, who bought him a new black satin robe that he could wear on the bench.[59]

When Bushrod took his place on the Supreme Court for the first time, he was joined by five colleagues who all had been appointed by his uncle. The chief justice of the United States was Oliver Ellsworth, who was chosen after Chief Justice John Jay resigned in 1795.[60] Chief Justice Ellsworth had been a member of the Constitutional Convention from Connecticut and one of the leading drafters of the Judiciary Act of 1789, the founding charter of the federal courts.[61] James Iredell had played a key role in persuading his home state of North Carolina to ratify the Constitution and was one of the original appointments to the Court in 1790.[62] (Iredell died in October 1799, and thus served with Bushrod for only a brief time.) William Cushing was another charter member of the Court and worked alongside Bushrod until 1810.[63] Justice Cushing was a crusty old Yankee, and as chief justice of the Supreme Judicial Court of Massachusetts made waves when he told a jury in 1783 that slavery was illegal under the new state constitution, which declared: "All men are born free and equal."[64] Next came Justice William Paterson, who was appointed in 1793 after representing New Jersey at the Constitutional Convention and serving as the state's governor.[65] Justice Paterson, who remained on the Court until his death in 1806, was born in Ireland and said that that he lived by the maxim "Laugh where we can."[66] Finally, there was Justice Samuel Chase, a signer of the Declaration of Independence from Maryland who reached the Court in 1796.[67] Justice Chase, nicknamed "Old Bacon Face," was a massive man (over six feet tall) with a massive temper, and he would be a lightning rod for the Court's critics.[68]

The Supreme Court was the least significant branch when Bushrod came on board. In part, the Court's weakness was a function of its limited appellate jurisdiction, which was set by Congress and was much narrower than at present.[69] There were also not many federal laws that could create Supreme Court cases and not many federal judges to decide those cases—the entire federal judiciary in February 1799 consisted of fifteen district court judges and the six justices.[70] And the Constitution was more restricted in scope initially. For instance, until 1868 there was no Fourteenth Amendment imposing the duties of "due process of law" and "equal protection of the laws" on the states.[71] Likewise, the first set of constitutional amendments, ratified in 1791 and now called the Bill of Rights, did not apply to the states.[72] Thus, in its early years, the Court did not have much to do. Indeed, only three cases were decided in Bushrod's first session on the Court, and he wrote an opinion in only one—*Fowler v. Lindsey*.[73] *Fowler* was a property dispute where the parties sought to invoke the Supreme Court's original jurisdiction (a trial where the justices find the facts and decide the case directly rather than hearing an appeal).[74] Washington wrote a crisp opinion holding that *Fowler* did not belong in the Court's original jurisdiction, and all the other justices who heard the case wrote separate opinions reaching the same conclusion.[75]

The Sedition Act

Upon his return to Virginia at the end of February, Bushrod visited Mount Vernon and then jumped into the campaign for Henry "Light-Horse Harry" Lee (the father of Robert E. Lee), who took Bushrod's place as the Federalist candidate for the House of Representatives from Westmoreland County.[76] Bushrod's political activism may sound incredible, for today a justice would never publicly support a political candidate. But in 1799, there was no sense that the justices should refrain from electioneering. Bushrod may have felt obliged to help Lee because he had been the previous Federalist nominee for the district, but a more important factor was that George Washington was eager for a Federalist victory.[77] The vote was scheduled for April (there was no uniform national election date then), and John Marshall was also in the thick of his race for the House of Representatives.

The pivotal issues of the campaign were the conflict with France and the validity of the Sedition Act.[78] This law, enacted at the peak of war hysteria in 1798, now stands condemned in the all-powerful court of history for making "false, scandalous and malicious" speech about the United States government, the president, or Congress a crime punishable by up to five years in prison.[79] The Sedition Act made an exception for critical speech about the vice president (in other words, Jefferson), which made the act an exercise in censorship and partisanship. In response, Jefferson and Madison anonymously wrote resolutions against the Sedition Act that were passed by the Kentucky and Virginia legislatures.[80] The Kentucky and Virginia Resolutions argued that the act was unconstitutional, with Jefferson's version adding that the states were justified in judging the constitutionality of a federal statute because the Constitution was a compact among the sovereign states that formed the ultimate authority of the Union.[81] His state compact theory was a forerunner of secession and would irritate Marshall and Bushrod throughout their judicial careers. As a House candidate in Virginia, though, Marshall was careful to say only that he did not support the Sedition Act, rather than comment on the compact theory or on the act's constitutionality.[82] In part, his caution might have been due to George Washington's support of the Sedition Act. When a federal district judge in Pennsylvania issued a grand jury charge defending the act, Washington sent Marshall a copy and told Bushrod that he doubted that any reasoning about the act's merits "will produce the least change in the conduct of the leaders of the opposition, to the measures of the General Government."[83] Though modern ideas about freedom of speech make the Federalist defense of the Sedition Act difficult to understand, the prevailing view of the First Amendment at the time was that the government was prohibited only from stopping expression, not from punishing that expression afterward.[84]

Justice Washington kept his uncle up to date on Lee's campaign. In early April, he reported: "I wish I could speak of the Congressional election in this District with any sort of confidence. The general opinion is, that the majority either way will be very inconsiderable, and this I believe will be the event. . . . There is but a small part of this County affected by Jacobin [pro-French] principles; I have been to every house in that neighborhood and endeavored to expose the many ridiculous and scandalous misrepresentations which had been made of the Government. I hope I was not entirely unsuccessful."[85] In the end, Lee and Marshall won narrowly—in Marshall's case by 114 votes—and gave Bushrod "the pleasure of announcing . . . the triumph of federalism in this Corner of the State."[86] George replied: "The Elections of Generals Lee and Marshall are grateful to my feelings. I wish however both of them had been Elected by greater majorities; but they are Elected, and that alone is pleasing. As the tide is turned, I hope it will come in with a full flow; but this will not happen if there is any relaxation on the part of the Federalists. We are sure there will be none of that of the Republicans, as they have very erroneously called themselves."[87]

After a brief Supreme Court session that resulted in no signed opinions, Justice Washington began a circuit court in Pennsylvania that included prosecutions under the Sedition Act.[88] He was substituting for Justice Iredell, who was ill and could not attend.[89] The district court judge who sat with Washington was Richard Peters, who became a friend after the justice was permanently assigned to the Pennsylvania circuit in 1803. The justice presided over the trial of Reverend Jacob Eyerman, who was charged with using his sermons for "seditious counseling."[90] Eyerman had no lawyer, presented no defense, and received the jury's guilty verdict.[91] Washington also charged grand juries that returned indictments against men who protested the Sedition Act with the words "the Constitution sacred, no gag law, liberty or death" and against two newspaper editors.[92] And he oversaw pretrial proceedings for William Duane, a leading Republican editor charged with publishing an article alleging that the British paid bribes to procure the nomination of America's ambassador to Britain.[93] All the actions taken by this circuit court, however, were invalidated when Washington and Peters belatedly realized that the federal marshal's term had expired before the session began, which, in effect, left the circuit court without jurisdiction.[94]

Justice Iredell's death in October scrambled the circuit assignments. President Adams nominated and the Senate confirmed Alfred Moore (who, at four feet five inches tall, was almost certainly the shortest justice ever) as Iredell's successor.[95]

In November, Bushrod held a circuit court in Virginia, though there is only one reported opinion from that circuit.[96] While the case raised a straightforward choice-of-law issue involving a contract, Washington went out of his way to say: "I am clearly of opinion that the general government derives its existence and power from the people, and not from the states."[97] His dictum was a shot at Jefferson's claim in the Kentucky Resolution that the federal government derived its power from the states. A basic question looming behind this debate was whether the states or the federal courts possessed the final authority to declare a law unconstitutional.

The Death of George Washington

On December 14, 1799, George Washington died after an excruciating final illness and repeated bleedings by his doctors.[98] Bushrod's immediate reaction to the news is unrecorded, and he was unable to get to Mount Vernon for the funeral. George's will, which he wrote himself in July 1799, named Bushrod as one of the executors and as his principal heir once Martha died.[99] No letters between George and Bushrod survive after May 1799, and the justice's last visit to Mount Vernon was in July.[100] There is nothing to indicate that they ever discussed the terms of the will or that Bushrod knew what he would receive, though the timing of the will's revision and his final visit could mean that there was a discussion. The items that the former president gave his nephew right away were a sword "accompanied with an injunction not to unsheathe [it] for the purpose of shedding blood, except it be for self-defense, or in defense of their Country and its rights," "all the Papers in my possession, which relate to my Civil and Military Administration of the affairs of this Country; [and] I leave to him also, such of private Papers as are worth preserving."[101] Upon Martha's death, Bushrod would get the mansion and the buildings at Mount Vernon, approximately 4,000 acres of land, and any books and pamphlets from the library that remained.[102]

Slaves were not part of Bushrod's inheritance. George directed that "upon the decease of my wife, it is my will and desire that all the slaves which I hold in my own right, shall receive their freedom."[103] Moreover, he provided that the freed elderly or ill Blacks be supported by the estate for the rest of their lives, and that any Black children without parents or unable to afford an education receive one and be freed when they turned twenty-five.[104] To remove any doubt about his intent, George wrote: "I do hereby expressly forbid the sale, or transportation out of the said Commonwealth, of any slave I may die possessed of, under any pretense whatever. And I do moreover most pointedly, and most solemnly enjoin it upon my Executors hereafter named . . . to see that this clause respecting slaves, and every part thereof be religiously fulfilled at the Epoch at which it is directed to take place; without evasion, neglect, or delay."[105] The ex-president was the only slave-owning Founding Father who emancipated his enslaved people after his death. No other notable slaveowner (including his nephew) followed his example. With this final act, George tried to reconcile his doubts about owning people with his lifelong practice of owning them, though he left the messy details for his heir to sort out. To take one example, an unintended consequence of George's decision to delay emancipation until after Martha's death was that she became fearful that his enslaved people might kill her to hasten their liberty. After visiting Mount Vernon in 1800, Abigail Adams said that her predecessor as First Lady "did not feel as though her life was safe in their hands."[106] Martha's insecurity could have been a product of grief or paranoia, but when a fire broke out at the estate she was suspicious of arson and summoned Bushrod to seek his advice.[107] Horace Binney recalled that Justice Washington cut short a circuit court in response to her plea and told her to free George's enslaved people as soon as possible.[108] She took that suggestion and let them go on New Year's Day in 1801.[109]

George Washington's passing was a profound event for the nation and for his nephew. In political terms, his departure marked the death knell of the Federalist Party. Without its leader, the party shattered into factions and would not win another presidential election. On a personal level, Bushrod would soon assume the mantle of the Washington name, with all its benefits and burdens. Carrying on the legacy of a man whose legend only grew with time would not be easy. Indeed, Bushrod's relationship with his uncle would prove far harder in death than in life.

The 1800 Presidential Campaign

Not long after George's death, Justice Washington returned to Philadelphia for a brief Supreme Court session and articulated a fundamental legal principle that would in time be closely associated with him. Chief Justice Ellsworth was absent, as President Adams had sent him to France to lead a new diplomatic team.[110] The only case that produced a signed opinion was *Cooper v. Telfair*.[111] Cooper was a Tory whose property had been confiscated by a 1782 Georgia statute that named him as a traitor.[112] He argued that a treason conviction without a trial violated his right to a jury trial, but the Court unanimously rejected his argument. Washington's opinion observed that Georgia's constitution did not bar bills of attainder (in other words, legislative convictions for crimes) and that no federal constitutional issue was present because the act against Cooper had been passed before the federal Constitution (with its prohibition on state bills of attainder) was ratified.[113] He ended his analysis with this point: "The presumption, indeed, must always be in favor of laws, if the contrary is not clearly demonstrated."[114]

Washington was not the first judge to state the "presumption of constitutionality" followed when the courts exercise judicial review, but he would be its most visible advocate on the Marshall Court.[115]

Washington was soon back on circuit holding more Sedition Act trials. The first involved Charles Holt, a newspaper editor in Connecticut, who criticized the military buildup launched by Congress and the president.[116] Holt said that this amounted to a standing army that would be led by Alexander Hamilton, an admitted adulterer, and asked if "our young officers and soldiers . . . like their general are . . . to be found in the bed of adultery."[117] Holt's lawyer argued that the Sedition Act was unconstitutional, but the justice rejected that claim.[118] The jury found Holt guilty, and Washington sentenced him to three months in prison.[119] The second case was the prosecution of William Durrell, a newspaper printer in New York who reproduced an article attacking the president.[120] Durrell presented no defense and was convicted by a jury in April 1800, but the justice and the district court judge recommended executive clemency, which President Adams granted.[121] Durrell's pardon brought Washington's encounters with the Sedition Act to a close. The act by its own terms expired in 1801, and President Jefferson pardoned those who were convicted.[122] Washington did not distinguish himself in these cases, though in fairness no federal judge at the time thought that there was merit in the constitutional arguments against the Sedition Act.

In August, the justices gathered for their final session before the election. Chief Justice Ellsworth was still in France negotiating with Napoleon's new regime and was now reporting to Secretary of State John Marshall, who had been appointed by President Adams in May.[123] Once again, only one Supreme Court case produced signed opinions—*Bas v. Tingy*.[124] *Bas* involved the ongoing naval conflict with France. An American ship was captured by a French privateer and then recaptured by a different American vessel. Under a law enacted in 1799, an American ship that recaptured an American vessel taken by "the enemy" more than four days afterward was entitled to a reward from the vessel equal to one-half the vessel's value. But was France an "enemy" of the United States given that Congress had not declared war? The Court unanimously held that France was an "enemy" for purposes of the statute.[125] Washington's opinion said that there were two kinds of wars. One was the "perfect kind," which was declared. "But hostilities may subsist between two nations more confined in its nature and extent; being limited as to places, persons, and things," he added, "and this is more properly termed imperfect war . . . Still, however, it is public war, because it is an external contention by force, between some of the members of the two nations, authorized by the legitimate powers."[126] The justice went on to explain why a state of imperfect war existed between the United States and France by carefully tracing the actions of Congress, concluding, "If they were not our enemies, I know not what constitutes an enemy" and that the contrary view was possible only if "the Court could wink so hard as not to see."[127] There was a political slant to the Court's ruling in that Federalists were much more likely to see France as the enemy, but even those who wanted France as an ally would be hard pressed to say that Congress treated France as a friend.

Washington's pragmatic distinction between perfect and imperfect war proved influential and is widely cited. While some of America's armed conflicts have been declared wars, in most cases the conflicts were initiated by the president and never formally declared. In 1901, the Court cited Washington's opinion in *Bas* as a legal justification for hostilities between the United States and Native American tribes.[128] During the Vietnam War, more than one federal court did the same to explain why the lack of a congressional declaration of war did not invalidate the military draft that was imposed during that conflict.[129] And as recently as 2015, Washington's imperfect-war concept was cited by a court in conjunction with the American intervention in Afghanistan.[130] There is a reasonable counterargument that Congress should be required to declare war before military might may be used abroad, but supporters of presidential power tend to disagree. Also, not all uses of armed force rise to the level of a war, and to require a declaration of war in each of those cases would have diplomatic consequences that may not be in the national interest.

Once the Supreme Court session ended, Washington began working for the president's reelection in his race against Vice President Jefferson.[131] He traveled to South Carolina and stumped for the Federalists in the midst of a circuit court.[132] This time the justice's partisanship cannot be chalked up to local concerns or to his uncle's influence. Simply put, Washington was horrified at the prospect of a President Jefferson. What he learned the hard way, though, was that the Federalists were hopelessly divided.[133] Part of the problem was that one faction of the party wanted war with France while President Adams was seeking peace.[134] (A treaty was signed with France at the end of 1800, but the news came too late to shape the election.)[135] Another sore point was the personal rivalry between Adams and Hamilton, culminating with a pamphlet in which Hamilton criticized the president for his "eccentric tendencies," "disgusting egotism," and "ungovernable temper;" terms that could be applied equally to Hamilton.[136] While Hamilton nevertheless gave Adams a lukewarm endorsement, behind the scenes he promoted Charles Cotesworth Pinckney, another member of the Constitutional Convention, who was running for vice president.[137] The president kept silent in public, but in private called Hamilton "a Creole bastard" and lambasted all his "fornications, adulteries, and incests."[138]

Upon reading Hamilton's tirade, Bushrod wrote Treasury Secretary Oliver Wolcott in disbelief. "We are all thunderstruck here by General Hamilton's pamphlet," he began. "If it was intended to promote the election of General Pinckney, it is seriously believed by his best friends here that it will produce quite a contrary effect. . . . It is feared that the effects of this attack upon Mr. Adams will be seriously exhibited in the Eastern States and particularly in Massachusetts. It may excite doubts in the minds of those disposed to support General Pinckney with Mr. Adams whether the friends of the former will everywhere and more especially in this State observe equal good faith toward the latter. Such apprehension ought at once to be dispelled. . . . It is most clear that should distrust take place between the friends of the two federal candidates, all must end in the election of Mr. J[efferson]—which God forbid."[139] While Washington assured Wolcott that things were still looking good for the Federalists in South Carolina, Jefferson ended up carrying the state and winning the presidency, with his party also making gains in Congress.[140]

America was now on the brink of its first transfer of power from one party to another. Twelve years of Federalist rule were about to end, and a struggle over judicial independence was about to begin.

6
The Marshall Court Begins

After spending over a year in France representing the United States, Chief Justice Ellsworth's failing health forced him to resign from the Court in December 1800.[1] Rather than leave the vacancy for the president-elect, John Adams decided to name the next chief justice.[2] When he was turned down by John Jay, the president turned to Secretary of State Marshall and said: "I believe that I must nominate you."[3] The Senate confirmed Marshall in February 1801, and he served as both secretary of state and chief justice until Jefferson took office in March.[4] While Marshall's appointment to the Court is now seen as a glorious moment in constitutional law, at the time his selection looked to many like just another partisan act. Over the next four years, Justice Washington found himself at the center of a fierce debate about the role of courts in a republic, and in the process he became the chief justice's right-hand man.

The reason Chief Justice Marshall's appointment reeked of politics was that the departing Congress and president were also expanding the federal courts and filling them with Federalist stalwarts under the Judiciary Act of 1801.[5] Nowadays, a lame-duck Congress and a defeated president do not take broad actions because the just-completed elections deprive them of legitimacy. In the 1800–1801 transition, though, the unwritten rules were still in their infancy, and no consensus existed about how power should be shared between outgoing and incoming administrations from different parties. The Judiciary Act of 1801 was, in many respects, a sound reform. The act abolished circuit riding by the justices and created a new set of federal judges for the circuit courts.[6] Having more federal judges was desirable due to the growth of the country, and ending circuit riding was a relief to the justices. They hated the extended travel and would no longer be troubled by the recusal issue created when the Supreme Court heard appeals in cases decided by a justice on circuit. Whatever the act's merits were, though, President Adams and the Senate tarnished the Judiciary Act by nominating and confirming all sixteen of the new circuit judges instead of leaving that task to Jefferson and the next Senate.[7] While most of these "midnight judges" were qualified, some were more like patronage appointments, including two of John Marshall's brothers-in-law and Treasury Secretary Wolcott.[8] The 1801 act also provided that the Supreme Court would shrink from six to five justices whenever the next vacancy arose, which meant that Jefferson would not be able to appoint a justice soon. Repeal

Washington's Heir. Gerard N. Magliocca, Oxford University Press. © Oxford University Press 2022.
DOI: 10.1093/oso/9780190947040.003.0007

of this Judiciary Act and the elimination of the midnight judges were high priorities for the new administration.

The New Captain

When John Marshall joined the Court, the justices were meeting in Washington, D.C., for the first time. The Court was assigned a makeshift courtroom in the Capitol basement, described by the architect as "a half-finished committee room meanly furnished and very inconvenient."[9] While the February 1801 session was brief and produced no signed opinions, the justices made a crucial change by living together in a boarding house—Conrad and McMunn's on Capitol Hill—where they ate, drank, slept, worked, and played cards while their spouses were back home.[10] It is impossible to overstate the importance of this social decision for the justices' ability to forge consensus in challenging cases over the next three decades. Years later, Justice Story wrote about his communal life when the Supreme Court was in session: "My brethren are very interesting men with whom I live in the most frank and unaffected intimacy. We are united as one, with a mutual esteem which makes even the labors of Jurisprudence light. . . . We moot every question as we proceed, and familiar conferences at our lodgings often came to a very quick and, I trust, a very accurate opinion, in a few hours."[11]

Justice Washington took charge of the boarding house arrangements.[12] This task may have fallen to Bushrod because of all the justices he lived the closest to the capital, but there is also the possibility that he initiated the idea with Marshall's support. When the British burned Washington, D.C., during the War of 1812, the chief justice's first impulse was to ask Bushrod if he could still find a suitable boarding house. "We must rely on you to make inquiries," Marshall wrote, "and if in your power to make arrangements for our accommodation. If it be practicable to keep us together you know how desirable this will be. If that be impracticable we must be as near each other as possible. Perhaps we may dine together should we even be compelled to lodge in different houses. . . . [G]ive me all the intelligence in your power on this interesting subject."[13] Bushrod's central role in maintaining the boarding house setting is strongly suggested by the fact that the custom ended when he died in 1829.

These efforts to build a team spirit among the justices began to bear fruit in August, when Marshall delivered his first unanimous opinion for the Court. *Talbot v. Seeman* was another case stemming from the recent conflict between France and the United States.[14] In 1799, the USS *Constitution* (now a floating museum nicknamed "Old Ironsides") seized a neutral merchant ship from a French vessel.[15] The captain of the *Constitution* claimed that he was entitled to a salvage award (in other words, compensation to a vessel that rescued another ship in distress) from the owner of the merchant vessel. Justice Washington heard the case on circuit and ruled against the captain following arguments by Alexander Hamilton (for the captain) and Aaron Burr (for the vessel owner).[16] The text of Washington's circuit opinion is lost, but in *Bas v. Tingy* he said that his ruling in *Talbot* rested on the conclusion that Congress did not authorize American ships to seize neutral vessels from the French.[17] Washington added that "my opinion remains unshaken; or rather has been confirmed by the very able discussion which the subject has lately undergone in this Court, on the appeal from my decree."[18] Nevertheless, he joined Chief Justice Marshall's opinion reversing his circuit decision. Marshall reasoned that although the merchant vessel was from a neutral state and could not be seized as a prize under international law, French law held that some neutral vessels could be captured as prizes.[19] As a result, the *Constitution* did (at least plausibly) rescue the merchant ship and was entitled to a salvage reward.[20] In calculating the award, though, the Court gave the captain an amount at the low end of the possible range.[21]

Talbot reads as a compromise in a close case. In isolation, the unanimity of the decision could be understood as the justices extending a courtesy to their new chief. Viewed in light of what happened afterward, though, *Talbot* was the next step in creating a new culture of consensus within the Court. The justices had issued some unanimous opinions before Marshall arrived, but that now became the norm. In the Court's December 1801 session, all the opinions were unanimous and all were written by the chief justice.[22] Justice William Johnson, who joined the Court in 1804, recalled that as a state court judge he "was accustomed to deliver my seriatim opinions in our appellate court [that is, each judge wrote a separate opinion], and was not a little surprised to find our Chief Justice in the Supreme Court delivering all the opinions in cases in which he sat, even, in some instances when contrary to his own judgment and vote."[23] "Some case soon occurred," Justice Johnson said, "in which I differed from my Brethren and I thought it a thing of course to deliver my opinion. But, during the rest of the session I heard nothing but lectures on the indecency of judges cutting at each other, and the loss of reputation which the Virginia appellate court had sustained by pursuing such a course [after the death of President Pendleton]. At length I found that I must either submit to circumstances or become such a cypher in our consultations as to effect no good at all. I therefore bent to the current."[24] The lectures against Virginia's shift from President Pendleton's practice of achieving unanimity whenever possible could have come only from the two justices who argued before that court—Marshall and Washington—which provides a clue about whose views carried weight within the Court. As Justice Story later explained, "Judge Washington thinks (and very correctly) that the habit of delivering dissenting opinions on ordinary occasions weaken[s] the authority of the Court."[25]

Talbot was the only signed opinion issued in the August session. With the end of circuit riding and little business before the Supreme Court, 1801 was undoubtedly the most leisurely year of Bushrod's professional life. And with Martha Washington still in residence at Mount Vernon, he did not yet have the burden of managing a complex plantation. Still, he was apprehensive about the future. Writing to Alexander Hamilton that November, the justice worried: "The system of intolerance and proscription which seems to be the order of the day from the General to many of the State Governments will I fear produce a fatal schism, which may probably divide the States as it already has the people."[26] "I do not think that it requires the gift of prophesy," he added, "to foretell the dissolution of the confederacy if a [constitutional] convention should be agreed to by two-thirds of the States at this, or perhaps at any other time."

Weighing a Judicial Strike

President Jefferson's inaugural address struck a bipartisan note in stating, "We are all Federalists; we are all Republicans," but the gloves came off as soon as Congress returned in December.[27] A bill was introduced to repeal the Judiciary Act of 1801 and unseat the midnight judges. But Federalists in Congress raised a powerful constitutional objection. Article III of the Constitution says that federal judges "shall hold their offices during good behavior," which was widely understood as life tenure.[28] The only way to remove a federal judge was impeachment by the House of Representatives and conviction in a Senate trial, which required a two-thirds vote.[29] Instead, Republicans were claiming that a statute—passed by a simple majority in each house of Congress—could remove a federal judge by wiping out his office.[30] The implication was that federal judges (including Supreme Court justices) did not, in fact, have life tenure. Hamilton urged that a suit be brought before the Supreme Court to challenge the repeal of the Judiciary Act of 1801 "as soon as possible."[31] In anticipation of such a challenge, Congress (for the first and only time) cancelled the upcoming session of the Court, decreeing that the justices would not meet again until February 1803 and then meet only once a year each February thereafter.[32]

When Jefferson signed the repeal in March 1802, the justices found themselves on the horns of a dilemma.[33] One consequence of the repeal was that circuit riding was restored, as there no longer were any federal circuit judges. While the justices were probably disgruntled about having to go back on the road to hear cases, there was a more fundamental problem. If the circuit judges did have life tenure and could not be ousted without an impeachment and a conviction, then how could the justices lawfully take their place? Some Federalists, including at least one of the circuit judges, urged the justices not to resume circuit riding and, in effect, to go on strike as a protest against the repeal of the Judiciary Act.[34] There was precedent for this kind of response. When Congress had assigned federal judges the task of reviewing military pension requests in 1792, subject to review by the secretary of war, some justices refused to comply on the grounds that judicial independence was inconsistent with the ability of a presidential appointee to overturn judicial decisions.[35] In that case, Congress modified the law in response, but noncompliance with the repeal of the Judiciary Act might have provoked a sharp backlash.[36] The justices would essentially be declaring a key plank of the Republican platform illegal without holding a hearing or writing an opinion. Furthermore, they would be doing this under circumstances that would look partisan, with Federalist justices protecting Federalist circuit judges. What might Congress or President Jefferson do in retaliation? The signs were ominous, given that Congress had already canceled the Supreme Court's upcoming session.

The deliberations among the justices about whether to go on strike against circuit riding provide a rare look at how the Marshall Court made decisions at its inception. Most of the time, the justices did their work over dinner and drinks at their boarding house. As a result, there is usually no written record of how opinions were drafted and edited. In this instance, though, the justices were not in session, were back in their home states, and hence could not hold face-to-face discussions. The picture that emerges from the surviving letters that were exchanged shows that Chief Justice Marshall did not dictate the Court's decisions. Instead, the justices carefully weighed what to do in search of consensus. Unanimity was especially important because of the gravity of the situation and the political impact that a split Court would have on any response contemplated by Congress. And in this debate, Justice Washington played a pivotal role in squelching the strike idea.

The chief justice wrote to all his colleagues, but the only one of these letters that survives was sent to Justice Paterson on April 19, 1802.[37] Marshall wrote that he held "an opinion that I cannot conquer" that resuming circuit riding would be unconstitutional, but that "my duty and my inclination in this as in all other cases [is] to be bound by the opinion of the majority of the Judges."[38] "This is a subject," he said, "not to be lightly resolved upon. The consequences of refusing to carry the law into effect may be very serious. For myself personally I disregard them, and so I am persuaded does every other Gentleman on the bench when put in competition with what he thinks his duty, but the conviction of duty ought to be very strong before the measure is resolved on."

Justice Chase was the first to respond to the chief justice.[39] He said that the repeal was unconstitutional for three reasons, one of which was that the circuit judges had life tenure and if "a Judge of the Supreme Court . . . should hold the Circuit Court, I think he would thereby, be instrumental to carry into effect an unconstitutional law." "I think," Chase went on, "it is in the power of the Judges to meet at Washington in July, or August next; and I wish you would urge it. . . . The burden of deciding so momentous a question, and under the present circumstances of our Country, would be very great on all the Judges assembled; but an individual Judge, declining to take a Circuit, must sink under it."

Washington was the next justice to reply, and he brought the strike momentum to a screeching halt. His response is lost, but Marshall described his views in another letter to Justice Paterson dated May 3. "Mr. Washington," the chief justice wrote, "states it as his opinion that the question respecting the constitutional right of the Judges of the supreme court to sit as circuit Judges ought to be considered as settled & should not again be moved."[40] Rather than accept Washington's decision as final, Marshall reiterated his constitutional doubts and said: "I have also received a letter from Judge Chase whose opinion is directly opposite to that of Judge Washington[,] but he expresses an earnest desire, which he has requested me to communicate to every member of the bench, that we should meet in Washington for the purpose of determining on the course of conduct to be pursued." But then Justice Paterson informed Marshall that "my opinion coincides with Judge Washington's."[41] Justice Cushing concurred with Washington and Paterson, and the debate was over.[42] No meeting was held, and the justices resumed circuit riding in the fall. When lawyers objected to the jurisdiction of the circuit courts, their objections were summarily dismissed.[43] Indeed, Washington was the first justice to address one of these constitutional challenges while riding circuit in Connecticut that September.[44] (Unfortunately, there is no record of what he said.) When a suit attacking the repeal reached the Supreme Court in 1803, the result was a foregone conclusion. The Court rejected the challenge in a brief opinion by Justice Paterson and upheld the repeal of the Judiciary Act of 1801.[45]

The strike deliberations are revealing. First, Chief Justice Marshall consulted with his colleagues before a decision was made. Historians, though, are split on Marshall's objective. Some contend that he was acting as an honest broker, laying out the arguments on both sides to see if there was any consensus for a strike.[46] Others think that the chief justice wanted to go on strike and was trying (unsuccessfully) to persuade the others.[47] The evidence points more to the latter view. First, Marshall could have said that he was against a strike but would bow to the wishes of the majority. But he did not. The chief justice could have dropped the strike idea once Washington announced his opposition. But he did not. He continued pressing the issue until Justice Paterson stated that he also was opposed. As a result, Marshall's preferred course of action was rejected. Second, Justice Washington's views carried weight in that rejection. If he had endorsed Justice Chase's support for the strike, then an irresistible bandwagon might have started. Justice Paterson might have been against a strike notwithstanding Washington's opinion, but it is also possible that his mind was changed or made up by that view. Washington's caution might have reflected his newfound experience as a judge, especially following the partisan furor created by the enforcement of the Sedition Act.

In hindsight, a strike probably would have been a disaster for the justices. In other words, Washington was right and Marshall was wrong. Today we know that government shutdowns to pursue a political goal are typically unpopular. A strike against holding courts is the judicial equivalent of a shutdown. Furthermore, the unelected justices would have been taking on a popular president and Congress at a time when federal courts were still relatively new and lacked the respect they now command. And by refusing to carry out their assigned duties, the justices would have given the House of Representatives a fine excuse to bring articles of impeachment. (Indeed, the House would impeach Justice Chase even in the absence of a strike, as we will see in a moment.) The political blowback against the Court probably would have been even greater if the justices—all Federalists—directly confronted the Republicans who controlled the other two branches. Judicial independence might not have survived.

Marbury v. Madison

When the justices finally reconvened in February 1803, they were under siege. A week before the Supreme Court's session, President Jefferson asked the House of Representatives to investigate Judge John Pickering, a federal district judge appointed by President Washington.[48] Pickering probably suffered from a mental illness, though he was impeached a month later for serving while "in a total state of intoxication, produced by the free and intemperate use of intoxicating liquors," and "in a most profane and indecent manner, invok[ing] the name of the Supreme Being, to the evil example of the good citizens of the United States."[49] The political message sent by Judge Pickering's impeachment inquiry, especially given its timing, was not subtle. The president was indicating that accepting the constitutionality of the Judiciary Act's repeal was not enough. Republicans were also looking to oust those whom they saw as Federalist partisans from the bench and to curtail the authority of the courts.

Part of the reason for Jefferson's dissatisfaction with the justices was that they were about to hear *Marbury v. Madison*, which is one of the Court's most famous cases.[50] William Marbury had been nominated by President Adams and confirmed by the Senate to be a justice of the peace in the District of Columbia. John Marshall, as secretary of state, was supposed to give Marbury his official commission, but he did not.[51] When James Madison, Marshall's successor as secretary of state, assumed office, he refused to send the commission and

Figure 6.1 Thomas Jefferson. Painting by Mather Brown. National Portrait Gallery.

claimed that Marbury was not a justice of the peace.[52] Marbury sued in the Supreme Court, invoking its "original jurisdiction" pursuant to Article III of the Constitution asking for an order (a writ of mandamus) directing Madison to deliver the commission.[53] In December 1801, the Court ordered Madison to respond to Marbury's lawsuit. The case did not attract much attention at first because Marbury's position was a minor one: the more pressing political question involved the federal circuit judges confirmed at the end of the Adams administration. By 1803, though, *Marbury* presented the best opportunity for the Federalists to attack the Republican assault on the courts. Federalists in the Senate introduced a petition raising Marbury's claim.[54] The president, in turn, ordered Madison to ignore Marbury's suit, which was a strong hint that any Court order telling the administration to act would be ignored.[55]

Dealt this bad hand, the Court's unanimous opinion found a clever excuse to avoid ordering Madison to deliver Marbury's commission. *Marbury* was read by Chief Justice Marshall on February 24 in the lobby of Stelle's Hotel, the boarding house where the justices were now staying.[56] After a lengthy statement denouncing the refusal to give Marbury his position, the Court explained that an order to Madison could not be issued because the Court lacked original jurisdiction over the case.[57] The opinion stated that the Judiciary Act of 1789 gave the Court such jurisdiction, but that in passing that section of the act, Congress violated the Constitution. The Court then made its landmark holding that the federal courts could hold an act of Congress unconstitutional and refuse to apply such an act. Judicial review was not a novel doctrine—Alexander Hamilton discussed the issue in Federalist #78—but *Marbury* marked the first time that the Court used that authority in a significant way.[58] Scholars generally think that the Court (perhaps deliberately) misread the statutory language: Congress did not, in fact, give the Court original jurisdiction beyond what the Constitution granted.[59] With this sleight of hand, though, the Court dodged having to create a humiliating precedent that a judicial order could be ignored by the president and instead created a principled one asserting that "it is emphatically the province and duty of the judicial department to say what the law is."[60] The mystery of *Marbury* is how the justices arrived at this solution. Since the chief justice wrote the opinion, a natural assumption is that the reasoning was all his. But there is no proof for that view. And the deliberations over the circuit court strike suggest that the justices worked together on important matters. Sometimes the drafting process for an opinion can be reconstructed, but that is not the case for *Marbury*.

The external threat to judicial authority probably made unanimity among the justices inevitable. All the opinions issued by the Court in 1803 were unanimous, and all but one of them were written by Chief Justice Marshall.[61] While unaminity may have started as a favor to the new chief justice, consensus became a habit once the justices became political targets. As Benjamin Franklin supposedly said about the signers of the Declaration of Independence, "We must, indeed, all hang together, or most assuredly we shall all hang separately."[62] The justices scattered for circuit court duty in March, with Washington taking up his permanent assignment to the circuit for Pennsylvania and New Jersey.[63] Meanwhile, an unexpected gaffe in another circuit gave the Republicans new momentum in their campaign against the Federalist judiciary.

The Impeachment of Justice Chase

In January 1804, the House of Representatives opened an impeachment inquiry into Justice Chase.[64] Chase was the easiest mark because he was the most outspoken justice. While riding circuit in May, Justice Chase delivered a charge to a grand jury in Baltimore and stated: "The late alteration of the Federal Judiciary by the abolition of the office of the sixteen circuit judges . . . will, in my judgment, take away all security for property and personal liberty. The independence of the national Judiciary is already shaken to its foundation, and the virtue of the people alone can restore it."[65] He also said in his charge that the consequence of allowing universal male suffrage in Maryland would be that "our republican constitution would sink into a mobocracy, the worst of all possible governments."[66] Jefferson wrote a Maryland congressman about this "seditious and official attack on the principles of our Constitution" and asked if Chase should "go unpunished."[67] After the inquiry began, Washington told Chase that he "was extremely anxious to know what was thought and said in that house about the impeachment . . . That you will repel and satisfactorily defeat [any charges] in the opinions of disinterested and candid men, I have no doubt, and I should hope that a majority of such men may be found in the body which will try them [in other words, the Senate]."[68] Following Jefferson's lead, the House impeached Justice Chase in March 1804 without bothering to draft articles of impeachment.[69] When the articles were finally drafted three weeks later, they charged Chase with high crimes and misdemeanors for his actions on circuit (including in some Sedition Act prosecutions) and for the grand jury charge, which was "highly indecent, extra judicial, and tending to prostrate the high judicial character with which he was invested to the low purpose of an electioneering partisan."[70] While the House was impeaching Justice Chase, the Senate was conducting the impeachment trial of Judge Pickering.[71] It was a trial in name only. The Senate did not permit Pickering to present a defense and swiftly convicted him by the necessary two-thirds vote.[72]

Against that backdrop, the Supreme Court's session in February 1804 was subdued. There were just four justices on the bench, as Justice Paterson was recovering from a coach accident and Justice Moore was ill.[73] As in 1803, all the opinions were unanimous and all but one of the signed decisions were issued by the chief justice.[74] While the Court was in session, Washington was deposed by the House committee investigating Chase.[75] During the deposition, he was asked about a comment that Chase had allegedly made to him at Stelle's Hotel about one of the Sedition Act cases involved in the impeachment.[76] Chase had supposedly told Washington that if he had realized that one of the journalists he tried was an enemy of Jefferson, he "would scarcely have fined him so high."[77] In reply to this inquiry into judicial bias, Washington deflected the point by saying that "he has not the slightest recollection of any such conversation" but that "he was in the habit for some years past to converse jocularly with the said Samuel Chase upon a variety of subjects, and is well satisfied that the conversation now alluded to, if it ever took place," was a joke.[78] What this line of questioning made clear was that Chase's colleagues could be called to testify in the Senate impeachment trial, and therefore, they needed to be very careful about their public actions and statements. One result of that caution was that none of the justices participated in the 1804 presidential campaign, in which Jefferson was reelected. Gone were the days when Washington knocked on doors for a Federalist congressional candidate to please his uncle or stumped for the reelection of President Adams.[79]

In January 1805, Justice Chase gave the Senate his formal answer to the articles of impeachment, and Washington described the news in a letter to a friend: "Mr. Chase appeared the first of the month, in obedience to summons and made his answer. In this he merely denied the truth of every charge against him and prayed for an extension of time to prepare his defense. We declared that it could not be done during this session of Congress. We stated reasons which, I thought, could not be denied—such as the precarious state of his health at this season of the year, the importance of the subject, and the difficulty of procuring counsel which the infirm state of his health would require."[80] "But his enemies," Washington continued, "impatient to get rid of him, would not grant his request. On the fourth of February they will renew his trial. You may suppose the issue when I tell you there were twenty-one members for present trial and only nine for postponement. A Judge is not more independent than a doorkeeper!" The justice's use of "we" to describe Chase's arguments indicates that he was advising Chase's legal defense team behind the scenes. The math was looking grim, as a 21–9 vote at the end of the trial (or anything comparable when all senators voted) would mean that Chase would be convicted and removed.

The impeachment trial commenced as scheduled on February 4. Vice President Aaron Burr, under indictment for the murder of Alexander Hamilton, presided.[81] Chase spoke in his own defense for over three hours and delivered a sympathetic performance.[82] Chief Justice Marshall was called as a defense witness and did his best to avoid saying anything under cross-examination by the House managers.[83] Still, Marshall was "plainly frightened" by the trial and wrote a letter suggesting that the principle of judicial review stated in *Marbury* would have to be sacrificed to preserve judicial independence if Chase was convicted.[84] In the end, a compromise proved unnecessary, as the Senate acquitted Chase on all counts.[85] Unlike later impeachment trials, the senators in the Chase trial did not explain their votes, so their motives are unknown. One explanation for the outcome is that the lead House manager, John Randolph, was at odds with Jefferson and that feud divided Republican senators.[86] Another view is that Randolph was not a lawyer and simply put on a poor case as compared with what Chase's very able attorneys presented.[87] Then there is the idea that the Court's concession to Congress on the validity of the repeal of the Judiciary Act of 1801, along with its decision not to issue an order to the president in *Marbury*, had bought just enough political goodwill for Chase to prevail. Whatever the reason, the Republican campaign against the judiciary suffered a decisive setback.

One Judge

While Chase's trial was ongoing, the justices held their 1805 term. Justice Moore had resigned in 1804 and Jefferson nominated William Johnson, a young state supreme court judge from South Carolina, as Moore's successor.[88] In time, Justice Johnson became the member of the Court most eager to speak out in separate opinions and dissent, though in his first term he wrote in only one case.[89] Consistent with the new practice, all the signed opinions in which the chief justice participated were unanimous—with one partial exception, discussed shortly. In the initial period of the Marshall Court, the justices seemed to follow an unwritten rule that the most senior justice wrote a unanimous opinion, though in cases where Marshall recused himself they had the option of each issuing a separate opinion.[90] Years later, Justice Johnson told Jefferson that this custom was mostly a result of his colleagues' shortcomings: "Cushing was incompetent, Chase could not be got to think or write—Paterson was a slow man and willingly declined the Trouble, and the other two Judges you know are commonly estimated as one Judge."[91]

Even if Johnson was exaggerating out of frustration, his comment about Marshall and Washington being one judge raises the question of what the working relationship was between these two leading justices. The difficulty with assessing their partnership is that there is little written documentation of their interactions prior to 1814. But the long professional connection between the two men going back to their days in Richmond belies the idea that Washington just followed Marshall's lead. John Marshall, for all his greatness, was not George Washington, to whom Bushrod did largely defer due to his family seniority and unique status as a national hero. The strike discussions also establish that Bushrod did not always agree with Marshall. If the correct reading of Justice Johnson's comment is that Washington was Marshall's equal, then he should be given more credit for the chief justice's opinions. We will never know what Bushrod may have contributed to them—none of Marshall's drafts survive—though we do know (as Chapter 7 explains) that Marshall and Bushrod worked together on Marshall's biography of George Washington. Justice Washington himself was not the author of a majority opinion until 1809 because the Court typically assigned opinion authorship to the most senior justice, and Washington was never the senior justice in a case until 1810.[92]

One piece of written evidence about Washington's relationship with Marshall is *United States v. Fisher*, an 1805 case in which they disagreed. *Fisher* concerned the interpretation of the federal bankruptcy law enacted in 1800, which Marshall had drafted when he was a member of Congress.[93] The chief justice wrote for the Court and held the act constitutional, arguing that under the Necessary and Proper Clause of Article One "Congress must possess the means, and must be

Figure 6.2 Justice William Johnson, Washington's independent-minded colleague for twenty-five years. Painting by unknown artist. Collection of the Supreme Court of the United States.

empowered to use any means which are in fact conducive to the exercise of a power granted by the Constitution."[94] (The Court would say more about this idea fourteen years later in *McCulloch v. Maryland*.)[95] Marshall then concluded that the act gave the United States priority over private creditors in collecting debts in a bankruptcy proceeding, though the statute did not expressly say so.[96] With this statutory holding, the Court overruled Washington's circuit decision holding that the United States did not have priority over other creditors.[97]

Bushrod recused himself from the case because his own ruling was under review, but he still wrote a statement criticizing the Court's ruling due to "the importance of the question."[98] Justice Washington began with this lament: "In any instance where I am so unfortunate as to differ with this court, I cannot fail to doubt the correctness of my own opinion. But if I cannot feel convinced of the error, I owe it in some measure to myself and to those who may be injured by the expense and delay to which they have been exposed to shew at least that the opinion was not hastily or inconsiderately given."[99] He then proceeded to shred Marshall's logic, writing that Congress did not intend to give the United States priority "because in every other section of the law they have declared a different intent; and secondly, because it would not only be productive of the most cruel injustice to individuals, but would tend to destroy more than any other act I can imagine all confidence between man and man. The preference claimed is not only unequal in respect to private citizens but is of a nature against which the most prudent man cannot guard himself."[100] *Fisher* was a strong case for deference to the chief justice because he was one of the drafters of the statute and presumably knew what was intended, but Washington refused and, in so doing, showed again that he made up his own mind. Bankruptcy law was an area where the "one judge" sometimes became two, as would happen again more than two decades later in *Ogden v. Saunders*.[101] Most of the time, though, the chief justice and Justice Washington were the spine of the Marshall Court, and that bond would only strengthen with time.

The political bitterness outside the Court that had begun with the Sedition Act now started to settle into an uneasy truce. The justices generally refrained from displaying their partisan feelings. In return, the elected branches expressed a willingness to influence the Court's rulings through less drastic techniques such as sound arguments in contested cases and the selection of new justices when vacancies arose. When the Supreme Court returned for its 1806 term, there was still some doubt in the air, as a constitutional amendment was introduced in the House of Representatives to allow the removal of federal judges by only a majority vote in each house of Congress, rather than through impeachment.[102] The Court continued to keep its head down, with all the signed opinions coming from the chief justice, and all but one of them unanimous.[103] The proposed constitutional amendment failed to pass the House, and the mood improved to the point that Washington and Marshall felt free to have a friendly dinner with Secretary of State Madison.[104] The heir of Mount Vernon was now firmly ensconced in the life of the capital that bore his family name.

7
Master of Mount Vernon

Martha Washington passed away in May 1802.[1] Her death capped a dramatic period of change in her nephew's personal life. Bushrod's mother, Hannah, had died a year earlier.[2] Not long afterward Bushrod sold his boyhood home at Bushfield.[3] By then, all his siblings and some of Nancy's were also dead. As a result, Bushrod and Nancy were raising many of their nephews and nieces.[4] Later in 1802, the Washington family traveled to take possession of their ancestral home along the rough roads that Bushrod knew so well from his visits when his uncle had been in residence. The mansion came into view on an elevation, standing two stories high and crowned by an octagonal cupola with a weathervane shaped like a dove representing peace.[5] The roof was rust red, with white walls made of wood but finished to look like stone. Two elliptical covered galleries linked the mansion to the kitchen and a building that welcomed visitors. At the rear of the mansion was a massive, covered veranda (called the piazza) with a sublime view of the Potomac. Inside the central passage was a twisting staircase, and on the wall at the foot of those stairs was the iron key to the Bastille given to George by the Marquis de Lafayette after the royal prison was stormed in 1789. Scattered on the grounds nearby were greenhouses, quarters for enslaved people, stables, and work buildings for doing laundry, smoking meat, spinning cloth, making shoes, and completing other essential tasks. A leisurely stroll from the mansion led to the tomb, a simple unmarked brick vault dug into a grassy knoll where George and Martha were buried.

When Bushrod and Nancy arrived, the mansion was empty. Tourists today see the interior of Mount Vernon recreated to look like it did in 1799 when George died. But Martha gave away almost all of their personal property and all of her enslaved people to other family members in her will, though Bushrod may have bought some items from the estate sale.[6] Consequently, far less is known about how the mansion looked inside when the justice's family lived there. Bushrod turned to his old friend Eliza Powel for a loan to furnish the house fully and buy the equipment required to run the farm.[7] The months between Martha's death and Bushrod's arrival were also a brief shining moment when Mount Vernon was free from slavery. George's slaves had been freed by Martha on Bushrod's advice, but the justice restored bondage to Mount Vernon by bringing his enslaved people there, including his unacknowledged relative West Ford, who was not yet twenty-one.[8] Oliver Smith's family, who had belonged to Jack Washington, were

Washington's Heir. Gerard N. Magliocca, Oxford University Press. © Oxford University Press 2022.
DOI: 10.1093/oso/9780190947040.003.0008

Figure 7.1 Mount Vernon. Mount Vernon Ladies' Association.

brought to the estate as part of a group including Sinah and her husband, Joe; her brother Ham and his wife, Pat (no last names recorded); and their children.[9] By 1815, the justice owned seventy-nine enslaved people at the plantation.[10]

The Life of George Washington

Even before Martha's death, Bushrod was grappling with how to handle the greatest treasure passed down by his uncle. George Washington was meticulous in all things, but he was especially careful with his personal papers. In retirement, he spent considerable time arranging his collection, which included more than thirty trunks for his Revolutionary War archive alone.[11] The former president was planning to construct a building at Mount Vernon to house them, but he never got further than ordering bookshelves. In a letter to a friend written two months after George's death, Bushrod explained: "As soon as I found myself the legatee of the papers of my late Uncle Gen[eral] Washington, I presumed that the public would expect from me the history of a life so conspicuously employed as his was in the civil and military affairs of this country. Your observations have impressed me very fully with the propriety of having such a history prepared for publication as speedily as circumstances will admit. A diffidence of my own talents for such an undertaking, together with weak eyes and want of time will probably forbid me from attempting it, but I trust that the selection of a fit character may be in my power, and this I shall endeavor to make immediately."[12]

Bushrod thought he knew the perfect person to write George Washington's biography—John Marshall. This was hardly the result of a thorough national search, but in 1800 (before he became chief justice) Marshall agreed.[13] They made a handshake deal under which they would divide the profits equally, with Washington providing the documents and taking care of the business arrangements.[14] When Bushrod was unsure about some of George's military actions in 1776, he wrote Alexander Hamilton (who had served in that campaign) and asked him a series of probing questions.[15] Washington later negotiated a contract with Caleb P. Wayne, the editor of a Federalist newspaper in Philadelphia, to publish the biography in five volumes.[16] The goal was to sell subscriptions where the buyer would agree to buy all the volumes before the first one was printed. As Justice Washington told Wayne, "Few will purchase afterwards because those who dislike the expense will calculate upon gratifying their curiosity by borrowing from their friend and neighbor."[17] The justice kept a close eye on the financial and legal details of the project over many years, including researching the Copyright Act to ensure that he knew its requirements for renewing a book copyright.[18]

Choosing Marshall to write the Washington biography was probably a mistake. The chief justice had never written a book and found the task slow going. "I had to learn," he said, "that under the pressure of constant exertion the spring of the mind loses its elasticity."[19] Another complication created by Bushrod's selection was that he and the chief justice were accused of preparing a partisan biography.[20] When he heard about the book, President Jefferson told a friend: "John Marshall is writing the life of General Washington from his papers. It is intended to come out just in time to influence the [1804] presidential election."[21] Bushrod rejected that claim, telling Wayne that Republicans "may say what they please and I have expected they would say a great deal, but this is at least not intended to be a party work, nor will any candid man have cause to make this charge."[22] The taint of political bias may have hurt sales, but a more concrete problem was that Marshall delivered the first volume rather late, which led some of the subscribers to cancel their orders.[23]

The editing process on the biography provides a glimpse of how Marshall and Bushrod worked together. Each volume's title page said that the work was "complied under the inspection of The Honorable Bushrod Washington."[24] When Marshall was working on the third book in the series, he told Bushrod he was "extremely anxious that you should give the volume an attentive reading and make all those corrections which I am sure will suggest themselves to you."[25] After receiving Washington's comments, the chief justice suggested changes to the wording of various passages, adding that "I very much regret that the manuscript is so voluminous."[26] He added that more comments were welcome, as "you mistake me very much if you think I rank the corrections of a friend with the bitter sarcasms of a foe, or that I should feel either wounded or chagrined at my inattentions and inaccuracies being pointed out by another. I know there are many and great defects in the composition." Washington also told Wayne that he "went to Richmond and continued with Mr. Marshall until we went through the reading and correcting of the third volume. I have just finished a second reading of it for the purpose of making a table of contents."[27] He then fact-checked the text and commented about the proposed battle maps, adding a thoughtful description of how British and American forces should be displayed.

The Life of George Washington was not completed until 1807, and the books were a disappointment to many contemporary readers. Some found Marshall's prose ponderous and felt that George did not come alive.[28] One review stated that the books were "unpardonably deficient in all that constitutes the soul and charm of biography" and there was no "anecdote that might fix a distinguishing feature of private character in the memory."[29] Others thought Marshall wrote a hagiography, with John Adams commenting that the books were "a mausoleum, 100 feet square and 200 feet high."[30] On the other hand, Madison thought the books were "highly respectable, as a specimen of historical composition."[31] Marshall and Washington each received about $20,000 in royalties, far less than they had expected.[32] They began publishing a second edition of *Life of Washington* in the 1820s and also worked together on those books.[33] And when Bushrod decided to publish a second edition of his two-volume series on the decisions of the Virginia Court of Appeals from the 1790s, Marshall reciprocated by serving as his research assistant, reviewing the record in one of the cases and helping him secure a new copyright for the book.[34]

The Archivist

With exclusive custody of such an important collection, Bushrod faced some ticklish questions about access to George's papers. One example came when Alexander Hamilton asked for some official cabinet memoranda that he had written for the president.[35] The justice said no. "On the one hand my esteem for you produces a correspondent wish to oblige you," he said, "whilst on the other I apprehend that a compliance would probably expose me to perhaps a just censure, as well as to future perplexity in consequence of similar applications. The opinions delivered to the President by the heads of departments were those I presume of a private council and intended for his information. They could therefore be obtained from no person but myself. Other measures of that administration may be again censured, discussed and condemned by one party, and vindicated by the other, whilst both must or at least resort to the same quiver for arms to fight with." "Acting with the fairness which shall always mark my conduct," he said, "I could not upon such a subject refuse to one what I have granted to the other party, and thus the papers might be used in a way very different from that which I am persuaded was intended by the person who confided them to my care." Washington told Marshall that he turned Hamilton down because "I formed a resolution shortly after the papers came to my possession, not to use or permit them to be used, for party purposes. If I opened them to my political friends, I could not refuse like access to those from whom I differed in opinion. How could I, without incurring imputations of unfairness and subjecting myself to charges which nothing but a resort to the papers could remove."[36] When a request came from someone seeking personal and unofficial letters written to George, Bushrod was more accommodating.[37] For instance, he loaned Madison and Lafayette some of their letters to his uncle so that they could make copies to replace their lost originals.[38]

Long after Hamilton's murder, his widow came calling in search of his correspondence with George Washington. Eliza Schuyler Hamilton, now famous as one of the Schuyler sisters from Lin-Manuel Miranda's musical *Hamilton*, visited Mount Vernon in 1818 seeking copies of some letters as part of a planned biography of her husband.[39] Seven years later, she contacted Bushrod again asking for documents proving that Hamilton had drafted President Washington's 1796 Farewell Address.[40] Hamilton's role in ghostwriting the address was a secret, but Eliza wanted the world to know as part of her lifelong effort to revive his reputation.[41] The justice replied that there was nothing in his collection on the Farewell Address.[42] Undaunted, she sued Rufus King—a member of the Constitutional Convention—to obtain any letters in his possession that might prove Hamilton's authorship.[43] Chief Justice Marshall told Bushrod: "I concur with you precisely in the course which ought to be pursued in the very unpleasant affair which Mrs. Hamilton has so unwisely brought before a court of chancery. It is said that Mrs. H[amilton] has demanded these letters and that you have withheld them. It is material to let the fact be known that no such letters were retained by General Washington. I can aver that I never saw them."[44]

In the 1820s, Marshall and Bushrod began working on a published collection of the Washington papers. Their inclination, at least on the chief justice's end, was that any letters reflecting badly on their patron should be excluded. For instance, Marshall believed that a letter from George that "expresses a good deal of dissatisfaction with General Greene" should be "suppressed," though he added that "I wish you would look at it and do what you think best."[45] Another letter that referred to George Mason "rather in terms of reprobation" during the debate on the Constitution's ratification should either be redacted "or the names left blank," but Marshall said he had not "executed this intention and suggest it to you for your consideration."[46] Ultimately, Washington and Marshall decided to ask Jared Sparks, who later became the president of Harvard, to oversee the project.[47] Marshall wrote Bushrod that "in addition to the obvious reasons for accepting [the Sparks offer] stated by yourself I suggested others of a nature somewhat delicate which I would not willingly submit to any eye but yours."[48] (He did not say what those delicate reasons were.) The book netted Marshall's and Washington's heirs another $15,000 each.[49]

By modern standards, Bushrod was a careless caretaker of his uncle's papers. He sometimes tore George's autograph from a letter and gave that scrap to a friend or collector.[50] While the justice's decision to keep the official papers from George's archive confidential was admirable, he did let one person see all those papers—John Marshall. Their duopoly over the archive may help explain their preeminence within the Supreme Court in certain cases.[51] Recall that Madison's notes on the Constitutional Convention were not published until after the chief justice and Justice Washington died.[52] Consequently, these two men possessed an advantage over their colleagues. They were the only two justices who had known George well. After 1810, they were the only two justices who had participated in the Constitution's ratification.[53] And they were also the only two who could claim special insights about what the Constitution meant due to their access to the former president's papers. Whether they ever played that trump card in the discussions among the other justices at the boarding house, though, is unknowable.

Living in a Fishbowl

Washington's routine did not vary much after he moved to Mount Vernon. Every February and part of March he stayed at a boarding house with the other justices in the capital. Nancy did not join him there, as Marshall gently discouraged his colleagues from bringing their spouses.[54] But when Washington went to Philadelphia and New Jersey to hear circuit cases, she almost always came with him.[55] This schedule meant that he was typically at Mount Vernon mainly during the summer or winter. One Christmas guest was Martin Van Buren, recently elected to the Senate, who wrote: "A closer acquaintance confirmed my impressions of the purity of the Judge's character, and I was agreeably surprised by the vivacity of his disposition. His mental qualifications were of a highly respectable order, and united to the simplicity and frankness of his manners made his society peculiarly agreeable."[56] Van Buren added: "In my experience of men, I have never known three men who received so nearly the same stamp from the hand of Nature as James Madison, Bushrod Washington and James Kent. In the simplicity, sincerity and inoffensiveness of their dispositions they were identical; each owned a delightful cheerfulness of temperament and an unvarying desire to develop that heaven-born quality in others. With a buoyancy of spirits and manners sometimes bordering on levity, they never for a moment hazarded the respect of their friends or of those about them." Van Buren then drew a contrast between Kent, an admired judge in New York, and Washington, concluding that Kent possessed a more powerful mind but inferior judgment.[57]

Washington may have been relieved to be away from Mount Vernon because the estate was an unrivaled tourist attraction. George had complained about the crush of visitors who came and (in keeping with the etiquette of the time) were entitled to free hospitality.[58] Now that people were coming to see the ex-president's tomb, the pilgrimage was relentless. Bushrod attempted to control the flow of people by requiring them to present a letter of introduction from someone he knew, though he did not always enforce this rule.[59] Visitors to Mount Vernon left behind many accounts, some of which caught Washington on a good day as a friendly host and others that found him out of sorts and surly. For instance, when a group of officers arrived for a tour, one of them wrote: "Judge Washington received us with the greatest kindness. He sent refreshments to the cadets and invited the officers and gentlemen who were present to his hospitality."[60] But another traveler said that the justice "received us coldly and reluctantly . . . and said 'I do not like to see people on [a Sunday], but you may walk around.' "[61]

The invention of the steamboat made Mount Vernon much more accessible. Ships carrying bands playing "marine music" to entertain the passengers were soon making regular stops there on their Potomac route.[62] Matters came to a head in 1822, when the justice posted this announcement: "The feelings of Mrs.

Figure 7.2 The interior foyer of Mount Vernon, with the key to the Bastille hanging on the left. Mount Vernon Ladies' Association.

Washington and myself, have been so much wounded by some late occurrences at this place, that I am compelled to give this PUBLIC NOTICE, that permission will not in future be granted to Steam-Boat Parties, to enter the gardens, or to walk over the grounds, nor will I consent that Mount Vernon, much less the lawns, shall be the place at which eating, drinking and dancing parties may assemble."[63] Bushrod also barred all uninvited visitors on Sundays, even turning away a party of congressmen who sought to visit the tomb and threatening to sue the steamboat captain who brought them.[64] Chief Justice Marshall wrote after that dust-up that he was "sorry to see in the papers your unpleasant altercation with some members of Congress," adding that he thought a rule against Sunday visits was entirely proper.[65]

A common theme of the eyewitness accounts was that Mount Vernon was dilapidated. When Justice Story went in 1821, he wrote his wife: "There were general symptoms of decay visible; and I was sorry that so little effort was made to repair the silent ravages of time. Were I the owner of this seat, I would preserve everything as nearly as could be in the style in which Washington left it, but I would not suffer anything to moulder away neglected and forgotten."[66] Another account observed that "every thing bespeaks the neglect and apathy of the present owner."[67] "The house contains nothing curious," the visitor continued, "save the huge old iron key of the French Bastille, kept in a glass case. . . . The furniture is mean and common and was brought here by Judge Washington." As for the exterior of the mansion, he said, "it suffers for want of paint, while bricks seem falling from the chimneys without being replaced. . . . The grass upon the lawn and garden, in front and rear of the house, is rotting and seeding down; it is never mown. The tomb containing the General, and his lady . . . might be mistaken for a dog-kennel."[68] The unkempt state of the tomb was a particular sore point, as one mourner said its appearance was a "stain of ingratitude, which, if not quickly removed, will become fixed, and forever remain an indelible stain and disgrace to the nation."[69]

Horace Binney captured Mount Vernon's fading glory during his visit in 1809. The justice had invited Binney and some other Philadelphia lawyers to spend a Sunday with him. They were met in Alexandria by Bushrod's coach, which Binney thought was "an heir loom of the Estate, antique, capacious, and showy."[70] The driver was dressed "with rather incomplete garments, a shabby hat, and his feet [were] wrapped up in a piece of old green baise [that is, coarse wool]."[71] And he "held the reins of four of the most raw-boned and ill groomed horses" imaginable. Shortly after leaving Alexandria, the group realized that these horses could not carry all of them, so some of the lawyers got out and walked back to town in search of another coach. Binney decided to press on, but soon the carriage Washington sent got stuck in the mud. Like almost all travelers, Binney did arrive at his final destination—eventually.

Mount Vernon's decline was probably inevitable. Bushrod was not a farmer. When he died, the justice's library was worth twice as much as all the livestock and equipment at Mount Vernon, which reveals his priorities.[72] Bushrod had told George in 1788 "that the cares of a plantation and the attention due to a professional life, are altogether incompatible with each other."[73] He was right. Richard Peters, his colleague on the circuit court in Philadelphia, told him: "You know that I do not hold in small estimation Virginian Talents, but your farming is deplorably *superficial*."[74] Much of the time the justice was away from Mount Vernon hearing cases. But even if he had concentrated on making the estate successful, he would have faced long odds. George had found turning a profit challenging in his later years, and he was a more skilled businessman working with an acreage twice as large as what he left to his nephew.[75] Virginia as a whole went through an agricultural malaise in the early nineteenth century due to soil exhaustion and falling crop prices, which left Jefferson and Madison mired in debt as their plantation income fell.[76] Bushrod said in 1821 that he "struggled for about 20 years to pay the expenses of my farm" and that "I would state upon my best judgment that the produce of the farm has in general fallen short of its support from $500 to $1000 annually."[77] One tourist correctly perceived that the "gift of Mount Vernon, from Washington to his nephew, was of no value; for probably, from the hour of his death to the present time, the planation has not supported itself."[78] The tourists themselves were partly to blame, as they paid nothing for the estate's upkeep while often inflicting damage by taking plants from the grounds or ripping cloth from the cover of George's coffin as souvenirs.[79]

Stories about the sorry state of Washington's tomb led Congress and Virginia to ask the justice for permission to build a new public resting place and to transfer George's remains from Mount Vernon.[80] Virginia's request came in 1816, in part because there was talk in Congress about building a giant mausoleum in the capital.[81] George Washington's will specified that his body be buried on the property "and it is my express desire that my Corpse may be interred in a private manner, without parade, or funeral Oration."[82] Accordingly, his nephew rejected all the transfer requests, stating that George's "will is to me a law which I dare not disobey."[83] Not long after Bushrod and Nancy were buried in the tomb, a disgruntled ex-gardener from Mount Vernon attempted to steal George's skull.[84] After that incident, the family decided to construct the more secure and elaborate tomb that remains today, following directions in George's will that stated: "The family vault at Mount Vernon requiring repairs, and being improperly situated besides, I desire that a new one of Brick, and upon a larger Scale, may be built at the foot of what is commonly called the Vineyard Inclosure."[85]

The greatest threat to Mount Vernon, apart from neglect, came during the War of 1812.[86] In August 1814, a British force burned down the Capitol and the White House. Bushrod was at Mount Vernon and watched anxiously from the piazza

Figure 7.3 George Washington's original tomb, which was relocated after Justice Washington's death. Painting by William Thompson Russell Smith. Mount Vernon Ladies' Association.

as a British fleet sailed up the Potomac. Instead of firing on George Washington's house, however, the squadron fired a salute. He later told a friend that the British "squadron lay at this place some days in its ascent and on its return, and yet I do not believe that during the whole time a single barge approached this shore. This distinguished forbearance I owe to the generous feeling of Commodore Gordon for a place which has once been the residence of my venerated Uncle."[87] The commodore had "an anxious desire to visit this spot but was so delicate as to declare his resolution not to do so, presuming that my official situation would render such a step peculiarly embarrassing and disagreeable to me. He further added that he would commit no act of hostility injurious to this place even [if] the militia should make their appearance on it." "I have much reason to thank him for such sentiments and conduct," Washington concluded, "and should it ever be my good fortune to see him in peace here or elsewhere, I should be proud to give him proof of my gratitude."

Domestic Life

A librarian of Congress who knew the justice wrote that he was "one of those men to whom the pleasures of the domestic circle are more seducing than the fitful though captivating splendor which surround the temples of the statesman or the warrior."[88] Faith was the center of Washington's family life. As there was no church in the immediate vicinity, the justice led prayers at Mount Vernon twice a day.[89] Writing to his great-nephews George and Spotswood in 1827, Washington said "never permit a morning or night to pass away without returning thanks to God for all his mercies to you, and imploring his divine assistance to promote your temporal and eternal happiness."[90] He remained an active Episcopalian, held pews in two churches located in Alexandria, and participated in church governance.[91] Some of Justice Washington's enslaved people, including Ham and Pat, joined the Alexandria Baptist Society, a church congregation that included whites, free Blacks, and slaves.[92]

Bushrod and Nancy did not socialize much at Mount Vernon, except for some dinners they held for his Supreme Court colleagues. This seclusion was probably a result of Nancy's health issues, as the justice was a reasonably sociable person.[93] In 1806, he told a friend about a stay in Annapolis over Christmas that included "charming ladies" and opined that the District of Columbia was "thronged with beautiful girls and other strangers. There are few but handsome women belonging to the City."[94] Much like the chief justice, Washington enjoyed wine and bought bottles for Marshall while receiving some from Madison.[95] He also loved sharing cured meats from Mount Vernon's smokehouse with Justice Story because "I know you are fond of old hams. . . . I trust you will find them as excellent as you ever tasted."[96] A friend explained that the justice had "a more decided inclination to the disengaged talk of a club supper-table, and a circulation of a temperate glass, than to anything else upon the round earth."[97] Less is known about how Washington spent time with his nieces and nephews, as no letters survive that describe them as children. Some of his nephews went to boarding school when they were old enough, with the justice paying their way.[98] George Corbin Washington became a member of Congress from Maryland. Charles Washington was a favorite who would receive George's papers and sword from Bushrod.[99] The justice's namesake nephew Bushrod, on the other hand, became a ne'er-do-well who racked up debts that Washington felt obliged to pay.[100] John Augustine Washington inspired the greatest confidence and would inherit (along with Nancy's niece Jane Charlotte, whom John Augustine married) Mount Vernon.[101] To his great-nephews, Washington dispensed wisdom not unlike what his uncle had given to him, telling them that they should study hard "both in and out of school, and be seen as seldom as possible in the streets."[102]

One remarkable facet of daily life at Mount Vernon was that enslaved people and free people of color lived and worked together, which was virtually unheard of elsewhere in the South. After West Ford became an adult and gained his freedom, he married Priscella Bell, a free Black woman, and worked at the estate while raising their children.[103] Ford also brought his mother, Venus, to live at Mount Vernon, though she remained enslaved.[104] Some former slaves of George also remained at the estate, though many of them were essentially retired.[105] One might think that this mix of free people of color and slaves made life better for the enslaved, but the opposite was probably true. This thought was confirmed by the upheaval that ripped Mount Vernon apart in 1821 (as Chapter 10 explains) when Justice Washington sold some of his enslaved people and broke up some of their families.

Being the lord of Mount Vernon was, in short, a mixed blessing. Washington was given memberships in the American Philosophical Society, the American Antiquarian Society, and the Bunker Hill Monument Association in part because he was George's heir.[106] But he also received letters like the one from a man calling himself "your most affectionate and living nephew," who explained that he was recently rescued from people who were "justly hanged for their crime of stealing me away and cutting open my head."[107] "I am at this time fat and well," the so-called nephew continued, so please "send for me as soon as possible, that I may come and receive the money and negroes which you have for me. I have had strong notions of marriage with Mary Nabb but have now determined that I will spite her by not marrying her and that I will marry no lady until I receive my fortune." "Let me know how your Judgeship is coming on," he ended, "and not fail to inform how much specie [gold or silver coins] you are saving for me." Scribbled on the back of the letter was this note from the justice: "From some impertinent fellow assuming the name of Samuel G. Washington."[108] Such was the price of fame.

8
Riding Circuit

Most of Justice Washington's work was as a circuit judge.[1] On average, he spent only about six weeks a year hearing cases on the Supreme Court. But he spent four months each year on circuit. Twice annually from 1803 until 1829, except when prevented by illness or by the War of 1812, Bushrod and Nancy traveled by coach from Mount Vernon to Philadelphia. The justice then stayed there (or sometimes in Trenton) for two months to conduct trials and hear appeals from Pennsylvania and New Jersey.[2] His obituary captured the truth that "Justice Washington belonged to two states—Virginia and Pennsylvania."[3] Each justice's individual temperament was revealed on circuit because he led that court. Washington's judicial craft is especially transparent because he kept a detailed journal on some of his circuit cases.[4] The justice demonstrated a knack for the art of instructing juries and a wise sensibility in written opinions covering a broad range of subjects. And when a showdown between Pennsylvania and the federal government reached his court in *United States v. Bright*, Washington did not hesitate to affirm national authority and the rule of law over the threat of armed force.

Setting the Scene

The circuit courts created by Congress in 1802 gave each justice and each district court judge within a part of each circuit limited criminal and civil jurisdiction. There were no federal appellate judges below the Supreme Court, as there are today. In criminal law, the circuit courts were given exclusive jurisdiction over federal felonies and concurrent jurisdiction with district courts over misdemeanors, although misdemeanor convictions from a district court could be appealed to circuit court.[5] In civil cases, circuit court jurisdiction was available for disputes worth more than $500 that involved the United States, an alien, or citizens of different states (now known as diversity jurisdiction), while maritime judgments from a district court could be appealed to a circuit court.[6] This meant that many, but not all, cases raising an issue of federal law could be heard in federal court. In one circuit opinion, Justice Washington said: "Whether it would have been wise in congress, to have vested in the national courts, the power of deciding, in some way or other, every national question, authorized by

Washington's Heir. Gerard N. Magliocca, Oxford University Press. © Oxford University Press 2022.
DOI: 10.1093/oso/9780190947040.003.0009

the constitution; is another point. I am one of those, I confess, who have always thought it would have been better, if the legislature of the Union, in allotting to the several courts the jurisdiction they were to exercise, had occupied the whole ground marked out by the constitution; but, I am not one of those, who think it a commendable quality in a judge, to enlarge, by construction, the sphere of his jurisdiction."[7] Circuit courts were often the final stop for litigants, as Congress did not give the Supreme Court broad appellate jurisdiction over the circuits until long after Justice Washington died.[8]

Washington's colleague during nearly his entire circuit career in Philadelphia was Richard Peters, a genial district court judge appointed by President Washington. Peters and Washington got along well, in part because Peters was a bon vivant with a lively (and vulgar) wit that the justice described as the "happy flow of spirits which you generally possess."[9] A lawyer who argued before Peters noted that he was famed for his skill with a "pun, quip, crank, or quiddit."[10] Judge Peters was a Federalist who served as Speaker of Pennsylvania's House of Representatives before joining the bench and was friendly with Chief Justice Marshall.[11] Attorneys who practiced in the circuit thought that Peters was not sharp, but Washington was fiercely loyal to him.[12] At one point, the justice even lobbied Senator Daniel Webster to give district judges a pay raise, mainly to help Peters.[13] Washington also became close to the judge's son, Richard Peters Jr., and turned to him to produce published reports of the justice's circuit cases.[14] When the Supreme Court reporter position became available in 1827, the justice recommended Richard Peters Jr. for the position, in which he served for many years.[15]

Justice Washington's circuit service was unusual because his circuit did not include his home state. Every other justice on the Marshall Court was assigned to a circuit that included his home state, to reduce travel and because many of the cases within a circuit involved subjects or state law that would be familiar to the justice from that circuit. But Washington could not take the Virginia circuit because Chief Justice Marshall was from Virginia (and, presumably, was entitled to pick first). Washington probably asked for Philadelphia because he was fond of the city from his days as an apprentice. Due to his choice, the justice was forced to learn unfamiliar state law and issues that he had not handled as a lawyer.[16] Philadelphia, after all, was a thriving port. Thus, many of the federal cases there involved maritime and commercial law, on which Washington became a leading authority.[17] He was also active in shaping patent and copyright law, as Philadelphia was a hub for innovation and the arts.[18] For example, Washington was one of the first judges to articulate the "doctrine of equivalents," a key patent concept holding that an invention that is practically the same as a patented technology violates a patent owner's rights.[19] Likewise, Washington was at the forefront of describing the "fixation" requirement to obtain a copyright, which meant

Figure 8.1 Judge Richard Peters, Justice Washington's colleague in the Philadelphia circuit. Painting by Ph. B. Wallace. University of Pennsylvania.

that an artistic or literary work must be drawn or written down in some form; an idea alone—no matter how creative—cannot be copyrighted.[20]

The records of what Washington did as a circuit judge are drawn almost exclusively from his notes taken during the cases.[21] In the 1790s, the justice was a leader in creating modern case reports for the Virginia Court of Appeals. In the 1810s, he began working on a similar project for his circuit decisions at a time when circuit decisions were not widely reported. Washington relied on Richard Peters Jr. as an editor, perhaps because his limited eyesight made him reluctant to produce his own volumes. He would send Peters revised versions of his notes, as he explained in an 1814 letter: "Soon after my return home from Philadelphia, I copied into my notebook all the written decisions which were delivered and which constituted about two-thirds of all the cases which were tried. . . . You will recollect that I rely upon you to correct the many errors of style . . . which in the hurried manner these notes were written will no doubt occur in great numbers."[22] Washington's edits were sometimes substantive, in part because some came years later, when other cases may have changed the law or his view.[23] "You will observe," he wrote Peters in 1816, "that the corrections which I have suggested are principally such as qualify expressions more general than it was safe to use or tend to expunge dicta where unnecessary to the points decided, the correctness of which might be doubted. If any of the opinions are wrong upon the point decided, they must stand so. As to arguments used merely for illustration, it is proper to correct them where they are doubtful, in the way I have adopted."[24]

One of Washington's notebooks is in the Chicago History Museum and gives us a backstage pass into his work at some crucial points.[25] This notebook, which is described as his journal in the rest of this book, contains fragments of letters, records on the illnesses among enslaved and free people at Mount Vernon, notes on other cases and subjects, and draft opinions. The precise date range of the journal is hard to ascertain, but one of the circuit court opinions that he prepared in the journal is from 1820 and one opinion from the Supreme Court is from 1827.[26] Acquired by the Chicago Historical Society, the journal came from the estate of Charles Gunther, a candy magnate and political memorabilia collector, who gave the society many items, such as the table upon which Ulysses S. Grant and Robert E. Lee signed Lee's surrender ending the Civil War.[27] The journal sometimes provides an unvarnished view of Washington's thoughts, much like a diary. On other pages, the journal is evidence of the justice's exhaustive review of the testimony in a trial or the cases cited by the attorneys. In later chapters, the journal will show Washington working through challenging legal problems, talking to himself about arguments made by other judges (such as Chief Justice Marshall) and, on occasion, changing his mind.

In addition to Washington's published opinions and his journal, the life of his circuit was described well by lawyers who regularly appeared there. The Philadelphia bar was an elite club, much like the one that Washington belonged to in Richmond when he was a lawyer. He referred affectionately to the younger attorneys in the circuit as "his boys" and to the senior ones as part of the "model bar of the United States."[28] Among its leaders was Jared Ingersoll, a member of the Constitutional Convention and the Federalist nominee for vice president in 1812.[29] Joseph Hopkinson represented Justice Chase during his Senate impeachment trial, served in the House of Representatives, and was someone who Washington said "would be an ornament and acquisition to any bench in the United States."[30] Horace Binney, whose memories of the justice were relayed in some earlier chapters, was later described by the Supreme Court as "one of the country's leading lawyers" of his era.[31] And David Paul Brown was the greatest anti-slavery lawyer in the city.[32] Washington took delight in the arguments these men made, commenting wryly in one case that a treatise writer "has been roughly handled by the counsel on one side, and highly eulogized on the other."[33]

They, in turn, praised Washington as an able administrator and a fine judge worth emulating.[34]

The best accounts of Washington's circuit court come from Binney and Brown. Binney's description especially rings true because he was not always complimentary. Indeed, the theme of Binney's reflection on the justice's life was that "he contained two different persons in the same man."[35] "In private life, and in general society," Binney said, "he was kind and good-humored, but not above the common level of educated men."[36] "His reading, except in the law, and in novels . . . did not appear to be extensive." (Indeed, David Paul Brown said that he did not think that the justice knew the author of *Macbeth*.)[37] "His taste," Binney went on, "particularly in music, of which he was passionately fond, and thought himself a judge, was rather unrefined. His opinions, whenever he expressed them upon political topics, or the occurrences of the day, or on points of social discussion, were of course sound, but in no way striking, either by their acuteness, or

Figure 8.2 Horace Binney, one of Philadelphia's leading lawyers and a close observer of Justice Washington. Drawing by Albert Newsam. National Portrait Gallery.

novelty, or the language in which he uttered them."[38] "But when his robes were upon him," Binney said, "he was an altogether different person."[39] "Without the least apparent effort, he made everybody see at first sight, that he was equal to all the duties of the place, ceremonial as well as intellectual. His mind was full, his elocution free, clear, and accurate, his command of all about him indisputable. His learning and acuteness were not only equal to the profoundest argument, but often carried the Counsel to depths which they had not penetrated."[40]

Binney called Washington the best trial judge he ever saw, "and I will refer to certain of Judge Washington's very striking qualities, which will enable others to comprehend the grounds of my opinion, if they do not fully show all the causes of his superiority."[41] One trait that "he possessed in absolute perfection—it was *attention*. This great faculty . . . is a turning difference between a good and a good-for-nothing Judge."[42] "Washington never interrogated a witness, nor asked Counsel to repeat what he had said, and but rarely called for documents after they had been read to him. He caught the important parts in a moment, and made a reliable note of them, before the Counsel was ready to proceed with further testimony."[43] Moreover, "he maintained, by his *equanimity*, a calm and equable temper in all parts of the Court. . . . He never interrupted Counsel—he never expressly told them that they had labored a point sufficiently, or that he wished them to consider another matter more, or that they were wasting time. But when that happened, his eye would have an expression, and occasionally he would give a short lift of the head, which they who saw much of him understood perfectly."[44] "He could be very sarcastic and severe," Binney said, "but this was far from his general bearing."[45]

Binney then described a typical day in Bushrod's court. For most of Justice Washington's tenure, the court met in Congress Hall, a building adjacent to Independence Hall that had housed Congress when the capital was in Philadelphia.[46] Binney continued:

> I now see him, beginning a jury trial, seated on that leathern cushion . . . with his box of rather Scotch snuff within his reach. There does he sit for five hours, perhaps six, without once leaving that chair, or changing his position in it, or ever taking his eye—that bright, steady, single eye—from the Counsel, or the witness that is on the floor, except to make a short note of the argument or the evidence, or to take a pinch of half Scotch snuff. During all this time, and so from day to day, if the trial shall last a week or even longer, he will never interrupt the speaker, or the reader, or the witness; nor disclose to the observer, by more or less attention, or in any other way, that the speaker is acceptable to him, or otherwise, or is speaking to a man who has an opinion of his own. He may smile at what Judge Peters whispers at his ear and go on as before. [Then] he will place before the Jury, this complicated case of fact and law and contradictory

> evidence, parol and written, so clearly, in such lucid order of parts, and with such masterly instructions . . . that it will have almost the air of inspiration. I have seen the same thing done many, many times; and never heard a suggestion from anybody, that he was either too concise, or too full, or in the least degree deficient or partial.[47]

David Paul Brown agreed with Binney's overall evaluation and said that Washington "stood among the judiciary as "THE JUDGE" par excellence.[48] Brown described him as "about five feet six inches high, with a finely chiseled, feminine face, and of a slender and feeble frame . . . His eyes were black, his hair brown, tinged with gray; his forehead expansive, and marked with thought."[49] "To the young and inexperienced members of the bar," Brown said, "he was always attentive and indulgent; he listened to them with great patience and marked courtesy."[50] He recalled one of his first trials, where he turned to call his witnesses to the stand and found that they were no longer in the courtroom. "I at once stated the difficulty to the Court," Brown said, "Judge Washington, who appeared to understand it as I did, replied in the kindest way, 'We will wait a moment, sir, perhaps they will return.' After waiting about ten minutes, which seemed like an hour, he turned towards me, and said: 'I believe the case must go on.' "[51] Brown also relayed an incident where two lawyers exchanged some harsh words, and Washington "placidly and mildly turned to the counsel and said in a subdued voice: 'Gentlemen, Philadelphia is celebrated throughout the Union, for the talents and courtesy of its bar; I trust, nay, I know, that you would not be willing to be considered exceptions to that character.' "[52] "In laying down the law, or in the explanations of its technical terms," Brown said, the justice "was unequalled."[53]

The heart of a circuit court's work, as Binney and Brown's stories show, was trials. Most judicial biographies are about appeals and the written opinions that those appeals produce, and this book will spend time addressing that aspect of Washington's work. But fewer studies exist of what makes someone a first-rate trial judge. Managing a jury trial and writing a fine opinion are different skills. Many justices who are considered great would not have been (or were not) great trial judges.[54] An important trait in a good trial judge, especially in Washington's day, was the ability to communicate the law in a way that ordinary jurors could understand.[55] Judges were also expected in this era to summarize the evidence and guide juries to a particular verdict in a way that is not done today.[56] Washington excelled at both tasks, in part, because he strongly believed in jury trials. He once said that the "theory of jury trials must necessarily imply a principle of compromises and concession, amongst the members of that body. In cases of conflicting evidence, where the credit of the witnesses must be weighed and decided upon, or where damages are to be assessed for the measure of which no legal rule is prescribed; it is inconceivable that twelve men should arrive precisely to the same result, unless upon the principle just stated."[57] In 1818, the justice told a jury on behalf of himself and Judge Peters: "It gives us great satisfaction, that, during the sixteen and seventeen years, in which we have presided in this court, this is [only] the second case, where, upon a dry point of law, a jury has given a verdict against the opinion of the court."[58]

In jury trials, Washington took pains to explain the law without using jargon. A few examples will have to suffice to give a sense of his style. In one criminal case, the justice gave the following instruction on manslaughter: "Manslaughter is the unlawful killing of another, without malice, either express or implied. It differs from murder in the important particular of the absence of malice; as where it happens in a sudden heat, when passion has obtained dominion over reason and the gentler feelings of the heart. From a respect to human infirmities, our law, in such a case, mitigates the offence of murder into manslaughter, as well as the punishment. Still, however, this offence is unlawful; the law not permitting any man to avenge his own wrongs, unless in a case of great emergency, by the death of the supposed offender."[59] In a contract case, he lucidly explained when a custom creates a binding obligation between parties: "What is called the custom or usage of trade, is the law of that trade; and to make it at all obligatory, it must be ancient, (sufficiently so at least, to be generally known,) certain, uniform, and reasonable. A usage of so doubtful authority as to be known only to a few, and where merchants engaged in the trade differ as they do in this case, as to the existence of it, can never be regarded."[60] Binney pointed out that "a jury never came back to ask what he meant, and Counsel were never at a loss to state the very point of their objection to his opinion or charge, if they had any objection to make."[61] And Brown added that when Washington gave a charge "his language was simple. He covered every topic that belonged to him as a judge and avoided everything like encroachments upon the just privileges of the jury."[62]

The Finer Points of Judging

Washington was a quick thinker during trials, but in deciding legal issues with an opinion, he was slow and meticulous. Joseph Hopkinson described him as "wise, as well as learned; sagacious and searching in the pursuit and discovery of truth, and faithful to it beyond the touch of corruption, or the diffidence of fear. He was cautious, considerate, and slow in forming a judgment; and steady, but not obstinate, in his adherence to it. No man was more willing to listen to an argument against his opinion; to receive it with candor; or to yield to it with more manliness, if it convinced him of an error."[63] Joseph Story believed that Washington's "mind was solid, rather than brilliant; sagacious and searching, rather than quick or eager; slow, but not torpid; steady, but not unyielding; comprehensive, and at the same time cautious; patient in inquiry, forcible in conception, clear in reasoning."[64] In calling the justice slow, Hopkinson and Story did not mean that he was dimwitted. Instead, they meant that he took his time before reaching any conclusion. Thinking slowly is an especially useful trait in an appellate judge. The Supreme Court's unofficial symbol (represented as a design motif outside the Court building) is a tortoise, which is meant as a reminder that justice should be deliberate.[65]

An example of Washington's detailed preparation for his decisions is *Le Tigre*, an 1820 maritime case that was ordinary except for the fact that the justice's journal contains his bench notes and his draft opinion.[66] His notes began by summarizing the claim and the response. Then, under the heading "Depositions," Washington crisply stated what each relevant witness had said at trial before the district court. Next came a description of crucial written evidence. After that, the justice wrote out an abstract of each of the leading cases cited by counsel. With all of that in hand, he then drafted an opinion in longhand that he edited on the page with various cross-outs. Washington affirmed the district court's award of salvage in *Le Tigre* but reduced the amount of the salvage award.[67] This intricate work was repeated in other circuit and Supreme Court cases that are in the journal and will be discussed in later chapters.

Le Tigre also illustrates Washington's respect for precedent. His opinions were usually filled with discussions of cases just like his notes, sometimes excessively so.[68] The justice's reliance on precedent was emblematic of his circumspect approach to judging and probably resulted from his institutional desire to raise the authority of circuit court decisions by citing other court decisions. As Hopkinson said: "He was, by no means, what is called a case hunting lawyer. He knew how far he should yield to authority, without giving himself up to it without examination or reflection. . . . He was, as every safe judge must be, respectful of the authority of decided cases, but equally discriminating and careful in applying them. He had not the weak and dangerous ambition, which would shape the law to its own notions and purposes, nor the contemptible vanity to disregard the wisdom and learning of others."[69]

Unlike the simple, everyday language that he used with juries, Washington's prose in his opinions was more formal. Nevertheless, from time to time he strove for eloquence or wit. In one case, he stated an idea about prejudice and education that applies to our time as well as his: "We all know, that prejudices become more inveterate, as they ripen by age, and in the soil of ignorance. We seldom recollect the particular facts and arguments, which have led our minds to particular prejudices. The impressions gather strength, and take deeper root, the longer they remain unremoved. The sooner, therefore, the attempt is made to remove them, the better."[70] Another opinion involving a disputed estate began this way: "Were a plain man, such as the writer of this will most certainly was, called

Figure 8.3 Joseph Hopkinson, another pillar of the Philadelphia bar who became Washington's colleague on the circuit court. Print by John Sartain. National Portrait Gallery.

upon to give a construction of it, he would probably be astonished to hear that gentlemen learned in the law had been perplexed by it; and he might seek in vain for those difficulties which great talents could alone discover."[71] And in a case on the meaning of a federal law, the justice gave voice to the frustration of parsing complicated legislation: "This is one of those cases which too frequently occur, in which the court is called upon to interpret legislative expressions of doubtful import, without a clue to ascertain, with precision, what was the real intention of the framers of the law. After the closest examination of the point on which the controversy hangs, we can truly say, that our mind rather inclines to the opinion which we shall deliver, than that we feel a full confidence in its correctness."[72]

This last comment was an example of a broader trend in Washington's most difficult cases, which was that he would freely admit if he doubted his conclusion. For instance, in one maritime case he wrote: "I feel cheered by reflecting that the error of my judgment, if I have committed one, can and will be corrected by a superior tribunal; for surely a question of such national importance as this is, ought not, and I hope will not, rest upon the decision of this court. I can at the same time truly declare that if I could be so wicked as to decide this case different from the opinion which I must sincerely entertain respecting it, my humble genius and talents would not enable me to give one single reason which my conscience or judgment could approve."[73] Similarly, he once told a jury that the "court has felt extreme doubt upon one of the points, and our opinion, which is now settled, has wavered considerably, during the very able discussion which we have heard."[74] And in another case, he said: "We are sensible of the difficulty of the question, as well as of its importance to the parties, in this and other similar cases; we derive consolation, however, from reflecting, that our opinion, if wrong, is subject to a revision elsewhere."[75] To some extent, these comments were a function of his role as a circuit judge whose rulings were sometimes subject to Supreme Court review.[76] But they also expressed a refreshing honesty about how judges think.[77]

When the justices were uncertain about how to resolve their circuit cases, they would turn to one another for help.[78] Many such letters were exchanged among Chief Justice Marshall, Justice Joseph Story, and Justice Washington. "A question which is new to me if not difficult was made on Saturday," Marshall wrote Washington in one note, "and I should like to know whether it has ever been raised before you."[79] "A case has occurred in this circuit which I have taken under advisement," the chief justice told Bushrod in another letter, "for the purpose of enquiring whether it has also occurred in other circuits."[80] Justice Story asked for Washington's advice on a patent issue and in a commercial law case, and Washington wrote Marshall asking about a decision from the chief justice's circuit.[81] Part of the motivation for these inquiries was to make circuit decisions uniform without resorting to Supreme Court review, though sometimes these exchanges made clear that the Supreme Court needed to hear arguments on a tough issue.[82]

These three justices also kept one another informed about the work in their respective circuits by writing reports summarizing their decisions. The most detailed of these reports were between Washington and Story.[83] "I have at length returned home, after an absence of between 4 and 5 months," Washington wrote in one, "and I employ the first moments of leisure in reporting to [Justice Smith Thompson] and brother Story the most interesting cases which came before me . . . during my late circuit."[84] These digests were largely free from commentary, though Washington once told Story that in a particular case "I hope to make a final decree in this case in April, and never again to be plagued with it, unless an appeal should be taken."[85] Sometimes Story or Washington would reply to the other's report with comments, though most of the time they just offered playful praise.[86] A running joke in Marshall's circuit reports to Washington was that one or more of his decisions would "be reversed by your Honors" when the Supreme Court reconvened.[87] An awkward fact about being a circuit judge and a justice was that all the justices were reversed at one point or another, and Washington was no exception.[88]

United States vs. Bright

Washington's nationalism burned brightest when private individuals or states attempted to obstruct federal officials from executing the law. In an 1808 case, the justice passed sentence on three men convicted of preventing a federal marshal from enforcing a court order on their land; they brandished weapons and threatened to kill the marshal.[89] Stating that the "conduct has evinced either great ignorance or great depravity," he declared in no uncertain terms: "The courts of justice are the sanctuaries of the law; and it is through the law that our government speaks and acts. Impair, by any means, the power of these tribunals in the lawful exercise of their functions, and you attack the majesty of the law, and sap, most essentially, the foundations of the republic. The government, in a degraded state, may survive the shock, but it ceases to be a government of laws; and liberty expires when force, the only remaining alternative, becomes necessary to coerce obedience to the will of the nation."[90]

When Pennsylvania engaged in a similar sort of armed obstruction a year later in *United States v. Bright*, Justice Washington treated that state's officials in a similar way.[91] As Joseph Hopkinson later explained, *Bright* is "a case which should never be forgotten by any citizen of this Republic—It is a lesson of duty so impressive, so honorable to all concerned in it, and most of all to the commonwealth of which we are immediate members."[92] "In the course of the trial, and in deciding the various questions of law which arose in it," Hopkinson said, "the extraordinary judicial qualifications of our Judge were shown in full relief. His learning; his patient hearing; his clear and discriminating sagacity; and, above all, his unhesitating fearlessness, were all conspicuous."[93]

Bright was based on an act of heroism during the Revolutionary War. In 1778, four Americans were captured by the British and forced to work on the *Active*, an enemy vessel bringing supplies to occupied New York.[94] The prisoners managed to seize the *Active* against overwhelming odds, but before they could find a safe port, the *Active* was met and brought to Philadelphia by the *Convention*, an American ship. There, both the *Convention*'s captain and the four ex-prisoners claimed that they had won the *Active* as a prize and were entitled to sell the vessel and keep the proceeds. A special prize court created by the Continental Congress held that the *Active* belonged to the ex-prisoners. But a state court refused to acknowledge Congress's authority, ordered the *Active* sold, and directed that the proceeds be held in escrow. Over two decades later, a former *Active* prisoner, Gideon Olmstead, sued in federal district court and demanded that the special prize court's judgment be enforced. Judge Peters ruled for Olmstead, but the Pennsylvania legislature enacted a law defying the federal court order.

On appeal to the Supreme Court, Chief Justice Marshall commanded Pennsylvania to let the federal judicial process go forward.[95] "If the legislatures of the several states may, at will, annul the judgments of the courts of the United States, and destroy the rights acquired under those judgments," he said, "the constitution itself becomes a solemn mockery; and the nation is deprived of the means of enforcing its laws by the instrumentality of its own tribunals.[96] But when Judge Peters sent a federal marshal to collect the money, the marshal found the location surrounded by state militia under the command of General Michael Bright, under orders from the governor to resist any federal enforcement. The marshal responded by forming a posse of 2,000 armed men to confront the state troops. In this explosive situation, the governor wrote President Madison asking the federal government to back down. The president refused. At that point, the governor retreated and gave Olmstead the money he was due.

Bright and some of his officers were arrested for obstructing federal judicial process and put on trial before Washington and Peters in circuit court.[97] Their trial in April 1809 was the talk of Philadelphia. David Paul Brown said that "there was the greatest popular agitation. Rumors, terrors, and threats of every kind were put into circulation. The States'-rights men affected to hold the power of the general government in contempt, and the authority of the Court in derision. It was publicly proclaimed, that Judge Washington would never dare . . . to pronounce sentence against them if they were convicted."[98] Bushrod told Nancy (who was back in Virginia): "I rise at 5 in the morning and get ready for work as soon as it is sufficiently light, and I seldom go to bed earlier than between 11 & 12 at night."[99] Prior to passing sentence, Brown said Washington told the court crier: "Adjourn the Court, to meet tomorrow morning, in the [larger] room on the ground floor of this building. This is an important case—the citizens manifest a deep interest in its result, and it is but right that they should be allowed, without too much inconvenience to witness the administration of the justice of the country; to which, all men, great and small, are alike bound to submit."[100] In this public show, the fact that the justice was George Washington's nephew may have mattered. He was, in that sense, a physical embodiment of the nation and the Revolution that no other justice could represent.

Washington's jury instruction in *Bright* contained several rhetorical flourishes that were in keeping with the extraordinary nature of the case. After discussing the facts and precedents supporting federal jurisdiction over the original conclusion that the *Active* belonged to Olmstead, he said: "Let me then put the question seriously to the jury: Will they have the vanity to think themselves wiser than all those who have passed opinions upon this important question of law? And will they undertake to decide that those opinions were erroneous? Miserable, indeed, must be the condition of that community where the law is unsettled, and decisions upon the very point are disregarded, when they again come, directly or incidentally, into discussion. In such a state of things good men have nothing to hope, and bad men nothing to fear."[101] The justice also rejected the claim that the Eleventh Amendment of the Constitution stripped the court of jurisdiction over the suit.[102] In part, he rested that conclusion on the commonsense observation that the Eleventh Amendment applied to cases in "law and equity."[103] "This was not a suit at law or in equity," Washington said, and was instead "a case of admiralty and maritime jurisdiction."[104] The justice did not think that "the court is bound to supply the words, 'or to cases of admiralty and maritime jurisdiction'" to the Eleventh Amendment. He asked: "Would we be justified by any rule of law in admitting such an interpolation, even if a reason could not be assigned for the omission of those words in the amendment itself? I think not. In our various struggles to get at the spirit and intention of the framers of the constitution, I fear that this invariable charter of our rights would, in a very little time, be entirely construed away, and become at length so disfigured that its founders would recollect very few of its original features."[105]

Justice Washington then delivered what amounted to a courtroom speech defending the authority of federal courts to decide legal questions even when states object to those decisions. "Have the people of the United States confided to the legislatures of the states, or even to that of the United States, the power to declare the judgments of the national courts null and void?"[106] The justice's answer was no, in language that would later be echoed by the Supreme Court:

> Could such a power be granted to them without sapping the foundations of the government and extinguishing the last spark of American liberty? It is a truth not to be questioned that the power to declare the judgments of your courts void can never be safely lodged with a body who may enforce its decision by the physical force of the people. This power necessarily resides in the judicial tribunals and can safely reside nowhere else. Whether a state court is competent to declare a judgment of a federal court void for want of jurisdiction need not now be considered. It may, however, be observed that, admitting the right in the first instance, the ultimate decision of the question belongs to the supreme judicial tribunal of the nation, if that decision be required; for the judicial power extends to all cases arising under the constitution and the laws of the United States made in pursuance thereof; and the twenty-fifth section of the judicial law [the Judiciary Act of 1789], with a view to secure to the national judiciary this important privilege, vests in the supreme court a power to review and affirm or reverse the decision of the highest court of law or equity in a state,

> where a question depending upon the construction of any clause in the constitution, treaty, or statute of the United States had been decided.[107]

Washington added that judicial authority was not a privilege for courts or judges: "It is the privilege of the citizen, and as long as I have the honor of a seat on the bench I will consider myself one of the guardians of this privilege (a very feeble one, I acknowledge), and with a steady and unvarying eye, fixed upon the constitution as my guide, I shall march forward, without entertaining the guilty wish to limit this privilege where the citizen may fairly claim it, or the desire, not less criminal, to enlarge its boundaries, because it is claimed."

Finally, the justice addressed Bright's argument that he could not be convicted because he was "just following orders" from Pennsylvania's governor. This should sound familiar because the Nazi leaders tried at Nuremberg for war crimes famously made that argument and lost.[108] Washington was scornful of that defense (as the Nuremberg tribunal would be), stating that "the doctrine appears to us monstrous; the consequences of it terrible." "In a state of open and public war where military law prevails," he said, "and the peaceful voice of municipal law is drowned in the din of arms, great indulgences must necessarily be extended to the acts of subordinate officers done in obedience to the orders of their superiors. But even there the order of a superior officer to take the life of a citizen, or to invade the sanctity of his house and to deprive him of his property, would not shield the inferior against a charge of murder or trespass, in the regular judicial tribunals of the country."[109] The justice understood the risk that if the defendants "had refused obedience to the order of the governor, they would have been punished by the state."[110] "It may, however, be observed that, had the defendants refused obedience, and been prosecuted before a military or state court, they ought to have been acquitted, upon the ground that the orders themselves were unlawful and void, and we ought, of course, to suppose that they would have been acquitted." In concluding his charge, he told the jury: "We enter not into the political discussions which have been so ably conducted on both sides, but we admonish you to discard from your minds all political considerations, all party feelings, and all federal or state prejudices. The questions involved in this case are in the highest degree momentous and demand a cool and dispassionate consideration. We rely upon your integrity and wisdom for a decision which you can reconcile to your consciences, and to the duties which you owe to God and to your country."

Bright's resolution also supplies a lesson in defusing a crisis. The jury delivered a verdict stating that Bright and his co-defendants had done what they were accused of doing but stopped short of declaring them guilty. Instead, the jury left that judgment to the court based on the law, which Washington made in finding Bright and his subordinates guilty and sentencing them to a month in jail and a fine. President Madison responded with a pardon.[111] All the relevant concerns were satisfied. A local jury was true to the facts without condemning one of their own; the court carried out its duty to the law without fear or favor; and the president exercised mercy in the interests of civil peace.

Golden v. Prince

Bright was Washington's most exciting trial, but his most incisive circuit opinion was probably *Golden v. Prince*, an 1814 decision addressing a Pennsylvania bankruptcy law as applied to a debt incurred before the law was enacted.[112] The federal bankruptcy statute that had sparked a disagreement between Chief Justice Marshall and Justice Washington in *Fisher* was repealed by Congress in 1803.[113] Some state bankruptcy laws were enacted in its place. The creditor in *Prince* argued that the Contracts Clause of the Constitution, which prohibits states from impairing the obligations of contracts, barred retrospective state bankruptcy statutes.[114] The creditor also claimed that Section 34 of the Judiciary Act of 1789 did not permit state laws enacted after 1789 to govern cases brought in federal court.[115]

Justice Story and Chief Justice Marshall wrote to Bushrod about *Prince* to express their delight (and perhaps envy) that Washington would be the first justice to rule on the validity of state bankruptcy laws. Story said, "I rejoice it has not fallen to my lot to make the first decision," before proceeding to offer his view that all state bankruptcy statutes were unconstitutional.[116] The chief justice was more circumspect: "Without examining the subject, I had taken it for granted that the power of passing bankrupt laws resided in the states. It now appears to me more doubtful than I had supposed it to be."[117] Unlike a retrospective law, a "prospective act presents a question of considerable difficulty. I have not thought of the question long enough, nor viewed it in a sufficient variety of lights to have a decided opinion on it, but the bias of my mind at the moment is rather in favor of the validity of the law though I acknowledge I feel very great doubts whether I shall retain that opinion. Your own judgment, you having heard the argument, is much more to be relied on than mine."

Justice Washington concluded that retrospective state bankruptcy laws did violate the Contracts Clause. He explained that a state "law prospective in its operation, under which a contract afterwards made, may be voided in a way different from that provided by the parties, would be clearly constitutional."[118] "But a law which authorizes the discharge of a contract, by a smaller sum, or at a different time, or in a different manner than the parties have stipulated," he said, "impairs its obligation, by substituting for the contract of the parties, one which they never entered into; and to the performance of which, they of course had never consented." In that case, "the old contract is completely annulled, and a legislative contract imposed upon the parties in lieu of it." If this did not impair the obligation of a contract, "then we should be curious to know by what means the obligation of a contract can be impaired?" The justice's distinction between retrospective state bankruptcy laws, which were unconstitutional, and prospective ones, which were not, was affirmed by the Supreme Court in an opinion written by Washington that Chapter 12 will discuss at some length.[119] The justice also commented that he thought states did not have the power to enact any bankruptcy laws because that authority resided exclusively with Congress, though he acknowledged that this point was not necessary for his decision about Pennsylvania's retrospective law.[120]

In rejecting the creditor's Section 34 claim, Washington offered a lucid analysis of how federal courts should stand in relation to state law. "The establishment of federal courts, and the jurisdiction granted to them in certain specified cases," he wrote, "could not, consistently with the spirit and provisions of the constitution, impair any of the obligations . . . imposed by the laws of the state; by setting up in those courts a rule of decision, at variance with that which was binding upon the citizens, if the suit had been instituted in the state court."[121] In other words, federal courts hearing cases that did not involve federal law should apply state law on substantive issues. "The injustice, as well as the absurdity of the former [a federal court] deciding by one rule, and the latter [a state court] by another," Washington stated, "would be too monstrous to find a place in any system of government."[122] But "with respect to rules of practice for transacting the business of the courts, a different principle prevails. These rules are the laws of the court and are, in relation to the federal courts, laws arising under the constitution of the United States, and consequently not subject to state regulations."[123] "Indeed," he wrote, "counsel for the plaintiff, in this case, seemed to admit the distinction between general laws affecting rights, and those which relate to the practice of the courts. . . . Now, it is most clear, that a law which discharges a contract is no more a law of practice, than one, under the sanction of which, the contract was made."

Prince's dicta on federalism and Section 34 of the Judiciary Act identified a controversy about the federal courts that all law students learn about in their first year of study. In 1842, the Supreme Court (in an opinion by Justice Story) rejected Washington's logic and held that federal courts should develop their own common law in civil cases involving disputes on subjects such as contracts, torts, and property.[124] As Justice Robert H. Jackson later said: "What was pronounced absurd and monstrous in 1814 became the law in 1842."[125] Over the next century, federal courts and state courts would sometimes apply different common law to the same set of facts, which led to criticism about the uncertainty that resulted, as well as questions about where the federal courts got their power to make civil common law.[126] In 1938, in *Erie Railroad Company v. Tompkins*, the Supreme Court overruled its prior holding and went back to *Prince*'s idea that federal courts should apply substantive state law in cases that do not involve the Constitution, a treaty, a federal statute, or federal maritime law.[127] This "*Erie* doctrine" is still the law and respects the proper role of states within our federal system. Though Washington was the first judge to discuss the substance of the *Erie* doctrine, he receives no credit from modern lawyers for his analysis of that point.

As a circuit judge, Washington mostly charted his own course. But in the Supreme Court, he was the consummate team player alongside Chief Justice Marshall and a new star colleague—Joseph Story.

9
The Supreme Court's Balance Wheel

With memories of the Chase impeachment still fresh, the justices kept a low profile as President Jefferson's second term wound down. In 1806, Justice Paterson died and was replaced by Henry Livingston, a New York judge who became a reliable ally of Chief Justice Marshall and Washington.[1] The Court's 1807 term with Justice Livingston was uneventful except for *Ex Parte Bollman*, a habeas corpus case growing out of an alleged plot by Aaron Burr to turn some of the western states into an independent country with assistance from Spain.[2] Marshall provoked the president's anger with his circuit rulings while presiding over Burr's treason trial, which ended with an acquittal.[3] Jefferson, who was convinced of Burr's guilt, asked Congress to examine Marshall's conduct of the trial, though nothing was done.[4] According to one account, some of the justices were so upset by the president's criticisms of their chief that they wanted to skip their annual social call at the White House, but Washington cast the tie-breaking vote in favor of breaking bread with Jefferson.[5]

Given that backdrop, the 1808 term was also subdued. There were now seven justices rather than six. An extra circuit had been created in 1807 for the growing nation, which meant that an extra justice was necessary for circuit riding.[6] The president appointed Thomas Todd, the chief justice of the Kentucky Supreme Court, to the new seat. Justice Todd later married the widow of Bushrod's cousin, which created a close bond between them.[7] Todd (like Justice Livingston) let Jefferson down by supporting Marshall and Washington over the next two decades, though his attendance was irregular.[8] All but four of the twenty-six cases decided by signed opinions in 1808 were unanimous, and almost all the opinions came from the chief justice. Sometimes this unanimity was a legal fiction in that the "unanimous" opinion said that only a "majority" of the justices agreed with its logic, but published dissents remained rare.[9] Washington wrote a concurrence in one of the four non-unanimous decisions—a maritime insurance case—and declared in his conclusion: "I hold the rules of law, when once firmly established, to be beyond the control of those who are merely to pronounce what the law is, and if from any circumstance it has become impolitic, in a national point of view, it is for the nation to annul or to modify it. Till this is done, by the competent authority, I consider the rule to be inflexible."[10]

One interested spectator at the Supreme Court in 1808 was a young attorney from Massachusetts, Joseph Story. In a letter to a friend, Story described the

Washington's Heir. Gerard N. Magliocca, Oxford University Press. © Oxford University Press 2022.
DOI: 10.1093/oso/9780190947040.003.0010

justices in detail and commented: "Judge Washington is of very short stature, and quite boyish in his appearance. Nothing about him indicates greatness; he converses with simplicity and frankness. But he is highly esteemed as a profound lawyer, and I believe not without reason. His written opinions are composed with ability, and on the bench he exhibits great promptitude and firmness in decision. It requires intimacy to value him as he deserves."[11] Little did Story know that he soon would gain that intimacy and contribute to the Marshall Court's most splendid era, in which George Washington's nationalist practices would be turned into constitutional law.

Mr. Madison's War

In 1808, James Madison was elected to succeed Jefferson as president amid another foreign policy crisis. The war between Britain and France (now ruled by Napoleon) and both nations' ongoing attacks on American shipping had led President Jefferson to impose a total embargo on exports so that the nation's ships could not be attacked.[12] Instead of bringing the belligerents to the bargaining table, though, the embargo created a severe recession and howls of protest from New England.[13] The embargo was modified shortly before Madison's inauguration, but the issue of how to navigate the Anglo-French conflict—a problem that had bedeviled each of Madison's three predecessors—would soon drag the United States into the War of 1812 with Britain. While this "Second War of Independence" caused the destruction of the Supreme Court's home inside the Capitol in 1814, the war would also rekindle the patriotic spirit of Washington's youth and give the Court a new lease on life in its contest with advocates of states' rights.

The case the Court heard during the week that President Madison was inaugurated was *Fletcher v. Peck.*[14] *Fletcher* invited the justices to take the bold step of invalidating a state law that violated the Constitution. In 1795, the Georgia legislature sold millions of acres of state land in exchange for bribes.[15] When the scandal was exposed, the rascals were voted out and the new legislature passed a law rescinding the sale. In the interim, though, many people who were unaware of the bribery scheme had bought land from the original purchasers, and now they were outraged that Georgia was stripping them of their property. After an unsuccessful effort to obtain relief from Congress that divided Federalists from Republicans for years, a suit was finally filed asking the federal courts to declare Georgia's rescission unconstitutional.[16] Taking on a state legislature and sanctioning a corrupt land deal was especially ambitious, as the controversy in Pennsylvania that produced *United States v. Peters* and the trial in *United States v. Bright* were raging. Perhaps in light of those considerations, the Court held off

Figure 9.1 James Madison. Painting by Chester Harding. National Portrait Gallery.

on making a decision in *Fletcher* and set the case for a new argument in 1810. The remainder of the 1809 term (other than *Peters*) largely followed the pattern of unanimous opinions written by the chief justice in a manner designed to avoid political controversy. Starting in 1807, the Court's practice was that either Marshall wrote the decision or the task was assigned to another justice without regard to seniority, possibly because the most senior associate justices (Cushing and Chase) were by then elderly and often unwell. As a result, Washington got to write his first majority opinion (over Justice Johnson's dissent) in a case denying a creditor's claim for enslaved people from a Virginia estate.[17]

When *Fletcher* came back to the Court the next term, Joseph Story was one of the lawyers arguing for the challengers to the repeal of the crooked land sale.[18] In a landmark ruling, the chief justice wrote for the Court holding that Georgia had violated the Contracts Clause of the Constitution and the "general principles which are common to our free institutions" by repealing a state land grant to private parties.[19] Marshall lamented "that corruption should find its way into the governments of our infant republics, and contaminate the very source of legislation."[20] Nevertheless, "the framers of the constitution viewed, with some apprehension, the violent acts which might grow out of the feelings of the moment; and that the people of the United States, in adopting that instrument, have manifested a determination to shield themselves and their property from the effects of those sudden and strong passions to which men are exposed. The restrictions on the legislative power of the states are obviously founded on this sentiment."[21] *Fletcher*, together with *Peters* and *Bright*, set vital precedents placing the federal judiciary above state legislatures in determining the meaning of the Constitution, though that achievement was still fragile.

Following *Fletcher*, the Court hibernated for two years. The rest of the 1810 term was routine, with unanimous decisions in every case but one. Washington wrote twice for the Court, once in a case involving a Virginia estate dispute and once in a case concluding that a state property confiscation from a Tory was lawful because it was complete before the Treaty of Paris was signed in 1783.[22] During its 1810 recess, the Court's new courtroom was finished.[23] And Washington took time away from his circuit duty to arrange an apprenticeship for Marshall's son John at an accounting firm in Philadelphia, to begin when John turned sixteen.[24] But when the justice returned to Washington in February 1811, the Court was unable (for the first and only time) to muster a quorum and was forced to cancel its term. Justice Cushing had died some months earlier, Justice Chase was ill and would pass away soon, and neither Justice Johnson nor Justice Todd was able to participate.[25] After the Court's abrupt adjournment, the president appointed Gabriel Duvall, Maryland's chief justice, to replace Chase, and he was confirmed.[26]

The search for Justice Cushing's replacement, however, gave Madison trouble. When circuit riding was restored in 1802, an unwritten rule developed that a Supreme Court vacancy should be filled by someone from the same circuit as the vacancy.[27] (For example, Justice Chase was from Maryland, and so was Justice Duvall.) Since Justice Cushing was from Massachusetts, his successor was expected to be from New England. The president, on Jefferson's advice, picked Levi Lincoln, the former attorney general, who was from Massachusetts.[28] Lincoln told Madison that he did not want the job because he was going blind, but Madison nominated him anyway and Lincoln was confirmed.[29] Lincoln then turned the position down cold. Madison next chose Alexander Wolcott, an undistinguished lawyer from Connecticut known mostly for party loyalty, but he was voted down by the Senate.[30] Madison's third choice was John Quincy Adams, who was the United States ambassador in Russia, and Adams was confirmed before he was told of his nomination.[31] (John Adams was a Federalist, but his son defied party labels.) Adams politely declined, as he was more interested in a diplomatic and political career.[32]

And so the president finally turned to Joseph Story, the nephew of one of Madison's longtime friends.[33] Story was only thirty-two years old, making him (even now) the youngest person ever named to the Court. He was a prodigy who graduated from Harvard at eighteen and then served in Congress and as Speaker of the Massachusetts House of Representatives.[34] Justice Story's reputation rests, in part, on his dazzling extrajudicial writings and lectures. He wrote many treatises, including one on constitutional law that is still widely cited.[35] Story was also a law professor at Harvard in his spare time. He inspired many students—most notably Charles Sumner, who became one of the greatest antislavery leaders.[36] As a judge, Story wrote many influential circuit opinions and became Chief Justice Marshall's most dependable ally after Justice Washington's death. When the chief justice died in 1835, Justice Story carried on Marshall's legacy (sometimes in dissent) until his own death in 1845.[37]

An unrecognizable Supreme Court reconvened for its 1812 term. The justices were finally meeting in their new quarters within the Capitol, which included a robing room and a courtroom under the Senate chamber.[38] Charles Ingersoll,

Figure 9.2 Joseph Story. Painting by Chester Harding. National Portrait Gallery.

who often argued before Washington on circuit, wrote that "the Judges in their robes of solemn black are raised on seats of grave mahogany; and below them is the bar; and behind that an arcade, still higher, so contrived as to afford auditors double rows of terrace seats thrown in segments around the transverse arch under which the Judges sit."[39] Justice Duvall and Justice Story were on the bench, but the chief justice was not—shortly before the Court's session began, Marshall's coach overturned on a trip and he broke his collarbone.[40] While he recovered, Washington presided for the first four cases and wrote two of those opinions.[41] Marshall then arrived wearing a sling, only for Washington to fall and miss several cases.[42] In late February, the Court's normal rhythm finally returned. Story told a friend that the justices heard arguments from eleven in the morning until four in the afternoon, then returned to their boarding house for dinner and a conference that lasted until eight in the evening to discuss the day's cases.[43] The Court maintained its outward unanimity, but the injuries and illnesses among the brethren meant that the term's opinions were distributed more widely than in the prior decade.[44] Washington wrote unanimous opinions in four cases overall.[45] Each justice wrote in at least one case. This group of justices would sit together until Justice Livingston's death in 1823, which was the longest stretch without any changes in the Supreme Court's membership until the twenty-first century.[46] During this second phase of the Marshall Court, the chief justice still wrote the greatest number of opinions, but he no longer exercised a near monopoly on writing, as before.[47]

In June 1812, the United States again declared war against King George III. The War of 1812 was partly the result of frustration with years of British attacks on American shipping and seizures of Americans for forced service in the Royal Navy. President Madison stressed these points in his message to Congress asking for a declaration of war, but left unsaid was that many Republicans saw Britain's preoccupation with Napoleon as their opportunity to seize Canada.[48] This objective helps explain why the United States did not declare war on France, which was also attacking American shipping. The dream of conquest did not pan out, largely due to America's lack of a professional army, which left bumbling state militias to wage unsuccessful attacks on British forts in Canada.[49] An ominous sign from the beginning was that Congress passed the war declaration in a partisan vote that reflected sharp sectional differences: New England voted for peace to avoid a loss of trade with Britain, but the rest of the country was eager to fight.[50] Propelled by war fever, President Madison was reelected in 1812.[51]

As the war unfolded, the Supreme Court's docket was increasingly filled with maritime cases arising from the capture of enemy vessels or from acts of Congress prohibiting trade with the enemy. The justices were largely unanimous in their thinking on these and other issues in the 1813 term, with Washington writing two opinions on the enforcement of the embargo and two in more humdrum cases.[52] In 1814, though, the "one for all and all for one" mentality forged by Congress's cancellation of the Court's 1802 term finally broke down. Wars inevitably lead to extraordinary exercises of federal power that can fracture even the most collegial court. The War of 1812 was no different, though the conflict may look insignificant to modern eyes. There were, of course, some maritime prize cases (that is, where someone captured an enemy ship or cargo and claimed ownership) in which the Court did reach consensus. Washington wrote four of those decisions.[53] But Marshall and Washington found themselves on opposite sides in two cases (and possibly three) in the same term for the only time.

The Venus marked the first great division within the Court over the prosecution of the war.[54] A ship named *The Venus* left Britain with goods bound for the United States after Congress had declared war, but before news of that action reached Britain.[55] An American vessel captured *The Venus* and claimed the ship as a prize. The vessel's owners objected in part on the ground that they were American citizens (though one of them was living in Britain) and that they had not known of the war when *The Venus* set sail. Washington wrote for a 3–2 majority affirming the circuit court's prize award, as Justice Johnson did not participate and Justice Story recused himself, having heard the case on circuit.[56] The Court's holding was that the property of an American citizen living in an enemy nation can be subject to prize confiscation as soon as war begins.[57] To hold otherwise, Washington said, would create too much uncertainty and allow such a citizen residing abroad to game the system to his advantage:

> If his property be taken trading with the enemy, shall he be allowed to shield it from confiscation, by alleging that he had intended to remove from the country of the enemy to his own, then neutral, and, therefore, that, as a neutral, the trade was lawful? If war exist between the country of his residence and his native country, and his property be seized by the former, or by the latter, shall he be heard to say in the former case, that he was a domiciled subject of the country of the captor, and in the latter, that he was a native subject of the country of that captor also, because he had declared an intention to resume his native character; and thus to parry the belligerent rights of both? It is to guard against such inconsistencies, and against the frauds which such pretensions, if tolerated, would sanction, that the rule above mentioned has been adopted.[58]

As for the argument that treating *The Venus* as a prize was unfair because the ship owners did not know when the vessel departed that war had been declared, Justice Washington replied that this "was altogether a novel theory" and contrary to the leading precedents in prize cases.[59]

Chief Justice Marshall dissented in *The Venus* because the opinion "subjects to confiscation the property of a citizen shipped before a knowledge of the war, and . . . disallows the defense founded on an intention to change his domicil and to return to the United States, manifested in a sufficient manner, and within a reasonable time after knowledge of the war."[60] While he conceded that the question was "undoubtedly complex and intricate," Marshall said that an American merchant living abroad should be presumed to want to return to the United States. "If such a person were required, on his arrival in a foreign country," he explained, "to declare his real intentions on the subject of residence, he would, most probably, say, if he spoke honestly, 'I come for the purpose of trade: I shall remain while the situation of the two countries permits me to carry on my trade lawfully, securely, and advantageously: when that situation so changes as to deprive me of these rights, I shall return.' "[61] "The character of his property shipped before a knowledge of the war," he thought, "ought not to be decided absolutely by his residence at the time of shipment or capture, but ought to depend on his continuing to reside and trade in the enemy country, or on his taking prompt measures for returning to his own."[62] In effect, the chief justice said that the line should be drawn when the expatriate merchant knew that war was declared and did nothing to leave, whereas Washington drew a bright-line rule when war had been declared. In his opinion, Washington rejected Marshall's "presumption that a person will certainly remove, before it can possibly be known whether he may elect to do so or not," to be "as unfounded in reason and justice, as it clearly is in law."[63]

In *Brown v. United States*, the chief justice prevailed. *Brown* involved a lumber cargo, owned by an American and bound for Britain before the war, that was claimed as a prize in the port of New Bedford.[64] Justice Story ruled on circuit that the lumber was a prize, but Marshall's opinion reversed that judgment because no specific act of Congress authorized the confiscation of enemy property on land. He denied that a declaration of war was self-executing, stating that "war gives the right to confiscate, but does not itself confiscate the property of the enemy."[65] In part, the chief justice relied on the fact that Article One, Section Eight of the Constitution gives Congress the power to declare war and "make rules concerning captures on land and water," which implied that a war declaration did not include those powers.[66] Justice Story dissented in defense of his circuit opinion, stating: "Nothing, in my judgment, is more clear from authority, than the right to seize hostile property afloat in our ports at the commencement of war. It is the settled practice of nations, and the modern rule of Great Britain herself, applied (as appears from the affidavits in this very cause) to American property in the present war."[67] Story also rejected Marshall's reading of the Constitution's War Clauses, explaining that the power to declare war "includes all the powers incident to war, and necessary to carry it into effect. If the constitution had been silent as to letters of marque and captures, it would not have narrowed the authority of congress. The authority to grant letters of marque and reprisal, and to regulate captures, are ordinary and necessary incidents to the power of declaring war. It would be utterly ineffectual without them. The expression, therefore, of that which is implied in the very nature of the grant, cannot weaken the force of the grant itself. The words are merely explanatory."[68]

We now come to the great mystery in *Brown*. Justice Story concluded his dissent on this note: "In the opinion which I have expressed I am authorized to state that I have the concurrence of one of my brethren."[69] He did not say, though, who concurred with him. Jean Edward Smith's biography of John Marshall in 1996 named Washington as the other dissenter, as "Washington's reasoning in *The Venus* conforms to the basic thrust of Story's dissent in *Brown*."[70] Why did Story not just say who joined his opinion? The answer is that he had a quirky practice at that point of not naming the justices who joined his dissents.[71] No direct evidence supports Smith's claim that Washington dissented in *Brown*, but there is a clue. In a third prize case decided in 1814, written by Justice Johnson and joined by the chief justice, Story dissented and said, "I have the concurrence of TWO of my brethren."[72] The unofficial Supreme Court reporter then added a note stating that Justices Washington and Todd were the two.[73] In general, when there was a close case on whether property should be subjected to prize, Washington and Story said yes and the chief justice said no. This does not prove that Washington joined the *Brown* dissent, though, as Justice Todd might have done so.[74]

The disagreements among the justices during the 1814 term paled in comparison to the danger presented by the invasion of Maryland and Virginia that August. After Napoleon's exile to Elba, British veterans were finally free to travel to the United States and get some revenge for 1776.[75] An expeditionary force of about 5,000 troops landed near Washington, D.C., and met a disorganized resistance that included the president and Secretary of State Monroe; they entered the city and burned the Capitol and the White House.[76] Stelle's Hotel, the boarding house at which the justices often stayed when in session, was spared, but the Court's furniture and many other official items were torched.[77] The disaster forced the Court into makeshift quarters until a new Capitol was built. Marshall wrote Washington that he was "anxious to know what our situation will be. Can you inform me what provision is made for us? Where and in what room are we to sit?"[78] For the next two terms, they convened in the front parlor of the Supreme Court clerk's house, while the clerk's eight children ran about not keeping quiet during oral arguments.[79]

Anti-war feeling in New England, exacerbated by the sack of the national capital, led some prominent Federalists in Massachusetts to summon a multistate convention in Hartford amid calls for secession from the Union. Washington was uneasy about this gathering, scheduled for December 1814, as he told a friend in a candid letter:

> The clouds which are gathering in the East alarm me more than all the other dangers united. The disunion of the States was the calamity which I most apprehended as likely to result from the declaration of this disastrous war. Should the convention at Hartford end in nothing beyond a recommendation of the meeting of a general convention for reforming the Constitution I shall be greatly relieved, nor should I object to any amendments which should give the eastern states a fair and equal representation and which should confine the limits of the government to such as they existed at the time the Constitution was formed. . . . I am satisfied that the best interests of this nation demand a President from one of the commercial states. I believe that we owe all of our present and past differences to the anticommercial principles which have influenced the hearts of our executive for the last 14 years.[80]

The Hartford Convention fizzled out, as only three states sent delegates and the body endorsed a set of rather mild reform proposals.[81] More importantly, the War of 1812 came to an end. In December 1814, British and American negotiators agreed to the Treaty of Ghent, which ended the hostilities by just restoring relations to where they had been before the war began.[82] With Napoleon's defeat, the Anglo-French fight was over, which meant that the reason for the War of 1812 also ended. Before news of the treaty reached the United States, though, a large British army attacked New Orleans and was wiped out by an American force led by Andrew Jackson.[83] Jackson became a national hero and would leverage that stature to become president in 1829.

The War of 1812 achieved little for the United States. But one consequence of the war was an increase in nationalism. The expression of secession and states' rights at the Hartford Convention was stigmatized as defeatism, which put aggressive proponents of state power on the defensive.[84] Likewise, the destruction of the Capitol and the poor performance of many national institutions during the war lent support to efforts to make those bodies stronger. For example, Congress allowed Hamilton's Bank of the United States to go out of business in 1811. The lack of a central bank, though, made borrowing money for emergencies difficult. Accordingly, Congress recreated the Bank in 1816 with President Madison's approval, much to the dismay of traditional Republicans.[85] The crisis conditions under which the Court met immediately following the war (in a crowded house) also probably renewed the spirit of unanimity that had prevailed at the start of the Marshall Court. All these war-related effects help explain the nationalist opinions that a unanimous Court issued over the next decade.[86]

Pulling Back the Curtain

The challenge in evaluating the Marshall Court is that there are few written records of the justices' internal deliberations: what was said in the boarding house stayed in the boarding house. After the War of 1812, though, there are a couple of hints about how the Court reached decisions or responded to political criticism. Peace returned calm to the Court, as the 1815 term was unanimous in all but two cases, even though prize cases still led the docket. Washington wrote four opinions, two in prize cases and two in civil cases.[87] But the eye-opener is *Terrett v. Taylor*, an opinion written by Justice Story that bears Washington's fingerprints.[88]

Terrett was the postscript to Virginia's successful effort to strip the Episcopal Church of the property that came from its status as the established religion of the state before 1776. In the 1790s, as Chapter 4 explained, Washington wrote a memo as a private attorney explaining why he thought a state effort to seize the church's property would be unlawful. After he joined the Court, the Virginia legislature proceeded with a repeal of the church's special privileges. An equally divided Virginia Court of Appeals upheld the repeal.[89] A parish in Alexandria then sued, claiming that it was not subject to the repeal because Alexandria became part of the District of Columbia before the state statute was enacted.[90] The Supreme Court agreed with this narrow point, but Justice Story used most of his opinion to attack Virginia's repeal as unconstitutional "upon the principles of natural justice, upon the fundamental laws of every free government, upon the spirit and the letter of the constitution of the United States, and upon the decisions of most respectable judicial tribunals."[91] Story also commented that the church's property rights were not inconsistent with the clause in Virginia's Declaration of Rights that "all men are equally entitled to the free exercise of religion according to the dictates of conscience."[92]

A comparison of Washington's memo and the Court's opinion in *Terrett* reveals more than a passing resemblance. In his 1797 memo, Washington held that Virginia's decision in 1776 to allow the church to retain its property did not violate the Declaration of Rights because "contemporaneous opinions, as to the true constructions of a law is in such case a fair and proper standard, by which ours should be formed. The first legislature which convened after the formation of [Virginia's] constitution, and composed chiefly of the same members, passed a law upon the very subject; which may be considered as a commentary upon the clause in question."[93] *Terrett* said that the 1776 law "is not only a contemporaneous exposition of the constitution, but has the additional weight that it was promulgated or acquiesced in by a great majority, if not the whole, of the very framers of the constitution."[94] Likewise, Washington's memo stated: "The law which vests the church property is either valid, or it is not. If the former then the legislature cannot divest such a right without establishing a precedent, by which they may revoke every grant the Commonwealth has ever made."[95] *Terrett* made the same point this way: "We have no knowledge of any authority which could support the doctrine that a legislative grant is revocable in its own nature. . . . Such a doctrine would uproot the very foundations of almost all the land titles in Virginia."[96] These and other parallels between the two documents could be explained by thoughtful lawyers independently reaching similar conclusions. But it is impossible to believe that Story and Washington did not collaborate given Bushrod's experience with the issue.[97] *Terrett* therefore forces us to consider again whether the opinions of the Marshall Court should be viewed as a result of teamwork rather than of individual authorship, or whether the team was often an inner circle made up of the three justices who regularly exchanged reports of their circuit work—Marshall, Washington, and Story.

One hint about how Washington may have influenced opinions such as *Terrett* comes from a letter by Chief Justice Marshall implying that Bushrod served as the unofficial secretary for Supreme Court arguments. A lawyer sent Marshall a written text of his upcoming argument to the Court and appears to have asked that this be submitted as part of the record.[98] The chief justice replied: "If Judge Washington will not consent to receive it; absolutely & unconditionally as an argument, it must be read over in court, & he must view it in the light of notes, and as a substitute for those which might be taken by himself."[99] At first glance Marshall's response is strange. He was the chief justice, so why did he need Bushrod's consent (and nobody else's) to agree to the attorney's request? The most plausible answer is that there was some understanding either between the two men or among the justices that Washington would keep the notes of the oral arguments for the Court's internal use. For whatever length of time Bushrod performed this role, he would have been able to shape opinions to the extent that his notes were used by other justices as a framework for discussion and drafting.

Consider a different example of teamwork from the Court's 1816 term—*Martin v. Hunter's Lessee*. Most of the 1816 term was unanimous and lackluster, with Washington writing three opinions for the Court.[100] *Martin*, by contrast, involved a bitter dispute with the Virginia Court of Appeals and Judge Spencer Roane, Marshall and Washington's classmate from William and Mary. In 1812, the Supreme Court reversed the Virginia Court of Appeals and held that the state's Revolutionary-era confiscation laws did not apply to a 730-acre property.[101] The chief justice recused himself because his brother owned some of the land at issue, so Justice Story wrote the Court's decision. When the case returned to Virginia, the state court refused to comply with Story's ruling on the ground that Section 25 of the Judiciary Act of 1789, which granted the Supreme Court the authority to review state court judgments in a certain set of cases, was unconstitutional.[102] The judges on the court of appeals, consistent with their practice since Edmund

Pendleton's death, gave their opinions seriatim. But the most strident explanation was by Judge Roane, who stated: "No calamity would be more to be deplored by the American people, than a vortex in the general government, which should ingulf and sweep away, every vestige of the state constitutions."[103] Justice Story then wrote a second opinion in *Martin* reversing the state court of appeals with a lucid analysis of the Constitution's text and structure.[104] *Martin* struck a nationalist tone for a postwar world that was similar to Justice Washington's rhetoric in *Bright*, stating that "the constitution of the United States was ordained and established, not by the states in their sovereign capacities, but emphatically, as the preamble of the constitution declares, by 'the people of the United States.' "[105]

The chief justice and Justice Washington had worked to bring *Martin* before the Court a second time as rapidly as possible. Marshall was disturbed by the Virginia ruling and did not want such an open repudiation of the Supreme Court's appellate jurisdiction to remain in doubt for over a year.[106] Instead, he wanted the case on the Court's docket in February 1816, even though the state decision was issued in December 1815. Consequently, the chief justice took the remarkable step of drafting the petition to appeal the decision himself, despite recusing himself from the case.[107] He then took that unsigned petition (in his own handwriting!) to Washington, the presiding justice in *Martin* given Marshall's "recusal," and Washington set the case for expedited argument.[108] The two friends almost certainly cooked up this scheme to blunt the impact of Roane's states' rights rhetoric, as they would plot again three years later in response to his criticisms of *McCulloch v. Maryland.*

While friction still existed between the Supreme Court and state courts, the justices were finally getting along well with Congress and the White House. In 1817, the Court moved from its clerk's front parlor into a temporary room in the new Capitol, and Congress appointed the first official court reporter to publish its opinions.[109] When James Monroe, who was elected to succeed President Madison, was inaugurated that March, all the justices attended the ceremony for the first time since 1797.[110] (Monroe and Marshall had been friends since childhood.)[111] Thus began the "Era of Good Feelings," in which partisanship diminished.[112] The absence of strife in the elected branches was also reflected in the judicial branch, as all but two of the cases decided by the Court in 1817 and in 1818 were unanimous. In the 1817 term, Washington wrote eight opinions—his largest tally in any single year.[113] In 1818, he wrote three.[114] Until 1821, the pattern after Justice Story's appointment was that he usually wrote the second-greatest number of opinions after the chief justice, and Washington was typically third.[115] Story's fluid pen was due to his ability and his vigor, as Washington's partial blindness probably made writing many decisions during the Court's compressed sitting schedule rather difficult.

The 1819 term was the Marshall Court's pinnacle, as the justices took up their new permanent quarters in the Capitol and brought their distinctive talents to bear in two landmark constitutional decisions.[116] *Dartmouth College v. Woodward* sparked disagreements that could not be reconciled and led to fascinating separate opinions by Marshall, Washington, and Story.[117] The case involved New Hampshire's attempt to turn Dartmouth from a private school into a state college by rewriting its royal charter. Daniel Webster, who had attended Dartmouth and was the greatest Supreme Court advocate of this era, contended that the state law violated the Contracts Clause, and (according to legend) he brought many to tears with his closing plea that he was defending only "a small college. And yet there are those who love it."[118] *Dartmouth College* was argued in 1818, but the Court was unable to reach a decision during that term. According to Webster, only the chief justice and Washington initially supported his stance.[119] During the recess, Marshall and some of his colleagues wrote opinions laying out their thoughts, and when the justices reconvened in 1819, they decided that another argument was unnecessary. The chief justice, writing for the Court over Justice Duvall's dissent, largely accepted Webster's position and held that Dartmouth's corporate charter was a contract that could not be transformed without its consent.[120] In typical Marshall fashion, he did not cite any cases in his analysis.

Washington's separate opinion in *Dartmouth College* reflected his more careful approach. For example, Marshall stated that "it can require no argument to prove, that the circumstances of this case constitute a contract."[121] Justice Washington did not assume that Dartmouth's charter was a contract and instead provided a discussion of that point, citing *Fletcher* as authority.[122] He then explained that charters for private entities like Dartmouth were entitled to protection from state interference—in contrast to those of public corporations. For that claim, he cited *Terrett*, which made sense given his long-standing objection to Virginia's effort to strip the Episcopal Church of the benefits of its legislative grant.[123] Washington also shied away from the broad pronouncements on the scope of the Contracts Clause that were in both Marshall's and Story's opinions. The most ingenious argument by New Hampshire was that the Contracts Clause should be read narrowly because a broad reading would render state divorce laws unconstitutional.[124] (Divorce law, of course, allows the parties to break their marriage contract.) The chief justice took the view that the Contracts Clause did not invalidate state divorce statutes because all the states required fault for a divorce (such as adultery); he reserved judgment on whether a state no-fault divorce law would be constitutional.[125] Justice Story, by contrast, went further and argued that a no-fault divorce law was probably unconstitutional because "a man has just as good a right to his wife, as to the property acquired under a marriage

Figure 9.3 Daniel Webster, who argued many of the landmark cases decided by the Marshall Court. Painting by Francis Alexander. National Portrait Gallery.

contract."[126] Washington did not take the bait, saying nothing about this difficult subject when no decision was necessary.[127]

The other milestone of 1819 was *McCulloch v. Maryland*, a unanimous opinion by the chief justice that upheld the constitutionality of the Second Bank of the United States and struck down Maryland's tax on the bank.[128] *McCulloch* is probably Marshall's most admired opinion and is still essential reading for law students. In that decision, the chief justice rejected Jefferson's state compact theory of the Constitution and gave the authority granted to Congress a reading that went beyond what was expressly listed in Article One, Section Eight of the text.[129] Even though the specific power to create corporations was not listed there, the chief justice explained that "the sound construction of the Constitution must allow to the national legislature that discretion, with respect to the means by which the powers it confers are to be carried into execution, which will enable that body to perform the high duties assigned to it, in the manner most beneficial to the people."[130] Such a flexible construction was essential "in a constitution, intended to endure for ages to come, and consequently, to be adapted to the various crises of human affairs."[131] Borrowing from Daniel Webster's argument to the Court, Marshall also said that "the power to tax involves the power to destroy" in concluding that Maryland could not impose a bank tax that applied only to the national bank and not to state banks.[132]

The blowback against *McCulloch* in Virginia was swift and fierce. *Dartmouth College* and *McCulloch* were nationalist opinions that either invalidated state legislation or downplayed states' rights. Coming on the heels of *Martin* and *Terrett*, the trend toward more federal power at Virginia's expense was unmistakable. Three weeks after *McCulloch* was issued, Marshall wrote Washington that "great dissatisfaction has been given to the politicians of Virginia by our opinion on the bank question. They have no objection to a decision in favor of the bank, since the good patriots who administer the government wished it and would probably have been seriously offended with us had we dared to have decided otherwise, but they required an obsequious, silent opinion without reasons. That would have been satisfactory, but our heretical reasoning is pronounced most damnable. We shall be denounced bitterly in the papers and as not a word will be said on the other side we shall undoubtedly be condemned as a pack of consolidating aristocrats. The legislature and executive who have enacted the law but who have power and places to bestow will escape with impunity, while the poor court who have nothing to give and of whom nobody is afraid, bears all the obloquy of the measure."[133] Over the week, the *Richmond Enquirer* published essays attacking *McCulloch* under the pen name of "Amphyction" that were written by William Brockenbrough, a state court judge.[134]

Marshall and Washington responded with a covert operation to defend *McCulloch*. The chief justice wrote two anonymous essays of his own, signed "A Friend to the Union," and asked Washington, who was in Philadelphia on his circuit, to give them for publication to the editor of the *Philadelphia Union*.[135] Unfortunately, the editor garbled the texts and made what Marshall called in another letter "a curious piece of work." "However good the ingredients may be," he told Washington, "when compounded as he has compounded them, [they] are rather nauseous to the intellectual palette."[136] The chief justice said that "this subject is not to drop. A very serious effort is undoubtedly making to have it taken up in the next [Virginia] legislature. It is said that some other essays written by a very great man are now preparing and will soon appear." He was referring here to Spencer Roane, who would soon publish four essays attacking *McCulloch* under the name "Hampden."[137] "On this account," Marshall said, "I am desirous that the answer to Amphyction should appear in its true shape and will be obliged to you to have it republished in the Alexandria paper [the *Gazette*]. I will give the instructions which I will thank you to copy and furnish with the papers I now send containing those essays marked—to the editor."[138]

Just two days after Roane published the first of his critical essays, Marshall began thinking about his rebuttal. He wrote Washington that "the storm which has been for some time threatening the Judges has at length burst on their heads and a most serious hurricane it is. . . . I find myself more stimulated on this subject than on any other because I believe the design to be to injure the Judges and impair the constitution. I have therefore thought of answering these essays and sending my pieces to you for publication in the Alexandria paper. I shall send them on in successive numbers but do not wish the first to be published till I shall have seen the last of Hampden. I will then write to you and request you to have the publications made immediately. As the numbers will be marked, I hope no mistake will be made by the printer and that the manuscript will be given to the flame."[139] (One wonders how many other sensitive letters Marshall asked Washington to burn during their relationship.) "I wish," Marshall continued, "two papers of each number to be directed to [his son] T. Marshall, Oak Hill, Fauquier. I do not wish them to come to me lest some suspicion of the author should be created." To further ensure that his authorship remained secret, the chief justice asked that the pseudonym for the new articles "be changed to 'A Constitutionalist.' A Friend of the Constitution is so much like a Friend of the Union that it may lead to some suspicion of identity."[140] Marshall ended up writing nine essays and asked Washington to retain copies to put "in the hands of some member of the assembly should an attempt be made to move the subject in the legislature."[141]

This cloak-and-dagger correspondence is remarkable for at least two reasons. First, the chief justice and Justice Washington did not consult with their Supreme Court colleagues before acting in defense of their unanimous *McCulloch* opinion.[142] What that omission suggests, when considered alongside the strange handling of the *Martin* petition, is that the two men whom Justice Johnson later labeled "one judge" decided some important matters themselves. Second, Marshall's letters to Washington indicate that they were both willing to enter the political arena if necessary, although they were cagier about such interventions in 1819 than during their early years on the Court. For all the drama of the secret *McCulloch* manuscripts, there is no reason to think that these essays moved public opinion or had any influence outside Virginia. Far more harmful to *McCulloch's* immediate standing was the onset of a financial panic in 1819 that coincided with the case and, as panics frequently do, made people angry at banks.[143]

Washington and Story Take Center Stage

When the justices returned for their 1820 term, Washington wrote three opinions, with *Houston v. Moore* leading the pack.[144] A member of the state militia in Pennsylvania was convicted by a state court-martial for refusing President Madison's call to muster for national service during the War of 1812.[145] The militiaman claimed that the state lacked the authority to punish what was, in reality, a federal crime.[146] Washington announced the judgment of the Court affirming the judgment of the court-martial, though he explained that his colleagues "do not concur in all respects in the reasons which influence my opinion."[147] Justice Story dissented along with an unnamed colleague.[148]

Houston is one of the rare instances where we know that the Court changed its mind after oral argument. The chief justice initially assigned the opinion to Justice Story, telling him the case "cannot be in better hands. I shall sketch my ideas for the purpose of examining them more closely but shall not prepare a regular opinion. . . . I do not think we shall differ."[149] But when the decision was issued, Washington had the opinion and Story was in dissent. Justice Story must have lost his majority after circulating an unpersuasive draft opinion or after Washington circulated a persuasive dissent. It also seems likely that Chief Justice Marshall was the unnamed colleague who joined Story's dissent given that Marshall said he did not think they would differ. It is also possible, though, that Marshall changed his mind after reading Bushrod's opinion.

Justice Washington said that *Houston* turned on when a state militia member entered into "the service of the United States" and thus became subject to exclusive federal jurisdiction under the Constitution's Militia Clause.[150] After reviewing the relevant acts of Congress, he concluded that "something more than organizing and equipping a detachment, and ordering it into service, was considered as necessary to place the militia in the service of the United States."[151] The something more was "the arrival of the militia at the place of rendezvous."[152] Houston did not arrive at his new camp because he refused to march at all. As a result, the justice reasoned that his offense fell within the state's concurrent constitutional authority to punish a violation of federal law, which the state exercised by passing a specific law for militia desertion cases.[153] While Congress could have vested jurisdiction over desertions exclusively to a federal court-martial, the federal statutory language spoke only about a "court martial," which meant in his view that state courts-martial could act.[154] Justice Story dissented on the ground that Congress's use of "court martial" must be understood to refer to a federal court-martial because state courts-martial were not mentioned.[155]

Washington then grappled with another constitutional puzzle: could a person be tried by two governments for the same offense? If the federal government and a state could court-martial a militia deserter, then could that deserter be punished twice for the same act or tried a second time if he was found not guilty the first time? Washington's answer was no. "If the jurisdiction of the courts be concurrent, the sentence of either court, either of conviction or acquittal, might be pleaded in bar of the prosecution before the other, as much so as the judgment of a State Court, in a civil case of concurrent jurisdiction, may be pleaded in bar of an action for the same cause, instituted in a Circuit Court of the United States."[156] He did not explain where this limit came from, though he stated that subjecting a person "to the operation of two laws upon the same subject, dictated by distinct wills, particularly in a case involving pains and penalties is, to my apprehension, something very much like oppression, if not worse."[157] In subsequent cases the justices debated whether Washington's analysis meant that the Double Jeopardy Clause of the Fifth Amendment should be read as barring all criminal defendants from being prosecuted by federal and state authorities for the same action.[158] In 2019, the Supreme Court reconsidered the issue in *Gamble v. United States* and maintained that *Houston* should not be read so broadly, though the dissenting opinions of Justice Ruth Bader Ginsburg and Justice Neil Gorsuch both argued that Washington did, in fact, condemn such successive prosecutions as unlawful.[159]

About six months after *Houston* was decided, Washington fell dangerously ill. He wrote to Judge Peters in September and said that he was suffering from "bilious fever" and could not attend the fall circuit.[160] (Bilious fever was a catchall term used then for any disease that caused diarrhea, vomiting, and a high temperature.) "My head is so confused and my hand so unsteady that I scarcely know what I am writing," he told Peters, and "Mrs. Washington is still under the dominion of the fever and her strength is so prostrated that she can with difficulty move across her room."[161] Washington was now fifty-eight, and his recovery was slow. Justice Story wrote to wish him well and offered this compliment: "I most earnestly hope and pray that a good Providence will restore you to health and enable you to attend at the February Term. I shall feel quite lost and uneasy without you and must say in all sincerity and frankness that I know not in whose judgment I have so implicit a reliance as in yours."[162] When February came, though, Washington felt unable to participate in the Court's work. Marshall told him that "however unwilling we may be to lose your aid, we all think that it would be madness to encounter the hazard of joining us, unless your health should be entirely restored," adding that "the wine is in fine order and we shall at dinner give a bumper [toast] to your better health."[163] Washington thus missed the entire 1821 term.[164] During a break in the Court's arguments, three of his colleagues (Livingston, Todd, and Story) traveled to Alexandria to visit him, with Justice Story writing to his wife that Washington's "health is somewhat improved, but he is still feeble."[165] By the spring, the justice was able to resume his circuit duty, reassuring Story in June that "I now feel as well as I have been for some years past."[166] But from then on, his letters would mention sickness more often. Washington was able to return to the Supreme Court for its 1822 term, but he wrote only one opinion, which suggests that he was still not back to normal.[167]

One of the cases decided in Washington's absence in 1821 was *Green v. Biddle*, which touched off a political firestorm that forced the justices to reconsider their decision. *Green* involved Kentucky property law, which was a tangled mess during the 1820s. Kentucky was originally part of Virginia. After Virginia gave Kentucky its independence in 1789, the two states entered into a formal agreement under which Kentucky promised to honor the property rights held there by Virginians.[168] But since much of the frontier was poorly surveyed, many farmers settled on what they thought was unowned land only to discover (sometimes years later) that their property was owned by a Virginian. The Kentucky legislature responded by enacting two laws that required absentee landlords to compensate the tenants for any improvements made to the land before an eviction could occur. If the landlord refused, then the tenant was allowed to purchase the land at a discounted rate. Some Virginians with title to land in Kentucky filed suit, and Justice Story held for a unanimous Court that the state laws were unconstitutional. His terse opinion was poorly received, in part because no lawyer appeared to defend the Kentucky statutes and because Story cited no cases, said almost nothing about the Constitution, and relied instead on "general principles of law" and "first principles of justice."[169] As a result, Senator Henry Clay of Kentucky, the former Speaker of the House of Representatives and a formidable Supreme Court advocate in his own right, urged the Court to hear a second argument in *Green* and then made a strong case for his state.[170] After that second argument, Washington wrote for the Court in 1823 and (over Justice Johnson's dissent) again held the Kentucky statutes unconstitutional.[171]

Washington's thought process in *Green* is accessible because his notes and a draft of the opinion are in his Chicago History Museum journal.[172] He began his notes with a summary of each of the two Kentucky statutes, the arguments made on their behalf, and the (fairly minor) differences between the two laws. Next, he briefed the leading cases (from the common law and from Virginia) on property rights, some of which he included in his opinion. In the draft opinion, Washington closed with this singular line: "I hold myself answerable to God, my conscience and my country to decide the question according to the dictates of my best judgment, be the consequences of the decision what they may."[173] In the final opinion, he used the plural: "We hold ourselves answerable to God, our consciences, and our country to decide the question according to the dictates of our best judgment, be the consequences of the decision what they may."[174] This distinction tells us something about how drafts were prepared in the Marshall Court and modified as justices joined an opinion. Washington did not assume in his draft that his colleagues would agree with him; he wrote initially for himself, and then must have sent the draft around or read his draft aloud at the boarding house and made changes as he garnered votes.

Washington's version of *Green* was longer than Story's and made clear that "our opinion is founded exclusively upon the Constitution of the United States."[175] He started by rejecting the argument that the interstate compact was unlawful because Congress did not give its approval as the Constitution requires.[176] *Green* replied that Congress expressly referred to the agreement with Virginia in granting Kentucky statehood, which was sufficient recognition.[177] The justice also pointed out that Kentucky was free to exercise eminent domain over the disputed title and pay fair market value to its owners before reallocating the title to the tenants.[178] Washington then offered a syllogism, which was (1) the interstate compact was a contract; (2) the Kentucky laws impaired the obligations of that contract by significantly diminishing the value of the Virginian titles; and therefore (3) the laws violated the Contracts Clause. "The terms compact and contract are synonymous," he explained, "and in *Fletcher v. Peck*, the Chief Justice defines a contract to be a compact between two or more parties. The principles laid down in that case are, that the constitution of the United States embraces all contracts, executed or executory, whether between individuals, or between a State and individuals; and that a State has no more power to impair an obligation into which she herself has entered, than she can the contracts of individuals."[179] He then commented: "Kentucky, therefore, being a party to the compact which guaranteed to claimants of land lying in that State, under titles derived from Virginia, their rights, as they existed under the laws of Virginia, was incompetent to violate that contract, by passing any law which rendered those rights less valid and secure." While the Court was always "favorable to the validity of the laws," the justice said, "the objections to them are fairly and clearly made out."[180]

Green teaches some additional lessons about the Marshall Court. First, Justice Washington's absence in *Green*'s first argument was followed by a tone-deaf opinion that the Court was, in essence, forced to retract. This fiasco suggests that Washington provided vital ballast to the Court's deliberations, and that Story's praise for his colleague's judgment (right before *Green* was issued in 1821) was not misplaced. Washington did his best to repair the damage from *Green*, but he was a general without troops. Only four justices participated in *Green*'s second argument, as Justices Livingston and Todd were ill, and Chief Justice Marshall recused himself.[181] Thus, the Kentucky courts argued that they were not bound by *Green* because less than a majority of the entire Court supported the judgment, given Justice Johnson's dissent.[182]

Second, *Green* illuminates a crucial difference between Story and Washington, which is that Justice Story was more brilliant but also more prone to error. In part, this was due to Story's penchant (which the chief justice shared) to reason from first principles rather than from cases and trusted authorities, as Washington preferred. Justice Story was somewhat self-aware of his tendency to write broadly, as he told Washington in one letter: "I dare say you will think me a bold Judge. Be it so, but I must ask your patience to read [my opinion] before you condemn me."[183] Another factor was that Story was a better writer than Washington, and judges who are great writers are often tempted to reach for a memorable quote at the expense of sound analysis. When Justice Robert H. Jackson (another quotable writer who sometimes succumbed to that temptation) was asked to compare two of the best circuit judges in his era, Learned Hand and his cousin Augustus "Gus" Hand, he replied that attorneys should "quote Learned but follow Gus."[184] The same advice could be applied to Story and Washington: Story wrote more memorable prose, while Bushrod was more surefooted. Their diverse gifts (along with those of their colleagues) complemented each other. Only when one justice was missing can we see how his absence changed the Court.[185]

Washington wrote three opinions other than *Green* during the 1823 term.[186] Shortly after the Court went into recess, Justice Livingston passed away.[187] The remarkable stability among the brethren after 1812 was over. In the first decade of the Marshall Court, Washington's work occurred mostly behind closed doors as the justices struggled to preserve their capacity to act in a hostile political environment. In the second decade, his labors were more public as the Court used its power to support national authority and contract rights. But change was again lapping at the Supreme Court's door by the 1820s, including challenging cases about slavery. And Justice Washington soon found himself in the midst of a reckoning with his complicity in that dreadful practice.

10
Southern Gentlemen Understand

Bushrod Washington was dependent on slaves from the day he was born until the year that he died.[1] He was responsible for returning slavery to Mount Vernon after his uncle put that evil on the path to extinction there. But the justice also served as the president of the American Colonization Society, which advocated emancipation and the resettlement of free Blacks in the new African nation of Liberia. Bushrod was an atypical slave owner in that he spent much of his time in free states (while riding circuit) and counted abolitionists among his close friends, most notably Eliza Powel. Yet he made national headlines for selling enslaved people in 1821 and bitterly rejecting the criticism that followed. To understand these conflicting impulses, let us look at how Washington handled slavery as a judge, as the president of the Colonization Society, and finally as an owner and seller of enslaved people.

The Rule of Law for Slaves

Justice Washington's first direct encounter with slavery on the bench came in the circuit case of *Butler v. Hopper*.[2] Pierce Butler, a wealthy South Carolina plantation owner, had been a member of the Constitutional Convention and then served in Congress.[3] Butler owned a house in Philadelphia and lived there several months a year. In 1805, his slave Ben claimed his freedom under a Pennsylvania law that said slavery was generally prohibited in the state. The statute provided exceptions for the enslaved people of foreign diplomats, members of Congress, and nonresidents who were in the state.[4] Washington first stated that this law did not violate the Fugitive Slave Clause of the Constitution because Ben had been voluntarily brought to a state by Butler.[5] Butler's main argument, though, was that he was not a Pennsylvania resident. A jury rejected that claim. Justice Washington held that the verdict was supported by the record. While there was sufficient evidence for a jury to conclude that Butler was not a state resident, "when they find only such facts as leave the question of law equivocal, and then draw a conclusion which the facts not found might have warranted, the court cannot say that their conclusion is against law."[6] Over a decade later in *Ex Parte Simmons*, the same law was invoked by a different enslaved person, and Washington again rejected the owner's defense.[7] Simmons was another South

Washington's Heir. Gerard N. Magliocca, Oxford University Press. © Oxford University Press 2022.
DOI: 10.1093/oso/9780190947040.003.0011

Carolina plantation owner living in Philadelphia.[8] His slave (who was not named in the case report) claimed his freedom under a provision in the Pennsylvania statute stating that a slave could not be kept by a nonresident for more than six months. Washington cited *Butler* for the proposition that the state law did not violate the Constitution and then stated that the enslaved person in question was free because he had been in the state for much longer than six months.[9]

Butler and *Simmons* probably hit close to home for Washington. First, he knew that he could bring his slaves to Philadelphia since he was not a resident of the state and did not stay for longer than two months at a time. There is no indication, however, that he ever brought enslaved people there. In part, that may be because doing so posed a risk that they would escape. Second, the justice may have also known about President Washington's efforts to evade Pennsylvania's law. When the capital was in Philadelphia, George brought enslaved people from Mount Vernon and, upon the advice of Attorney General Edmund Randolph, took care to rotate them so that none stayed in Pennsylvania for more than six months at a time.[10] Some of his enslaved people, though, managed to flee before being rotated, leading the president to complain in one case about "the ingratitude of the girl, who was brought up and treated more like a child than a servant (and Mrs. Washington's desire to recover her) [and] ought not to escape without impunity if it can be avoided."[11]

Other circuit cases before the justice involved fugitive slaves. In *Hill v. Low*, a slave named Ezekial escaped to Pennsylvania from Maryland.[12] When Ezekial's owner arrived in Philadelphia and seized him, another man prevented the owner from bringing Ezekial to a place where he could be detained until a custody hearing was held.[13] The owner sued the man and a jury awarded him $500. Washington reversed that judgment. First, he said that the district court erred in instructing the jury that they could not consider if Ezekial was, in fact, an enslaved person, as the owner was required to prove that fact under the Fugitive Slave Act.[14] Second, Washington ruled that only hindering the arrest of a fugitive created liability under the relevant federal provision.[15] "No subsequent obstruction," he said, "whilst the custody continues, although it should afford an opportunity for escape, or be a restraint upon the free will of the claimant, can constitute the offence of obstruction or hinderance mentioned in, or intended by, the fourth section of the [Fugitive Slave] act."[16] While Washington stated that such interference might give rise to an action under state law or violate another part of the Fugitive Slave Act if force were employed, those issues were not before the court.[17] Three years later, in *Worthington v. Preston*, he explained to a jury that his practice when an owner brought an alleged fugitive slave before him was to keep the person in custody for some period before holding a hearing "or else the fugitive could not safely be indulged with time to get witnesses to disprove the claim of the asserted owner."[18] The justice added that the Fugitive Slave Act gave judges no power to issue arrest warrants for fugitive slaves or to confine them after the judge determined that the owner had a valid claim; a hearing under the Fugitive Slave act gave the owner only the right to remove the enslaved person from the state.[19] Privately, Washington was critical of the Fugitive Slave Act, mostly on the ground that the law did not give slave owners enough protection. In an undated entry in his journal, he said that the act was "practically unenforceable."[20] One issue was that Pennsylvania eventually prohibited state judges from enforcing the act, which meant that "no small portion of my time, after the adjournment of the Court, has been employed in attending to those cases."[21] Setting aside his administrative complaint, Washington said that there were not enough federal judges to handle all the fugitive slave cases and therefore Congress should appoint more magistrates. Moreover, he thought that federal judges should be authorized to order a United States marshal to take an enslaved person back to his owner's state at the expense of the owner.[22] Congress took no action, and the justice voiced his criticisms to others.[23] In an 1826 letter, he said that the law "in relation to fugitive slaves, is a shameful, and a fraudulent, execution of the injunction of the constitution, which declares, that they *shall* be delivered up on claim to the owner; whereas the Act of Congress provides, that the owner may recover his slave, if he can find him, and get him before a Judge, and from the State, against the obstructions to which he may be exposed. Nevertheless, there is no chance, I understand, to get the law amended."[24]

The third type of slavery case that Washington addressed involved the international slave trade and led to his only Supreme Court opinion on slavery. Beginning in the 1790s, Congress enacted a series of measures to restrict and abolish commerce in enslaved people on the high seas. In 1806, the justice referred to the international slave trade as "inhuman and unjustifiable traffic" in a circuit opinion.[25] Eighteen years later, *The Merino* came before the Marshall Court.[26] The case involved American vessels carrying enslaved people from Cuba to Florida, which was then part of Spain.[27] The district court concluded that these vessels were guilty of violating federal law; hence, the vessels and the enslaved people should be forfeited. Washington wrote for a unanimous Court affirming in part and reversing in part. He rejected the argument that the slave trade statutes only reached "bringing into bondage those persons who were free in their own country."[28] "The language of the acts of 1800 and 1818," he said, "leaves no reasonable doubt that the intention of the legislature was to prevent citizens of, or residents within, the United States, from affording any facilities to this trade."[29] Applying the law to the facts, the Court affirmed the forfeiture of one vessel and its enslaved people, reversed and remanded for two other ships due to a technical error in the pleadings that Washington said could be corrected, and reversed as to some of the enslaved people on the ground that the acts of

Congress did not permit the forfeiture of slaves themselves when the vessels were captured by warships, which was the case for some of the vessels in *The Merino*.[30]

Justice Washington's slavery decisions were rather favorable to enslaved people even though he did not oppose slavery. One simple explanation for this result is that he just applied the law as written. When the law favored freedom in a case, he ruled that way. And because the Fugitive Slave Act was written narrowly, he applied the statute narrowly, rather than twisting its words to suit his view of what the act should say. A more complex rationale comes from *Justice Accused*, a widely acclaimed book written by Robert Cover.[31] In the book, Professor Cover talked about the paradox that judges who were personally against slavery—including Joseph Story—were often the strongest defenders of slavery in their judicial capacity. Cover argued that anti-slavery judges, tortured by the moral dilemma posed by the legality of slavery, responded by claiming that they lacked discretion to give a narrower construction to slave laws. To admit that they had discretion would mean that they were at times choosing not to exercise that authority on behalf of freedom, which seemed worse than simply pretending that they lacked the authority. Washington presents the opposite case. He accepted the institution of slavery, and therefore was free to issue decisions that softened its blow to individuals without compromising his beliefs. The justice also believed that slavery could be reformed for the better, though his vision of what that reform could be was extremely limited.

The American Colonization Society

The justice's personal attitude toward slavery was clarified by his role as the first President of the American Colonization Society (ACS), from 1816 until 1829. The ACS was established with the goal of supporting the gradual emancipation of enslaved people and the emigration of free Blacks to a new nation in Africa dubbed Liberia.[32] Liberia's capital was named Monrovia (after President James Monroe). A significant part of Monrovia—even today—is called Bushrod Island because of Washington's leadership on colonization. Membership in the Society was a status symbol of sorts for establishment figures. The roll included Chief Justice Marshall, his successor Roger Taney, James Madison, Andrew Jackson, and Henry Clay.[33] Why Washington was chosen as the first president is unknown, though his family name was probably a crucial factor. Equally unclear is why he accepted the job. The Christian mission of the ACS's founder, Reverend Robert Finley, may have appealed to the justice's faith.[34] Washington told one visitor to Mount Vernon that the ACS was an "instrument in the conversion of Africans to Christianity" and would help establish "the kingdom of the Messiah in every quarter of the globe."[35]

But the Society's manifesto, issued in Washington's name and delivered as a petition to Congress, revealed deep divisions about the organization's goals. "It is now reduced to be a maxim," the petition began, "equally approved in philosophy and practice, that the existence of distinct and separate castes, or classes, forming exceptions to the general system of policy adapted to the community, is an inherent vice in the composition of society; pregnant with baneful consequences, both moral and political, and demanding the utmost exertion of human energy and foresight to remedy or remove it. If this maxim be true in the general, it applies with peculiar force to the relative condition of the free people of color in the United States; between whom and the rest of the community, a combination of causes, political, physical, and moral, has created distinctions, unavoidable in their origin, and most unfortunate in their consequences."[36]

The manifesto's first sentence about separate classes sounded like a condemnation of slavery, but the second sentence focused on the problem posed by "free people of color." "The actual and prospective condition of that class of people," the manifesto said, "their anomalous and indefinite relations to the political institutions and social ties of the community, their deprivation of most of those independent, political, and social rights, so indispensable to the progressive melioration of our nature; rendered, by systematic exclusion from all the higher rewards of excellence, dead to all the elevating hopes that might prompt a generous ambition to excel; all these considerations demonstrate . . . [the need] to provide some adequate and effectual remedy." This sounded like a call to make free Blacks equal citizens, but the next line rejected that notion: "The evil has become so apparent, and the necessity for a remedy so palpable, that some of the most considerable of the slaveholding states have been induced to impose restraints upon the practice of emancipation, by annexing conditions, which have no effect but to transfer the evil from one state to another; or . . . end in the total abrogation of a right, which benevolent or conscientious proprietors had long enjoyed under all the sanctions of positive law and of ancient usage." In other words, the evil that required a remedy was not racial inequality but the presence of free Blacks in the United States, which was leading slave states to restrict the right of owners to emancipate. Thus, the solution was to create "a colony, to be composed of such of the above description of persons as may choose to emigrate."[37]

One problem with the ACS was that the group meant different things to different whites. Some saw the Society as the best first step toward emancipation, and even as late as the 1860s, Abraham Lincoln advocated colonization as the most realistic solution for slavery.[38] Others took the view that colonization was about removing free Blacks from the United States, either to make the nation more white or to ensure that all Blacks were enslaved. John Quincy Adams, for instance, refused to support the ACS because "the mass of coloured people who

Figure 10.1 James Madison's membership certificate in the American Colonization Society. Library of Congress.

may be removed to Africa, by the Colonization Society, will suffer more and enjoy less than they would if they should remain in their actual Condition in the United States."[39] John Marshall, however, wrote to the secretary of the ACS in 1831 that the "removal of our colored population is, I think, a common object, by no means confined to the slave States, although they are more immediately interested in it. The whole Union would be strengthened by it, and relieved from a danger, whose extent can scarcely be estimated."[40] Needless to say, no leading members of the Society were the free Blacks who were the organization's supposed beneficiaries. Indeed, a recent book shows that free Blacks overwhelmingly opposed colonization and made their opinions known with petitions and civic activism against the ACS.[41]

Washington's understanding of colonization is partially revealed by journal notes for remarks at one of the Society's meetings.[42] After stating it was "not my intention" to make "a long address," Washington urged his "fellow Christians [to] be not discouraged if the work of benevolence in which we are engaged should be more tardy with accomplishment than our wishes would have it be."[43] Though he initially discussed the goal of introducing free Blacks "to the religion of Christ into the country which gave birth to their fathers," the justice said that "if I be mistaken in the opinion I have always entertained that Africa is to be enlightened," the Society was driven "by other additional motives."[44] Washington then listed those motives: "Arresting the progress of the slave trade—providing an asylum for those who may choose and be at liberty to accept it—and [getting] remaining difficulties out of the way of those who would want to emancipate their slaves but who are now either morally or legally restrained from doing so." "I know," he then explained, "in many respects the objects of this society are misunderstood and often unkindly misrepresented." At that point, the notes end with a list of the misrepresentations: (1) "coercive banishment," (2) "coercive emancipation," and (3) "prevention of emancipation—the reverse of the former." Here he was expressing the moderate's creed—nobody was being required to do anything. Free Blacks could stay or leave. Slave owners could keep their enslaved people or let them go. Change would be slow, if any occurred at all.

Another window into Bushrod's cautious mindset about slavery comes from a draft letter that he wrote after the ACS was founded.[45] Someone had sent the justice an essay arguing that the federal government should use the power of eminent domain to free all enslaved people and give their former enslavers compensation. Washington expressed doubt both that there was a federal power of eminent domain and that Congress would spend such a large sum.[46] While he had "no hesitation in declaring that I concur in . . . the policy of giving freedom to our slaves under such modifications as may insure their happiness and promote the well-being of our country," he did not see how that could be accomplished. Since southern agriculture was dependent on slavery, ending that practice would bring about "the most disastrous consequences" unless "an equally efficient white population" could farm the land. (Washington did not, evidently, think that ex-slaves would want to stay and work for wages.) But the justice believed that few such whites would move to the South "so long as the western sections of the US offer to foreign emigrants . . . fertile lands upon the moderate terms on which they can now be purchased or rented."[47] His hope was that emancipation "may be gradually brought about by voluntary emancipation and the advance of natural sentiment and feeling upon the subject as rapidly as the present circumstances will bear." "There exist difficulties in the way of many who anxiously wish to emancipate their slaves," he concluded, "which I fondly hope the experts of the Colonization Society, should they be helpful, will remove." The ACS was meant "to satisfy those inquiries and to remove these obstacles, and I am persuaded that by the cooperation of our fellow citizens, without which nothing can be done, these benefits will be realized."

The American Colonization Society failed in its mission. Only about 13,000 free Blacks moved to Liberia.[48] Instead of bringing the United States together to solve its most horrific problem, the Society foundered in the face of growing sectional divisions.[49] Part of the problem was that the ACS suffered a blow to its credibility when a journalist broke the story that its president was selling enslaved people rather than freeing them.[50]

A Cruel Fate

In August 1821, a brief story in a Leesburg, Virginia, newspaper described Washington's sale and highlighted the brutal reality of enslavement. "On Saturday last a drove of negroes," the article said, "consisting of about 100 men, women, and children, passed through this town for a southern destination. *Fifty-four* of the above unhappy wretches were sold by *Judge Washington*, of Mount Vernon, *president of the mother colonization society*."[51] A few days later, an unsigned letter to the editor of a Baltimore paper added details to the story. "I was at Mount Vernon a few days since," the author explained, "and was told by the slaves, whose countenances were remarkably indicative of despondency and dejection, that more than fifty of their companions (59 I believe) had been sold but a week before to go to New Orleans, for ten thousand dollars, the whole. One would have thought that the poor creatures who were left, the aged and blind, had lost every friend on earth."[52] "I inquired the reason," he said, and "they answered that husbands had been torn from their wives and children, and that many relations were left behind. Take the following comment: I asked an old slave if he was living at Mount Vernon when GEORGE WASHINGTON died. His answer was 'no sir—not so lucky—I should not be a slave *now* if I had.'" Among those sold were enslaved people who had lived at Mount Vernon since the justice moved there, including Sinah and her husband, Joe; her brother Ham and his wife, Pat; and all of their children and grandchildren.[53] "Judge Washington," the author said, "certainly has as much right to sell his slaves as any other owner of them has, but there is something excessively revolting in the fact that a herd of them should be driven from Mount Vernon, sold by the nephew and principal heir of GEORGE WASHINGTON, as he would dispose of so many hogs or horned cattle; violating every tie that fastens on the human heart, and dissolving the connection of husband and wife, mother and child. We do hope that there is some mistake in this matter."[54]

An event that might have disappeared from history was instead inflamed by the justice's decision to respond publicly to the charge that he was immoral. Before examining what Washington said in his defense, the first question worth asking is why he bothered replying at all.[55] His answer was that these stories were an attack on "the Colonization Society, through the president of that institution . . . I take no exception, *individually*, to the statement of the Leesburg paper. The simple fact that a sale was made of fifty-four negroes, to two gentlemen of Louisiana, is true. The covert attack upon the Colonization Society, the tendency and object of which, it would not be difficult to unfold, ought not, *in this way*, to have been made."[56] This was, at best, a half-truth. The justice was probably concerned about the impact of the articles on the ACS, but the tone of his reply suggests that he bristled at the criticism against him. Maybe he also felt a need to justify his actions because of his personal relationships with people who were opposed to slavery. Most notably, Eliza Powel supported the Pennsylvania Abolition Society, even though women were excluded from membership.[57] In her will, Powel gave that group an annual annuity of $100, proclaiming: "I abhor slavery under any modification and consider the practice of holding our fellow creatures in bondage alike inconsistent with the principles of humanity and free republican institutions. . . . I feel it to be the duty of every individual to cooperate by all honorable means in the Abolition of Slavery, and in the restoration of freedom to that important part of the family of mankind, which has so long groaned under oppression."[58] What would friends like Eliza think of Bushrod if he stayed silent?

Washington's response came in a long letter to the editor of the *Federal Republican*, a friendly newspaper in Baltimore, which the justice penned "for the purpose of refuting certain illiberal remarks, which have appeared in other journals of the day, respecting a sale of negroes which it was my good fortune to effect during the last month."[59] Before correcting what he called the "misrepresentations" in the articles, Washington stated: "I take the liberty, on my own behalf, and on that of my southern fellow citizens, to enter a solemn protest against the propriety of any person questioning our right, *legal or moral*, to dispose of property which is secured to us by sanctions equally valid with those by which we hold every other species of property." But he then said: "I acknowledge, at the same time, that if, in the exercise of it, I have disregarded the dictates of humanity, or unnecessarily given pain to those who were affected by it, my conduct is justly open to public reprehension." He expressed no regret about owning people or selling them, as he had done both throughout his life.[60] Instead, he focused on the claim "that husbands had been torn from their wives and children, and that many relations were left behind."[61] "If the writer," he contended, "meant to insinuate that I had *voluntarily* separated husbands from their wives and children, he has been misled by false information. In making out the list of those negroes which, as it will presently appear, I was under the necessity of parting with, I took care so to arrange it, so as to avoid the separation of families. . . . The charge that parents were torn from their children, if it be meant that I might have prevented such separations, and failed to do so, is equally without foundation." Only his friends knew "what sacrifices I submitted to, in order to keep the families entire, and to relieve the members of them from every regret which their change in situation might otherwise have occasioned." "I parted with a few negroes, the sons of some of those who were sold, and whose services I knew not how to dispense with, at prices greatly below what I would accept for them from others" to keep some families together.[62] He said that he accepted $2,500 less than the market value of his enslaved people overall to ensure that as many families as possible could stay together.[63]

The inadequacy of this explanation may have led the justice to try another, which was that family separation was not so bad. "It is, after all," he wrote, "an extraordinary circumstance, that whilst emigration to this country of parents who have voluntarily separated themselves from their children, and of children who have left behind their parents, never to revisit their native homes, pass daily before our eyes, without observation, so much sensibility should be felt, when similar occurrences take place in relation to this particular class of people."[64] Comparing family separations arising from voluntary emigration with ones caused by the sale of enslaved people was absurd. Moreover, this argument contradicted the previous one in which he said that he had tried hard not to separate families. If he did not think "so much sensibility should be felt" about that result, then why did he make so many "sacrifices" to keep that from happening?

"I may be permitted to add," Washington said, "that I have never heard a sigh or a complaint, from the parents of the two most valuable servants I ever owned, that their sons had abandoned them, and my service, and sought new habitations in the northern states where they now are." Once again, the justice was comparing apples and oranges in a way that should have been obvious. Enslaved people were probably happy when a family member escaped to freedom but would not have felt anything remotely similar when one was sold to another owner far away. Washington offered some personal testimony to support his view that no harm was done. "It is well-known to those who were witnesses of the separation that those who were sold, carried with them no feelings of despondency or regret. In answer to a short address which I made to them, the elders admitted the necessity which compelled me to part with them and confiding in the assurances made to them by the respectable gentlemen to whom they were sold, as to the treatment they might expect, they expressed their belief that their situation would be improved, and cheerfully consented to go with them." Since these elders remained enslaved, though, they were in no position to complain.

Next, Bushrod responded to the criticism that George Washington had freed his slaves and was therefore a better man. This point probably cut deep and resulted in a passage that betrayed a certain degree of resentment toward his uncle's ghost. "I pass by the *insinuation* that because general Washington thought proper to emancipate his slaves, his nephew ought to do likewise," he explained, "with the single observation, that I do not admit the right of any person to decide for me on this point. I am the last man in the world who would attempt to deprecate that, or any other act, of this most revered relative. He was influenced on that, as on all other occasions, by that moral rectitude which invariably governed him through life. He believed the measure to be right, and this was always decisive with him." (Tellingly, Bushrod did not say that he thought George was right to free his enslaved people.) He declined to discuss "the reasons which influence my conduct on this particular subject. It is possible that they may have misled my judgment; but I am conscious of the purity of my motives, and I trust that those at least who know me, will in this respect do me justice." Not long after that ambiguous line, Washington returned to the point that "my negroes [held] upon their minds the belief that, as the nephew of general Washington, or as president of the colonization society, or for other reasons, I could not hold them in bondage, and particularly that they would be free at my *death*." The presence of free Blacks at Mount Vernon (George's ex-slaves and West Ford) helped created this expectation of liberty, though Bushrod blamed outside visitors to Mount Vernon, whom he called "unworthy persons," for convincing his enslaved people that freedom was coming because that was the Washington tradition.

While the justice's main explanation for why he needed to sell people was that Mount Vernon was losing money at an alarming rate, he made the further claim that the ones who were sold deserved their fate because they were not loyal or hardworking.[65] "The insubordination of my negroes," he commented, "and their total disregard of all authority, rendered them worse than useless to me. Southern gentlemen understand, and well know how to appreciate the force of this motive, and I therefore forbear to enlarge upon it." Here the justice was probably alluding to an incident shortly after (and probably in retaliation for) the sale, in which Hannah, the daughter of his longtime slave Oliver Smith, was accused of poisoning Leland Seal, the manager of Mount Vernon.[66] To squelch any rumors that his enslaved people would be freed, Washington stated:

> I called the negroes together in March last, and after stating to them what I'd heard, and that they had been deceived by those who had neither their or my good in view, I assured them most solemnly that I had no intention to give freedom to any of them, and that nothing but a voluntary act of mine could make them so. That the disappointment caused by this declaration should lead to the consequences which followed . . . was to be expected.[67]

The consequences that followed were that many of these enslaved people tried to flee. "During my last circuit," Washington wrote, "and soon after my return, three of them eloped without the pretense of a cause—one of them, a valuable cook [named Emanuel], is at this time a fugitive in one of the northern states; the other two were retaken on their way to Pennsylvania—but I had to pay about $250."[68] "I had good reason," he said, "for anticipating the escape of all the laboring men of any value, to the northern states, so soon as I should leave home." Selling them made that someone else's problem, though two of the enslaved people whom he chose to keep, Oliver Smith's sons George and Ned, escaped shortly afterward before being recaptured.[69]

The most astonishing statement in Washington's letter was that he told his Mount Vernon slaves that he would never free them. Even the most imaginative writer would strain to recreate such a dispiriting speech and scene. Washington did, though, retain a letter in his files, written partly in French, that excoriated him for the sale: "Je take la libertie of writing to vous," the note began. "Je have heard of votre character in Louisiana, where vous rend votre Slaves. . . . Vous suppose you are great because [you are] named Washington—you imagine you may commit crimes with impunitee. Wretched being le time is coming when vous have to answer for votre base crimes. . . . Le Spanish Pirate is better than vous. You send votre fellow mortals to a land of miserie. Vile petit villain how can vous look a manly man in le face. Votre withered hellish countenance black with le deeds of hell . . . Your brains ought to be blown out, vous stinkin Cur . . . Adieu, Je remain votre implacable enemy."[70] (Washington made a notation on the letter that read "impertinent.")

The Genius of Universal Emancipation, an abolitionist publication under the leadership of Benjamin Lundy, reprinted Washington's letter and offered a more refined, although just as vehement, attack on his justification for selling people and splitting their families. Lundy was a Quaker who wanted to purchase enslaved people and free them.[71] His assessment was that "the explanation offered by the judge, appears to me as a very lame apology; a most sorry excuse for so glaring an act of inconsistency and so wide a departure from the rules of justice and Christian benevolence, which it was reasonable to expect would have been adhered to by a man who has had such excellent examples set him by his relatives, as Bushrod Washington."[72] He was particularly scornful of Washington's comparison between voluntary emigration and selling people to a new owner: "Who would have believed that the learned judge of the Supreme Court of the United States could have *descended* to the use of such pitiable sophistry? It must indeed be a bad cause that avails itself of such support as this." "Few will believe that he was *necessitated* to *sell* his negroes," Lundy added. "Had he freed them all, he would, no doubt, still have been rich. It may fairly be presumed that avarice had a much greater influence on his mind than philanthropy." He then made a final point, which was that Lawrence Augustine Washington, Bushrod's first cousin, had freed all his enslaved people in the 1810s.[73] "Which of these two gentlemen," he said, "must now possess the most pleasant feelings?"[74]

The Founding Fathers who enslaved people felt free to ignore any criticism on that ground. Justice Washington, by contrast, did feel the need to respond, which was a sign that the debate about slavery was beginning to change. As the editor of *Niles' Weekly Register* said in his preface to Washington's letter: "It is pleasant . . . to observe that he has not thought himself superior to a trial at the bar of public reason."[75] The justice lost that trial hands down. But soon thereafter he wrote an opinion that would become one of the greatest assets for free Blacks and women fighting for their liberties after the Civil War.

11
Corfield v. Coryell

Justice Washington's most important circuit opinion was *Corfield v. Coryell*. *Corfield* was the first decision to discuss the "privileges and immunities of citizens" protected by Article Four, Section Two of the Constitution.[1] Washington's views on what was included among these rights became a touchstone for the Congress that enacted the Civil Rights Act of 1866 and proposed the Fourteenth Amendment to secure equal justice to free Blacks. His opinion was also the first to say that voting was an essential right, which made *Corfield* a favorite of the women's suffrage movement. While *Corfield*'s substance deserves careful attention, the way in which Washington decided the case also shows how judges think through complex problems and change their minds, sometimes with profound consequences.

A Judge's First Impression

In 1820, New Jersey enacted a statute restricting the harvesting of oysters within state waters to prevent exhaustion of a natural resource.[2] Oyster harvesting was barred from May until September. During the rest of the year, only state residents were allowed to take oysters. The plaintiff in *Corfield*, who was not a New Jersey resident, owned a vessel that harvested oysters in New Jersey state waters.[3] The vessel and its contents were seized by state authorities and sold. The plaintiff brought a trespass action in federal court and made two substantial constitutional claims in alleging that his ship had been wrongfully seized.[4] First, the state oyster harvesting statute was "contrary to that part of the constitution which vests in congress the power to regulate trade and commerce between the states." Second, the law was "contrary to the second section of the fourth article of the constitution of the United States, by denying to the citizens of other states, rights and privileges enjoyed by those of New Jersey."[5] A trial was held and the justice, "after stating to the jury the great importance of many of the questions involved in this cause, recommended to them to find for the plaintiff and assess the damages."[6] The jury followed the court's advice and found for plaintiff in the amount of $560.[7]

To understand why the court advised the jury to rule for the plaintiff, let us look at Washington's notes on the case. In his journal, under the heading

Washington's Heir. Gerard N. Magliocca, Oxford University Press. © Oxford University Press 2022.
DOI: 10.1093/oso/9780190947040.003.0012

"Corfield v. Coryell," he began with the plaintiff's Commerce Clause argument. In 1823, no Supreme Court precedent existed on that part of the Constitution, which gives Congress the power "to regulate Commerce with foreign Nations, and among the several States, and with the Indian Tribes."[8] Instead, the justice turned to a recent Commerce Clause discussion by the governor of Connecticut, Oliver Wolcott Jr., in a veto that he issued against a bill that barred steamboat navigation in state waters by anyone licensed to operate steamboats in New York.[9] The bill retaliated against a New York law that granted a steamboat monopoly in that state's waters to Robert Fulton and Robert Livingston.[10] Wolcott vetoed the bill because he thought that New York lacked the authority to pass its steamboat law under the Commerce Clause (either on its own or as applied by Congress in various statutes) and thus Connecticut lacked the authority to respond in kind.[11] The only remedy, he wrote, lay in a constitutional challenge to the New York law in the Supreme Court.[12] The justice summarized Wolcott's argument in his notes:

> Governor Wolcott's reasons ag[ainst] the Connecticut Bill—The Constitution of the U.S. vests in Cong[ress] the right to regulate commerce between the States. This right is necessarily exclusive. If then N.Y. can constitutionally forbid the navigation of her waters for commercial or other purposes, by steam boats, she may equally forbid to all vessels of any description. The power to regulate includes a right to make regulations regarding the use of navigable waters not the objects of commerce [that] may be attained. A state may make regulations respecting ferries, bridges, etc. and take tolls for the use of them for this is in furtherance of the power vested in Congress. The grant by a State of the exclusive right to use them does not interfere with the right vested in Congress. But the exclusive right to the use of navigable *waters for all purposes* does. By this grant to Cong[ress] the navigable waters of the U.S. are thrown open to all its citizens for navigation [and] commerce [and] no state can prohibit the use of them to any citizen. The N.Y. law equally interferes with the collection of the revenue by imports etc. As Congress has passed laws regulating the commercial intercourse between the States, as these are bottomed upon the principle that such intercourse may be carried on without interruption by all the citizens of the U.S. The above law would be void even tho[ugh] the power was concurrent.[13]

In this summary, Justice Washington was grappling with two points that were in tension. The Commerce Clause gives Congress broad authority to regulate commerce. But the states take many actions that affect interstate commerce, such as regulating ferries, bridges, and tolls for roads. How can these two ideas be reconciled? One solution was to say that the commerce power is concurrent (in other words, shared) between Congress and the states in some fashion. Another option

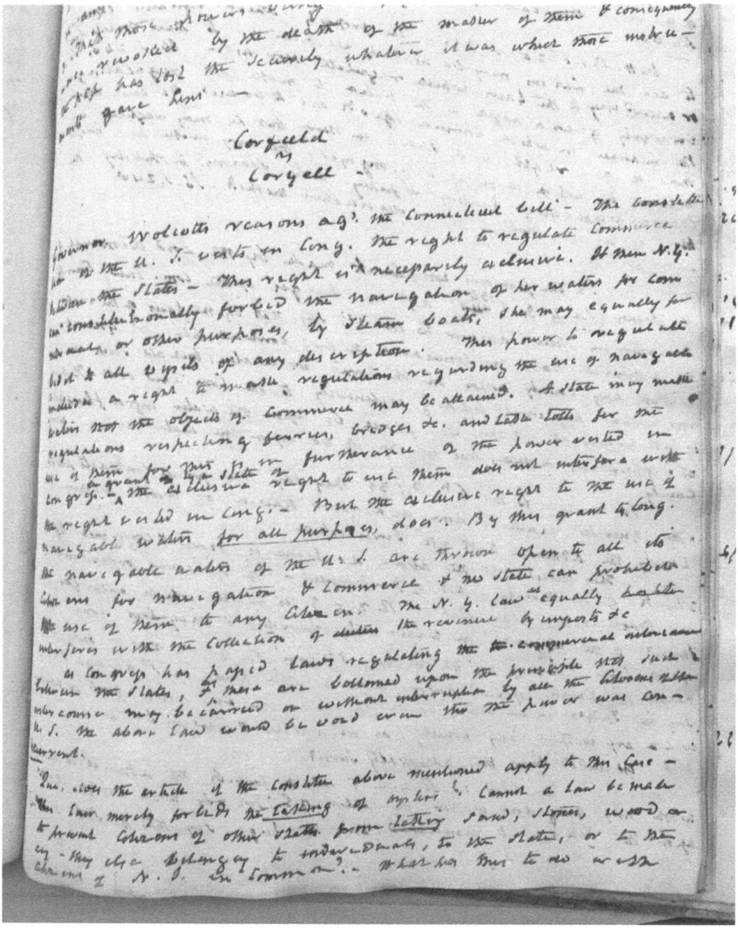

Figure 11.1 The first page of Bushrod Washington's notes on *Corfield*. Photo by the author. Chicago History Museum.

was to say that some state actions are not commercial regulations and hence do not tread on Congress's authority over commerce.

In the next part of his notes, Washington opted for the latter interpretation and argued to himself that the harvesting of oysters was not commerce:

> Does the article of the Constitution above mentioned apply to the case—The law merely forbids the *taking* of oysters. Cannot a law be made to prevent citizens of other states from *taking* sand, stones, wood, or anything belonging to individuals, to the state, or to the citizens of N.J. in common? What has that to do with commerce, which consists in bartering, buying [and] selling. The

> prohibition is not of the use of the waters for navigation [and] trade, but of the taking of oysters within the waters. Could not a law forbid the citizens of other states from taking the fish or oysters from a several fishery? Or from a free fishery? If she could why not forbid the same in relation to a common fishery?[14]

Put another way, Washington's tentative view was that the New Jersey law was more like a typical state law regulating property or torts than a regulation of commerce. In his opinion in *Corfield* (which will be discussed in greater detail later), he cleaned up his notes and explained: "Paving stones, sand, and many other things, are as clearly articles of trade as oysters; but can it be contended, that the laws of a state, which treats as tortfeasors those who shall take them away without the permission of the owner of them, are commercial regulations?"[15] The bottom line is that the justice was not persuaded by the plaintiff's Commerce Clause argument, though he did not reach a conclusion on whether the commerce power was exclusive or concurrent.

Next, Washington took up the plaintiff's second argument, which was that the New Jersey oyster law violated the Privileges and Immunities Clause, which states: "The citizens of each State shall be entitled to all privileges and immunities of citizens in the several States."[16] There was no Supreme Court precedent on this provision either, but a decision from New York's highest court discussed privileges and immunities in upholding that state's steamboat monopoly law.[17] In his notes, Washington stated: "I am inclined to the opinion of the [New York court] in *Livingston v. Van Ingen*, that the meaning of this article is that the citizens of each State shall within every other State have *equal* privileges or rights as the citizens of such State have, the words *all privileges of citizens* being equivalent to equal privileges."[18] The New Jersey oyster law, though, did not give out-of-state residents the same rights as state residents. Then the justice asked himself the next logical question:

> Is the right which a citizen has to enjoy the common property belonging to the citizens of the state a privilege or immunity? . . . I am inclined to think that it is a privilege within the meaning of this article of the Constitution. If it be not, then the rights to navigate the waters would not be, because they also are common property, and yet it would look to violate this article to make a law forbidding citizens of other states to navigate the waters of that State.[19]

Here the justice was saying that he could not sensibly distinguish the constitutional privilege to use the navigable waters of any state from the plaintiff's asserted privilege to take oysters from those same waters. A state might be free to ban oyster harvesting but could not do so only for out-of-state residents—that was unequal and unconstitutional.

Accordingly, Washington's notes on *Corfield* indicate that he instructed the jury to find for the plaintiff because the New Jersey law violated the Privileges and

Immunities Clause. But the jury's verdict was not the final word. After the trial in *Corfield*, Washington wrote Justice Story that the case involved "more constitutional questions than I have ever met with in any one cause. Those arising out of the steamboat cause are to be met with in this, and many others."[20] The Supreme Court was about to weigh in on New York's steamboat monopoly law and on the Commerce Clause.

Gibbons v. Ogden

The justices returned to action in February 1824 with a new colleague. To replace Justice Livingston, President Monroe selected Smith Thompson, the secretary of the navy and a former chief justice of New York.[21] Chief Justice Marshall wrote Washington to celebrate after learning of Thompson's appointment, stating: "I had been so alarmed about the successor to our lamented brother Livingston that I am truly rejoiced to find Mr. Thompson is appointed."[22] Anticipation was high for the argument in *Gibbons v. Ogden*, a case challenging the New York steamboat monopoly.[23] Daniel Webster and Attorney General William Wirt thundered that the monopoly was unlawful under the relevant acts of Congress and unconstitutional under the Commerce Clause.[24] A week after the arguments ended, Marshall fell and dislocated his shoulder, which forced Washington to preside while the chief justice recuperated.[25] Judge Peters wrote when he heard about the accident, and Justice Washington said in March that "the accident which befell him is deeply felt by us all, and I do not think that you express yourself too strongly in saying that 'the nation is in danger.' He is now, thank God, nearly recovered."[26]

The chief justice delivered the Court's unanimous opinion in *Gibbons* while still wearing a sling.[27] In striking down New York's monopoly, Marshall was careful to rest his holding on the ground that the state law conflicted with federal statutes concerning free navigation.[28] He seized the opportunity, though, to comment on the meaning of the Commerce Clause and give that text a broad nationalist interpretation. Marshall rejected the view that commerce should be limited "to traffic, to buying and selling, or to the interchange of commodities . . . Commerce, undoubtedly, is traffic, but it is something more; it is intercourse."[29] "The word used in the constitution, then, comprehends, and has been always understood to comprehend navigation within its meaning."[30] In describing the commerce power more generally, he stated: "This power, like all others vested in Congress, is complete in itself, may be exercised to its utmost extent, and acknowledges no limitations, other than are prescribed in the constitution."[31] "The wisdom and the discretion of Congress," he said, "their identity with the people, and the influence which their constituents possess at elections, are, in this, as in many other instances, as that, for example, of declaring war, the sole restraints on which they have relied, to secure them from its abuse."[32]

The chief justice did acknowledge that the states retained the authority to regulate aspects of the economy that indirectly influenced commerce: "Inspection laws, quarantine laws, health laws of every description, as well as laws for regulating the internal commerce of a State, and those which respect turnpike roads, ferries, &c., are component parts of this mass. No direct general power over these objects is granted to Congress; and, consequently, they remain subject to State legislation."[33] Judge Peters wrote Washington praising *Gibbons*, and the justice replied that "your approbation of the decision in the Steamboat cause is highly gratifying to the Chief Justice and his associates, to whom I took the liberty of showing your letter. The answer of the former, upon returning it to me was 'may he live a thousand years!' "[34] The rest of the 1824 term was business as usual, with the Court largely unanimous and Bushrod writing five opinions.[35]

Washington's notes on *Corfield* suggest that he was unusually well prepared for *Gibbons*, though we do not know what he may have contributed to the opinion. He was thinking about the constitutional issues raised by the New York steamboat monopoly before the case was heard in the Supreme Court. He was also mulling over the issue of where the line between Congress's commerce power and the state's domestic authority should be drawn before the Court addressed that question. His views on both of these points were shaped by the Wolcott Veto, and he may have brought that reasoning into the Court's conference. What is unclear is how the justice processed his conflicting views about commerce to reach a conclusion. In his notes, he seemed to accept the narrow definition of commerce as just "bartering, buying, and selling," which Marshall's opinion rejected. On the other hand, Washington twice jotted down in his journal that Wolcott used "intercourse" to define commerce.[36] Perhaps the justice decided that Wolcott's more expansive definition was correct; perhaps he was swayed by Daniel Webster's argument for a broader definition; or perhaps he was persuaded by his colleagues.[37] Whatever the answer, he was not done thinking through these questions.

On Second Thought

Now let us return to Philadelphia for round two of *Corfield*. In October 1824, the defendant asked the circuit court to declare the jury's verdict contrary to law.[38] The case report does not explain the legal arguments that were made, but an obvious thought was that *Gibbons* required Justice Washington to reconsider his conclusion that the state oyster law did not violate the Commerce Clause. Six months later, he issued his opinion. The justice almost never spent six months on a circuit opinion, which indicates that he gave *Corfield* extra attention. Moreover, he showed a draft of the opinion to Justice Story during the Supreme Court's 1825 term, which suggests that he was still tinkering with *Corfield* while sitting on the High Court.[39] (This is the only known example of Washington showing another justice a draft opinion in a circuit case.)

Justice Washington's opinion began by reaffirming his initial view that the defendant's Commerce Clause claim was without merit. He commented that the commerce power "does by no means impair the right of the state government to legislate upon all subjects of internal police within their territorial limits . . . even though such legislation may indirectly and remotely affect commerce." "Inspection, quarantine, and health laws; laws regulating the internal commerce of the state; laws establishing and regulating turnpike roads, ferries, canals, and the like" were valid state statutes. After quoting from *Gibbons*, Washington explained that "if the power which congress possesses to regulate commerce does not interfere with that of the state to regulate its internal trade, although the latter may remotely affect external commerce . . . much less can that power impair the right of the state governments to legislate, in such manner as in their wisdom may seem best, over the public property of the state."[40] The fact that oysters were themselves articles of commerce did not mean that a state law regulating their harvest came within the commerce power. "The law," he explained, "does not inhibit the buying and selling of oysters after they are lawfully gathered, and have become articles of trade, but it forbids the removal of them from the beds in which they grow (in which situation they cannot be considered articles of trade)."[41] Justice Washington distinguished between potential and actual trade articles due, in part, to a line in *Gibbons* that said state inspection laws were not commercial regulations since "they act upon the subject before it becomes an article of foreign commerce, or of commerce among the states, and prepare it for that purpose."[42] "Is this not," *Corfield* asked, "precisely the nature of those laws which prescribe the seasons when, and the manner in which, the taking of oysters is permitted?" Washington thought that the answer was clearly yes, and hence "we deem it superfluous to pursue this subject further."

But then *Corfield* made a U-turn. The justice changed his mind and decided that the New Jersey law was constitutional after all. His notes say that he initially thought that the state law was contrary to the Privileges and Immunities Clause because the right to take oysters from navigable waters was like the right to travel on navigable waters. Now he wrote that "we cannot accede to the proposition which was insisted on by the counsel, that, under this provision of the constitution, the citizens of the several states are permitted to participate in all the rights which belong exclusively to the citizens of any other, merely upon the ground that they are enjoyed by those citizens."[43] Washington rejected the argument that "in regulating the use of the common property of the citizens of such state, the legislature is bound to extend to the citizens of all the other states the same advantages as are secured to their own citizens." "It would," he stated, "be going quite too far to construe the grant of privileges and immunities of citizens, as amounting to a grant of a co-tenancy in the common property of the state, to the citizens of all of the other states." To do so, he said, "would, in many instances, be productive of the most serious public inconvenience and injury, particularly, in regard to those kinds of fish, which, by being exposed to too general use, may be exhausted." In language that a modern environmental lawyer might use, Washington explained: "The oyster beds belonging to a state may be abundantly sufficient for the use of the citizens of that state, but might be totally exhausted and destroyed if the legislature could not so regulate the use of them as to exclude the citizens of the other states from taking them, except under such limitations and restrictions as the laws may prescribe." As a result, he held that the jury's verdict should be set aside and that the defendant should win.[44]

The famous part of *Corfield* is where Washington described what was included among the privileges and immunities of citizens if oyster harvesting in navigable waters was not one of them. Here is what he said, with some numbering added for ease of reading:

1. We feel no hesitation in confining these expressions to those privileges and immunities which are, in their nature, fundamental; which belong, of right, to the citizens of all free governments; and which have, at all times, been enjoyed by the citizens of the several states which compose this Union, from the time of their becoming free, independent, and sovereign. What these fundamental principles are, it would perhaps be more tedious than difficult to enumerate.
2. They may, however, be all comprehended under the following general heads: Protection by the government; the enjoyment of life and liberty, with the right to acquire and possess property of every kind, and to pursue and obtain happiness and safety; subject nevertheless to such restraints as the government may justly prescribe for the general good of the whole.
3. The right of a citizen of one state to pass through, or to reside in any other state, for purposes of trade, agriculture, professional pursuits, or otherwise; to claim the benefit of the writ of habeas corpus; to institute and maintain actions of any kind in the courts of the state; to take, hold and dispose of property, either real or personal; and an exemption from higher taxes or impositions than are paid by the other citizens of the state; may be mentioned as some of the particular privileges and immunities of citizens, which are clearly embraced by the general description of privileges deemed to be fundamental:
4. [T]o which may be added, the elective franchise, as regulated and established by the laws or constitution of the state in which it is to be exercised.

5. These, and many others which might be mentioned, are, strictly speaking, privileges and immunities, and the enjoyment of them by the citizens of each state, in every other state, was manifestly calculated (to use the expressions of the preamble of the corresponding provision in the old articles of confederation) "the better to secure and perpetuate mutual friendship and intercourse among the people of the different states of the Union."[45]

Why did the justice change his view that oyster taking was encompassed by the "right of a citizen of one state to pass through . . . any other state for purposes of trade, agriculture, professional pursuits; or otherwise"? He left no clues behind. What seems clear, though, is that his doubts on that point drove him to discuss the category of privileges and immunities more than was necessary to resolve the case before him. Uncertainty led to greater self-reflection.

Some observations are in order about Washington's definition of privileges and immunities in *Corfield*. One is that he was speaking in aspirational terms. History does not support the notion that the rights in *Corfield* had "at all times, been enjoyed by the citizens of the several states which compose this Union, from the time of their becoming free, independent, and sovereign."[46] Indeed, part of Washington's statement was probably drawn from the ideals set forth in the Virginia Declaration of Rights of 1776, which was that all men possess certain basic rights—"namely, the enjoyment of life and liberty, with the means of acquiring and possessing property, and pursuing and obtaining happiness and safety."[47] Next, *Corfield*'s list of rights came mainly from the common law rather than from the Constitution. The right of citizens to travel, to dispose of property, to bring civil actions, and to seek habeas corpus were well settled at common law.[48] While some of these rights can be inferred from the Constitution, *Corfield* did not say that the founding text was the source of rights that belonged to citizens of all free governments. The exception was the opinion's comment about the right to vote, which was neither a common-law right nor a write secured by the 1787 Constitution.

Washington's statement on voting rights, though qualified by the word "may" and by the power of the state to regulate suffrage, was revolutionary. No prior case had said that voting was a basic right of any sort, and no leading political figure took that view. While the Declaration of Independence said that "the consent of the governed" was necessary for legitimate authority, there was no sense that consent meant individual voting or that citizenship included a right to vote. *Corfield*'s position on voting rights was so radical that even strong proponents of equal citizenship during Reconstruction could not accept Washington's logic, as we shall see shortly. Only in the twentieth century would *Corfield*'s ideal approach reality, though universal suffrage in practice remains a work in progress.

Why the justice included voting rights in *Corfield* is also a mystery. Two decades earlier, he had told a friend that he was skeptical about a proposal to extend voting rights in Alexandria.[49] Maybe he changed his mind on this issue as well. Or maybe he did not anticipate the implications of his comment.

Corfield and Reconstruction

Until 1866, *Corfield* received little attention. When courts cited the case, they did so mainly for the unremarkable point that the Privileges and Immunities Clause meant that a state could not discriminate against out-of-state citizens.[50] After the Civil War, though, Republicans in Congress wanted to ensure that free Blacks would have the rights of free whites. But what were those basic rights? To frame the Civil Rights Act of 1866 and the Fourteenth Amendment to the Constitution, many members of Congress cited Justice Washington's discussion of privileges and immunities as guidance.[51] They treated *Corfield* as a list of rights that every citizen was entitled to in every state. This was almost certainly not what Washington meant.[52] He was instead describing the rights that every state was required to give to out-of-state citizens *if* state citizens were given that right. Nevertheless, *Corfield* was open to the broader, or more nationalist, reading that was given to the opinion during Reconstruction, the period of egalitarian reform that immediately followed the Civil War.[53]

The debate on the Civil Rights Act of 1866 was the first appearance of this new and improved *Corfield*. Senator Lyman Trumbull quoted the opinion and said the case "enumerates the very rights belonging to a citizen of the United States which are set forth in the first section of this bill."[54] Likewise, Representative James Wilson relied on *Corfield* for the proposition that the Civil Rights Act "merely affirms existing law" on the rights of citizens, which made the proposal sound moderate.[55] Democratic critics replied that Justice Washington's "views were uttered in reference alone to white citizens" and so could not support the act.[56] Realizing that Black male voting was politically unpopular, these critics also seized on *Corfield*'s statement on suffrage as proof that the Civil Rights Act would give many free Blacks voting rights even though voting was not mentioned in the bill. As Representative Andrew Rogers said: "The bill, then, would prevent a State from refusing negro suffrage under the broad acceptation of the term 'civil rights or immunities.' In fact, it has been decided by the circuit court of the United States, in the case of *Corfield v. Coryell* . . . that the elective franchise is included in the words privileges and immunities."[57] Senator Trumbull's rebuttal was that Washington went "further than the bill under consideration" when he gave "as his opinion that under this clause of the Constitution, securing to the citizen of each State all the privileges and immunities of citizens of the several States of the United States, a person who is a citizen in one State and goes to another is even entitled to the elective franchise."[58] The Civil Rights Act was enacted over President Andrew Johnson's veto and borrowed from *Corfield*'s analysis in guaranteeing free Blacks the right "to make and enforce contracts, to sue, be parties, and give evidence, to inherit, purchase, sell, and convey real and personal property, and to full and equal benefit of all laws and proceedings for the security of person and property, as is enjoyed by white citizens."[59]

When the debate turned to the Fourteenth Amendment, leading members of Congress still looked to *Corfield* as inspiration for the Privileges or Immunities Clause in Section One of the proposal while continuing to disavow Washington's statement about voting rights. Senator Jacob Howard's introduction of the Fourteenth Amendment quoted at length from what Washington—"that very learned and excellent judge"—said about the privileges and immunities of citizens in describing what the equivalent provision in Section One would mean.[60] But Senator Howard then stated: "The right of suffrage is not, in law, one of the privileges or immunities thus secured by the Constitution. It is merely a creature of law. It has always been regarded in this country as the result of positive local law, not regarded as one of those fundamental rights lying at the basis of all society and without which a people cannot exist except as slaves, subject to a despotism." To make clear that voting was not yet a constitutional right for all Americans, the drafters of the Fourteenth Amendment provided in Section Two that states denying suffrage to eligible "male" voters would suffer only a representation penalty in the House of Representatives and in the Electoral College, which meant that the states were still able to deny the vote to free Black men.[61]Women, white and Black, could be excluded from voting without penalty.

After the Fourteenth Amendment was ratified in 1868, though, advocates of female suffrage insisted that *Corfield* meant that women, as citizens, were entitled to vote. In 1871, Victoria Woodhull, a colorful champion of sex equality, petitioned the House of Representatives and argued that the Privileges or Immunities Clause of the Fourteenth Amendment gave women voting rights.[62] Woodhull's attorney, Albert Riddle, told the National Women's Suffrage Convention that her petition was supported by *Corfield* and observed that "Bushrod Washington, the favorite nephew of our Washington, made the decision, ladies. He was the Washington who got all of the brains of the family outside of its great chief, and he put them to good use."[63] In a written opinion, the House Judiciary Committee rejected the petition even while quoting *Corfield*'s passage about privileges and immunities.[64] Though left unstated, the Committee might have reasoned that *Corfield*'s comment that voting rights were subject to state regulation meant that states could bar women from voting, an inference that was especially powerful given that Section Two of the Fourteenth Amendment used the word "male" to describe presumptively eligible voters.

Figure 11.2 Victoria Woodhull presenting her suffrage petition to the House Judiciary Committee.
Originally published in *Frank Leslie's Illustrated Newspaper*. Library of Congress.

Two dissenting members of the House Judiciary Committee issued their own opinion, relying, in part, on *Corfield*.[65] After quoting Washington's dicta, the dissenters stated: "This case is cited by the majority of the committee as sustaining their view of the law, but we are unable to so understand it. It is for them an exceedingly unfortunate citation."[66] In *Corfield*, "the court enumerated some of the 'privileges of citizens,' such as are '*in their nature fundamental and belong of right to the citizens of all free governments*' (mark the language), and among those rights, place the 'right of the elective franchise' in the same category with those great rights of *life, liberty, and property*. And yet the committee cites this case to show that this right is not a fundamental right of the citizen!"[67] The dissent conceded that *Corfield* explained that suffrage "is to be enjoyed as regulated and established by the State in which it is to be exercised," but rejected the view that "these words are supposed to qualify this right, or rather take it out of the list of fundamental rights, where the court had just placed it."[68] A right was either fundamental or not; *Corfield* could not be read to say that something is a " 'fundamental right of the citizen,' but it does not exist, unless the laws of the State give it. A singular species of 'fundamental rights'! Is there not a clear distinction between the regulation of a right and its destruction? The State may regulate the right, but it may not destroy it." The dissent restated the problem with voting rights that *Corfield* had recognized fifty years earlier. Suffrage is a fundamental right, but the states retain considerable control over its exercise. Subsequent constitutional amendments barred states from engaging in types of voting discrimination (on the bases of race, sex, poll taxes, and age), but local officials still determine district boundaries, the implementation of most election procedures, and eligibility for voting on other grounds.[69] What, then, does calling voting a fundamental right mean, when the states are given significant latitude in enforcement? America still struggles with the paradox that Washington first identified in *Corfield.*

When the Supreme Court issued its first Fourteenth Amendment opinion in 1873, *Corfield* was given a narrower reading. In the *Slaughter-House Cases*, the Court omitted the specific rights contained in Justice Washington's list and stated that the sole purpose of Article Four's Privileges and Immunities Clause "was to declare to the several States, that whatever those rights, as you grant or establish them to your own citizens, or as you limit or qualify, or impose restrictions on their exercise, the same, neither more nor less, shall be the measure of the rights of citizens of other States within your jurisdiction."[70] Put another way, *Slaughter-house* gave *Corfield* its antebellum interpretation as an anti-discrimination case against out-of-state citizens instead of a decision about fundamental rights secured for every citizen in every state.[71] Justice Stephen Field's dissent in *Slaughter-House* rejected this view and included most of the specific rights *Corfield* had described, stating that Justice Washington described the privileges and immunities that "belong to the citizens of all free governments."[72] Justice Joseph Bradley's dissent also gave *Corfield* the broader reading, but neither Field nor Bradley dared to mention Washington's statement on voting rights.[73] Indeed, the Court did not touch that part of *Corfield* until the end of the nineteenth century.[74] In 1900, when voters in St. Louis brought an equal-protection challenge against a registration statute in Missouri that singled out the city for special treatment, the Court unanimously rejected the claim, declaring: "The elective franchise, if one of the fundamental privileges and immunities of the citizens of St. Louis, as citizens of Missouri and of the United States, is clearly such franchise 'as regulated and established by the laws or Constitution of the state in which it is to be exercised.' "[75] The quoted language in support of this state restriction on suffrage came from *Corfield.*

The fundamental rights that Justice Washington said belonged to all citizens were not part of the law in his lifetime. But *Corfield* remains a guiding light for those who think that all Americans enjoy constitutional rights that are not expressly written in the Constitution.[76] Since the existence of unspecified rights will be contested for as long as the Republic endures, the legacy of Washington's willingness to reconsider his decision in *Corfield* will also endure.

12
A Long Judicial Life

Age was gaining on Washington by the mid-1820s. A journalist at the oral argument in *Gibbons* described him as having "a sallow countenance, not very strongly marked, but deeply furrowed by the hand of time and bearing the marks of infirm health."[1] During his circuit in 1824, Washington told Justice Story that he "was attacked by a highly inflammatory rheumatism in my chest which confined me to my room for a fortnight. I then made an effort to proceed with business of the court, but the copious bleeding to which [his doctor] found it necessary to subject me, together with the other remedies which had been used, so totally debilitated me, that by the advice of my brother Judge and the Bar, I adjourned the court."[2] "My health is now better," he said, "[b]ut I dare not expect that it will ever be entirely reestablished." John Marshall was also feeling old, telling Washington in 1825 that "when you reach my age you will find that when a man is engaged as I am at present, a thing postponed is very apt to slip the memory and to be longer neglected than it ought to be."[3] Nonetheless, they were still plugging away on a revised edition of *Life of Washington*, with Marshall asking his friend at one point to track down an obscure Anti-Federalist essay for him.[4]

In the 1824 presidential election, Virginia lost the stranglehold on national power that had been the state's birthright since the American Revolution. Four candidates, each hailing from a different part of the country, campaigned to succeed James Monroe.[5] Andrew Jackson won the largest number of popular votes, but none of the four contenders received a majority in the Electoral College. The final choice was therefore made by the House of Representatives, and it selected John Quincy Adams, who had come in second behind Jackson in the national poll.[6] This result outraged Jackson's supporters, especially because they thought that their man lost because of a "Corrupt Bargain" involving Adams and Henry Clay, the fourth-place finisher, who threw his support to Adams in the House and was named secretary of state soon thereafter.[7] The Era of Good Feelings was over, as Jackson spent the next four years harboring bad feelings and planning revenge.

The Supreme Court's 1825 term got under way while the House was still picking the new president.[8] All the cases decided during that term were unanimous, with Washington writing three opinions for the Court.[9] In one of the three, *McCormick v. Sullivant*, he penned one of his more widely quoted comments

Washington's Heir. Gerard N. Magliocca, Oxford University Press. © Oxford University Press 2022.
DOI: 10.1093/oso/9780190947040.003.0013

about federal courts. Although Article Three of the Constitution describes what Congress designated circuit and district courts as "inferior," Washington said that their final judgments were still legal authority that the Supreme Court must respect.[10] Any view to the contrary "proceeds upon an incorrect view of the character and jurisdiction of the inferior courts of the United States. They are all of limited jurisdiction, but they are not on that account, inferior courts, in the technical sense of these words, whose judgments taken alone, are to be disregarded."[11] The fact that the justices sat on these inferior courts made Washington's point more obvious in his day than in ours. In between, the Court cited his maxim in several cases to remind litigants that the judgments of the inferior courts were still binding on the parties.[12]

Shortly after the 1826 term began, Justice Todd (who had not participated much in the Supreme Court's work in the prior few years) died in Kentucky.[13] The remaining six justices were again able to reach unanimity in every case, with Bushrod writing for the Court four times.[14] President Adams selected Robert Trimble, the federal district judge in Kentucky, as Justice Todd's replacement.[15] In the same year, John Adams and Thomas Jefferson died on the fiftieth anniversary of the Declaration of Independence.[16] Perhaps it was the final illness of these contemporaries of George Washington, along with the death of Justice Todd, that prompted Bushrod—now sixty-four years old—to update his will in July 1826.[17]

Ogden v. Saunders

When the justices returned to action in January 1827, they were asked to decide if the states were permitted to enact bankruptcy statutes.[18] Recall that in *Golden v. Prince*, Justice Washington had held on circuit that retrospective state bankruptcy laws were unconstitutional under the Contracts Clause. He also stated in dicta that states could not enact valid bankruptcy laws at all because that authority was exclusive to Congress. After Washington wrote *Prince*, Justices Johnson and Livingston rejected his dicta in their respective circuits and held that the states did have some power to regulate bankruptcies.[19] In 1819, the issue came before the Supreme Court in *Sturges v. Crowninshield*.[20] Chief Justice Marshall wrote a unanimous opinion that papered over the stark differences among the justices. The Court held that retrospective state bankruptcy laws were invalid, as Washington had held in *Prince*, but did not decide the broader issue of whether states could enact any bankruptcy law.[21] This holding avoided what Marshall called "the delicate inquiry respecting the precise limitations which the several grants of power to congress, contained in the constitution, may impose on the state legislatures."[22] The chief justice included language in *Sturges* suggesting that states might be free to have bankruptcy laws if they were not inconsistent with the Contracts Clause. The explanation for this ambiguity was given afterward by Justice Johnson: "The Court was, in that case, greatly divided in their views of the doctrine, and the judgment partakes as much of a compromise, as of a legal adjudication. The minority thought it better to yield something than risk the whole."[23]

Justice Johnson did not divulge which of his colleagues joined him in the minority who "thought it better to yield something than risk the whole." What is clear is that Washington was not among them. He later said that he concurred with the holding of *Sturges* and with "the reasoning of the learned Judge who delivered that opinion . . . although I did not then, nor can I now bring my mind to concur in that part of it which admits the constitutional power of the State legislatures to pass bankrupt laws."[24] *Sturges* confirms that the Marshall Court's unanimity was sometimes the result of give-and-take, and that an opinion's author was sometimes stating what other justices thought rather than his own view.

Sturges only postponed the inevitable showdown. In 1824, the justices heard argument in *Ogden v. Saunders*, which challenged the validity of New York's prospective bankruptcy law, with Daniel Webster arguing against its constitutionality.[25] Washington wrote to Judge Peters after the arguments to say that the justices were "now engaged in considering the validity of State bankrupt laws in their operation on *subsequent* contracts, and are not a little puzzled by the question which they present," adding that this information was "entre nous" (just between us).[26] The Court was evenly divided in *Ogden*, as Justice Todd was absent, and thus ordered that the case be reargued when there was a full bench. Webster renewed his plea in 1827, but this time the justices rejected his argument by a 4–3 vote. Closely divided votes in the Supreme Court now occur regularly, but *Ogden* was the first case in which the Court announced a major constitutional decision by a majority of one.[27] The surprise in *Ogden* was that Washington wrote the lead opinion upholding the New York statute, in spite of his decision in *Prince* holding that the states lacked the power to enact bankruptcy statutes.[28] The chief justice, Justice Story, and Justice Duvall dissented.[29] *Ogden* was, in a sense, Washington's swan song, and it was another fine example of his mature approach to judging and his respect for precedent.

Early in his opinion, Washington explained how he saw his task. "I have examined both sides of this great question with the most sedulous care," he wrote, "and the most anxious desire to discover which of them, when adopted, would be most likely to fulfill the intentions of those who framed the constitution of the United States. I am far from asserting that my labors have resulted in entire success. They have led me to the only conclusion by which I can stand with any degree of confidence; and yet, I should be disingenuous were I to declare, from this place, that I embrace it without hesitation, and without a doubt of its correctness. The most that candor will permit me to say upon the subject is, that I see, or think

I see, my way more clear on the side which my judgment leads me to adopt, than on the other, and it must remain for others to decide whether the guide I have chosen has been a safe one or not."[30] With this opening, the justice exhibited the intellectual humility that marked many of his most difficult circuit opinions. Even though he was one of the men who had ratified the Constitution, he did not claim that he knew what the Constitution meant. But Washington did point out that "not one voice was raised against [the Contracts Clause], in any of those conventions, by the jealous advocates of State rights, nor even an amendment proposed, to explain the clause, and to exclude a construction which trenches so extensively upon the sphere of State legislation."[31]

The justice's journal contains his notes on *Ogden* and gives us one final look into his mind in an important case. He began by recognizing that *Sturges* was binding precedent. In a form of shorthand, Washington asked himself whether Webster's argument was "conclusive to prove that the power is exclusive in Congress that all bankruptcy law must of necessity violate the obligation of contracts on which ground *Sturges v. Crowninshield* proceeded."[32] Put another way, the creditors in *Ogden* were arguing that only Congress could enact bankruptcy laws, which was what Washington had said in *Prince*. But the best reading of *Sturges* was that the states could enact bankruptcy laws as long as those laws did not violate the Contracts Clause. Washington stated in *Ogden* that *Prince* was correct in stating that only Congress could regulate bankruptcy, but "it becomes me to believe that this opinion was, and is incorrect, since it stands condemned by the majority of the Court, solemnly pronounced."[33] "After making this acknowledgement," he said, "I refer again to [*Sturges*] with some degree of confidence, in support of the opinion to which I am inclined to come." What is important about this passage is that the justice set his reading of the Constitution aside in favor the Court's collective judgment. This sacrifice was in keeping with his actions throughout his tenure, which were designed to strengthen the authority of the Court and ensure that the rule of law was different from the views of any single judge.

With *Sturges* in mind, Washington's notes then homed in on the central question in *Ogden*: "What is the obligation of a contract?"[34] A little later, he jotted down: "The parties are morally bound to perform their contracts. Municipal law adds no additional sanction to this obligation but by affording a legal remedy to enforce this obligation instead of leaving it to the forum of conscience. The terms on which the remedy is afforded rests with the legislature and it is no violation of the contract to deny the remedy after so many years—can it be so, then, to deny it if the party surrenders all his property?" A sticking point for the justice in thinking about the Contracts Clause was that every state had a statute of limitations for a contract action, and these laws denied some parties a legal remedy after a certain period of time even when a contractual promise was broken. Since a statute of limitations "does not impair the obligation," then how, he asked, could a prospective state bankruptcy law do so? Washington did consider that *Sturges* described the Contracts Clause as barring "any law discharging a contract without performance," and told himself: "The general manner in which the proposition is expressed would seem to cover subsequent as well as prior contracts."[35] But he then commented: "Statutes of limitations and usury laws [prohibiting loan contracts charging an excessive interest rate] unless retroactive in their effect do not impair the obligations of contracts." After quoting further from *Sturges*, Washington scribbled: "The above opinion clearly distinguishes between the legal obligations of a contract and the remedy given by law to enforce it and admits that the remedy may be modified without impairing the obligation unless it operates on past contracts."

The justice's opinion in *Ogden* presented a polished version of this analysis. "It has constantly appeared to me that the error of those who controvert the constitutionality of the bankrupt law under consideration . . . if they be in error at all, has arisen from not distinguishing accurately between a law which impairs a contract, and one which impairs its obligation."[36] "What is it, then, which constitutes the obligation of a contract? The answer is given by the Chief Justice, in the case of Sturges v. Crowninshield, to which I readily assent now, as I did then; it is the law which binds the parties to perform their agreement."[37] "But the question, which law is referred to in the above definition, still remains to be solved," he said. "It cannot, for a moment, be conceded that the mere moral law is intended, since the obligation which that imposes is altogether of the imperfect kind, which the parties to it are free to obey, or not, as they please."[38] Washington conceded that the "law of nations" could create an "obligation of contract made upon a desert spot, where no municipal law exists."[39] "But can it be seriously insisted that this," he asked, "was exclusively in the contemplation of those who framed this constitution? What is the language of this universal law? It is simply that all men are bound to perform their contracts. The injunction is as absolute as the contracts to which it applies. It admits of no qualification." "If it be true," he wrote, "that this is exclusively the law to which the constitution refers us, it is very apparent, that the sphere of State legislation upon subjects connected with the contracts of individuals, would be abridged beyond what it can for a moment be believed the sovereign States of this Union would have consented to; for . . . there are few laws which concern the general police of a state, or the government of its citizens, in their intercourse with each other, or with strangers, which may not in some way or other affect the contracts which they have entered into, or may thereafter form."[40]

The justice then gave several examples of state laws that limited contracts and remedies, such as statutes of limitation, statutes of frauds, bans on usury, "and those [laws] that limit the fees of professional men and the charges of tavern keepers."[41] (In his notes, Washington also mentioned state bans on "contracts by married women.")[42] "If it be conceded that *those laws* are not repugnant to the constitution, so far as they apply to subsequent contracts, I am yet to be instructed how to distinguish between those laws, and the one now under consideration."[43] "I confidently believe," he added, "that none exist that will bear the test of a critical examination."[44]

Chief Justice Marshall's dissent rejected Washington's principle that the obligation of contracts protected by the Constitution necessarily included prospective state laws. He argued that contracts instead reflected a "pre-existing intrinsic obligation which human law enforces. If, on tracing back the right to contract, and the obligations created by contract, to their source, we find them to exist anterior to, and independent of society, we may reasonably conclude that those original and pre-existing obligations are, like many other natural rights, brought with man into society, and, although, they may be controlled, are not given by human legislation."[45] And "the framers of our constitution were intimately acquainted with the writings of those wise and learned men, whose treatises on the laws of nature and nations have guided public opinion on the subjects of obligation and contract. If we turn to those treatises, we find them to concur in the declaration, that contracts possess an original intrinsic obligation, derived from the acts of free agents, and not given by government. We must suppose, that the framers of our constitution took the same view of the subject, and the language they have used confirms this opinion."[46] Marshall then said that state laws preventing some contract formation (for instance, because the contract was not written) were valid because no obligation of contract was impaired unless the contract existed in the first place.[47] As for a statute of limitations, he argued that this should be understood more like a rule of evidence creating a conclusive presumption of satisfactory performance rather than the denial of a remedy for non-performance.[48] (In other words, if a party did not complain about a contract breach after a certain amount of time, then the state could just assume that no breach occurred.) Washington rejected Marshall's first point on the ground that state usury laws did not just prevent the creation of those loan contracts; they could also limit the interest rate of a lender in a way that radically altered a contractual obligation.[49] As for statutes of limitations, he said that these so-called rules of evidence could not be applied retrospectively according to *Sturges*, which indicated that the "distinction [was] between those which operate prospectively and those which operate retrospectively."[50] In his notes, the justice added that "statutes of limitation are not grounded altogether on a presumption of performance but on political reasons."[51]

The dueling portions of *Ogden* were a forerunner of the subsequent debate within the Supreme Court about whether the Constitution protected a "liberty of contract" from some state and federal regulation. Proponents of the liberty of contract sometimes defended that doctrine by referring—much as Marshall did—to natural rights and to the Declaration of Independence.[52] The dissenting view, championed most forcefully by Justice Oliver Wendell Holmes Jr., was that there was no constitutional liberty of contract because contracts were wholly a creature of state law. Justice Holmes specifically mentioned usury laws and statutes of frauds as examples in one of his liberty-of-contract dissents, just as Washington did in *Ogden*.[53] While the liberty of contract was later repudiated, constitutional jurisprudence remains divided between those who are willing to invoke natural law principles and those who hew more closely to positive or written law. Washington was in the positivist camp, as demonstrated by his rejection of federal civil common law in *Prince* and by his reasoning in *Ogden*.[54] Even *Corfield*, which broadly defined the privileges and immunities of citizens, did so based on well-settled common law.

Washington and Marshall also engaged in a sharp volley about how the Contracts Clause should be read in conjunction with the rest of Article One, Section Ten of the Constitution. Washington began in typical low-key fashion: "I come now to a more particular examination and construction of the section under which this question arises; and I am free to acknowledge, that the collection of the subjects for which it provides, has made an irresistible impression upon my mind, much stronger, I am persuaded, than I can find language to communicate to the minds of others."[55] He reasoned that the first relevant part of Section Ten, which said: "No State shall . . . coin money, emit bills of credit, make any thing but gold and silver a tender in payment of debts," was meant "to provide a fixed and uniform standard of value throughout the United States" and "will admit of no construction which would confine it to State laws which have a retrospective operation."[56] The next portion of Section Ten barred states from enacting bills of attainder and ex post facto laws, which were criminal penalties applied retroactively that were "oppressive, unjust, and tyrannical" according to "the universal sentence of civilized man."[57] Then came the Contracts Clause, which Washington said prohibited retroactive state laws that impair contract obligations. Reading the Contracts Clause as sharing the purpose of the Ex Post Facto and Attainder Clauses made sense because "there is nothing unjust or tyrannical about punishing offenses prohibited by law and committed in violation of that law. Nor can it be unjust, or oppressive, to declare by law, that contracts subsequently entered into, may be discharged in a way different from that which the parties have provided, but which they know, or may know are liable, under certain circumstances, to be discharged in a manner contrary to the provisions of their contract."[58] The justice rejected the argument that the Contracts Clause should be read together with the first part of Section Ten—the ban on all legal tender—because both provisions were about contracts. This would rearrange the order of the constitutional text in a way that "falls little short, in my opinion, of begging the whole question in controversy."[59]

Chief Justice Marshall's dissent rested his reading of the Contracts Clause in part on the absence of any reference to retrospective laws in that provision. "The first impression which the words make on the mind," he wrote, "would probably be that the prohibition is intended to be general."[60] "Had the intention been to confine the restriction to laws which were retrospective in their operation, language could have been found, and would have been used, to convey this idea. The very word would have occurred to the framers of the instrument, and we should probably have found it in the clause. . . . [T]he State legislatures would have been forbidden 'to pass any *retrospective* law impairing the obligations of contracts,' or 'to pass any law impairing the obligation of contracts previously made.' "[61] "In instruments prepared on great consideration," Marshall concluded, "general terms, comprehending a whole subject, are seldom employed to designate a particular, we might say, a minute portion of that subject." Washington's textual retort was that if the Framers had wanted to bar prospective state bankruptcy laws, they would have said "impairing contracts, instead of the obligation of contracts," in the Contracts Clause, but they did not use that phrase because it would have "*hazarded* [that is, jeopardized], to say the least of it, the adoption of the constitution by the State conventions."[62]

Justice Washington's most famous statement in *Ogden* came at the end. "I shall now conclude this opinion," he began, "by repeating the acknowledgment which candor compelled me to make in its commencement, that the question which I have been examining is involved in difficulty and doubt. But if I could rest my opinion in favor of the constitutionality of the law on which the question arises, on no other ground than this doubt so felt and acknowledged, that alone would, in my estimation, be a satisfactory vindication of it."[63] Then came this pearl of wisdom: "It is but a decent respect due to the wisdom, the integrity, and the patriotism of the legislative body by which any law is passed to presume in favor of its validity until its violation of the Constitution is proved beyond all reasonable doubt." Nearly a century later, Justice Louis Brandeis picked up on this comment and quoted the line in three cases to warn the Court against exercising judicial review too aggressively.[64] Justice Brandeis may have gotten the idea from James Bradley Thayer, one of his professors at Harvard Law School, who cited Washington's closing statement in *Ogden* in his scholarship arguing for judicial restraint.[65]

In 1937, President Franklin D. Roosevelt repeated Washington's mantra during one of his most anticipated fireside chats. The president's radio address to the nation concerned his plan to increase the number of justices on (or "pack") the Supreme Court in response to a series of cases invalidating aspects of his New Deal program.[66] To justify his proposal, Roosevelt gave listeners a brief history lesson about judicial review: "Congress passed a statute which, in 1803, the Court said violated an express provision of the Constitution. The Court claimed the power to declare it unconstitutional [in *Marbury*] and did so declare it. But a little later the Court itself admitted that it was an extraordinary power to exercise and through Mr. Justice Washington laid down this limitation upon it."[67] He then quoted *Ogden*'s punch line and stated: "But since the rise of the modern movement for social and economic progress through legislation, the Court has more and more often and more and more boldly asserted a power to veto laws passed by the Congress and State Legislatures in complete disregard of this original limitation." Why FDR selected the quote from *Ogden* and singled out Justice Washington is unclear. Bushrod was not a household name in 1937, as the *New York Times* felt the need to put an Associated Press blurb in its coverage of the speech explaining who Justice Washington was.[68] The president may have wanted simply to invoke the name of Washington—any Washington—on the side of his controversial plan. Once the Supreme Court started upholding the constitutionality of the New Deal and the proposal to pack the Court was shelved, neither Roosevelt nor any justice cited this part of *Ogden* again.

Ogden was not the only skirmish over creditors' rights during the 1827 term. In *Mason v. Haile*, the Supreme Court held that a debtor in Rhode Island was lawfully discharged from debtors' prison when the state legislature granted his petition for release by enacting a special relief law just for him.[69] The creditor's constitutional objection (made by Daniel Webster) was that imprisonment for default was in the debt contract and that the release was a retrospective law altering that term. *Haile* rejected that argument, reasoning that private legislative petition relief was part of state practice when the contract was made and thus the exercise of discretion to grant this debtor's petition was not retrospective in a constitutional sense.[70] Justice Washington dissented alone, with this disclaimer: "It has never been my habit to deliver dissenting opinions in cases where it has been my misfortune to differ from those which have been pronounced by a majority of this Court. Nor should I do so upon the present occasion, did I not believe, that the opinion just delivered is at variance with the fundamental principles upon which the cases of *Sturges v. Crowninshield*, and *Ogden v. Saunders*, have been decided. A regard for my own consistency, and that, too, upon a great constitutional question, compels me to record the reasons upon which my dissent is founded."[71] He explained that the "great, the intelligible principle, upon which those cases were decided, is that a retrospective State law, so far as it operates to discharge, or to vary the terms of an existing contract, impairs its obligation, and is, for that reason, a violation of the tenth section of the first article of the constitution of the United States; but that a law, which is prospective in its operation, has not this effect, and, consequently, is not forbidden by that instrument." Washington argued that a legislative grant "for the purpose of benefitting a particular individual, is the enactment of a new law" and that this law was giving retrospective relief for an existing debt contract.[72] If there was a distinction between

Haile and the recent bankruptcy precedents, "the course of reasoning by which it is to be effected is quite too subtle for my mind to comprehend it."[73]

The Finishing Canter

Sometime after the end of this busy term, Washington sat for his final portrait. The painting, which now hangs in the Supreme Court, was executed by Chester Harding, a popular artist who painted many of the portraits included in this book. Gone is the boy of twenty-one, who asked his mother if he looked too pensive in his first portrait. In this image of Washington as an old man, his blind eye is off-center and his hair is wispy and unkempt. He is wearing his judicial robes, but the image is a realistic one instead of the more heroic depictions of George Washington. Artistic tastes change, of course, so perhaps the difference reflects nothing more than that. But there is an underlying truth to Justice Washington's official portrait. He was a man, not a legend. The same idea was expressed by Bushrod's graveside marker at Mount Vernon. In 1850, a modest obelisk was erected there as a memorial. At the same time, construction was under way not far away on the tallest obelisk in the world at the time—the Washington Monument.

The Court's 1828 term was uneventful, but one of the cases shows how the justices worked together to achieve consensus when possible. *Bell v. Morrison* was a contract case from Kentucky that turned on the interpretation of that state's statute of limitations.[74] Shortly after the argument, Washington wrote Justice Story a note stating that: "The Chief Justice informs me that you are to draw the opinion in the Case of Bell."[75] He then explained that "a night's reflection has induced me to change my opinion on the Kentucky decisions" on the statute of limitations. "The view which Justice Trimble takes of the doctrine, as settled and understood by the Supreme Court of *his own state*, is, as it ought to be, conclusive with me. I should be very sorry if the settled construction of a Statute in one state should be unsettled by the S[upreme] Court of the United States." "You may therefore," Washington concluded, "consider me as uniting with Messers Trimble, Duvall, and yourself on *that point*. On every other, I remain as firm as a rock."

Justice Story's opinion held that the Kentucky decisions on that state's statute of limitations must be followed even though they were at odds with English decisions interpreting nearly identical statutory language.[76] Story went out of his way to comment that the English decisions were more soundly reasoned, adding that "this opinion thus expressed [in *Bell*], is not unanimous, but of the majority of the Court; and as is apparent, from the preceding reasoning, it has been principally, although not exclusively, influenced by the course of decisions in Kentucky

Figure 12.1 Bushrod Washington. Painting by Chester Harding. National Portrait Gallery.

upon this subject."[77] His compromise language can be traced back directly to what Washington's letter revealed about the differences among the justices.

The 1828 term was less interesting than the events that followed.[78] That summer, Washington fell sick again.[79] He recovered, but in August received the news that his longtime circuit partner Richard Peters was dead. Washington wrote Richard Peters Jr., who was now the Supreme Court reporter, to say: "I was shocked on receiving the information and yet I had endeavored for more than twelve months to prepare myself for it."[80] Joseph Hopkinson, the mainstay of the Philadelphia bar who had argued many cases before the justice, was appointed by President Adams to replace Peters and sat with Washington during his final circuits.[81] That August, Justice Trimble also died, though his demise was unexpected.[82] The ensuing vacancy came at a delicate moment, as President Adams and Andrew Jackson were in the midst of a presidential campaign that is widely regarded as the nastiest in the United States before the twenty-first century.[83] Jackson emerged victorious, which prompted Justice Story to write

Washington: "I deeply regret the overthrow of Mr. Adams's administration. But we must submit with as good a grace as we may and hope for the best."[84] After his defeat, President Adams nominated John Crittenden, a senator from Kentucky, to replace Justice Trimble in the Court's "Kentucky seat," but Jackson's supporters in the Senate blocked the nomination so that the new president could fill the vacancy.[85]

Since the 1829 term began before Jackson's inauguration, only six justices were on the Court. Washington issued six opinions, the most he had written in a single term for years.[86] In one of his cases, *Satterlee v. Mathewson*, the justice returned to the Contracts Clause and to what state actions impaired contractual obligations. *Satterlee* presented the issue of whether a state law that broadened the definition of a valid contract could be lawfully applied to transactions that occurred prior to the statute and, in effect, retroactively convert nonenforceable agreements into binding obligations.[87] While "this law may be censured, as it has been, as an unwise and unjust exercise of legislative power," Washington explained that "it is not easy to perceive how a law which gives validity to a void contract can be said to impair the obligation of that contract."[88] "It surely cannot be contended," he continued, "that to create a contract, and to destroy or impair one, mean the same thing."[89] The justice commented that the fact that "the effect of [the state law] was to divest rights that were vested by law" did not make the law void. He then pivoted away from the Court's reference to natural law in *Fletcher v. Peck*, stating that while the chief justice did suggest that "the nature of society and of government power" might condemn a law that transferred property rights without compensation, "it is nowhere intimated in that opinion, that a state statute, which divests a vested right, is repugnant to the *constitution of the United States*."[90] Washington's italics for the Constitution reinforced the theme of his *Ogden* opinion, which was that the text was the only proper source of authority for judicial review. Washington then left Washington, never to see Chief Justice Marshall or his colleagues again.

The justice held his usual spring circuit and went back to Philadelphia for the fall cases. His new district court colleague Joseph Hopkinson recalled that Washington arrived at the end of September "on his way to Trenton, where he was to hold a Circuit Court on the first day of October. I called upon him in the afternoon of the day after his arrival—he was full of animation and apparent health—he was, indeed, highly exhilarated. He spoke of his late visit to the Springs; of the severe exercise he was able to undergo there; of his climbing the high hills, without the least inconvenience, or any symptoms of the shortness of breath that had formerly afflicted him."[91] Hopkinson then added this poignant note: "I remember well that, speaking of the business of his approaching courts, he made a quick movement, and said—'I am now ready for anything.' "[92] But the next morning, "he was entirely changed; he looked wearied and distressed; he said he had passed a disturbed and sleepless night. He however attributed his indisposition to a supper he had eaten, which he thought had produced indigestion; and we both expressed a confidence that this derangement of his system would be but temporary. The next day he went on to Trenton, and got through the business of that Court, although laboring under sickness and pain. On his return to Philadelphia, his appearance bespoke how much he had suffered; but we nevertheless hoped, from day to day, he would yet be able to attend his duties here. That hope was never realized."

On November 26, 1829, Justice Washington died in the city that was his second home. He was sixty-seven years old, the same age that his uncle had been when he died. Nancy was with her husband when he passed away, but—in an astonishing coincidence—she joined him in death two days later while on her way back to Virginia.[93] Tributes poured in when the sad news arrived. The Philadelphia bar, which provided Washington with his legal training and then relied upon him as a judge, placed a tablet in Congress Hall praising his "simplicity of manners and purity of heart: Fearless, dignified, and enlightened, as a Judge; No influence or interest could touch his integrity, or Bias his Judgment."[94] He left "to his professional brethren, A spotless fame; And to his country, The learning, labor, and wisdom, of a long judicial life." Writing from Boston, Justice Story paid tribute to his colleague.[95] "He read to learn, and not to quote; to digest and master, and not merely to display," Story said.[96] "He was not easily satisfied. If he was not as profound as some, he was more exact than most men. . . . He indulged not the rash desire to fashion the law to his own views; but to follow out its precepts with a sincere good faith and simplicity. Hence, he possessed the happy faculty of yielding just the proper weight to authority, neither, on the one hand, surrendering himself blindfold to the dictates of other judges, nor, on the other hand, overruling settled doctrines upon his own private notion of policy or justice." "In short," Justice Story concluded, "he was exemplary and able, one whom all may reverence, and but few may hope to equal."

The most illuminating response to Bushrod's death came from John Marshall. Upon hearing the news, the chief justice told James Madison simply: "I need not say how much I regret his loss."[97] Marshall later sent a letter to Joseph Hopkinson praising his eulogy for Washington: "He was indeed one of the worthiest and best, and therefore one of the most beloved of men. In amiableness of manners, in excellence of heart, in professional acquirements and in soundness of intellect, he was all that you have represented him. His loss is deplored by no person more than myself."[98] Even after Bushrod's death, Marshall still wanted his friend's counsel. At one point, he asked Justice Story about a difficult legal issue, saying, "I recollect a conversation between you and Judge Washington on some question connected with this in which I believe, though I am not certain, you did not concur. . . . I did not attend to the conversation and do not recollect it with any sort of accuracy. Will you, if you have any recollection on this subject, or if you have any fixed judgement on the question, drop me a line."[99]

An official memorial was held for Washington when the justices gathered for their 1830 term, but the most telling sign of his absence came when the chief justice returned to the capital.[100] Marshall learned that his colleagues were not all together in a boarding house for the first time in thirty years. Justice John McLean, named by President Jackson to fill Justice Trimble's seat, was staying with his family, and Justice Johnson also chose to live separately.[101] While the breakup of communal living may have been inevitable, Washington's death hastened the change. He was, in so many ways, the glue of the Marshall Court.

Epilogue

Half-Blind Justice

Bushrod and Nancy were laid to rest in the family crypt at Mount Vernon alongside George and Martha. The mansion and the estate, now reduced to 1,225 acres after the justice had parceled out his land to various relatives, passed to his nephew John Augustine Washington.[1] In 1850, Bushrod's niece Jane Charlotte erected a modest obelisk for him that still stands outside the tomb. On the grave marker was inscribed: "As a Judge, he was wise and just . . . Firm in every honorable purpose and pursuit. Yet gentle, humane, and condescending." Describing someone as "condescending" in his epitaph may seem strange. In Washington's day, however, "condescending" was a compliment. To be condescending meant that a superior person talked to inferior people as if they were equal, which demonstrated generosity and humility.[2] Today "condescending" is a criticism because the assumption is that no person is inherently superior to another. This turnaround in the meaning of a word that involves social commentary points out the distance between our world and Bushrod Washington's. While that distance should soften any conclusions about Justice Washington's life, some closing observations are still appropriate.

Bushrod Washington cared more about legal institutions than about personal glory. In this respect, he shared one of his uncle's best traits. At Virginia's ratifying convention for the Constitution, Bushrod held his tongue in public and concentrated on getting the proposal over the finish line. As an appellate lawyer, he took on the thankless task of publishing detailed reports about decisions of the Virginia Court of Appeals for the benefit of the profession. As a circuit judge, he was a gifted administrator and a master of instructing juries in a manner that gave attorneys and their clients confidence that they received impartial justice. On the Supreme Court, Justice Washington often refrained from expressing his views publicly so that the chief justice could speak for the Court with one voice at a time when unity was crucial for judicial authority. Yet at a pivotal moment, he probably saved judicial independence by privately counseling his colleagues to avoid a confrontation with Congress and President Jefferson. When Washington did write Supreme Court opinions, he took pains to cite cases and treatises far more than Chief Justice Marshall did, to emphasize that his reasoning drew from the law and not from his personal beliefs. And in *Ogden v. Saunders*, Justice

Washington's Heir. Gerard N. Magliocca, Oxford University Press. © Oxford University Press 2022.
DOI: 10.1093/oso/9780190947040.003.0014

Washington provided an early example of applying stare decisis in a principled manner when he set aside his reading of the Bankruptcy Clause on circuit in favor of the Supreme Court's subsequent decision on that issue. If, as Ralph Waldo Emerson said, an institution is the lengthened shadow of one man, the federal judiciary owes much of its character to Bushrod Washington.

Yet Washington did not just lead by example. His judicial opinions left behind a rich legacy. *Corfield v. Coryell* is his most important contribution because of its influence on the Fourteenth Amendment and its groundbreaking invocation of an individual right to vote. The justice's cogent articulation of the presumption of constitutionality and the deference owed by courts to legislative action remain bedrock tenets of judicial review. Washington's opinion in *Golden v. Prince* anticipated the *Erie* doctrine and the proper relationship between federal courts and state law by over a century. Finally, his defense of federal supremacy and reading of the Eleventh Amendment in *United States v. Bright* was an eloquent statement of constitutional first principles that provides valuable insights for modern

Figure E.1 West Ford in 1858. Drawing by Benson Lossing. Originally published in *Harper's Weekly*. Mount Vernon Ladies' Association.

jurists. Washington was not perfect. His rejection of the argument that the Sedition Act violated the First Amendment was an unfortunate blind spot traceable to his political partisanship in the 1790s. All in all, though, Washington's decisions across many subjects reveal a steady hand and sound judgment.

Against all these public virtues, there is the moral stain of Washington's unapologetic ownership and sale of enslaved people. As Bushrod promised in 1821, he did not free anyone. In this respect, he did not follow his uncle's example. West Ford did receive 160 acres and used the proceeds from selling that land to buy freedom for some members of his family, though others remained enslaved at Mount Vernon.[3] Ford and some of his free children and grandchildren kept working at Mount Vernon in various capacities until the 1860s.[4]

In 1858, John Augustine Washington III, the justice's great-nephew, sold the estate to the Mount Vernon Ladies' Association, which still runs the museum there.[5] Shortly before the sale, Benson Lossing, a historian and journalist, came to Mount Vernon and interviewed West Ford.[6] After their interview, Lossing "left him with an engagement to meet him the next morning for breakfast, for the purpose of delineating his likeness with a pencil. I found him prepared, having on a black satin vest, a silk cravat, and his curly gray hair arranged in the best manner. 'For,' he said, 'the artists make colored people look bad enough anyhow.'"[7] Five years later, with the Civil War raging in Virginia, Ford was brought back to Mount Vernon during his final illness. He died on July 30, 1863, the last Washington to reside at the family home.[8] Ford may have been buried in the slave cemetery a stone's throw from George's and Bushrod's crypt. But his final resting place, like his parentage, will probably never be known.

How should Bushrod Washington's achievements be weighed alongside his personal record on slavery? Perhaps the answer is that we are all George Washington's heirs. Heirs of the soldiers whom he commanded, heirs of the people whom he enslaved, and heirs of the nation that he led. Justice Washington was the first person who was forced to make choices about this complex inheritance. He was not the last. Now these choices fall to all Americans to decide, as the justice said in *Corfield,* which liberties are "fundamental and belong, of right, to the citizens of all free governments" and how they should be regulated for "the good of the whole."

Notes

Introduction

1. "Judge Washington," *Niles' Register*, Sept. 29, 1821, 21:72; see Scott E. Casper, *Sarah Johnson's Mount Vernon: The Forgotten Memory of An American Shrine* (New York: Hill and Wang, 2008), 15. The book usually refers to people who were owned as "enslaved people." On occasion, though, I deviate from that usage and say "slave," largely because using that word just makes a particular sentence read better.
2. See, e.g., Jean Edward Smith, *John Marshall: Definer of a Nation* (New York: Henry Holt & Co., 1996), 290.
3. Last Will and Testament, July 9, 1799, in *The Papers of George Washington: Retirement Series*, ed. W. W. Abbot and Dorothy Twohig (Charlottesville: University Press of Virginia, 1998–99), 4:480.
4. See *Morning Chronicle and Baltimore Advertiser*, Aug. 24, 1821, 2 (reprinting the article leveling the charge); "Judge Washington," *Niles' Register*, Sept. 29, 1821, 21:70–72 (issuing his response). For the best accounts of slavery at Mount Vernon, see Casper, *Sarah Johnson's Mount Vernon* and Mary V. Thompson, *"The Only Unavoidable Subject of Regret": George Washington, Slavery, and the Enslaved Community at Mount Vernon* (Charlottesville: University of Virginia Press, 2019).
5. See *Corfield v. Coryell*, 6 F. Cas. 546, 551–52 (C.C.E.D. Pa. 1825) (No. 3,230); Kurt Lash, *The Fourteenth Amendment and the Privileges and Immunities of American Citizenship* (New York: Cambridge University Press, 2014), 27; see also *Congressional Globe*, 39th Cong., 1st Sess. 2765 (1866) (statement of Sen. Howard) (quoting from the opinion of the "very learned and excellent judge" Washington to explain the Privileges or Immunities Clause of the Fourteenth Amendment).
6. In addition to many letters and primary documents, this book draws upon excellent secondary sources for the basic facts on Justice Washington. See, e.g., David A. Faber, "Justice Bushrod Washington and the Age of Discovery in American Law," *West Virginia Law Review* 102 (2000): 735–807; Herbert A. Johnson, "Bushrod Washington," *Vanderbilt Law Review* 62 (2009): 447–90; James R. Stoner, "Heir Apparent: Bushrod Washington and Federal Justice in the Early Republic," in *Seriatim: The Supreme Court Before John Marshall*, ed. Scott Douglas Gerber (New York: New York University Press, 1998), 322–50.
7. Ron Chernow, *Washington: A Life* (New York: Penguin Books, 2010), 604.
8. There are two unpublished biographies of Justice Washington. See David Leslie Annis, "Mr. Bushrod Washington, Supreme Court Justice on the Marshall Court," PhD diss., Notre Dame University, 1974, and William Robert Emmons, "Mr. Justice Bushrod Washington and the American Constitution," unpublished manuscript,

1991, Mount Vernon Library. Only one hard copy of the Emmons manuscript is available at Mount Vernon; there is no digital copy.

9. Letter from William Johnson to Thomas Jefferson, Dec. 10, 1822, https://founders.archives.gov/?q=William%20johnson%201822%20Author%3A%22Johnson%2C%20William%22&s=1511311111&r=3.

Chapter 1

1. Last Will and Testament, in *Papers of George Washington: Retirement Series*, 4:487. Throughout the book, I have taken the liberty of modernizing some of the spelling, punctuation, and capitalization in documents to make them easier to read. The early chapters often refer to the principals by their first names (for instance, Jack, George, Bushrod, or Hannah) because just saying "Washington" would cause confusion. By contrast, the later chapters tend to use "Washington" to mean Bushrod Washington, as all of the other leading family members were dead by then. Finally, I use the word "heir" in the title and throughout the book in a colloquial sense. Legally speaking, someone who inherits property is more properly described as a "legatee" or a "devisee" depending on what is being given by the benefactor.
2. Ibid. The history of Mount Vernon, which is one of America's most famous homes, is recounted in many fine books. My primary sources about the estate are Robert F. Dalzell Jr. and Lee Baldwin Dalzwell, *George Washington's Mount Vernon: At Home in Revolutionary America* (New York: Oxford University Press, 1998); Jean B. Lee, ed., *Experiencing Mount Vernon: Eyewitness Accounts, 1784–1865* (Charlottesville: University of Virginia Press, 2006); and Mary V. Thompson, *"The Only Unavoidable Subject of Regret": George Washington, Slavery, and the Enslaved Community at Mount Vernon* (Charlottesville: University of Virginia Press, 2019).
3. Letter from George Washington to Henry Knox, April 27, 1787, in *The Papers of George Washington: Confederation Series*, ed. W. W. Abbot and Dorothy Twohig (Charlottesville: University Press of Virginia, 1997), 5:157. The basic facts in the text and in the notes about Jack's youth and his relationship with George until 1758 come from Ron Chernow, *Washington: A Life* (New York: Penguin Books, 2010) and Henry Wiencek, *An Imperfect God: George Washington, His Slaves and the Creation of America* (New York: Farrar, Straus, and Giroux, 2003). Unfortunately, there is no authentic image of Jack Washington. A painting of him can be found online and in at least one old book, but no original source or artist is cited. As a result, I cannot establish to my satisfaction that this image is a genuine likeness.
4. For recent accounts of Mary Ball Washington that are more positive, see Martha Saxton, *The Widow Washington: The Life of Mary Washington* (New York: Farrar, Straus, and Giroux, 2017); see also Alexis Coe, *You Never Forget Your First: A Biography of George Washington* (New York: Viking Press, 2020), xxxiv–xl.
5. Letter from George Washington to John Augustine Washington, May 31, 1754, in *The Papers of George Washington: Colonial Series*, ed. W. W. Abbot, Dorothy Twohig,

and Philander Chase (Charlottesville: University Press of Virginia, 1983), 1:118–19 (noting the death of Ensign de Jumonville, the French commander); see Joseph J. Ellis, *His Excellency: George Washington* (New York: Vintage Press, 2004), 13–14, 17–18 (explaining how this became a global incident because French troops were killed after allegedly attempting to surrender).

6. Ellis, *His Excellency*, 119. George's comment to Jack was leaked to the press and reported in London, where King George II is said to have replied: "He would not say so, if he had been used to hear many." See John Rhodehamel, *George Washington: The Wonder of the Age* (New Haven, CT: Yale University Press, 2017), 51. The leak may have been orchestrated by George with Jack's cooperation. See David O. Stewart, *George Washington: The Political Rise of America's Founding Father* (New York: Dutton, 2021), 43.
7. Lawrence Washington inherited Mount Vernon from Augustine Washington but died in 1752. See Chernow, *Washington*, 26; Stewart, *Political Rise*, 51. Mount Vernon was named after Admiral Edward Vernon, under whom Lawrence served in the Royal Navy.
8. See letter from George Washington to John Augustine Washington, May 14, 1755, in *Papers of George Washington: Colonial Series*, 1:257–58. Jack also managed George's property on Bullskin Creek in Frederick County. See Stewart, *Political Rise*, 25, 80. Unfortunately, no letters from Jack to George survive from this period.
9. Letter from George Washington to John Augustine Washington, May 28, 1755, in *Papers of George Washington: Colonial Series*, 1:291.
10. Ibid. George was instead listed on the ballot in Frederick County and lost. See Stewart, *Political Rise*, 72–73 (explaining that it is unclear whether he wanted to run for the House of Burgesses there or was entered by friends without his consent). In 1758, though, he was elected to the House of Burgesses. He was then reelected in 1761 and many times thereafter. See Chernow, *Washington*, 129 (stating that Jack voted for George in 1761).
11. The essential facts about Hannah Bushrod Washington come from David Leslie Annis, "Mr. Bushrod Washington, Supreme Court Justice on the Marshall Court," PhD diss., Notre Dame University, 1974, 17, 20–21. There is one painting of Hannah (by an unknown artist) in a private collection, but I was unable to obtain a copyright permission to use that image here.
12. Augustine Washington Jr. inherited Pope's Creek, George's birthplace, from his father and lived in Westmoreland County when he served in the House of Burgesses.
13. See Coe, *You Never Forget Your First*, 27–38 (describing the courtship and marriage of George and Martha). It is unclear when the move occurred. Jack and Hannah were not at Mount Vernon during the winter of 1757–58, when George was there and suffering from dysentery. See Stewart, *Political Rise*, 1–7. Thus, they probably moved to Bushfield in 1757, though they could have returned to Mount Vernon during George's courtship of Martha in 1758.
14. See John W. Wayland, *The Washingtons and Their Homes* (Staunton, VA: McClure, 1944), 111 (describing John Bushrod's will).

15. *Journal and Letters of Philip Vickers Fithian, 1773–1774: A Plantation Tutor of the Old Dominion*, ed. Hunter Dickinson Farish (Williamsburg, VA: Colonial Williamsburg, 1943), 89.
16. See Wayland, *Washingtons and Their Homes*, 125.
17. See Scott E. Casper, *Sarah Johnson's Mount Vernon: The Forgotten Memory of An American Shrine* (New York: Hill and Wang, 2008), 9.
18. For some background of the Stamp Act and the Boston Port Bill, see Alison L. LaCroix, *The Ideological Origins of American Federalism* (Cambridge, MA: Harvard University Press, 2010), 30–32, 100–101.
19. Wayland, *Washingtons and Their Homes*, 114–15.
20. Bushrod's older sister Jane married her cousin William Augustine Washington and died in 1791. Mildred Washington, Bushrod's second sister, married a son of Richard Henry Lee and died in 1796. His brother Corbin married a daughter of Richard Henry Lee and died in 1799. And his brother Augustine died in a gun accident in 1784.
21. In 1818, Justice Washington briefly described his education in response to a request for biographical information. See letter from Bushrod Washington to Joseph Delaplaine, March 12, 1818, Tulane University Library (stating that "I received 4 years of my classical education . . . from about the year 73 to 77 having been previously educated by Mr Balmain at the house of Colo. Richard H. Lee in the same County . . . I was entirely educated under the care of my father altho' I lived at home only the 4 years above mentioned").
22. Ibid.; see *Philip Vickers Fithian*, 55 and n. 78 (describing Lowe). Many secondary sources incorrectly state that Bushrod received an undergraduate degree from William and Mary. The justice did not mention this in his autobiographical letter and there is no record of his attendance. The mistake probably stems from the fact that he did attend William and Mary to study law and other subjects in 1780, though he received no degree.
23. Letter from Bushrod Washington to Hannah Bushrod Washington, July 1, 1783, Mount Vernon Library.
24. See *The Diaries of George Washington*, ed. Donald Jackson (Charlottesville: University Press of Virginia, 1978), 3:322–23 (noting John's visit with Bushrod's brother William).
25. Letter from George Washington to John Augustine Washington, June 20, 1775, in *The Papers of George Washington: Revolutionary War Series*, ed. Philander Chase (Charlottesville: University Press of Virginia, 1985), 1:19.
26. See, e.g., letter from George Washington to John Augustine Washington, October 13, 1775, in *Papers of George Washington: Revolutionary War Series*, 2:160–62; see also letter from George Washington to John Augustine Washington, March 31, 1776, in *Papers of George Washington: Revolutionary War Series*, 3:567–69 (discussing the British evacuation from Boston and stating: "No man perhaps since the first institution of armies ever commanded one under more difficult circumstances than I have done").
27. See Brent Tarter, ed., *Revolutionary Virginia: The Road to Independence* (Charlottesville: University Press of Virginia, 1983), 7:21–25 (listing all the

convention delegates). In context, there is no doubt that Jack Washington rose on his own merits. Until 1775, George was just one of many notable Virginians. As a result, Jack's public service was not a function of George's fame. After 1775 that premise is open to question, but I uncovered nothing to suggest that Jack's selection for the Fifth Virginia Convention as an alternate delegate was attributable to George.

28. *See* Ralph Ketcham, *James Madison: A Biography* (Charlottesville: University Press of Virginia, 1990), 69–75 (summarizing the convention proceedings); Tarter, *Revolutionary Virginia*, 7:654–55 (noting Henry's election as governor). On the importance of the Virginia Declaration of Rights and George Mason's role in drafting that text, see Gerard N. Magliocca, *The Heart of the Constitution: How the Bill of Rights Became the Bill of Rights* (New York: Oxford University Press, 2018), 17–19.
29. See letter from George Washington to John Augustine Washington, April 12, 1777, in *Papers of George Washington: Revolutionary War Series*, 9:144–45 ("The ridiculous, and inconsistent Orders given by the Executive Powers in some of the States, and even by the Officers therein for the Rendezvous of their Men, is scarcely to be thought of with patience"); letter from George Washington to John Augustine Washington, July 4, 1778, in *Papers of George Washington: Revolutionary War Series*, 16:25–26 (describing the Battle of Monmouth); letter from George Washington to John Augustine Washington, May 12, 1779, in *Papers of George Washington: Revolutionary War Series*, 20:462 ("The depreciation of our money, is alarming beyond measure. Something must be done, and effectually done, to give it more value").
30. Letter from Bushrod Washington to Hannah Bushrod Washington, March 13, 1778, Mount Vernon Library. A few years later, Bushrod wrote to Hannah about a situation in which he considered proposing marriage to a young woman but later realized he was just infatuated. See letter from Bushrod Washington to Hannah Bushrod Washington, April 12, 1783, George Washington Masonic National Memorial Association. The woman in question may have been the same one described by Bushrod in 1778, but there is no way to know for certain.
31. Wythe's background and his teaching methods are drawn mainly from Davison M. Douglas, "The Jeffersonian Vision of Legal Education," *Journal of Legal Education* 51 (2009): 200–202; see also Jean Edward Smith, *John Marshall: Definer of a Nation* (New York: Henry Holt, 1996), 77–80 (describing Marshall's experience and his class notes).
32. See Merrill D. Peterson, *The Great Triumvirate: Webster, Clay, and Calhoun* (New York: Oxford University Press, 1987), 9–10 (stating that Henry Clay was Wythe's apprentice in the 1790s).
33. See generally William Blackstone, *Commentaries on the Laws of England*, 4 vols. (1765) (Chicago: University of Chicago Press, 1979) (attempting to categorize the common law).
34. Smith, *Marshall*, 79.
35. Marshall's brief stay at William and Mary is chronicled in Smith, *Marshall*, 75–80, and R. Kent Newmyer, *John Marshall and the Heroic Age of the Supreme Court* (Baton Rouge: Louisiana State University Press, 2001), 77–78. For a brisk overview

of Marshall's military career, see Joel Richard Paul, *Without Precedent: John Marshall and His Times* (New York: Riverhead Books, 2018), 5–11, 17–19.

36. See "Original Records of the Phi Beta Kappa Society," *William and Mary Law Quarterly* 4 (1896): 215 (listing Marshall and Washington among the members). At a meeting held in June 1780, Marshall discussed the subject "whether any form of Government is more favourable to public virtue than a Commonwealth" (ibid., 236), while at the next meeting Washington tackled "whether the rape of the Sabine Women [a famous story from Roman mythology] was just" (ibid., 237). Some accounts say that Marshall stayed at William and Mary for just six weeks, but others say that he stayed for somewhat longer, which is why the text says "less than three months."
37. See Smith, *Marshall*, 450–51 (providing additional background on Roane and his contentious relationship with Marshall).
38. Letter from Bushrod Washington to Hannah Bushrod Washington, July 16, 1780, Chicago History Museum. The Phi Beta Kappa records indicate that Bushrod was present at William and Mary in late October ("Original Records," 239), but he appears to have returned to Bushfield sometime in November (ibid., 240, not noting Bushrod's presence at a December 5 meeting of the society).
39. See letter from Bushrod Washington to Joseph Delaplaine, March 12, 1818, Tulane University Library.
40. Some sources give the figure as 1,600 troops. For the basics on Arnold's initial raid, I rely mainly on Richard Ketchum, *Victory at Yorktown: The Campaign that Won the Revolution* (New York: Henry Holt, 2004), 125–27, and Jon Meacham, *Thomas Jefferson and the Art of Power* (New York: Random House, 2012), 133–34. John Marshall was part of the regiment that restored order in Richmond after Arnold withdrew. See Paul, *Without Precedent*, 23–24.
41. Ironically, the capital was moved from Williamsburg because Richmond was seen as a more defensible city. See, e.g., Meacham, *Jefferson*, 133.
42. "Original Records," 240.
43. See Stanley D. M. Carpenter, *Southern Gambit: Cornwallis and the British March to Yorktown* (Norman: University of Oklahoma Press, 2019), 217–20; Louis Gottschalk, *Lafayette and the Close of the American Revolution* (Chicago: University of Chicago Press, 1942), 233.
44. See Ellis, *His Excellency*, 132; Rhodehamel, *George Washington*, 181.
45. Bushrod briefly served as Mercer's legal apprentice before enlisting. See letter from Bushrod Washington to Joseph Delaplaine, March 12, 1818, Tulane University Library. The exact date of Bushrod's enlistment is unknown. A letter from Jack Washington establishes that Bushrod was in the militia in early July, as Jack referred to the movements of the enemy and said that he and Hannah were looking forward to his discharge. See letter from John Augustine Washington to Bushrod Washington, July 3, 1781, Mount Vernon Library.
46. Letter from William Garvard to Bushrod Washington, March 18, 1825, Mount Vernon Library.
47. See letter from Bushrod Washington to Joseph Delaplaine, March 12, 1818, Tulane University Library.

48. The account of the Battle of Green Spring draws largely from Gottschalk, *Lafayette*, 264–67, and Thomas J. Fleming, *Beat the Last Drum: The Siege of Yorktown, 1781* (New York: St. Martin's Press, 1963), 30–33.
49. One version of the battle says that Colonel Mercer's cavalry, which was conducting reconnaissance, was divided on whether the British had crossed the James, with Bushrod being one of the men who thought that they had. See Gottschalk, *Lafayette*, 264.
50. Letter from William Garvard to Bushrod Washington, March 18, 1825, Mount Vernon Library.
51. Letter from Bushrod Washington to Joseph Delaplaine, March 12, 1818, Tulane University Library.
52. See Ketchum, *Yorktown*, 240–55 (discussing the surrender negotiations and the ceremony). Many secondary sources claim that Bushrod was at Yorktown, but this is wrong. A letter from Jack does say that Bushrod witnessed the British evacuation from New York in November 1783. See letter from John Augustine Washington to Bushrod Washington, January 17, 1784, Mount Vernon Library. Perhaps someone along the way mixed up Bushrod's presence at Yorktown with his presence at this other significant British withdrawal.

Chapter 2

1. Letter from George Washington to James Wilson, Mar. 19, 1782. This letter is not yet part of the official edition of Washington's papers, but can be found at the National Archives: https://founders.archives.gov/?q=James%20wilson%20Author%3A%22Washington%2C%20George%22%20Recipient%3A%22Wilson%2C%20James%22&s=1111311111&r=2.
2. Letter from George Washington to James Wilson, Mar. 22, 1782, https://founders.archives.gov/?q=James%20wilson%20Author%3A%22Washington%2C%20George%22%20Recipient%3A%22Wilson%2C%20James%22&s=1111311111&r=3. Explaining the value of money from the distant past is difficult because so many variables are involved. But in 1782 the United States lacked a stable currency due to the Revolution, so British money was especially desirable and scarce.
3. For an example of George Washington visiting Bushfield, see *The Diaries of George Washington*, ed. Donald Jackson (Charlottesville: University Press of Virginia, 1978), 2:87–88 (noting a visit in August 1768). It is hard to say when or how often Bushrod visited Mount Vernon as a child. For example, when Martha's daughter Patsy died in 1773, Jack and his family attended her funeral at Mount Vernon. See David O. Stewart, *George Washington: The Political Rise of America's Founding Father* (New York: Dutton, 2021), 176 (citing George Washington's diary from June 21, 1773). Presumably Bushrod was among those mourners, but he was not mentioned by name as a Mount Vernon visitor until he was an adult.

4. Letter from George Washington to John Augustine Washington, Jan. 16, 1783, https://founders.archives.gov/?q=John%20augustine%20washington%20%20Recipient%3A%22Washington%2C%20John%20Augustine%22&s=1111311111&r=38.
5. This was not the only time that George helped Jack. In 1784, he asked George Mason to give Jack a loan. See letter from George Washington to George Mason, Dec. 13, 1784, in *The Papers of George Washington: Confederation Series*, ed. W. W. Abbot and Dorothy Twohig (Charlottesville: University Press of Virginia, 1997), 2:180 ("My brother John is much in want of four, five, or six hundred pounds which he is desirous of borrowing on interest. If it is in your power to supply him, I will become security for the fulfillment of his agreement").
6. Letter from John Augustine Washington to Bushrod Washington, Apr. 1, 1782, Mount Vernon Library. Bushrod probably lived at Bushfield between his discharge from the militia and his move to Philadelphia early in 1782. His journey to Philadelphia was almost certainly his first trip outside of Virginia.
7. Letter from Bushrod Washington to Levy Hollingsworth, Historical Society of Pennsylvania. The letter is dated 1782 and one source claims that the letter was written in November, but my review of the document discloses no month or day. There is a word crossed out next to 1782 on the letter that could be "November," but that is not clear. An undated letter from Bushrod to his father refers to Hollingsworth and says that a delay in some hemp sent up from Virginia meant "I was obliged to borrow." See letter from Bushrod Washington to John Augustine Washington, Huntington Library. This is probably referring to the loan request that is discussed in the text, though I cannot be certain.
8. Letter from George Washington to Bushrod Washington, Jan. 15, 1783, https://founders.archives.gov/?q=george%20washington%20to%20bushrod%20washington%2015%20january%201783&s=1511311111&sa=&r=9&sr=. There is no record of Bushrod's response to his uncle's letter.
9. Letter from George Washington to John Augustine Washington, Jan. 16, 1783, https://founders.archives.gov/?q=John%20augustine%20washington%20Recipient%3A%22Washington%2C%20John%20Augustine%22&s=1511311111&r=41.
10. The brief biography of Wilson in the text draws from William Ewald, "James Wilson and the Drafting of the Constitution," *University of Pennsylvania Journal of Constitutional Law* 10 (2008): 902–15.
11. See James Wilson, "Considerations on the Nature and Extent of the Legislative Authority of the British Parliament," in *Collected Works of James Wilson*, ed. Kermit L. Hall and Mark David Hall (Indianapolis, IN: Liberty Fund, 2007), 1:3–31.
12. The best discussion of these trials is Carlton F. W. Larson, *The Trials of Allegiance: Treason, Juries, and the American Revolution* (New York: Oxford University Press, 2019).
13. For some background on Wilson's contributions to the Constitution, see Pauline Maier, *Ratification: The People Debate the Constitution, 1787–1788* (New York: Simon and Schuster, 2010), 78 (stating that Wilson spoke more often at the Constitutional Convention than all but one of the delegates "and some of his speeches—condemning the small states' insistence on equal representation, for example—are

among the Convention's most memorable"); Gerard N. Magliocca, *The Heart of the Constitution: How the Bill of Rights Became the Bill of Rights* (New York: Oxford University Press, 2018), 28–29 (discussing Wilson's pathbreaking discussion of enumerated powers at the Pennsylvania ratifying convention).

14. Wilson is probably underappreciated because he defaulted on his debts from real estate speculation and was thrown into debtors' prison shortly before he died. Wilson remains the only sitting Supreme Court justice to spend time in jail.
15. Charles Warren, *A History of the American Bar* (Boston: Brown, Little, and Company, 1911), 167. Bushrod took on apprentices when he was a lawyer, though there is no evidence about his training methods. His most successful apprentice was Walter Jones, who argued more than 300 cases before the Supreme Court, including *McCulloch v. Maryland.*
16. Letter from John Augustine Washington to Bushrod Washington, Sept. 4, 1783, Mount Vernon Library.
17. See letter from Bird Wilson to Bushrod Washington, Aug. 19, 1822, Historical Society of Pennsylvania. The book was written in 1822 by Justice William Johnson, Bushrod's Supreme Court colleague. See William Johnson, *Sketches of the Life and Correspondence of Nathanael Greene, Major General of the Armies of the United States in the Revolution* (Charleston, SC: A. E. Miller, 1822).
18. Letter from Bushrod Washington to Bird Wilson, Oct. 26, 1822, Historical Society of Pennsylvania.
19. For a biography of Powel, see David W. Maxey, *A Portrait of Elizabeth Willing Powel, 1743–1830* (Philadelphia: American Philosophical Society, 2006), 15–32, 51–58.
20. Ron Chernow, *Washington: A Life* (New York: Penguin Books, 2010), 528.
21. See letter from Elizabeth Willing Powel to George Washington, Nov. 17, 1792, in *The Papers of George Washington: Presidential Series*, ed. W. W. Abbot, Dorothy Twohig, Philander D. Chase, David R. Hoth, Christine Sternberg Patrick, and Theodore J. Crackel (Charlottesville: University Press of Virginia, 1985–), 11:395–97; Joseph J. Ellis, *His Excellency: George Washington* (New York: Vintage Press, 2004), 220.
22. See Chernow, *Washington*, 528, 539. The Powel House Museum website is at https://www.philalandmarks.org/powel-house. Elizabeth Powel was the person to whom Benjamin Franklin allegedly said, in response to her question about what the Convention had produced: "A republic, madam, if you can keep it." See Chernow, *Washington*, 539 (stating that she had no recollection of this comment); Maxey, *Elizabeth Willing Powel*, 30 (same).
23. See letter from Elizabeth Willing Powel to Hannah Bushrod Washington, Apr. 17, 1783, Mount Vernon Library (noting the introduction).
24. See Maxey, *Elizabeth Willing Powel*, 23 (stating that both Powel children died in infancy).
25. Letter from Bushrod Washington to Hannah Bushrod Washington, June 11, 1782, University of Virginia, Special Collections.
26. Letter from Elizabeth Willing Powel to Hannah Bushrod Washington, Apr. 17, 1783, Mount Vernon Library.

27. See Stephen A. Patrick, "'I Have at Length Determined to Have My Picture Taken': An Eighteenth-Century Young Man's Thoughts About His Portrait by Henry Benbridge," *American Art Journal* 22 (1990): 68–81, 74 (noting the occasion of Bushrod's twenty-first birthday and Franklin's praise for Benbridge); letter from Bushrod Washington to Hannah Bushrod Washington, undated, Library of Congress (stating that Powel suggested Benbridge due to the artist's "strong Genius").
28. Reuben Gold Thwaits, ed., *Early Western Travels, 1748–1846* (Cleveland: Arthur H. Clark Co., 1905), 12:126 (quoting a diary entry from a visitor).
29. See Chernow, *Washington*, 124 (quoting Jefferson's opinion that Washington was "the best horseman of his age"); Ellis, *His Excellency*, 68 (stating that contemporaries agreed that "he was physically majestic"); Weincek, *Imperfect God: George Washington, His Slaves and the Creation of America* (New York: Farrar, Straus, and Giroux, 2003), 65 (reproducing a description of him as a young man that said he was "six feet two inches in his stockings and weighing 175 pounds . . . His frame is padded with well-developed muscles, indicating great strength").
30. Letter from Bushrod Washington to Hannah Bushrod Washington, July 1, 1783, Mount Vernon Library.
31. Letter from Bushrod Washington to Hannah Bushrod Washington, July 1, 1783, Mount Vernon Library.
32. Letter from Bushrod Washington to unknown recipient, undated, Library of Congress. This letter was probably written to Hannah, but I am not absolutely sure.
33. Letter from Elizabeth Willing Powel to Bushrod Washington, Jan. 3, 1785, Historical Society of Pennsylvania.
34. See Maxey, *Elizabeth Willing Powel*, 51. The niece's recollection was written on the back of a letter that Eliza wrote Hannah. See letter from Elizabeth Willing Powel to Hannah Bushrod Washington, Apr. 17, 1783, Mount Vernon Library. Samuel Powel died during a yellow fever epidemic in 1793. See Chernow, *Washington*, 701. Eliza did not remarry.
35. Maxey, *Elizabeth Willing Powel*, 29. Eliza Powel died two months after Bushrod, in January 1830; ibid., 3.
36. *Nancy Shippen Her Journal Book: The International Romance of a Young Lady of Fashion of Colonial Philadelphia with Letters to Her and About Her*, ed. Ethel Armes (Philadelphia: J. B. Lippincott Co., 1935), 170. Bushrod's first recorded outing with Nancy Shippen was in May 1783. See ibid., 142.
37. Ibid., 142, 172, 174, 183–84.
38. Ibid., 184; Mary Beth Norton, *Liberty's Daughters: The Revolutionary Experiences of America's Women, 1750–1800* (Ithaca, NY: Cornell University Press, 1980).
39. Letter from Bushrod Washington to Nancy Shippen, Apr. 28, 1784, in *Journal Book*, 310.
40. Letter from John Augustine Washington to Bushrod Washington, Feb. 16, 1784, Mount Vernon Library (stating that "a young Man at Delemans Academy trifling with a loaded gun" caused the weapon to fire "and y[ou]r Brother setting before the fire re[ading], [was hit by] the whole load in his breast of which he expired in a few minutes").

41. Letter from John Augustine Washington to George Washington, Apr. 4, 1784, in *Papers of George Washington: Confederation Series*, 1:261. This is the first letter from Jack to George that survives.
42. Shippen, *Journal Book*, 179–80.
43. See letter from John Augustine Washington to Bushrod Washington, Mar. 10, 1784, Mount Vernon Library ("Your presence would greatly contribute to your Mother's tranquility").
44. See letter from George Washington to John Augustine Washington, June 30, 1784, in *Papers of George Washington: Confederation Series*, 1:478. For background on the negotiations that led to the Treaty of Paris, see Walter Issacson, *Benjamin Franklin: An American Life* (New York: Simon and Schuster, 2003), 399–415.
45. Letter from George Washington to John Augustine Washington, June 30, 1784, in *Papers of George Washington: Confederation Series*, 1:478.
46. Letter from John Augustine Washington to George Washington, July 8, 1784, in *Papers of George Washington: Confederation Series*, 1:491.
47. Letter from John Augustine Washington to George Washington, July 24, 1784, in *Papers of George Washington: Confederation Series*, 2:8.
48. See Chernow, *Washington*, 479–81; Stewart, *Political Rise*, 284–85. The friend was Dr. James Craik, who was George's physician and "cared" for him with bleedings in 1799, shortly before he died. See Stewart, *Political Rise*, 285, 410–12.
49. The date range for West Ford's birth are established by four documents. The first is a slave list from Bushfield in March 1783 that lists the members of Ford's family (Venus and her parents) but not West Ford. See Mary V. Thompson, "*The Only Unavoidable Subject of Regret*": *George Washington, Slavery, and the Enslaved Community at Mount Vernon* (Charlottesville: University of Virginia Press, 2019), 149. The second is a similar list from 1786 or 1787 that does list West Ford, which strongly suggests that his omission from the 1783 list meant that he was not yet born then. See ibid. (giving the date of this second list as "early in 1787"); Weincek, *Imperfect God*, 299 (giving the date as 1786). Third is Hannah's will, which states that West was born before Jack Washington made his will. Finally, there is Jack's will, which was written in June 1784 and then amended in November 1785. See Last Will and Testament of John Augustine Washington, June 22, 1784, Mount Vernon Library; Thompson, *Subject of Regret*, 150. It is not clear whether Hannah was referring to the original will or to the amended will when she said that Ford was born before Jack's will was written. What must be true, though, is that West was born before Jack amended his will in November 1785.
50. See Scott E. Casper, *Sarah Johnson's Mount Vernon: The Forgotten Memory of An American Shrine* (New York: Hill and Wang, 2008), 9; Weincek, *Imperfect God*, 301.
51. Last Will and Testament of Hannah Bushrod Washington, April 1801, Mount Vernon Library. Jack may have made his will in response to Augustine's death a few months earlier, but that could have been a coincidence.
52. See Casper, *Sarah Johnson's Mount Vernon*, 24–25.
53. The sketch was donated to Mount Vernon in 1985 with a notation that states: "The enclosed picture [of the drawing] was always said by Mrs. R. P. Chew to be of West Ford." Bushrod's great-great-niece Louisa Fontaine Washington married Robert

Preston Chew and probably met West Ford when he was elderly, as she was born at Mount Vernon in 1844. I thank Dawn Bonner for explaining the provenance of the sketch.

54. See Last Will and Testament of Bushrod Washington, July 19, 1828, Mount Vernon Library.
55. See Casper, *Sarah Johnson's Mount Vernon*, 26; Chernow, *Washington*, 493; Thompson, *Subject of Regret*, 151; Weincek, *Imperfect God*, 310.
56. Thompson, *Subject of Regret*, 147; see Casper, *Sarah Johnson's Mount Vernon*, 58; see letter from West Ford to Bushrod Washington, Aug. 29, 1829, Mount Vernon Library (updating the justice on repairs at the estate); see also Casper, *Sarah Johnson's Mount Vernon*, 56 (describing Ford as the manager of Mount Vernon's enslaved people).
57. See Casper, *Sarah Johnson's Mount Vernon*, 76; Thompson, *Subject of Regret*, 147; Weincek, *Imperfect God*, 298.
58. Weincek, *Imperfect God*, 293.
59. Benson J. Lossing, "Mount Vernon as It Is," *Harper's New Monthly Magazine* 18 (March 1859): 444; see Casper, *Sarah Johnson's Mount Vernon*, 76.
60. See Casper, *Sarah Johnson's Mount Vernon*, 76; Weincek, *Imperfect God*, 298. See also *Dred Scott v. Sandford*, 60 U.S. (19 How.) 393 (1857) (holding that Blacks could not be citizens of the United States).
61. See Weincek, *Imperfect God*, 291–92; Nicholas Wade, "Descendants of Slave's Son Contend That His Father Was George Washington," *New York Times*, July 7, 1999, A14.
62. Corbin's will made clear that he was dismissive of enslaved people, though this does not prove anything with respect to West Ford. See Weincek, *Imperfect God*, 351 (quoting the will as follows: "As it is not uncommon for Negroes to become disobedient to their Mistresses after the Death of their Masters . . . I do hereby give my said dear Wife full powers and authority to sell and dispose of any of them so offending in her Opinion").
63. The fact that Bushrod had no children with his wife could mean that he was sterile. But the absence of legitimate children does not mean that Bushrod was incapable of having children.

Chapter 3

1. See letter from George Washington to Marquis de Lafayette, Feb. 15, 1785, in *The Papers of George Washington: Confederation Series*, ed. W. W. Abbot and Dorothy Twohig (Charlottesville: University Press of Virginia, 1997), 2:365 ("Bushrod Washington, sensible of your polite invitation, but unable to avail himself of it, wrote you a letter of grateful acknowledgment and thanks"). Bushrod never ended up traveling outside of the United States.
2. See letter from George Washington to Bushrod Washington, Dec. 29, 1787, in *Papers of George Washington: Confederation Series*, 5:513 (discussing an ejectment case

involving some of his lands); letter from George Washington to Bushrod Washington, Dec. 3, 1787, in *Papers of George Washington: Confederation Series*, 5:473–75 (asking Bushrod to look into a tax claim on some of his lands); letter from George Washington to Bushrod Washington, Apr. 3, 1785, in *Papers of George Washington: Confederation Series*, 2:474–75 (asking Bushrod to give notice for a meeting of the Dismal Swamp Company, in which George was an investor); letter from George Washington to Bushrod Washington, Jan. 22, 1785, in *Papers of George Washington: Confederation Series*, 2:284–85 (asking Bushrod to present a note to someone for payment and find a copy of an ordinance). There is not much information on Bushrod's early practice, but he seems to have handled routine matters. See letter from Bushrod Washington to Thomas Stone, Oct. 17, 1786, Morristown National Historical Park Library (discussing with another attorney the possible scheduling of depositions).

It is not clear where Bushrod lived prior to his marriage. In February 1785 he was at Mount Vernon for six days on his way to Bushfield. See *The Diaries of George Washington*, ed. Donald Jackson (Charlottesville: University Press of Virginia, 1978), 4:93, 96. George Washington told Edmund Randolph that he "conceived Bushrod Washington was living at Richmond, but the establishment of circuit Courts it seems has changed his plan: he intends to live at Fredericksburg." Letter from George Washington to Edmund Randolph, March 19, 1785, in *Papers of George Washington: Confederation Series*, 2:451. It appears that he did move to Fredericksburg, based on a letter he wrote from there to Hannah in April stating that "I am very anxious to hear from Bushfield." See letter from Bushrod Washington to Hannah Bushrod Washington, Apr. 7, 1785, Chicago History Museum. At some point thereafter he moved back to Bushfield, but when that occurred is uncertain.

3. See Horace Binney, *Bushrod Washington* (Philadelphia: C. Sherman & Son, 1858), 24. Their joint tombstone at Mount Vernon says that Mrs. Washington died two days after her husband.
4. See letter from Bushrod Washington to Hannah Bushrod Washington, July 1, 1783, Mount Vernon Library.
5. The original home at Rippon Lodge still stands and is now a museum. The website can be found at https://www.pwcgov.org/government/dept/park/hp/Pages/Rippon-Lodge.aspx.
6. See David Leslie Annis, "Mr. Bushrod Washington, Supreme Court Justice on the Marshall Court," PhD diss., Notre Dame University, 1974, 46. Thomas Blackburn's obituary, which confirms his wound at the Battle of Germantown, can be found in the *Virginia Gazette* of August 29, 1807.
7. See Annis, "Bushrod Washington," 47; see also James R. Heintze, "Music of the Washington Family," *Music Quarterly* 56 (1970): 292 (describing Nancy's extensive music collection). Her grave marker at Mount Vernon says that she was sixty when she died. This means that she was sixteen when she wed in 1785.
8. Last Will and Testament of Bushrod Washington, July 28, 1828, Mount Vernon Library.
9. See letter from George Washington to Thomas Blackburn, Oct. 10, 1785, in *Papers of George Washington: Confederation Series*, 3:301 ("General and Mrs. Washington

present their compliments to Colonel and Mrs. Blackburne; are much obliged to them for their kind invitation to the Wedding on Thursday. They would attend with pleasure, but for the indisposition of the latter; and the particular engagements of the former. . . . The General and Mrs. Washington will always be happy to see the young couple at Mount Vernon").

10. See *Diaries of George Washington*, 4:208.
11. The only two letters that survive were written from Philadelphia when Bushrod was hearing cases on circuit and Nancy did not come with him. See letter from Bushrod Washington to Julia Blackburn Washington, Apr. 23, 1814, Library of Congress; letter from Bushrod Washington to Julia Blackburn Washington, Apr. 24, 1809, Mount Vernon Library.
12. See Ron Chernow, *Washington: A Life* (New York: Penguin Books, 2010), 814; Weincek, *Imperfect God: George Washington: His Slaves and the Creation of America* (New York: Farrar, Straus, and Giroux, 2003), 358. I cannot prove that Hannah and Bushrod's heirs destroyed their marital correspondence, but the dearth of letters is suggestive.
13. Letter from Bushrod Washington to Samuel Hodgon, Feb. 1, 1786, New York Public Library.
14. See Chernow, *Washington*, 104 (pointing out that George and Martha raised nearly a dozen orphaned relatives).
15. See, e.g., letter from Bushrod Washington to George Washington, July 3, 1796, in *The Papers of George Washington: Presidential Series*, ed. W. W. Abbot, Dorothy Twohig, Philander D. Chase, David R. Hoth, Christine Sternberg Patrick, and Theodore J. Crackel (Charlottesville: University Press of Virginia, 1985–), 20:364 ("Mrs. Washington's health is so bad during the summer in this lower Country, that I shall (inconvenient as it is for me to leave Town) endeavor to carry her up to the Berkley Springs").
16. See *The Autobiography of Martin Van Buren*, ed. John C. Fitzpatrick (Washington, DC: Government Printing Office, 1920), 2:177. Van Buren said that this visit occurred during President Monroe's second administration, which meant between 1821 and 1824.
17. See letter from Horace Holley to Mary Austin Holley, Apr. 15, 1818, William L. Clements Library, University of Michigan.
18. See Binney, *Bushrod Washington*, 23.
19. Ibid., 24.
20. Ibid., 8; see David Paul Brown, *The Forum: Or, Forty Years Full Practice at the Philadelphia Bar* (Philadelphia: Robert H. Small, Law Bookseller, 1856), 1:366 ("Mrs. Washington was an accomplished woman, but of a highly excitable and nervous temperament").
21. See R. Kent Newmyer, *John Marshall and the Heroic Age of the Supreme Court* (Baton Rouge: Louisiana State University Press, 2001), 34; Joel Richard Paul, *Without Precedent: John Marshall and His Times* (New York: Riverhead Books, 2018), 111.
22. See letter from Martha Jefferson Carr to Thomas Jefferson, Feb. 26, 1787, in *The Papers of Thomas Jefferson*, ed. Julian P. Boyd (Princeton, NJ: Princeton University

Press, 1958), 15:635 ("Mrs. Marshal [*sic*], once Miss Ambler, is Insane, the loss of two Children is thought to have Occasioned it").

23. See Paul, *Without Precedent*, 178; Jean Edward Smith, *John Marshall: Definer of a Nation* (New York: Henry Holt, 1996), 375–76.
24. Smith, *Marshall*, 376.
25. See Paul, *Without Precedent*, 333; Smith, *Marshall*, 375.
26. *Martin Van Buren*, 2:177.
27. For an excellent account of the defects in the Articles of Confederation, see Michael J. Klarman, *The Framers' Coup: The Making of the United States Constitution* (New York: Oxford University Press, 2016), 11–72.
28. Letter from Bushrod Washington to Samuel Hodgdon, Sept. 15, 1786, New York Public Library.
29. Letter from Bushrod Washington to George Washington, Sept. 27, 1786, in *Papers of George Washington: Confederation Series*, 4:274.
30. Letter from George Washington to Bushrod Washington, Sept. 30, 1786, in *Papers of George Washington: Confederation Series*, 4:278.
31. Letter from Bushrod Washington to George Washington, Oct. 31, 1786, in *Papers of George Washington: Confederation Series*, 4:322.
32. Letter from George Washington to Bushrod Washington, Nov. 15, 1786, in *Papers of George Washington: Confederation Series*, 4:368.
33. For information on the Annapolis meeting that led to the Constitutional Convention, see Mary Sarah Bilder, *Madison's Hand: Revising the Constitutional Convention* (Cambridge, MA: Harvard University Press, 2015), 38–40.
34. See Joseph Hopkinson, *Eulogium in Commemoration of the Hon. Bushrod Washington, Late One of the Justices of the Supreme Court of the United States* (Philadelphia: T. S. Manning, 1830), 11; James R. Stoner Jr., "Heir Apparent: Bushrod Washington and Federal Justice in the Early Republic," in *Seriatim: The Supreme Court Before John Marshall*, ed. Scott Douglas Gerber (New York: New York University Press, 1998), 326.
35. See Smith, *Marshall*, 111–12. There was discussion in the state legislature about any conditions that should be attached to the call for a ratifying convention, but (as a freshman member) Bushrod played no significant role in that debate. See Klarman, *The Framers' Coup*, 456–60 (describing these parliamentary maneuvers); Smith, *Marshall*, 112–14, 117 (same).
36. Letter from George Washington to David Stuart, Nov. 30, 1787, in *Papers of George Washington: Confederation Series*, 5:467.
37. *Diaries of George Washington*, 5:93.
38. For some references to Jack's gout, see letter from John Augustine Washington to George Washington, Apr. 4, 1784, in *Papers of George Washington: Confederation Series*, 1:261; letter from John Augustine Washington to Bushrod Washington, Nov. 11, 1782, Mount Vernon Library; letter from John Augustine Washington to Bushrod Washington, July 3, 1781, Mount Vernon Library.
39. Letter from George Washington to Bushrod Washington, Jan. 10, 1787, in *Papers of George Washington: Confederation Series*, 4:509–10. A month after Jack's death,

Bushrod and his brother Corbin visited Mount Vernon. See *Diaries of George Washington*, 5:102–3.

40. See Last Will and Testament of John Augustine Washington, June 22, 1784, Mount Vernon Library; see also Scott E. Casper, *Sarah Johnson's Mount Vernon: The Forgotten Memory of an American Shrine* (New York: Hill and Wang, 2008), 9 (describing Oliver and Doll as part of Bushrod's inheritance from Jack). The properties Bushrod received included 643 acres at Berkley, 400 acres in Stafford County, and two other tracts each measuring 320 acres.
41. See Chernow, *Washington*, 540 (noting Washington's return to Mount Vernon on September 22); *Diaries of George Washington*, 5:249 (noting Bushrod's arrival on October 7 and departure on October 10).
42. See letter from George Washington to Bushrod Washington, Nov. 9, 1787, in *Papers of George Washington: Confederation Series*, 5:420–25.
43. Letter from Bushrod Washington to Robert Carter, Nov. 3, 1787, in *The Documentary History of the Ratification of the Constitution*, ed. John P. Kaminski and Gaspare J. Saladino (Madison: State Historical Society of Wisconsin, 1988), 8:142–43.
44. See Klarman, *Framers' Coup*, 458 (giving March 1788 as the date of the elections).
45. Letter from James Madison to Thomas Jefferson, Apr. 22, 1788, in *The Papers of James Madison*, ed. Robert A. Rutland and Charles F. Hobson (Charlottesville: University Press of Virginia, 1977), 11:28.
46. See letter from Elizabeth Willing Powel to Bushrod Washington, April 14, 1789, Historical Society of Pennsylvania (stating that she sent the transcript a year earlier, as "I thought it might be agreeable to you see in how masterly a Manner Mr. Wilson had treated the Science of Government").
47. See Pauline Maier, *Ratification: The People Debate the Constitution, 1787–1788* (New York: Simon and Schuster, 2010), 256; David O. Stewart, *Madison's Gift: Five Partnerships That Built America* (New York: Simon and Schuster, 2015), 63.
48. See Maier, *Ratification*; 259; see also Smith, *Marshall*, 131–32, 137–38 (describing Marshall's major speeches to the convention).
49. See Klarman, *Framers' Coup*, 472; Maier, *Ratification*, 260–61.
50. See Chernow, *Washington*, 539–40; Klarman, *Framers' Coup*, 468; Maier, *Ratification*, 230; see generally Jon Kukla, *Patrick Henry, Champion of Liberty* (New York: Simon & Schuster, 2017) (providing a thorough account of Henry's life).
51. Letter from Bushrod Washington to George Washington, June 7, 1788, in *Papers of George Washington: Confederation Series*, 6:315.
52. This is the only letter that we have from Bushrod during the convention. One wonders if there were others, as there is something odd about Bushrod writing a detailed report once and then saying nothing else.
53. Letter from George Washington to Bushrod Washington, Nov. 9, 1787, in *Papers of George Washington: Confederation Series*, 5:424.
54. See Jonathan Elliott, ed., *The Debates in the Several State Conventions on the Adoption of the Federal Constitution as Recommended by the General Convention at Philadelphia in 1787* (Philadelphia: J. B. Lippincott, 1891), 3:655.

Chapter 4

1. Letter from Bushrod Washington to George Washington, Nov. 20, 1788, in *The Papers of George Washington: Presidential Series*, ed. W. W. Abbot, Dorothy Twohig, Philander D. Chase, David R. Hoth, Christine Sternberg Patrick, and Theodore J. Crackel (Charlottesville: University Press of Virginia, 1985–), 1:119. In the same letter, Bushrod explained that he was renting out the properties that he had inherited from Jack and was confident that Hannah could keep living at Bushfield for the rest of her life (1:120).
2. See letter from George Washington to Bushrod Washington, Nov. 25, 1788, in *Papers of George Washington: Presidential Series*, 1:126–27. Bushrod declined the offer. See letter from Bushrod Washington to George Washington, Dec. 12, 1788, in *Papers of George Washington: Presidential Series*, 1:175, though he did end up using one of George's stables; see letter from Bushrod Washington to George Washington, Jan. 18, 1789, in *Papers of George Washington: Presidential Series*, 1:249–50. Bushrod and Nancy lived on Duke Street in Alexandria. In 2021, their former home was listed for $1.9 million.
3. See *The Diaries of George Washington*, ed. Donald Jackson (Charlottesville: University Press of Virginia, 1978), 5:439.
4. See Act to Establish the Judicial Courts of the United States, ch. 20, § 35, 1 Stat. 85 (1789) (hereinafter Judiciary Act of 1789).
5. Jared Sparks, whom Bushrod worked with to produce the first official set of George Washington's papers, included a letter in that set from Bushrod to President Washington dated July 1, 1789, requesting the appointment. See *The Writings of George Washington*, ed. Jared Sparks (Boston: Ferdinand Andrews, 1839), 10:24n*. The original letter, though, is no longer in any collection that I can find. As a result, I cannot verify if what Sparks printed is accurate.
6. Letter from George Washington to Bushrod Washington, July 27, 1789, in *Papers of George Washington: Presidential Series*, 3:34.
7. The Judiciary Act of 1789 was enacted in September of that year. See 1 Stat. 85 (1789).
8. See letter from Bushrod Washington to George Washington, Dec. 27, 1789, in *Papers of George Washington: Presidential Series*, 4:453–54.
9. In the letter, Bushrod said that he hurt his right hand, which presumably means that he was right-handed if he could not write. See ibid.
10. The Constitution states that Congress may delegate the appointment of some inferior officers in the executive branch to "the courts of Law." U.S. Const., art. II, § 2.
11. Bushrod's ill-considered letter may have created a chill in his relationship with George. No other letters between them can be found until 1792. Other explanations can be given for this lengthy gap. George Washington was, after all, occupied being president: Bushrod was trying to build a practice. And there are many letters from this era that were just lost or destroyed. But the possibility remains that George was silently expressing his disappointment in Bushrod.
12. See letter from Bushrod Washington to Joseph Delapaine, March 12, 1818, Tulane University Library. In the introduction of his book of reports on the cases of the

Virginia Court of Appeals. Bushrod said that his notes began in 1792 and that the cases discussed prior to that year came from notes provided by President Pendleton, which confirms that Washington did not live in Richmond before 1792. See Bushrod Washington, "To the Reader," in *Cases Argued and Determined in the Court of Appeals of Virginia* (Richmond, VA: Thomas Nicolson, 1798), 1:n.p.

13. See Jean Edward Smith, *John Marshall: Definer of a Nation* (New York: Henry Holt, 1996), 148–52 (describing one example), 153–58 (discussing another case that Henry and Marshall worked on together before the circuit court in Richmond).
14. See Ron Chernow, *Washington: A Life* (New York: Penguin Books, 2010), 732–35 (discussing how Randolph resigned from President Washington's cabinet following a scandal); see also *Spencer v. Moore*, 8 Va. 423 (1798); *Hooe v. Marquess*, 8 Va. 416 (1798); *Commonwealth v. Banks*, 8 Va. 338 (1798); *Wood v. Baughan*, 5 Va. 329 (1798); *Carter v. Tyler*, 5 Va. 165 (1797); *Chichester v. Vass*, 5 Va. 83 (1797); *Gibson v. Fristoe*, 5 Va. 62 (1797); *M'Call v. Peachy*, 5 Va. 55 (1797); *Warder v. Arell*, 2 Va. 282 (1796); *Norton v. Rose*, 2 Va. 233 (1796); *Mackie's Ex'r v. Davis*, 2 Va. 219 (1796). In these cases, Washington and Randolph were on opposite sides, though sometimes with other lawyers.
15. *The Life and Selected Writings of Thomas Jefferson*, ed. Adrienne Koch and William Peden (New York: Modern Library, 1993), 38 (quoting from Jefferson's unpublished autobiography).
16. See letter from Bushrod Washington to George Washington, July 3, 1796, in *Papers of George Washington: Presidential Series*, 20:363–64 (describing a chancery case involving the president); see also R. Kent Newmyer, *John Marshall and the Heroic Age of the Supreme Court* (Baton Rouge: Louisiana State University Press, 2001), 74–75 (stating that Wythe was the chancellor). Broadly speaking, equity referred to civil cases in which a party was seeking a remedy other than money (usually, an injunction or a court order).
17. Other notable lawyers working in Richmond at that time included John Taylor of Caroline, who later wrote an influential book on Jeffersonian constitutional theory, and John Wickham, who defended Aaron Burr in his treason trial and was Bushrod's opponent in some cases. See John Taylor, *An Inquiry into the Principles and Policy of the Government of the United States* (Fredericksburg, VA: Green and Cady, 1814); Smith, *Marshall*, 147, 359; Newmyer, *Heroic Age*, 75.
18. *The Virginia Journals of Benjamin Henry Latrobe, 1795–1798*, ed. Edward C. Carter II (New Haven, CT: Yale University Press, 1977), 1:132 (quoting Latrobe's diary entry from May 31, 1796). The other attorney that Latrobe mentioned was James Innes, who died in 1798.
19. Letter from Bushrod Washington to George Washington, Feb. 13, 1794, in *Papers of George Washington: Presidential Series*, 15:231.
20. Letter from George Washington to Bushrod Washington, Feb. 23, 1794, in *Papers of George Washington: Presidential Series*, 15:266–67. A point worth making is that Bushrod did not become successful because he was George's nephew. The cases that Bushrod took had nothing to do with the federal government or the president. And having George's relative as a lawyer in state court would not have given clients an edge.

21. Horace Binney, *Bushrod Washington* (Philadelphia: C. Sherman & Son, 1858), 27; see also 12 (calling Washington "as accomplished a Nisi Prius Judge as ever lived").
22. See James R. Stoner Jr., "Heir Apparent: Bushrod Washington and Federal Justice in the Early Republic," in *Seriatim: The Supreme Court Before John Marshall*, ed. Scott Douglas Gerber (New York: New York University Press, 1998), 327 (stating that these books were "a pioneering effort in an age when there were no official court reporters or systematic written opinions"). Bushrod did not report every case decided by the Virginia Court of Appeals in the relevant period. He exercised judgment about which to include and exclude.
23. See John Langbein, Renee Lettow Lerner, and Bruce P. Smith, eds., *History of the Common Law: The Development of Anglo-American Legal Institutions* (New York: Aspen, 2009), 817–23.
24. Washington, "To the Reader."
25. Bushrod Washington, "Dedication," in *Cases Argued and Determined in the Court of Appeals of Virginia* (Richmond, VA: Thomas Nicolson, 1798), 1:n.p.
26. Washington's book of reports lists the judges who served on the Court of Appeals, and states that Spencer Roane joined the Court in April 1795.
27. See Pauline Maier, *Ratification: The People Debate the Constitution, 1787–1788* (New York: Simon and Schuster, 2010), 256 (describing Pendleton at the Virginia ratification convention).
28. *Life and Selected Writings of Thomas Jefferson*, 38–39.
29. See M. Todd Henderson, "From Seriatim to Consensus and Back Again: A Theory of Dissent," *Supreme Court Review* 2007 (2007): 304 (stating that Pendleton got the idea from Lord Mansfield, one of the greatest English common law judges).
30. See ibid., 292–308.
31. See, e.g., *Chichester*, 5 Va. 83 (assumpsit action); *Carter*, 5 Va. 165 (disputed estate); *Warder*, 2 Va. 282 (debt action); *Doe v. Northern*, 1 Va. 282 (1794) (disputed deed); *Barnett v. Watson*, 1 Va. 372 (1794) (contract action); *McWilliams v. Willis*, 1 Va. 199 (1793) (contract action); *Thornton v. Spotswood*, 1 Va. 142 (1792) (disputed estate). In one case, Washington represented the Commonwealth of Virginia in a suit brought against the state for its seizure of some property during the Revolution. See *Commonwealth*, 8 Va. 338.
32. See 1 Va. 266 (1794); Newmyer, *Heroic Age*, 90–91. *Shermer* is one of the cases in which John Marshall and Bushrod Washington were on opposite sides. See *Shermer*, 1 Va. at 267–72.
33. See *Spencer*, 8 Va. 423–29.
34. See ibid. at 423.
35. See ibid. at 424.
36. See ibid. at 425–28; cf. *M'Call*, 5 Va. at 57 (quoting John Wickham) (stating in one case: "Mr. Washington's idea is ingenious, but I believe not tenable").
37. See *Tate v. Tally*, 7 Va. 354, 358 (1802). An amusing exception was recalled by Henry Clay, who was George Wythe's apprentice in Richmond before embarking on his remarkable political career. See Benjamin Blake Minor, *"Memoir of the Author" from Decisions in Virginia by the High Court of Chancery* (Richmond, VA: J. W. Randolph,

1852), xxxiii–xxxiv (quoting a letter from Henry Clay to Minor dated May 3, 1851). Clay said that Bushrod appeared before Chancellor Wythe on behalf of President Washington seeking to enjoin the collection of a debt. But the argument that George was not obligated to pay the debt was weak, and after reading the motion Wythe handed it to Bushrod "enquiring with an ineffable smile upon his countenance, 'do you think, sir, that I ought to grant this injunction?' Mr. Washington blushed and observed, that he had presented the bill at the earnest insistence of his client" (xxxiv).

38. For the cases in which Marshall and Washington went head-to-head, see *Tuberville v. Self*, 8 Va. 580 (1795); *Lee v. Tuberville*, 2 Va. 162 (1795); *Turner v. Moffett*, 2 Va. 70 (1795); *Brock v. Phillips*, 2 Va. 68 (1795); *Tuberville v. Self*, 2 Va. 71 (1795); *Currie v. Donald*, 2 Va. 58 (1795); *Wroe v. Washington*, 1 Va. 357 (1794); *Burnley v. Lambert*, 1 Va. 308 (1794); *Pendleton v. Vandevier*, 1 Va. 381 (1794); *Roy v. Garnett*, 2 Va. 9 (1794); *Shermer*, 1 Va. 267; *Taylor's Adm'x v. Peyton's Adm'x*, 1 Va. 252 (1794); *Carr v. Gooch*, 1 Va. 260 (1794); *Brown's Adm'x v. Garland*, 1 Va. 221 (1793); *Eustace v. Gaskins*, 1 Va. 188 (1793); *Stevens v. Taliaferro*, 1 Va. 155 (1793); *Hunter's Ex'rs v. Spotswood*, 1 Va. 145 (1792). In some of these cases, other lawyers worked with Washington, Marshall, or both men. For cases where Marshall and Washington collaborated, see *Hooe v. Marquess*, 8 Va. 416 (1798); *Stephens v. White*, 2 Va. 203 (1796); *Shelton v. Barbour*, 2 Va. 64 (1795); *Watson v. Alexander*, 1 Va. 340 (1794).

The only reference from Marshall about Washington when they were private lawyers comes in a cryptic letter. See letter from John Marshall to an unknown person, Mar. 14, 1796, in *The Papers of John Marshall Digital Edition*, ed. Charles Hobson (Charlottesville: University of Virginia Press, 2014) ("I have seen Mr. Washington and conversed with him on the subject of your letter. We both think the agreement very carelessly and incautiously drawn but yet suppose your construction to be the right one").

39. In one case, the Court of Appeals listened to Marshall's argument and told Bushrod "that there was no necessity [for him] to say anything, as there was no difficulty in the case" before ruling against Marshall. See *Stevens*, 1 Va. at 156.

40. See letter from Bushrod Washington to George Washington, Oct. 20, 1797, in *The Papers of George Washington: Retirement Series*, ed. W. W. Abbot and Dorothy Twohig (Charlottesville: University Press of Virginia, 1998–99), 1:417 ("I was sent for not long ago by a man of the name of Pearson who I found at Mr. Marshall's office. He was consulting Mr. Marshall respecting some very extensive claims upon the town of Alexandria and its vicinity, in which he also wished to employ me. I refused to engage it, knowing that many of my friends in that place would be involved in the dispute").

41. Marshall's house is now a museum. Bushrod's first house in Richmond was previously owned by Albert Gallatin, who served as the treasury secretary for President Jefferson and for President Madison. See *Yearbook of the Association for the Preservation of Virginia Antiquities for 1898 and 1899* (Richmond, VA: Wm. Ellis Jones, 1900), 29; see also Jon Meacham, *Thomas Jefferson and the Art of Power* (New York: Random House, 2012), 354 (providing some background on Gallatin). In 1795, the Washingtons moved to Belvidere, a home on the outskirts of Richmond. See Contract Between Bushrod Washington and Henry Lee, Jan 29, 1798, Mount Vernon Library (detailing

the sale of Belvidere and Washington's purchase of an office in Richmond that he had previously been renting from Lee).

42. See Common Hall Records, 1793–95, Library of Virginia, 2:58, 69–70, 60 (stating that Marshall and Bushrod were on a committee "to revise and amend the police ordinance of the city"), and 64 (stating that they were on a committee that proposed a change to the appointment method for the city treasurer). Marshall served on the city council for a much longer period of time. Bushrod was elected in 1794 and resigned in 1795 after he moved to Belvidere, which was just outside the city limits.
43. See William Walter Henning, *The Statutes at Large: Being a Collection of All the Laws of Virginia* (Richmond, VA: Samuel Pleasants, 1809), 1:vii.
44. See letter from Bushrod Washington to Corbin Washington, Feb. 25, 1796, Morristown National Historical Park Library ("Mr. Marshall and myself have brought a very important case in the Court of Chancery which will try the question"). What happened to this suit is not clear, but the issue was under what circumstances enslaved people belonged to a man's wife rather than to his male heirs when a married man died.
45. See *Shelton*, 2 Va. at 64–68. The name of the enslaved man is not in the case report.
46. Ibid. at 65–66.
47. Ibid. at 66.
48. Ibid. at 67.
49. Paul Finkelman, *Supreme Injustice: Slavery in the Nation's Highest Court* (Cambridge, MA: Harvard University Press, 2018), 5.
50. See *Hooe*, 8 Va. 416 (deed dispute in which enslaved people were involved that both Marshall and Washington argued); *Burnley*, 1 Va. 308 (detinue action for enslaved people involving both Washington and Marshall); Contract Between Bushrod Washington and Henry Lee, Jan 29, 1798, Mount Vernon Library (stating that Bushrod would receive "a valuable young Negro fellow between 20 and 40 years of age"); see also Finkelman, *Supreme Injustice*, 36–47 (establishing that Marshall owned more than 150 enslaved people near the end of his life).
51. *Chapman v. Turner*, 5 Va. 280, 283 (1798). In one instance, Bushrod petitioned the governor for clemency on behalf of a slave who was convicted of a crime and sentenced to death. See letter from Bushrod Washington to Henry Lee, Dec. 22, 1793, Virginia State Library. The petition (which was granted) was more about saving the slaveowner's property than about helping the enslaved person.
52. For some examples of the work that Bushrod did for his uncle while he was president, see, e.g., letter from George Washington to Bushrod Washington, Jan. 8, 1792, in *Papers of George Washington: Presidential Series*, 9:410–13 (asking Bushrod to bring a trespass action against squatters on his land); letter from Bushrod Washington to George Washington, Apr. 22, 1794, in *Papers of George Washington: Presidential Series*, 15:633–34 (asking George to respond to an injunction issued by the High Court of Chancery); letter from George Washington to Bushrod Washington, Apr. 30, 1794, in *Papers of George Washington: Presidential Series*, 15:688–90 (providing answers for the litigation). Bushrod also handled at least one legal matter for his old cavalry commander, Colonel John Mercer. See

letter from Bushrod Washington to John Francis Mercer, June 14, 1796, Historical Society of Pennsylvania.

53. Letter from Thomas Jefferson to Thomas M. Randolph, Feb. 26, 1795, in *The Papers of Thomas Jefferson*, ed. Julian P. Boyd (Princeton, NJ: Princeton University Press, 1958), 28:283.
54. See letter from Thomas Jefferson to Bushrod Washington, Sept. 23, 1795, in *Papers of Thomas Jefferson*, 28:479.
55. Jefferson observed that his neighbor could get loans to build the dam, but not to tear it down. See ibid.
56. Letter from Bushrod Washington to Thomas Jefferson, Nov. 2, 1795, in *Papers of Thomas Jefferson*, 28:518–19.
57. See letter from Thomas Jefferson to Bushrod Washington, Oct. 9, 1796, in *Papers of Thomas Jefferson*, 29:189–90 (asking Bushrod to take on one of his friends as a client); letter from Bushrod Washington to Thomas Jefferson, Apr. 26, 1796, in *Papers of Thomas Jefferson*, 29:91 (updating Jefferson on some other matters where Bushrod was his attorney); see also letter from Thomas Jefferson to Daniel Call, Aug. 15, 1799, in *Papers of Thomas Jefferson*, 31:165 (stating that "Mr. Washington has left under your care [after being confirmed to the Supreme Court] a suit of mine in Chancery").
58. The basic facts of the glebe land dispute described in the text come from *Terrett v. Taylor*, 13 U.S. (9 Cranch) 43, 46–49 (1815) and from a legal memorandum by Bushrod that is held by the University of Virginia. See Opinion of Bushrod Washington, Esq. on the Subject of the Glebes and Churches, Dec. 27, 1797, University of Virginia Library, Special Collections.
59. Va. Decl. of Rights, § 16.
60. My assumption is that he wrote this opinion for the church or for a church member, but there is nothing in the document that discloses the client.
61. Opinion of Bushrod Washington, 1.
62. Ibid., 4.
63. Ibid., 4. Bushrod framed this as a separation-of-powers argument, though modern lawyers might describe the point as an issue of due process of law.
64. Ibid., 2.
65. See ibid., 2–3 ("Contemporaneous opinions, as to the constructions of a law is in such case a fair and proper standard, by which ours should [be] formed. The first legislature which convened after the formation of our constitution, and composed chiefly of the same members, passed a law upon the very subject; which may be considered as a commentary upon the clause in question").
66. See ibid., 4.
67. See *Turpin v. Locket*, 10 Va. 113 (1804) (upholding the acts revoking the church's grant); see also *Terrett*, 13 U.S. (9 Cranch) at 46–55 (implicitly criticizing that decision and denying its applicability to the churches within the District of Columbia).
68. Letter from Joseph Story to Richard Peters, Dec. 10, 1829, in *Life and Letters of Joseph Story*, ed. William Wetmore Story (Boston: Little & Brown, 1851), 2:32.
69. Letter from Bushrod Washington to Hannah Bushrod Washington, June 21, 1789, Mount Vernon Library.

70. See Stoner, "Heir Apparent," 328.
71. In a letter to the Bible Society, Justice Washington explained that the goal was "to spread, throughout his dominions upon earth, a knowledge of the words of Divine Life." Letter from Bushrod Washington to the American Bible Society, Mar. 8, 1820, reprinted in the 1820 Annual Report of the Society, 99–100 (hereinafter Bible Society Letter). I thank the American Bible Society for scanning this letter for me from its archives.
72. Letter from Bushrod Washington to George Washington, Jan. 21, 1797, https://founders.archives.gov/?q=bushrod%20pleuresy&s=1511311111&r, 1 ("I received your favor of the 10th during my confinement under a severe attack of the Pleuresy. I am now on the recovery, though very weak, nor have a I left my room").
73. Letter from Hannah Bushrod Washington to Bushrod Washington, Feb. 3, 1797, Mount Vernon Library.
74. See letter from Timothy Pickering to John Adams, Sept. 20, 1798, https://founders.archives.gov/?q=%20pickering%20%20Author%3A%22Pickering%2C%20Timothy%22%20Recipient%3A%22Adams%2C%20John%22&s=1111311111&r=78.
75. Charles Warren, *The Supreme Court in United States History* (Boston: Little, Brown, and Company, 1926), 1:466.
76. Bushrod rarely discussed his disability, though in his 1820 letter to the Bible Society he did say that "my sight is not good" but that he was able to read some stereotype plates "with less fatigue to the eye than print of the same size in most other books." Bible Society Letter, 99.

Chapter 5

1. See, e.g., Barry Friedman, *The Will of the People: How Public Opinion Has Influenced the Supreme Court and Shaped the Meaning of the Constitution* (New York: Farrar, Straus, and Giroux, 2009), 46–47.
2. See U.S. Const., art. II, § 3; Ron Chernow, *Alexander Hamilton* (New York: Penguin Books, 2004), 514–15. The Twelfth Amendment altered this arrangement in 1804 following the deadlock between Jefferson and Aaron Burr in 1800. See U.S. Const., amend. XII; Bruce Ackerman, *The Failure of the Founding Fathers: Jefferson, Marshall, and the Rise of Presidential Democracy* (Cambridge, MA: Harvard University Press, 2005), 31–34, 203–6.
3. Letter from Joseph Story to Richard Peters, Dec. 10, 1829, in *Life and Letters of Joseph Story*, ed. William Wetmore Story (Boston: Little & Brown, 1851), 2:32. A secondary source written long after Bushrod died says that he was a candidate in 1796 to be Virginia's attorney general—an officer then elected by the state legislature—and lost. See St. George Tucker Brooke, "The Brooke Family," *Virginia Historical Magazine* 19 (1911): 101. I cannot find any contemporary corroboration for this claim.
4. See Jonathan Gienapp, *The Second Creation: Fixing the American Constitution in the Founding Era* (Cambridge, MA: Harvard University Press, 2018), 251–53; John

Rhodehamel, *George Washington: The Wonder of the Age* (New Haven, CT: Yale University Press, 2017), 281–85 (discussing the Jay Treaty, signed by Britain and the United States in 1795).

5. See Ron Chernow, *Washington: A Life* (New York: Penguin Books, 2010), 671; Gerald Leonard and Saul Cornell, *The Partisan Republic: Democracy, Exclusion, and the Fall of the Founders Constitution, 1780s–1830s* (New York: Cambridge University Press, 2019), 44–48.
6. See Chernow, *Hamilton*, 347–55; Gienapp, *Second Creation*, 202–09.
7. See Chernow, *Washington*, 793; Joseph J. Ellis, *His Excellency: George Washington* (New York: Vintage Press, 2004), 246–49.
8. See Chernow, *Washington*, 691; David O. Stewart, *George Washington: The Political Rise of America's Founding Father* (New York: Dutton, 2021), 375–86.
9. See David McCullough, *John Adams* (New York: Simon and Schuster, 2001), 477; Jean Edward Smith, *John Marshall: Definer of a Nation* (New York: Henry Holt and Company, 1996), 183.
10. Letter from Alexander Hamilton to Oliver Wolcott Jr., June 15, 1796, in *The Papers of Alexander Hamilton*, ed. Harold C. Syrett (New York: Columbia University Press, 1974), 20:223.
11. See McCullough, *Adams*, 485–86; Smith, *Marshall*, 184.
12. See Chernow, *Washington*, 783; McCullough, *Adams*, 495–96.
13. See McCullough, *Adams*, 503; Joel Richard Paul, *Without Precedent: John Marshall and His Times* (New York: Riverhead Books, 2018), 176–78. XYZ was the coded reference to the three French agents who would receive Talleyrand's bribe. See Paul, *Without Precedent*, 172–73; see also letter from Benjamin Latrobe to Giambattista Scandella, Apr. 17. 1798, in *The Papers of Benjamin Henry Latrobe: Correspondence and Miscellaneous Papers*, ed. Edward C. Carter II (New Haven, CT: Yale University Press, 1984), 1:85 ("Even the peaceful fireside of Mr. Washington is disturbed by political fanaticism. What news? . . . XYZ and the Lady, &c., was my answer").
14. *Virginia Gazette and General Advertiser* (Richmond), Aug. 14, 1798.
15. See *The Diaries of George Washington*, ed. Donald Jackson (Charlottesville: University Press of Virginia, 1978), 6:254. George's diaries omit any mention of Bushrod between 1789 and 1797. Thus, they probably did not see each other during his presidency, though I cannot be sure.
16. See letter from George Washington to Bushrod Washington, Jan. 30, 1798, in *The Papers of George Washington: Retirement Series*, ed. W. W. Abbot and Dorothy Twohig (Charlottesville: University Press of Virginia, 1998–99), 2:60–61; letter from Bushrod Washington to George Washington, Jan. 9, 1798, in *Papers of George Washington: Retirement Series*, 2:12–13; letter from Bushrod Washington to George Washington, Nov. 13, 1797, in *Papers of George Washington: Retirement Series*, 1:473–74; letter from Bushrod Washington to George Washington, Oct. 25, 1797, in *Papers of George Washington: Retirement Series*, 1:428; letter from George Washington to Bushrod Washington, Oct. 30, 1797, in *Papers of George Washington: Retirement Series*, 1:445–46.

17. Letter from George Washington to Bushrod Washington, Oct. 9, 1797, in *Papers of George Washington: Retirement Series*, 1:398; see also 397–98 (asking Bushrod a series of questions about a pending lawsuit).
18. Letter from George Washington to Bushrod Washington, Oct. 23, 1797, in *Papers of George Washington: Retirement Series*, 1:422.
19. Letter from George Washington to Bushrod Washington, Nov. 3, 1797, in *Papers of George Washington, Retirement Series*, 1:455; see letter from Bushrod Washington to George Washington, Oct. 27, 1797, in *Papers of George Washington, Retirement Series*, 1:422 (stating that a Mrs. Forbes, the housekeeper under consideration, "is honest, industrious, and well acquainted with nice as well as common Cooking, and other subjects of domestic employment necessary in her profession"); letter from Bushrod Washington to George Washington, Oct. 30, 1797, in *Papers of George Washington, Retirement Series*, 1:446 (stating that she wanted $150 per year); letter from George Washington to Bushrod Washington, Dec. 18, 1797, in *Papers of George Washington: Retirement Series*, 1:522 (stating that he did hire Mrs. Forbes).
20. See Chernow, *Washington*, 785; McCullough, *Adams*, 507.
21. Letter from Bushrod Washington to George Washington, Aug. 7, 1798, in *Papers of George Washington, Retirement Series*, 2:496.
22. Letter from George Washington to Bushrod Washington, Aug. 12, 1798, in *Papers of George Washington, Retirement Series*, 2:515.
23. See letter from Bushrod Washington to George Washington, Apr. 10, 1799, in *Papers of George Washington, Retirement Series*, 3:479–80; letter from George Washington to Bushrod Washington, Dec. 31, 1798, in *Papers of George Washington, Retirement Series*, 3:303; letter from Bushrod Washington to George Washington, Sept. 21, 1798, in *Papers of George Washington, Retirement Series*, 2:31–32; letter from Bushrod Washington to George Washington, Aug. 20, 1798, in *Papers of George Washington, Retirement Series*, 2:546.
24. Letter from George Washington to Bushrod Washington, Aug. 27, 1798, in *Papers of George Washington, Retirement Series*, 2:565.
25. See Smith, *Marshall*, 176.
26. See Chernow, *Washington*, 780; Smith, *Marshall*, 239–41.
27. See *The Autobiography of Martin Van Buren*, ed. John C. Fitzpatrick (Washington, DC: Government Printing Office, 1920), 177–78; see also *Diaries of George Washington*, 6:314 (noting that Bushrod and Marshall arrived on September 3, 1798), 315 (indicating that they left on September 6). There are other versions of the story with colorful details about how Bushrod and Marshall arrived at Mount Vernon, but the variety creates doubt about whether any of these more elaborate tales are true.
28. In Marshall's telling, he resisted George's request for a few days and gave in only after more face-to-face chats. See Paul, *Without Precedent*, 183; Smith, *Marshall*, 241. Perhaps this is more accurate, though one wonders if Marshall was exaggerating to create a better story.
29. See letter from Bushrod Washington to George Washington, Mar. 13, 1798, in *Papers of George Washington, Retirement Series*, 2:140 ("Having sold Belvidere, that I might with more convenience pursue my practice in Town (where I now reside)"); Contract

Between Bushrod Washington and Henry Lee, Jan. 29, 1798, Mount Vernon Library (selling Belvidere). Until they moved to Mount Vernon, Bushrod and Nancy also spent part of their year at Walnut Farm in Westmoreland County. Bushrod's ownership of this land allowed him to run for the House of Representatives from a district outside of Richmond.

30. See James D. Richardson, ed., *A Compilation of the Messages and Papers of the Presidents* (New York: Bureau of National Literature, Inc., 1897), 1:250 (making the appointment that was declined). Washington declined due to unspecified conflicts of interest that the post would create with clients, but this could have been an excuse to avoid taking time away from private practice. See David Leslie Annis, "Mr. Bushrod Washington, Supreme Court Justice on the Marshall Court," PhD diss., Notre Dame University, 1974, 65 (quoting a letter from Bushrod to the secretary of war stating: "My professional engagements are of such a nature, as to render my acceptance as it respects the interests of others improper and therefore impossible").
31. Marshall's opponent was John Clopton, a popular Republican. See Paul, *Without Precedent*, 183. Bushrod would have run against Walter Jones, another incumbent who was aligned with Jefferson. See letter from Thomas Jefferson to Benjamin H. Latrobe, Sept. 22, 1798, in *The Papers of Thomas Jefferson*, ed. Julian P. Boyd (Princeton, NJ: Princeton University Press, 1958), 30:524. Jones was the father of Walter Jones Jr., who was Bushrod's apprentice.
32. Letter from Thomas Jefferson to Benjamin H. Latrobe, Sept. 22, 1798, in *Papers of Thomas Jefferson*, 30:524.
33. See Smith, *Marshall*, 160–61 (describing Marshall's role in organizing the first social club in Richmond and his fondness for playing quoits with club members).
34. See R. Kent Newmyer, *John Marshall and the Heroic Age of the Supreme Court* (Baton Rouge: Louisiana State University Press, 2001), 21–23.
35. See *Collected Works of James Wilson*, ed. Kermit L. Hall and Mark David Hall (Indianapolis, IN: Liberty Fund, 2007), 1:xxv (giving the date of Wilson's death as August 21, 1798). George Washington, Bushrod, and John Marshall were unaware of this news when they met at Mount Vernon to discuss the upcoming elections.
36. Letter from John Adams to Timothy Pickering, Sept. 13, 1798, https://founders.archives.gov/?q=bushrod%20Author%3A%22Adams%2C%20John%22&s=1511311111&r=5.
37. There is no indication that George knew that Bushrod was under consideration for the Court or offered his views to Adams prior to the nomination.
38. See letter from John Adams to Timothy Pickering, Sept. 14, 1798, https://founders.archives.gov/?q=wilson%20Author%3A%22Adams%2C%20John%22&s=1511311111&r=71 ("As Virginia has no [Supreme Court] judge at present, she is as much entitled as Pennsylvania to attention").
39. Letter from Timothy Pickering to John Adams, Sept. 20, 1798, https://founders.archives.gov/?q=%20Recipient%3A%22Adams%2C%20John%22&s=1111312111&sa=pickering&r=79. In a letter to Pickering a week later, Adams reiterated his view that Marshall was at the top of his list with Bushrod second, though this time he mentioned Marshall's service in France as a reason to name him. See letter from

John Adams to Timothy Pickering, Sept. 26, 1798, https://founders.archives.gov/?q=%20Author%3A%22Adams%2C%20John%22%20Recipient%3A%22Pickering%2C%20Timothy%22&s=1111311111&r=38.

40. A famous example was Daniel Webster, one of the greatest constitutional lawyers of his era, who litigated cases while serving in Congress. See Merrill D. Peterson, *The Great Triumvirate: Webster, Clay, and Calhoun* (New York: Oxford University Press, 1987), 179–81 (noting that right after giving his famous "Reply to Hayne" oration in the Senate, Webster returned home and defended a wealthy Massachusetts merchant against a murder charge).
41. See Smith, *Marshall*, 245.
42. Justice Washington was a recess appointment, which meant that he became a justice immediately upon his nomination by the president because the Senate was not in session. See U.S. Const., art. II, § 2, cl. 3 ("The President shall have Power to fill up all Vacancies that may happen during the Recess of the Senate"); Annis, "Bushrod Washington," 71 (noting that the recess appointment was made on September 29, 1798). The Senate confirmed Washington in December, though there is no record of any debate, if one even took place. See Horace Binney, *Bushrod Washington* (Philadelphia: C. Sherman & Son, 1858), 5 (stating that Justice Washington's official commission was dated December 20, 1798). In those days, most Supreme Court confirmations were unanimous and routine.
43. Bushrod visited Mount Vernon again on October 6, which probably means that he did not receive President Adams's request until after that date. See *Diaries of George Washington*, 6:319. Otherwise, there would have been no need to write a letter stating that he had been picked.
44. Letter from Bushrod Washington to George Washington, Oct. 19, 1798, in *Papers of George Washington, Retirement Series*, 3: 113–14.
45. Letter from George Washington to Bushrod Washington, Oct. 24, 1798, in *Papers of George Washington, Retirement Series*, 3: 138.
46. See Van Buren, *Autobiography*, 178 (quoting Bushrod as stating: "I had entered upon the steps deemed advisable to qualify myself to represent Westmoreland when I received a letter from the Secretary of State informing me that President Adams had appointed me one of the Justices of the Supreme Court of the United States, and I was advised by the same letter that a circuit court was to be held in Georgia in so short a time that it would be necessary to start immediately for that state if I accepted the office. I took the official oath immediately, threw myself into the stage coach, proceeded to Georgia and informed the General from that place of what I had done and my reasons for doing it"); letter from William Cushing to James Iredell, Nov. 9, 1798, in *Life and Correspondence of James Iredell: One of the Associate Justices of the Supreme Court of the United States*, ed. Griffith J. McRee (New York: D. Appleton & Co., 1858), 2: 539 ("You have heard that Mr. Bushrod Washington is appointed to the bench, and I am told he has gone on for the Southern Circuit").
47. See Act of Mar. 2, 1793, ch. 22, § 1, 1 Stat. 333–34 (hereinafter Judiciary Act of 1793).
48. See Judiciary Act of 1789, ch. 20, § 4, 1 Stat. 73.

49. In the absence of the district judge the Supreme Court justice could hold a circuit court by himself (see Judiciary Act of 1793, ch. 22, § 2, 1 Stat. 334), but the district judge could not hold a circuit court without a justice.
50. Letter from George Washington to Bushrod Washington, Oct. 24, 1798, in *Papers of George Washington, Retirement Series*, 3:138.
51. See Smith, *Marshall*, 336 (giving several examples of these accidents); letter from Joseph Story to Bushrod Washington, May 8, 1813, New York Historical Society (stating that Justice Livingston was injured in a carriage accident due to poor roads).
52. Letter from Joseph Story to Bushrod Washington, May 8, 1813, New-York Historical Society.
53. In a letter to Justice Iredell, Bushrod stated that he arrived in Charleston too late to hold court there and so proceeded to Augusta. See letter from Bushrod Washington to James Iredell, Dec. 5, 1798, in *Life and Correspondence of James Iredell*, 2:541. We do know that the justice decided a case about Revolutionary War debts and the obligation to pay them under the treaties negotiated with Great Britain, but his opinion went unreported. See *Williamson v. Kincaid*, 4 U.S. (4 Dall.) 20 (1800). Regular reporting of Washington's circuit opinions did not begin until 1803, though in 1800 he did try to interest someone in publishing his cases. See letter from Bushrod Washington to J. B. Wallace, Nov. 5, 1800, Historical Society of Pennsylvania (asking Wallace to consider reporting his circuit cases).
54. See letter from George Washington to Bushrod Washington, Dec. 31, 1798, in *Papers of George Washington: Retirement Series*, 3:302 ("It gave me pleasure to hear by Judge Cushing, that you had returned from your Southern Circuit in good health").
55. The date can be pinpointed through two sources. The first is that Binney's recollection says that he first met the justice in January 1799; see Binney, *Bushrod Washington*, 5. The other is that Bushrod dined at Mount Vernon on January 23, 1799; see *Diaries of George Washington*, 6:331. Thus, Bushrod must have arrived at the boarding house in late January.
56. See Paul, *Without Precedent*, 67. The National Park Service offers tours of the room in which the Court met until 1800. See https://www.nps.gov/inde/planyourvisit/oldcityhall.htm.
57. Binney, *Bushrod Washington*, 6–7.
58. Ibid., 7.
59. See letter from Elizabeth Willing Powel to Bushrod Washington, April 28, 1799, Mount Vernon Library. Eliza's purchase confirms the conclusion of a recent article that some of the justices wore black robes in the 1790s. See Matthew Hofstedt, "The Switch to Black: Revisiting Early Supreme Court Robes," *Supreme Court Historical Journal* 46, no. 1 (2021): 13–41. The oft-told story that John Marshall was the first justice to don black robes is therefore a myth. See Paul, *Without Precedent*, 234; Smith, *Marshall*, 285–86.
60. See Chernow, *Washington*, 757; Paul, *Without Precedent*, 223. John Rutledge received a recess appointment from President Washington after Chief Justice Jay resigned, but the Senate rejected Rutledge's nomination and so the president turned to Ellsworth.

61. See Chernow, *Hamilton*, 280; Michael J. Klarman, *The Framers' Coup: The Making of the United States Constitution* (New York: Oxford University Press, 2016), 144–45.
62. See Klarman, *Framers' Coup*, 511–14, 516; Pauline Maier, *Ratification: The People Debate the Constitution, 1787–1788* (New York: Simon and Schuster, 2010), 410–13, 469.
63. See Chernow, *Washington*, 602; Smith, *Marshall*, 397.
64. See Klarman, *Framers' Coup*, 260; Smith, *Marshall*, 287; see also Massachusetts Declaration of Rights of 1780, art. I.
65. See Klarman, *Framers' Coup*, 189; Smith, *Marshall*, 287–88.
66. See Paul, *Without Precedent*, 298; Smith, *Marshall*, 288.
67. See Frank O. Bowman III, *High Crimes and Misdemeanors: A History of Impeachment for the Age of Trump* (New York: Cambridge University Press, 2019), 129; Smith, *Marshall*, 288.
68. See Bowman, *High Crimes*, 135; Chernow, *Hamilton*, 118; Smith, *Marshall*, 289.
69. See, e.g., Akhil Reed Amar, *America's Constitution: A Biography* (New York: Random House, 2005), 216 (explaining that Congress did not give the Court general federal question jurisdiction in criminal cases until the 1890s).
70. The figure comes from the data compiled by the Federal Judicial Center (www.fjc.gov), a research agency created by Congress, which has information on every federal judge confirmed.
71. See U.S. Const., amend. XIV, § 1.
72. See *Barron v. Baltimore*, 32 U.S. (7 Pet.) 24 (1833) (confirming the Framers' view that the first set of constitutional amendments did not apply to state governments); Gerard N. Magliocca, *The Heart of the Constitution: How the Bill of Rights Became the Bill of Rights* (New York: Oxford University Press, 2018), 53–57 (describing the status of the first set of amendments into the nineteenth century and their exclusive application to federal action).
73. 3 U.S. (3 Dall.) 415 (1799). Chief Justice Ellsworth delivered the unanimous opinion of the Court in one (see *Clarke v. Russel*, 3 U.S. [3 Dall.] 415 [1799]), and in the other he gave the Court's opinion with one separate concurrence (see *Sims' Lessee v. Irvine*, 3 U.S. [3 Dall.] 425 [1799]). I am more comprehensive about the decisions of the Ellsworth Court because that period gets less attention. When the text reaches the Marshall Court, I will focus on the major decisions and the ones that directly involved Bushrod.
74. See U.S. Const., art. III, § 2; *Fowler*, 3 U.S. (3 Dall.) at 411; James R. Stoner Jr., "Heir Apparent: Bushrod Washington and Federal Justice in the Early Republic," in *Seriatim: The Supreme Court Before John Marshall*, ed. Scott Douglas Gerber (New York: New York University Press, 1998), 328.
75. See *Fowler*, 3 U.S. (3 Dall.) at 412–13 (opinion of Washington, J.); Stoner, "Heir Apparent," 328 (describing Washington's opinion as "the most thorough"). Only three justices participated, as Chief Justice Ellsworth recused himself and two others were ill. See *Fowler*, 3 U.S. (3 Dall.) at 412, 413–14 (opinion of Paterson, J.), and 414–15 (opinion of Cushing, J.).

76. See Kurt Lash and Alicia Harrison. "Minority Report: John Marshall and the Defense of the Alien and Sedition Acts," *Ohio State Law Journal* 68 (2007): 461–62. During the campaign, a series of anonymous essays entitled "Plain Truth" were published defending the Federalists by a "citizen of Westmoreland County" (462). These essays are attributed to Henry Lee, but Lash and Harrison argue that the real author was Bushrod Washington (476–79). In part, their claim rests on reasons why Lee could not have written the essays, but they also point out that Washington was the most prominent citizen of Westmoreland County who could have written them. I was intrigued by this idea and researched the question at length, but I found nothing to confirm or refute Bushrod's authorship of "Plain Truth."
77. Lee also needed help because he was absent from the campaign trail much of the time, though whether that was due to illness or financial problems is unclear. See ibid., 470–71.
78. The Sedition Act was part of a package (known as the Alien and Sedition Acts) passed by the Federalist Congress and signed by President Adams. The other statutes lengthened the residency period necessary to become a naturalized citizen, enhanced the president's power to deport aliens (noncitizen immigrants) deemed hostile to the United States, and essentially made all French citizens living here enemy aliens. See Chernow, *Hamilton*, 570; McCullough, *Adams*, 505. These acts did not come before Justice Washington and did not play a significant role in the 1799 campaign, and thus I do not discuss them in the text.
79. See Sedition Act, ch. 74, §2, 1 Stat. 596 (1798); *New York Times v. Sullivan*, 376 U.S. 254, 276 (1964) ("Although the Sedition Act was never tested in this Court, the attack upon its validity has carried the day in the court of history"); see also Wendell Bird, *Press and Speech Under Assault: The Early Supreme Court Justices, the Sedition Act of 1798, and the Campaign Against Dissent* (New York: Oxford University Press, 2016), 253–63 (providing a fine overview of the Sedition Act).
80. See Chernow, *Hamilton*, 573; David O. Stewart, *Madison's Gift: Five Partnerships That Built America* (New York: Simon and Schuster, 2015), 177–78.
81. See, e.g., Daniel A. Farber, "The Fourteenth Amendment and the Unconstitutionality of Secession," *Akron Law Review* 45 (2012): 488.
82. See Paul, *Without Precedent*, 180–81; Smith, *Marshall*, 244.
83. Letter from George Washington to Bushrod Washington, Dec. 31, 1798, in *Papers of George Washington, Retirement Series*, 3:303; see letter from George Washington to John Marshall, Dec. 30, 1798, in *Papers of George Washington, Retirement Series*, 3:297.
84. See Jud Campbell, "The Invention of First Amendment Federalism," *Texas Law Review* 97 (2019): 552–53.
85. Letter from Bushrod Washington to George Washington, Apr. 10, 1799, in *Papers of George Washington, Retirement Series*, 3:479.
86. Letter from Bushrod Washington to George Washington, Apr. 26, 1799, in *Papers of George Washington, Retirement Series*, 4:25; see Smith, *Marshall*, 250.
87. Letter from George Washington to Bushrod Washington, May 5, 1799, in *Papers of George Washington: Retirement Series*, 4: 51.

88. See letter from Bushrod Washington to James Iredell, Aug. 20, 1799, in *Life and Correspondence of James Iredell*, 2:583 (informing Justice Iredell, who missed the session due to illness, that "fortunately there was no business brought on which involved any question of importance or difficulty, and the term was consequently short"). Due to a yellow fever epidemic, this circuit was held in Norristown rather than Philadelphia.
89. See ibid. (asking Iredell for his notes about any pending cases).
90. See Wendell Bird, "New Light on the Sedition Act of 1798: The Missing Half of the Prosecutions," *Law and History Review* 34 (2016): 564–65.
91. See ibid., 565.
92. See ibid., 561–62, 581.
93. See Annis, "Bushrod Washington," 89–90; Bird, "New Light on the Sedition Act," 581.
94. See Bird, "New Light on the Sedition Act," 581; see also Judiciary Act of 1789, §27 (stating that "a marshall [*sic*] shall be appointed in and for each district for the term of four years"). Evidently, the term of the marshal in Judge Peters's district had lapsed, and thus all the orders that the marshal executed in the cases for the October 1799 circuit were unlawful.
95. See Paul, *Without Precedent*, 234; Smith, *Marshall*, 290.
96. See *Banks v. Greenleaf*, 2 F. Cas. 756 (C.C.D. Va. 1799) (No. 959).
97. Ibid. at 759. The case raised the issue whether Maryland or Virginia law applied to a contract made in Virginia between a citizen of Virginia and a citizen of Maryland. See ibid. at 757. Washington held that Virginia law applied and that Maryland bankruptcy law could not, therefore, absolve Greenleaf of his debt under the contract. See ibid. at 758.
98. See Chernow, *Washington*, 808–9; Rhodehamel, *Wonder of the Age*, 299.
99. Last Will and Testament, in *Papers of George Washington: Retirement Series*, 4:479–91 Washington's will was a complex document with many bequests that spawned considerable litigation not unlike the cases that Bushrod handled as a lawyer. See, e.g., letter from Bushrod Washington to George Lewis, Jan. 26, 1804, Huntington Library (regarding a deed that was part of the estate); letter from Tobias Lear to Bushrod Washington, June 24, 1803, Huntington Library (submitting a receipt for reimbursement by the estate).
100. See *Diaries of George Washington* 6:357 (describing Bushrod as "Judge Washington").
101. Last Will and Testament, in *Papers of George Washington: Retirement Series*, 4:485.
102. See ibid., 488 ("I give and bequeath [to Bushrod] all that part thereof which is comprehended within the following limits . . . containing upwards of four thousand acres, be the same more or less—together with the Mansion house and all other buildings and improvements thereon"). Some parcels of the plantation went to other family members.
103. See ibid., 480; Mary V. Thompson, "*The Only Unavoidable Subject of Regret*": *George Washington, Slavery, and the Enslaved Community at Mount Vernon* (Charlottesville: University of Virginia Press, 2019), 294; Weincek, *Imperfect God*: George Washington, His Slaves and the Creation of America, (New York: Farrar,

Straus, and Giroux, 2003), 4. Some of Mount Vernon's enslaved people were owned by Martha as a life estate and by her heirs through the estate of her first husband; George could not free them. See Thompson, *Subject of Regret*, 309; Weincek, *Imperfect God*, 354. The only person freed immediately upon George's death was Billy Lee, his personal slave since the Revolution. See Chernow, *Washington*, 802.

104. See Thompson, *Subject of Regret*, 294; Ellis, *His Excellency*, 263.
105. Last Will and Testament, in *Papers of George Washington: Retirement Series*: 4:480.
106. Thompson, *Subject of Regret*, 311; see Chernow, *Washington*, 815.
107. See Chernow, *Washington*, 815; Thompson, *Subject of Regret*, 311.
108. See Binney, *Bushrod Washington*, 25–26. In Binney's telling, John Marshall was also called to Mount Vernon by Martha. I cannot find any confirmation for Binney's assertion about Marshall, nor can I establish which circuit session was truncated. There is a letter proving that Bushrod advised Martha immediately after George's death and discussed his view of the will with Marshall. See letter from Bushrod Washington to Martha Washington, Jan. 26, 1800, Mount Vernon Library.
109. See Chernow, *Washington*, 815; Weincek, *Imperfect God*, 358.
110. See Smith, *Marshall*, 252n* (noting Ellsworth's appointment and his dispatch to France in November 1799); see also McCullough, *Adams*, 525 (discussing Ellsworth's selection).
111. 4 U.S. (4 Dall.) 14 (1800). All the other cases in the session were disposed of with brief orders or per curiam opinions.
112. See *Cooper*, 4 U.S. (4 Dall.) at 15.
113. See ibid. at 19 (opinion of Chase, J.) (making the point that judicial review probably did not apply to state statutes enacted before 1788); see also U.S. Const., art. I, § 10, cl. 1 (prohibiting state bills of attainder).
114. *Cooper*, 4 U.S. (4 Dall.) at 18.
115. See *Ogden v. Saunders*, 25 U.S. (12 Wheat.) 213, 270 (1827); *Green v. Biddle*, 21 U.S. (8 Wheat.) 1, 93–94 (1823); Randy E. Barnett, *Restoring the Lost Constitution: The Presumption of Liberty* (Princeton, NJ: Princeton University Press, 2004), 151 (noting that Justice Washington was one of the first judges to articulate the presumption of constitutionality).
116. See Bird, *Press and Speech*, 308.
117. Ibid.; see Chernow, *Hamilton*, 533–36, 540–44 (describing the Maria Reynolds affair).
118. See *Connecticut Journal* (New Haven), Apr. 24, 1800, 3 ("Judge Washington in his charge to the jury, (which was given in an unrivalled manner) established the act to be constitutional, by a train of reasoning too powerful to be resisted"); Bird, *Press and Speech*, 308–9. There is no transcript of Washington's charge, and so we can only speculate about what he may have said. The Federalist newspaper account (quoted earlier) also said that he "proved the publication to be libelous, beyond even the possibility of doubt" and at sentencing described "the heinous and aggravating circumstances which attended the publication of the libel" in a way "as to make the prisoner blush for his crime, and be satisfied with his punishment"; *Connecticut Journal* (New Haven), Apr. 24, 1800, 3. The last portion raises doubts

about the account's reliability, as common sense says that Holt would not have been "satisfied with the punishment." Perhaps the journalist exaggerated Washington's statements, although I do not doubt that the justice upheld the constitutionality of the Sedition Act.

119. See Bird, *Press and Speech*, 309.
120. See ibid., 306–7.
121. See ibid., 307; Phillip I. Blumberg, *Repressive Jurisprudence in the Early American Republic: The First Amendment and the Legacy of English Law* (New York: Cambridge University Press, 2010), 132. Durrell was bankrupt, which may explain the clemency recommendation.
122. See Jon Meacham, *Thomas Jefferson and the Art of Power* (New York: Random House, 2012), 357; Michael Stokes Paulsen, "The Most Dangerous Branch: Executive Branch to Say What the Law Is," *Georgetown Law Journal* 83 (1994): 255.
123. See Paul, *Without Precedent*, 194–96; Smith, *Marshall*, 266–67, 275–76.
124. 4 U.S. (4 Dall.) 37 (1800).
125. See ibid. at 39–46.
126. Ibid. at 40.
127. Ibid. at 41–42.
128. See *Montoya v. United States*, 180 U.S. 261, 267 (1901).
129. See *Massachusetts v. Laird*, 451 F.2d 26, 33, and n. 11 (1st. Cir. 1971); *Berk v. Laird*, 317 F. Supp. 715, 722 (S.D.N.Y. 1970); cf. *Davi v. Laird*, 318 F. Supp. 478, 481 (W.D. Va. 1970) (doing the same to reject an attack on military spending in Vietnam).
130. See *Anderson v. Carter*, 802 F.3d 4, 8–9 (D.C. Cir. 2015).
131. Some secondary sources say that the justice backed Charles Pinckney for president in 1800 (see Stoner, "Heir Apparent," 331), but this claim is mistaken. Pinckney was from South Carolina and was the draw for the Federalists there; thus Washington's praise for Pinckney in his only surviving letter about the campaign was about how to deliver the Federalist vote to John Adams. See letter from Bushrod Washington to Oliver Wolcott Jr., Nov. 1, 1800, Connecticut Historical Society. Moreover, there is no indication that he did not support the president who appointed him to the Court.
132. See letter from Bushrod Washington to Oliver Wolcott Jr., Nov. 1, 1800, Connecticut Historical Society (writing from Charleston). I am not certain that Washington was holding a circuit court there, but I cannot otherwise explain why he was in South Carolina.
133. For an insightful explanation of that split and its broader significance, see Stephen Skowronek, *The Politics Presidents Make: Leadership from John Adams to Bill Clinton* (Cambridge, MA: Harvard University Press, 1997), 66–69.
134. See Chernow, *Hamilton*, 593–94; McCullough, *Adams*, 544.
135. See McCullough, *Adams*, 552; Paul, *Without Precedent*, 209.
136. McCullough, *Adams*, 449; see Chernow, *Hamilton*, 622–23, 525 (describing Adams and Hamilton as "hasty, erratic, impulsive men capable of atrocious judgment").
137. See Chernow, *Hamilton*, 612, 616–18; McCullough, *Adams*, 550; see also Mary Sarah Bilder, *Madison's Hand: Revising the Constitutional* Convention (Cambridge,

MA: Harvard University Press, 2015), 59–61 (describing Pinckney's draft at the Convention).

138. Chernow, *Hamilton*, 522.
139. Letter from Bushrod Washington to Oliver Wolcott Jr., Nov. 1, 1800, Connecticut Historical Society.
140. See ibid.; Paul, *Without Precedent*, 217; Smith, *Marshall*, 277. Jefferson and Aaron Burr tied in the Electoral College, and the election was decided by the House of Representatives. See Bruce Ackerman, *The Failure of the Founding Fathers: Jefferson, Marshall, and the Rise of Presidential Democracy* (Cambridge, MA: Harvard University Press, 2005), 30–108 (providing a detailed account). I pass over the Jefferson/Burr crisis in the text because Justice Washington played no role in that affair.

Chapter 6

1. See Barry Friedman, *The Will of the People: How Public Opinion Has Influenced the Supreme Court and Shaped the Meaning of the Constitution* (New York: Farrar, Straus, and Giroux, 2009), 49; Joel Richard Paul, *Without Precedent: John Marshall and His Times* (New York: Riverhead Books, 2018), 221–22. Today a justice would never retire during a transition period between administrations of different parties, and any attempt to replace a justice who died during that interregnum would provoke a political crisis.
2. Legend says that Jefferson would have named Spencer Roane chief justice if given the chance, but there is no direct evidence for that claim. See Jean Edward Smith, *John Marshall: Definer of a Nation* (New York: Henry Holt and Company, 1996), 450.
3. See Bruce Ackerman, *The Failure of the Founding Fathers: Jefferson, Marshall, and the Rise of Presidential Democracy* (Cambridge, MA: Harvard University Press, 2005), 123–27; David McCullough, *John Adams* (New York: Simon and Schuster, 2001), 560. Why did Marshall accept the nomination when he had declined the associate justice offer in 1798? Maybe the allure of being the chief justice was a draw, though Marshall also knew that the Judiciary Act of 1801 would become law and end circuit riding. To the extent that circuit riding was a burden that he did not want in 1798, that appeared to no longer be a concern. Another curious aspect of Marshall's selection was that Virginia then had two of the six seats on the Court, which meant that nobody else from Virginia could be named until after Bushrod's death. But there is no indication that anyone objected to Marshall on the ground that there could not be a second justice from Virginia.
4. See Paul, *Without Precedent*, 224–25; Smith, *Marshall*, 279–80. Prior to the ratification of the Twentieth Amendment, the presidential term ended in March. See U.S. Const., amend. XX, § 1 (changing the date to January 20).
5. Judiciary Act of 1801, ch. 4; 2 Stat. 89 (repealed 1802).

6. See Ackerman, *Failure of the Founding Fathers*, 128–29; Joshua Glick, "On the Road: The Supreme Court and the History of Circuit Riding," *Cardozo Law Review* 24 (2003): 1782. The act also expanded federal jurisdiction and said that the Supreme Court would shrink to five justices once a new vacancy arose, but the act was repealed before that Court-related provision could be invoked.
7. See Smith, *Marshall*, 303; see also Robert H. Jackson, *The Struggle for Judicial Supremacy: A Study of a Crisis in American Power Politics* (New York: Alfred A. Knopf, 1941), 25 (providing some background).
8. See Ackerman, *Failure of the Founding Fathers*, 132–34. The circuit judges were dubbed "midnight judges" by critics, though President Adams did not literally appoint them on his last day in office.
9. Smith, *Marshall*, 285.
10. See Paul, *Without Precedent*, 235; Smith, *Marshall*, 286.
11. Letter from Joseph Story to Samuel P. P. Fay, Feb. 24, 1812, in *Life and Letters of Joseph Story*, ed. William Wetmore Story (Boston: Little & Brown, 1851), 1:215.
12. For an example of Washington acting as the Court's travel agent, see letter from Bushrod Washington to William Cranch, Dec. 27, 1816, Cincinnati History Museum and Library (stating that "the judges appeared to be all pleased with their situation last winter" but that he would try to arrange a stay with "Mrs. Wadsworth. We require 7 bedrooms and one dining room").
13. Letter from John Marshall to Bushrod Washington, Dec. 29, 1814, in *The Papers of John Marshall Digital Edition*, ed. Charles Hobson (Charlottesville: University of Virginia Press, 2014).
14. 5 U.S. (1 Cranch) 1 (1801). *Talbot* was the only opinion of the August 1801 session.
15. See *Talbot*, 5 U.S. (1 Cranch) at 27; Smith, *Marshall*, 291–92.
16. See *Talbot*, 5 U.S. (1 Cranch) at 3–4; Smith, *Marshall*, 292.
17. See *Bas v. Tingy*, 4 U.S. (4 Dall.) 37, 42 (1800).
18. Ibid. The case was argued in the Supreme Court prior to Marshall's appointment but was not decided. See *Talbot*, 5 U.S. (1 Cranch) at 24n*; see also *The Amelia*, 4 U.S. (4 Dall.) 34 (1800) (describing the inconclusive first argument).
19. See *Talbot*, 5 U.S. (1 Cranch) at 36–43. There was a dispute about whether French law was properly part of the record in the case, which may explain why Bushrod ruled the other way on circuit (at 37–38). If only international law was considered, then no salvage was warranted (at 43).
20. The Court conceded that there was no proof that France did, in fact, treat neutral ships as prizes, but said that such proof was unnecessary. See ibid. at 40.
21. See ibid. at 43–45 (awarding one-sixth of the net value of vessel and its cargo with costs subtracted, rather than one-half with no costs subtracted); Smith, *Marshall*, 294 (pointing out that in salvage cases subtracting costs was unusual).
22. The case tallies going forward come from a review of the Supreme Court's opinions in the official compilation of the *United States Reports*. I will not cite each and every case.
23. Letter from William Johnson to Thomas Jefferson, Dec. 10, 1822, https://founders.archives.gov/?q=William%20johnson%201822%20Author%3A%22Johnson%2C%20William%22&s=1511311111&r=3.

24. Following President Pendleton's death in 1803, the Virginia Court of Appeals resumed the practice of issuing seriatim opinions. See M. Todd Henderson, "From Seriatim to Consensus and Back Again: A Theory of Dissent," *Supreme Court Review* 2007 (2007): 304.
25. Letter from Joseph Story to Henry Wheaton, Apr. 18, 1818, in *Letters of Joseph Story*, 1:303–4.
26. Letter from Bushrod Washington to Alexander Hamilton, Nov. 21, 1801, in *The Papers of Alexander Hamilton*, ed. Harold C. Syrett (New York: Columbia University Press, 1974), 25:433.
27. See Thomas Jefferson, "First Inaugural Address," in James D. Richardson, ed., *A Compilation of the Messages and Papers of the Presidents* (New York: Bureau of National Literature, Inc., 1897), 1:311.
28. U.S. Const., art. III, § 1; Akhil Reed Amar, *America's Constitution: A Biography* (New York: Random House, 2005), 222.
29. See U.S. Const., art. I, § 3, cl. 6.
30. For a rich discussion of these competing arguments, see Ackerman, *Failure of the Founding Fathers*, 149–57. One finesse could have been if Congress had continued to pay the circuit judges while giving them nothing to do. Congress, though, refused even to pay their salaries, despite efforts to get it to do so. See generally Jed Glickstein, "After Midnight: The Circuit Judges and the Repeal of the Judiciary Act of 1801," *Yale Journal of Law and the Humanities* 24 (2012): 543–78 (describing the political efforts and short-lived litigation over the salary issue).
31. Letter from Alexander Hamilton to James A. Bayard, Apr. 16–21, 1802, in *Papers of Alexander Hamilton*, 25:609. The precise date of this letter is unknown.
32. See Ackerman, *Failure of the Founding Fathers*, 159; R. Kent Newmyer, *John Marshall and the Heroic Age of the Supreme Court* (Baton Rouge: Louisiana State University Press, 2001), 153. Another possible objective of the cancellation was to make it more difficult for the justices to agree on a strike, to the extent that a face-to-face discussion would have led to that choice.
33. See Newmyer, *Heroic Age*, 153 (noting the date of the repeal); see also Judiciary Act of 1802, ch. 31; 2 Stat. 256 (setting forth the details of the court system in the aftermath of repeal).
34. See Ackerman, *Failure of the Founding Fathers*, 277–97 (reprinting the essays written by Judge Richard Bassett arguing that the repeal was unconstitutional and advocating a strike).
35. See *Hayburn's Case*, 2 U.S. (2 Dall.) 409 (1792); see Maeva Marcus and Robert Teir, "*Hayburn's Case*: A Misinterpretation of Precedent," *Wisconsin Law Review* 1988 (1988): 529–41 (explaining how the dispute unfolded).
36. See Marcus and Teir, "*Hayburn's Case*," 539–41 (describing the revision in 1793).
37. See letter from John Marshall to William Paterson, Apr. 19, 1802, in *Papers of John Marshall Digital Edition*. Justice Moore's response to the chief justice is unknown.
38. Marshall's stated concern was that the Constitution prohibited Supreme Court justices from also serving as circuit judges. See ibid.; see also letter from John Marshall to William Paterson, Apr. 6, 1802, in *Papers of John Marshall Digital Edition*

("I confess I have some strong constitutional scruples. I cannot well perceive how the performance of circuit duty by the Judges of the supreme court can be supported"). In part, this concern rested on the fact that the Constitution specified the circumstances under which the justices could hear cases in original jurisdiction, but as circuit judges they did so in circumstances well beyond what Article III described. The problem was that the justices had served as circuit judges prior to 1801, and thus the question was what weight that practice should receive.

39. Letter from Samuel Chase to John Marshall, Apr. 24, 1802, in *Papers of John Marshall Digital Edition*.
40. Letter from John Marshall to William Paterson, May 3, 1802, in *Papers of John Marshall Digital Edition*.
41. Letter from William Paterson to John Marshall, June 18, 1802, in *Papers of John Marshall Digital Edition*; see Ackerman, *Failure of the Founding Fathers*, 170; Smith, *Marshall*, 308.
42. See Ackerman, *Failure of the Founding Fathers*, 170; Smith, *Marshall*, 307–8.
43. See Ackerman, *Failure of the Founding Fathers*, 173–75; Paul, *Without Precedent*, 247.
44. See Paul, *Without Precedent*, 247; Smith, *Marshall*, 310.
45. See *Stuart v. Laird*, 5 U.S. (1 Cranch) 299 (1803). Chief Justice Marshall recused himself from *Stuart* because he heard the case on circuit (at 308), though he may have used this as an excuse to avoid writing an opinion that capitulated to Congress. Justice Paterson wrote the opinion because Justice Cushing was ill, making Paterson the senior associate justice hearing the case. After resuming circuit riding, the justices would have found declaring the repeal of the Judiciary Act of 1801 unconstitutional nearly impossible. For instance, all the acts taken by the circuit courts with the justices since the resumption would have been invalidated, which would have been incredibly disruptive.
46. See Newmyer, *Heroic Age*, 154–56; Smith, *Marshall*, 305–9.
47. See Albert J. Beveridge, *The Life of John Marshall* (Boston: Houghton & Mifflin, 1919), 3:122 (stating that Marshall proposed that the justices go on strike but that his colleagues "had not the courage to adopt the heroic course Marshall had recommended . . . So Marshall reluctantly abandoned his bold plan"); see also Ackerman, *Failure of the Founding Fathers*, 164–71 (interpreting the internal correspondence as an effort at persuasion).
48. See Ackerman, *Failure of the Founding Fathers*, 200; Paul, *Without Precedent*, 251; see also letter from Thomas Jefferson to the House of Represenatives, Feb. 3, 1803, in *The Papers of Thomas Jefferson*, ed. Julian P. Boyd (Princeton, NJ: Princeton University Press, 1958), 39:443–44 (referring Judge Pickering's case to the House).
49. Frank O. Bowman III, *High Crimes and Misdemeanors: A History of Impeachment for the Age of Trump* (New York: Cambridge University Press, 2019), 137–38 (quoting from the articles of impeachment against Judge Pickering), 138–39 (discussing the case). Pickering was not accused of committing a crime, which raises a question about whether his impeachment and removal were appropriate. He was probably just incapable of carrying out his responsibilities due to illness, which is hard to describe as a "high crime and misdemeanor." U.S. Const., art. II, § 4.

50. See *Marbury v. Madison*, 5 U.S. (1 Cranch) 137 (1803). The academic literature on *Marbury* is enormous and my research yielded no new information about the case, so the text provides only a summary of the facts and the decision. For a stimulating overview of *Marbury* and its relationship to the appropriate role of judges, see Lawrence Lessig, *Fidelity and Constraint: How the Supreme Court Has Read the American Constitution* (New York: Oxford University Press, 2019), 23–33.
51. The reason is unclear. Marshall's brother Thomas submitted an affidavit stating that the secretary of state delegated the task to him, but that he had to deliver many commissions and just did not get to Marbury's. But there are lingering doubts about whether Thomas Marshall's affidavit was accurate. See Newmyer, *Heroic Age*, 159, 160–62; see also Paul, *Without Precedent*, 253–54.
52. Given Marshall's direct role in the facts of the case, there is a strong argument that he was ethically bound to recuse himself. See Friedman, *Will of the People*, 63. Recusal standards were not the same then as they are now, but Marshall was probably just bound and determined to participate in *Marbury*.
53. See U.S. Const., art. III, § 2, cl. 2 ("In all Cases affecting Ambassadors, other public Ministers and Consuls, and those in which a State shall be [a] Party, the Supreme Court shall have original Jurisdiction").
54. See Smith, *Marshall*, 314–15.
55. Evidently this boycott did create any ill will between Washington and Madison, as a month after *Marbury* was decided the justice wrote a note thanking the secretary of state for a recent book loan. See letter from Bushrod Washington to James Madison, Mar. 28, 1803, in *Papers of James Madison: Secretary of State Series*, ed. Mary Hackett, J. C. A. Stagg, Jeanne Kerr Cross, Susan Holbrook Perdue, and Ellen J. Barber (Charlottesville: University Press of Virginia, 1998), 4:455–56.
56. The justices announced *Marbury* at the boarding house because Justice Chase was ill. See Paul, *Without Precedent*, 254–55; Smith, *Marshall*, 318–19. Stelle's Hotel was located at what is now part of the Library of Congress.
57. See *Marbury*, 5 U.S. (1 Cranch) at 153–80. The statement about Marbury's right to the commission was gratuitous, as the Court held that jurisdiction was lacking.
58. See Jacob E. Cooke, ed., *The Federalist* (Hanover, NH: Wesleyan University Press, 1961), 521–30.
59. See, e.g., Amar, *America's Constitution*, 232; Robert H. Bork, *The Tempting of America: The Political Seduction of the Law* (New York: The Free Press, 1990), 23–24; see also Judiciary Act of 1789, ch. 20, § 13, 1 Stat. 77 (stating that the Supreme Court may issue mandamus writs in the exercise of its appellate jurisdiction, not its original jurisdiction).
60. *Marbury*, 5 U.S. (1 Cranch) at 177.
61. The exception was *Stuart v. Laird*, which was discussed in an earlier note and was written by Justice Paterson.
62. Walter Isaacson, *Benjamin Franklin: An American Life* (New York: Simon and Schuster, 2008), 313.
63. Justice Washington did not hold a circuit court in the fall of 1803 due to a yellow fever epidemic. See letter from Bushrod Washington to Richard Peters, Sept. 25, 1803,

Historical Society of Pennsylvania (discussing the outbreak in Philadelphia and deciding to adjourn the court).

64. See Smith, *Marshall*, 336–37. For a thorough overview of the Chase impeachment, see William H. Rehnquist, *Grand Inquests: The Historic Impeachments of Justice Samuel Chase and President Andrew Johnson* (New York: William Morrow, 1992), 15–134.
65. Ackerman, *Failure of the Founding Fathers*, 202. In this era, judges exercised influence over grand juries in a way that they do not today and commented on the issues under review. See Bowman, *High Crimes and Misdemeanors*, 134.
66. Friedman, *Will of the People*, 66.
67. Jon Meacham, *Thomas Jefferson and the Art of Power* (New York: Random House, 2012), 375.
68. See letter from Bushrod Washington to Samuel Chase, Jan. 24, 1804, Historical Society of Pennsylvania.
69. See Ackerman, *Failure of the Founding Fathers*, 202.
70. 13 *Annals of Congress* 1239 (1804) (quoting the seventh article of impeachment against Justice Chase), and 1237–38; see also Bowman, *High Crimes and Misdemeanors*, 128–36 (discussing the Chase impeachment).
71. See Ackerman, *Failure of the Founding Fathers*, 201.
72. See ibid., 200–201; Paul, *Without Precedent*, 251.
73. See Smith, *Marshall*, 336, 338.
74. The exception was *Ogden v. Blackledge*, a brief decision by Justice Cushing (the senior associate justice present) in a case where Marshall recused himself because he heard the case on circuit. See *Ogden v. Blackledge*, 6 U.S. (2 Cranch.) 272 (1804); Smith, *Marshall*, 632n90.
75. See *National Intelligencer and Washington Advertiser*, Mar. 16, 1804, 1.
76. See ibid.; see also Smith, *Marshall*, 342 (stating that Marshall was deposed about the same alleged conversation).
77. See Smith, *Marshall*, 342. Chase's alleged comment was about James Callender, who was a fierce critic of the Adams administration but later turned against Jefferson and disclosed Jefferson's sexual relationship with Sally Hemings. See Meacham, *Art of Power*, 378–79; see also Annette Gordon-Reed, *The Hemingses of Monticello* (New York: W. W. Norton & Company, 2008), 554–59 (discussing the background).
78. *National Intelligencer and Washington Advertiser*, Mar. 16, 1804, at 1; see Smith, *Marshall*, 342 (stating that Marshall took the same line).
79. Washington maintained a studied political neutrality in public for the rest of his life. In 1828, a newspaper erroneously reported that the justice had endorsed President John Quincy Adams for reelection; the paper confused the justice with his nephew Bushrod, who did endorse President Adams and also lived at Mount Vernon. See "Judge Washington," *Delaware Journal*, June 27, 1828 (quoting another article referring to a "Bushrod Washington Jr." who was "expecting soon to leave the country, not to return until after the election has passed"). See also *Alexandria Gazette*, Nov. 22, 1827 (listing Bushrod Washington Jr. as among a group of Fairfax County citizens opposed to Andrew Jackson's election as president).

80. Letter from Bushrod Washington to Edward S. Burd, Jan. 7, 1805, in "The Letters of Bushrod Washington (1762–1829) in the Hampton L. Carson Collection of the Free Library of Philadelphia," ed. Howell J. Heaney, *American Journal of Legal History* 2 (1958): 165. Heaney dated this letter as January 1804, but that cannot be correct given the start date of Chase's trial.
81. See Bowman, *High Crimes and Misdemeanors*, 128; Ron Chernow, *Alexander Hamilton* (New York: Penguin Books, 2004), 719.
82. See Smith, *Marshall*, 344.
83. See Paul, *Without Precedent*, 279–81; Smith, *Marshall*, 344–55.
84. See Jackson, *Struggle for Judicial Supremacy*, 28. Specifically, Marshall stated that permitting Congress to overrule court decisions was preferable to the impeachment and removal of judges for their decisions. See also Ackerman, *Failure of the Founding Fathers*, 220.
85. See Bowman, *High Crimes and Misdemeanors*, 135; Friedman, *Will of the People*, 67. The largest vote against Chase on an article of impeachment was 19–15, which was well short of the two-thirds support required.
86. See Ackerman, *Failure of the Founding Fathers*, 212–13; see also Stephen Skowronek, *The Politics Presidents Make: Leadership from John Adams to Bill Clinton* (Cambridge, MA: Harvard University Press, 1997), 80–81 (providing background on the fracture within Republican ranks over the Yazoo land deal that would lead to the Supreme Court's decision in *Fletcher v. Peck*).
87. See Friedman, *Will of the People*, 67–68.
88. See Paul, *Without Precedent*, 298; Smith, *Marshall*, 342.
89. See *Lambert's Lessee v. Paine*, 7 U.S. (3 Cranch) 97, 126–130 (1805) (opinion of Johnson, J.); at 130–33 (Washington, J., dissenting); at 133–38 (opinion of Paterson, J.); at 138–39 (opinion of Cushing, J.). Marshall recused himself because in private practice he had been a lawyer for one of the parties (at 117), and Chase was absent due to the impeachment trial.
90. See *Marine Ins. Co. v. Wilson*, 7 U.S. (3 Cranch) 187 (1805) (contract case decided seriatim by Cushing, Paterson, and Washington in which the chief justice recused himself); see also *Randolph v. Ware*, 7 U.S. (3 Cranch) 503 (1806) (insurance case decided seriatim by four justices); *United States v. Heth*, 7 U.S. (3 Cranch) 399 (1806) (statutory interpretation applying to customs collectors decided seriatim by four justices); *The Marine Ins. Co. of Alexandria v. Tucker*, 7 U.S. (3 Cranch) 357 (1806) (marine insurance case decided seriatim by four justices). Justice Chase missed many cases in 1806 due to illness.
91. Letter from William Johnson to Thomas Jefferson, Dec. 10, 1822, https://founders.archives.gov/?q=William%20johnson%201822%20Author%3A%22Johnson%2C%20William%22&s=1511311111&r=3.
92. See *Pierce v. Turner*, 9 U.S. (5 Cranch) 154 (1809). Marshall participated in *Pierce*, and thus the seniority custom must have been relaxed by this point.
93. See Newmyer, *Heroic Age*, 90; Smith, *Marshall*, 348; see also *United States v. Fisher*, 6 U.S. (2 Cranch) 358 (1805).
94. *Fisher*, 6 U.S. (2 Cranch) at 396.

95. 17 U.S. (4 Wheat.) 316 (1819).
96. *Fisher*, 6 U.S. (2 Cranch) at 385–96.
97. See *United States v. Fisher*, 25 F. Cas. 1087 (No. 15,103) (C.C.D. Pa 1803), reversed by 6 U.S. (2 Cranch) 358 (1805).
98. *Fisher*, 6 U.S. (2 Cranch) at 397 (statement of Washington, J.). Today no justice would make a statement when recused, but in this era recusal could mean only not voting on the case.
99. Ibid. at 397–98 (statement of Washington, J.).
100. Ibid. at 403 (statement of Washington, J).
101. 25 U.S. (12 Wheat.) 213 (1827).
102. See Ackerman, *Failure of the Founding Fathers*, 224–26.
103. The exception was *Simms v. Slacum*, where Justice Paterson offered a partial dissent. See 7 U.S. (3 Cranch) 300 (1806).
104. Ralph Ketcham, *James Madison: A Biography* (Charlottesville: University Press of Virginia, 1990), 447. Justice Johnson and John Quincy Adams also attended the dinner.

Chapter 7

1. See Ron Chernow, *Washington: A Life* (New York: Penguin Books, 2010), 816; Robert F. Dalzell Jr. and Lee Baldwin Dalzwell, *George Washington's Mount Vernon: At Home in Revolutionary America* (New York: Oxford University Press, 1998), 225. Bushrod's father-in-law, Thomas Blackburn, died a year after Martha. See David Leslie Annis, "Mr. Bushrod Washington, Supreme Court Justice on the Marshall Court," PhD diss., Notre Dame University, 1974, 128; letter from Caleb P. Wayne to Bushrod Washington, Nov. 27, 1803, Historical Society of Pennsylvania (expressing condolences for "the demise of the worthy Colonel Blackburn"). Family lore says that Bushrod attended Martha's funeral, but I cannot confirm this.
2. Hannah Washington's will made clear that she was fearful of being buried alive, as she set forth lengthy instructions to prevent that fate, such as "when it is thought I am dead that I remain in my bed quite undisturbed in every respect my face to be uncovered" and that she stay that way until "putrefaction." Last Will and Testament of Hannah Bushrod Washington, Apr. 26, 1801, Mount Vernon Library.
3. See Scott E. Casper, *Sarah Johnson's Mount Vernon: The Forgotten Memory of An American Shrine* (New York: Hill and Wang, 2008), 25; see also Articles of Agreement between Bushrod Washington and George Lewis, Aug. 18, 1802, Historical Society of Pennsylvania (describing the sale of Bushfield). Washington sold Walnut Farm and his other family properties after he inherited Mount Vernon. See letter from Bushrod Washington to William Frederick, July 5, 1804, Huntington Library (describing these transactions).
4. See Casper, *Sarah Johnson's Mount Vernon*, 26.

5. My account is drawn in part from a description of the mansion by a visitor who was there two days before Martha died. See Jean B. Lee, ed., *Experiencing Mount Vernon: Eyewitness Accounts, 1784–1865* (Charlottesville: University of Virginia Press, 2006), 97–98 (quoting a diary entry by Thomas Pim Cope); see also Chernow, *Washington*, 476–78 (describing the exterior of Mount Vernon). The exterior of the house that tourists visit today looks much the same as in 1802, as the goal of the Mount Vernon Ladies' Association, which now runs the estate as a museum, is to restore the house to its 1799 appearance.
6. See Dalzell and Dalzell, *Mount Vernon*, 225 (describing the auction). The only items that Bushrod inherited were the Bastille key and a portrait of Lawrence Washington (George's half-brother), which still hang on the walls of Mount Vernon.
7. See letter from Bushrod Washington to Elizabeth Willing Powel, May 10, 1804, Mount Vernon Library. Years later, while he was living at Mount Vernon, Eliza sent him a muffin recipe. See letter from Elizabeth Willing Powel to Bushrod Washington, Nov. 13, 1816, Mount Vernon Library.
8. See Casper, *Sarah Johnson's Mount Vernon*, 24; Mary V. Thompson, "*The Only Unavoidable Subject of Regret*": *George Washington, Slavery, and the Enslaved Community at Mount Vernon* (Charlottesville: University of Virginia Press, 2019), 147.
9. See Casper, *Sarah Johnson's Mount Vernon*, 6, 8–10 (describing the household enslaved people); Thompson, *Subject of Regret*, 147.
10. See Casper, *Sarah Johnson's Mount Vernon*, 10.
11. See Chernow, *Washington*, 777.
12. Letter from Bushrod Washington to Doctor Morse, Feb. 18, 1800, Historical Society of Pennsylvania.
13. See Jean Edward Smith, *John Marshall: Definer of a Nation* (New York: Henry Holt and Company, 1996), 328; letter from Bushrod Washington to Caleb P. Wayne, April 1800, Historical Society of Pennsylvania (indicating Marshall's interest in writing the book).
14. See Smith, *Marshall*, 328; letter from Bushrod Washington to unknown recipient, Sept. 16, 1801, Harvard University Library (describing the transfer of some papers to Marshall).
15. See letter from Bushrod Washington to Alexander Hamilton, Apr. 15, 1802, in *The Papers of Alexander Hamilton*, ed. Harold C. Syrett (New York: Columbia University Press, 1974), 25:602–5.
16. See Articles of Agreement between Bushrod Washington and Caleb P. Wayne, Sept. 22, 1802, Historical Society of Pennsylvania (stating the terms of the agreement and copyright).
17. Letter from Bushrod Washington to Caleb P. Wayne, Mar. 1, 1803, Historical Society of Pennsylvania.
18. See letter from Bushrod Washington to Caleb P. Wayne, Jan. 22, 1802, Historical Society of Pennsylvania (discussing the European copyright for the biography); see also letter from Bushrod Washington to Caleb P. Wayne, May 27, 1817, Historical Society of Pennsylvania (advising Wayne about renewing the copyright).

19. Smith, *Marshall*, 329.
20. See Joel Richard Paul, *Without Precedent: John Marshall and His Times* (New York: Riverhead Books, 2018), 250; Smith, *Marshall*, 331.
21. Letter from Thomas Jefferson to Joel Barlow, May 3, 1802, in *The Papers of Thomas Jefferson*, ed. Julian P. Boyd (Princeton, NJ: Princeton University Press, 1958), 37: 401.
22. Letter from Bushrod Washington to Caleb P. Wayne, Nov. 19, 1802, Historical Society of Pennsylvania.
23. See Paul, *Without Precedent*, 248; Smith, *Marshall*, 330. Bushrod wondered if the nation's postmasters, who were patronage appointees of President Jefferson, "will feel a disposition to advance the work." See letter from Bushrod Washington to Caleb P. Wayne, Mar. 1, 1803, Historical Society of Pennsylvania.
24. John Marshall, *The Life of George Washington*, 5 vols. (Philadelphia: C. P. Wayne, 1804–7).
25. Letter from John Marshall to Bushrod Washington, Mar. 25, 1804, in *The Papers of John Marshall Digital Edition*, ed. Charles Hobson (Charlottesville: University of Virginia Press, 2014). The letters concerning volume three of the biography are the only ones between Marshall and Washington that are available prior to 1814.
26. Letter from John Marshall to Bushrod Washington, Apr. 20, 1804, in *Papers of John Marshall Digital Edition*.
27. Letter from Bushrod Washington to Caleb P. Wayne, June 22, 1804, University of Virginia Library, Special Collections.
28. See Chernow, *Washington*, 814; see also Paul, *Without Precedent*, 248 (observing that almost the entire first volume inexplicably addressed the history of the colonies with nary a mention of George Washington).
29. Smith, *Marshall*, 331.
30. Chernow, *Washington*, 814.
31. Smith, *Marshall*, 331.
32. See Paul, *Without Precedent*, 250; Smith, *Marshall*, 329–30.
33. See, e.g., letter from Bushrod Washington to G. P. Wayne, Esq., Feb. 14, 1822, Morristown National Historical Park Library (discussing a second edition of the book); letter from John Marshall to Bushrod Washington, Dec. 27, 1821, in *Papers of John Marshall Digital Edition* (discussing a second edition); letter from John Marshall to Bushrod Washington, Sept. 2, 1820, in *Papers of John Marshall Digital Edition* (asking Bushrod questions about a letter referring to George's youth); see also Smith, *Marshall*, 486–87 (discussing publication of the first volume of the second edition).
34. See letter from John Marshall to Bushrod Washington, Apr. 15, 1822, in *Papers of John Marshall Digital Edition* (discussing the chief justice's research); letter from John Marshall to Bushrod Washington, May 3, 1823, in *Papers of John Marshall Digital Edition* (stating that he "deposited with the clerk of the district court the copy of the title of your reports").
35. See letter from Bushrod Washington to Alexander Hamilton, Nov. 21, 1801, in *Papers of Alexander Hamilton*, 25: 433–34.
36. Letter from John Marshall to William Paterson, May 3, 1802, in *Papers of John Marshall Digital Edition*. Marshall was quoting from a letter that he received from

Washington—the same one in which the justice expressed his opposition to going on strike.

37. The justice received many requests for personal items that had belonged to his uncle. See letter from Bushrod Washington to Captain Bliss, Dec. 24, 1811, American Philosophical Society Library (stating that he was sharing "a sprig of cedar from one of the trees which shade the tomb" and stating that he might provide "the flannel morning gown which was worn by my uncle to [the] time of his death").
38. See, e.g., letter from James Madison to Bushrod Washington, Aug. 18, 1819, in *The Papers of James Madison: Retirement Series*, ed. David Mattern, J. C. A. Stagg, Mary Parke Johnson, and Anne Mandeville Colony (Charlottesville: University of Virginia Press, 2009), 1:500 (making the initial request); letter from Bushrod Washington to James Madison, Sept. 14, 1819, in *Papers of James Madison: Retirement Series*, 1:513–14 (granting the request); letter from James Madison to Bushrod Washington, Oct. 14, 1820, in *Papers of James Madison: Retirement Series*, 2:130–31; see also letter from Marquis de Lafayette to Bushrod Washington, Aug. 13, 1825, Indiana University, Lilly Library Collection (stating that Lafayette's copies were "lost in the French Revolution"); letter from Marquis de Lafayette to Bushrod Washington, Sept. 11, 1827, Indiana University, Lilly Library Collection (thanking the justice and informing him that the letters relating to "the Virginia Campaign, 1781" were being returned); Laura Auricchio, *The Marquis: Lafayette Reconsidered* (New York: Alfred A. Knopf, 2014), 297–301 (describing Lafayette's visit to America as an old man, which included a trip to Mount Vernon in 1824).
39. See letter from Eliza Schuyler Hamilton to Bushrod Washington, month and date unknown, 1818, Mount Vernon Library (thanking the justice for his help and inviting him and Nancy to stay with her in New York); letter from Bushrod Washington to John Marshall, Aug. 10, 1818, Mount Vernon Library (stating that "Mrs. Hamilton stayed for a fortnight"); letter from Bushrod Washington to Eliza Schuyler Hamilton, Nov. 27, 1818, Mount Vernon Library (stating that "immediately after you left Mount Vernon" he had written to Chief Justice Marshall to obtain some letters).
40. See letter from Eliza Schuyler Hamilton to Bushrod Washington, Sept. 19, 1825, Mount Vernon Library; John Avlon, *Washington's Farewell: The Founding Father's Warning to Future Generations* (New York: Simon & Schuster, 2018), 223–26.
41. See Avlon, *Washington's Farewell*, 224; cf. Chernow, *Hamilton*, 2–3 (describing Eliza's effort to rehabilitate Hamilton after his death).
42. Letter from Bushrod Washington to Eliza Schuyler Hamilton, Nov. 27, 1825, Mount Vernon Library.
43. See Avlon, *Washington's Farewell*, 225; Michael J. Klarman, *The Framers' Coup: The Making of the United States Constitution* (New York: Oxford University Press, 2016), 38–39n, 40 (describing King).
44. See letter from John Marshall to Bushrod Washington, Oct. 3, 1825, in *Papers of John Marshall Digital Edition*; see also letter from John Marshall to Bushrod Washington, June 20, 1825, in *Papers of John Marshall Digital Edition* ("It may also be thought that this correspondence was among the General's papers and was concealed by you and myself. The fact undoubtedly is that we have never seen it").

45. Letter from John Marshall to Bushrod Washington, Apr. 9, 1825, in *Papers of John Marshall Digital Edition*. No letters from Washington to Marshall about the papers project survive.
46. Letter from John Marshall to Bushrod Washington, Dec. 11, 1824, in *Papers of John Marshall Digital Edition*.
47. See letter from Bushrod Washington to Jared Sparks, Sept. 6, 1827, Morristown National Historical Park Library (putting Sparks in charge of the project); Chernow, *Washington*, 814; see also letter from Bushrod Washington to Jared Sparks, Mar. 13, 1826, Morristown National Historical Park Library ("A part of the work which you now contemplate writing has for some years past engaged the attention and commanded the labours of [the] Chief Justice and myself")
48. Letter from John Marshall to Bushrod Washington, Dec. 27, 1826, in *Papers of John Marshall Digital Edition*.
49. See Smith, *Marshall*, 425.
50. See letter from Bushrod Washington to Joseph Hopkinson, Mar. 30, 1824, Historical Society of Pennsylvania; letter from Bushrod Washington to General Jan Pieter van Suchtelen, Aug. 10, 1818, Mount Vernon Library; Alexis Coe, *You Never Forget Your First: A Biography of George Washington* (New York: Viking Press, 2020), 249n7.
51. I am indebted to Professor John Mikhail for first raising this point to me.
52. See Mary Sarah Bilder, *Madison's Hand: Revising the Constitutional* Convention (Cambridge, MA: Harvard University Press, 2015), 236–37.
53. Justice Cushing (who died in 1810) served in the Massachusetts ratifying convention for the Constitution. See Pauline Maier, *Ratification: The People Debate the Constitution, 1787–1788* (New York: Simon and Schuster, 2010), 193–94; Paul, *Without Precedent*, 307.
54. See Herbert A. Johnson, "Bushrod Washington." *Vanderbilt Law Review* 62 (2009): 450.
55. See Horace Binney, *Bushrod Washington* (Philadelphia: C. Sherman & Son, 1858), 24 (stating that Nancy "uniformly attended him upon his Circuit").
56. *The Autobiography of Martin Van Buren*, ed. John C. Fitzpatrick (Washington, DC: Government Printing Office, 1920), 2:177. This was the visit where Bushrod relayed the story (told in Chapter 5) about how his uncle had talked him into running for Congress.
57. See ibid., 2:63–64; see generally James Kent, *Commentaries on American Law*, 4 vols. (New York: O. Halsted, 1826) (providing one of the leading discussions prior to the Civil War).
58. See Chernow, *Washington*, 708–9; Dalzell and Dalzell, *Mount Vernon*, 196–97; see also Coe, *You Never Forget Your First*, 116 (quoting George's letter to his mother that described Mount Vernon as "a well resorted tavern").
59. See Matthew R. Costello, *Property of the Nation: George Washington's Tomb, Mount Vernon, and the Memory of the First President* (Lawrence: University Press of Kansas, 2018), 52.
60. Lee, *Experiencing Mount Vernon*, 129–30.

61. Reuben Gold Thwaites, ed., *Early Western Travels, 1748–1846* (Cleveland: Arthur H. Clark Co., 1905), 12:123 (quoting a diary entry from the visitor).
62. See Costello, *Property of the Nation*, 54.
63. Lee, *Experiencing Mount Vernon*, 118–19.
64. See ibid., 127–28; see also *Richmond Enquirer*, May 30, 1826 (containing an initial description of the incident, Washington's reply alleging "misrepresentations" in the story, and a follow-up report). The crux of the dispute was that some of the congressmen felt that Bushrod was rude to them (the congressional view was that "they were never asked to go into the house or take a seat" and that "the manner of the Judge was violent"). He offered a semi-apology, in effect saying that he was sorry if they were offended ("I should feel very much mortified if I could suppose that my conduct was so understood by the members of that body; but if it was, I beg them to believe that . . . I had no intention to treat them otherwise than with respect").
65. Letter from John Marshall to Bushrod Washington, May 31, 1826, in *Papers of John Marshall Digital Edition*. Some religious publications cheered Bushrod's effort to keep the Sabbath holy. See Costello, *Property of the Nation*, 58.
66. Letter from Joseph Story to Sarah Wetmore Story, Feb. 27, 1821, in *Life and Letters of Joseph Story*, ed. William Wetmore Story (Boston: Little & Brown, 1851), 1:398–99; see Lee, *Experiencing Mount Vernon*, 117 ("The changes which have taken place are, however, chiefly produced by decay"). Bushrod did make some additions to the house, including a summerhouse near the Potomac that was shaped like a gazebo. See Costello, *Property of the Nation*, 158–59; Dalzell and Dalzell, *Mount Vernon*, 225.
67. Thwaites, *Early Western Travels*, 12:124.
68. In a similar vein, see letter from Horace Holley to Mary Austin Holley, Apr. 15, 1818, University of Michigan, William L. Clements Library (stating that the gardens are "in a bad condition, and so are all the grounds, and all the buildings").
69. Lee, *Experiencing Mount Vernon*, 105 (quoting a newspaper account from 1818).
70. Costello, *Property of the Nation*, 52–53 (quoting from Binney's unpublished autobiography, which is held by the Historical Society of Pennsylvania).
71. Ibid., 53.
72. See Casper, *Sarah Johnson's Mount Vernon*, 11. Bushrod did experiment with new crops (such as millet) in an attempt to improve the farm's yields. See letter from Bushrod Washington to Richard J. Peters, June 21, 1822, Historical Society of Pennsylvania.
73. Letter from Bushrod Washington to George Washington, Nov. 20, 1788, in *The Papers of George Washington: Presidential Series*, ed. W. W. Abbot, Dorothy Twohig, Philander D. Chase, David R. Hoth, Christine Sternberg Patrick, and Theodore J. Crackel (Charlottesville: University Press of Virginia, 1985–), 1:119.
74. Letter from Richard Peters to Bushrod Washington, July 30, 1810, Historical Society of Pennsylvania.
75. See Chernow, *Washington*, 705–9, 750–51, 778–79, 803. In fairness, George's extended absences from Mount Vernon during the Revolution and as president made supervising the estate very challenging.

76. See Casper, *Sarah Johnson's Mount Vernon*, 11; Jon Meacham, *Thomas Jefferson and the Art of Power* (New York: Random House, 2012), 478–79, 485–86, 496; David O. Stewart, *Madison's Gift: Five Partnerships That Built America* (New York: Simon and Schuster, 2015), 331–34; see also letter from Bushrod Washington to Richard Peters, May 27, 1817, Historical Society of Pennsylvania ("The farms of Virginia from one corner to the other of the state exhibit a sense of universal desolation").
77. "Judge Washington," *Niles' Register*, Sept. 29, 1821, 21:71.
78. Lee, *Experiencing Mount Vernon*, 130.
79. See Casper, *Sarah Johnson's Mount Vernon*, 12–13; Lee, *Experiencing Mount Vernon*, 131 (quoting a visitor who said "visitors plunder it of branches and shrubs").
80. See Casper, *Sarah Johnson's Mount Vernon*, 67; Lee, *Experiencing Mount Vernon*, 107 (quoting a visitor who mentioned Congress's request and Bushrod's refusal); see also letter from Louisa Catherine Johnson Adams to Charles Francis Adams, Mar. 27, 1823, https://founders.archives.gov/?q=%22Judge%20Washington%22&s=1511311111&r=11 ("Judge Washington received and entertained us with great politeness. We visited the tomb, the sight of which shocked me more than I can express—It is a disgrace to the Nation").
81. See Annis, "Mr. Bushrod Washington," 167–68; see also "The Memory of Washington," *Alexandria Gazette, Commercial and Political*, Feb. 29, 1816, 3 (discussing the debate in Congress that followed Virginia's request). There was also some concern that Washington's remains were not safe at Mount Vernon, especially since British forces got close to the estate in 1814. See Costello, *Property of the Nation*, 27.
82. Last Will and Testament, July 9, 1799, in *The Papers of George Washington: Retirement Series*, ed. W. W. Abbot and Dorothy Twohig (Charlottesville: University Press of Virginia, 1998–99), 4:491.
83. Annis, "Mr. Bushrod Washington," 170.
84. See Chernow, *Washington*, 811; Thomas J. Craughwell, *Stealing Lincoln's Body* (Cambridge, MA: Belknap Press, 2007), 77–79
85. Last Will and Testament, July 9, 1799, in *Papers of George Washington: Retirement Series*, 4:491.
86. There was a fire at Mount Vernon in 1804 that Bushrod attributed to arson, though no culprit was identified. See letter from Bushrod Washington to Richard Peters, May 21, 1804, Mount Vernon Library.
87. Letter from Bushrod Washington to Chancellor Henry DeSaussure, Nov. 29, 1814, New York Public Library. In 1814, the justice wrote secretary of state James Monroe to express his concerns about how British operations in Virginia were restricting supplies to Mount Vernon. See letter from Bushrod Washington to James Monroe, Sept. 15, 1814, National Archives.
88. Casper, *Sarah Johnson's Mount Vernon*, 12.
89. See ibid.
90. See letter from Bushrod Washington to George and Spotswood Washington, Feb. 25, 1827, University of Virginia Library, Special Collections; cf. letter from Bushrod Washington to unknown recipient, Nov. 14, 1824, Morristown National Historical

Park Library (praising a manuscript on "Letters on the Sacrament in the Lord's Supper").

91. See Casper, *Sarah Johnson's Mount Vernon*, 14; Annis, "Mr. Bushrod Washington," 171.
92. See Casper, *Sarah Johnson's Mount Vernon*, 14.
93. See Binney, *Bushrod Washington*, 10 ("In later years, in consequence of his devotion to Mrs. Washington, then a valetudinarian, both in mind and body, he very much diminished the opportunity of his friends to see him in mixed society"); David Paul Brown, *The Forum: Or, Forty Years Full Practice at the Philadelphia Bar* (Philadelphia: Robert H. Small, Law Bookseller, 1856), 1:366 ("Say until 1810, before her infirmity became confirmed, he entered into social and convivial parties, and shared fully in their enjoyments; but the moment that he found that even his temporary absence disturbed his wife, he abandoned those scenes entirely").
94. Letter from Bushrod Washington to Edward S. Burd, Jan. 14, 1806, Mount Vernon Library.
95. See Paul, *Without Precedent*, 235 (noting Marshall's love of Madeira); letter from Bushrod Washington to John Marshall, May 2, 1810, in *Papers of John Marshall Digital Edition*; letter from Bushrod Washington to James Madison, Nov. 12, 1807, https://founders.archives.gov/?q=bushrod%20wine%20Author%3A%22Washington%2C%20Bushrod%22&s=1511311111&r=1.
96. Letter from Bushrod Washington to Joseph Story, June 18, 1824, Massachusetts Historical Society.
97. Binney, *Bushrod Washington*, 9. The author owns a copy of a brief letter from the justice to one of his wine merchants. See letter from Bushrod Washington to unknown recipient, June 14, 1808, on file with author (enclosing $29 for "a jug of Madeira wine and a jug of rum").
98. See letter from Bushrod Washington to James Rew, Mar. 10, 1807, Mount Vernon Library (discussing education expenses for his nephews John and Bushrod). The justice later supported his grandnephews at boarding school. See letter from Bushrod Washington to Gustavus H. Scott, Dec. 28, 1825, Morristown National Historical Park Library (discussing payments for the school).
99. See Last Will and Testament of Bushrod Washington, July 19, 1828, Mount Vernon Library.
100. See letter from Bushrod Washington to George Carter, Feb. 9, 1814, Huntington Library; letter from Bushrod Washington to George Carter, Jan. 19, 1813, University of Virginia Library, Special Collections.
101. See Casper, *Sarah Johnson's Mount Vernon*, 27, 29, which also notes that Jane and John Augustine spent part of their youth at Mount Vernon. See also Last Will and Testament of Bushrod Washington, July 19, 1828, Mount Vernon Library.
102. Letter from Bushrod Washington to George and Spotswood Washington, Feb. 25, 1827, University of Virginia Library, Special Collections.
103. See Casper, *Sarah Johnson's Mount Vernon*, 26.
104. See ibid., 25.
105. See Chernow, *Washington*, 815–16; Thompson, *Subject of Regret*, 311–12.

106. See letter from Bushrod Washington to Thomas C. James, Sept. 13, 1805, American Philosophical Society Library (expressing thanks for his election); Bushrod Washington's Membership in the American Antiquarian Society, Dec. 22, 1813, Chicago History Museum; letter from Edward Everett to Bushrod Washington, Mar. 29, 1825, Mount Vernon Library.
107. Letter from "Samuel George Washington" to Bushrod Washington, Sept. 19, 1823, Mount Vernon Library.
108. Ibid. A man with the same name wrote another letter a year later claiming to be Bushrod's son, which led the justice to complain about "some fool or knave calling himself Samuel G. Washington and my son." See letter from "Samuel George Washington" to Bushrod Washington, June 20, 1824, Mount Vernon Library.

Chapter 8

1. The best book on circuit riding by the Marshall Court justices is David Lynch, *The Role of the Circuit Courts in the Shaping of United States Law in the Early Republic: Supreme Court Justices Washington, Livingston, Story and Thompson on Circuit and on the Court* (Portland, OR: Hart Publishing, 2018). I do not agree with all of Lynch's conclusions, but his research is careful and his analysis thoughtful, especially as he was himself a former judge.
2. The Judiciary Act of 1802 provided that the Third Circuit would meet in April and October each year. See Judiciary Act of 1802, § 4, ch. 31; 2 Stat. 256. The Washingtons always traveled by coach, apparently because Nancy was fearful of going by either steamboat or train. See David Paul Brown, *The Forum: Or, Forty Years Full Practice at the Philadelphia Bar* (Philadelphia: Robert H. Small, Law Bookseller, 1856), 1:366–67. Little is known about how Bushrod spent his time when he was in New Jersey. Virtually all the descriptions of his circuit duty are about Philadelphia. The only interesting reference to his New Jersey service that I can find is about a dinner that the justice attended at Bispham's Hotel in Trenton with some of lawyers during one of his circuits there (ibid., 1:363–65).
3. "Obituary," 28 U.S. (3 Pet.) viii (1830). In Philadelphia, Bushrod and Nancy lived in various boarding houses. See letter from Bushrod Washington to Caleb P. Wayne, Oct. 15, 1811, Historical Society of Pennsylvania (stating that he was then living on Market Street).
4. The journal is described later in the chapter. But I should explain why I think that the manuscript is genuine. First, the script looks the same as the handwriting in other letters and documents that I have examined that were drafted by Justice Washington. Second, there is no reason to think that anyone would have forged a Bushrod Washington journal. The journal contains esoteric material of interest only to scholars, though no scholar took notice of those contents until recently. Justice Washington was also not a well-known figure such that there would have been a

market for fakes of his work. Finally, the journal has a rough quality (with cross-outs and marginal notes) that is inconsistent with a forgery.

5. See Lynch, *Role of Circuit Courts*, 39–41. When the circuit justice was absent, litigants could choose between filing their action in federal district court (if jurisdiction was available) or filing it in circuit court pending the circuit justice's return.
6. See, e.g., *Bank of the United States v. Northumberland Bank*, 2 F. Cas. 726, 727 (C.C.E.D. Pa. 1824) (No. 931) ("To the circuit courts was assigned original cognizance, concurrent with the state courts, of all suits of a civil nature, at common law or in equity, of a certain value, and the United States are plaintiffs, or an alien is a party, or the suit is between a citizen of the state where the suit is brought, and a citizen of another state. . . . It will be observed that this section bestows upon the circuit courts original jurisdiction only in civil suits at common law, and in equity, where the value in dispute exceeds the sum or value of $500, and where the parties to the suit are the United States, aliens, or citizens of different states").
7. Ex Parte *Cabrera*, 4 F. Cas. 964, 966 (C.C.D. Pa. 1805) (No. 2,278) (denying habeas corpus relief due to lack of jurisdiction); see *Kirkpatrick v. White*, 14 F. Cas. 685, 687 (C.C.D. Pa. 1826) (No. 7,850) ("We very truly regret that the authorities and the course of reasoning which has been stated, lead us inevitably to the conclusion, that the jurisdiction cannot be sustained in this case against the Lehigh Coal and Navigation Company; and we freely acknowledge, that we have struggled, as far as duty would sanction, to discover such reasons as we could safely and conscientiously abide by, to authorize us in coming to a different conclusion. Our duty is to follow where the rules of law or equity, and right reason lead, without looking to consequences; although, from a view of those consequences, we may be permitted, as we have done, to express our regret that the law is as we have stated it, or as we apprehend it to be").
8. Without getting too deep into the weeds on the Supreme Court's appellate jurisdiction, the Judiciary Act of 1802 stated that when the circuit justice and the district judge disagreed on a point of law, the point could be appealed to the Supreme Court. See Judiciary Act of 1802, § 6, ch. 31; 2 Stat. 256. In practice, this meant that the Supreme Court could exercise discretion and hear an appeal in almost any circuit case by having a circuit justice arrange a disagreement with a district judge. The frequency of that practice is hard to gauge from a modern vantage point.
9. Letter from Bushrod Washington to Richard Peters, Oct. 3, 1815, in "The Letters of Bushrod Washington (1762–1829) in the Hampton L. Carson Collection of the Free Library of Philadelphia," ed. Howell J. Heaney, *American Journal of Legal History* 2 (1958): 168; see letter from Richard Peters to Bushrod Washington, July 30, 1810, Historical Society of Pennsylvania (comparing Chief Justice Marshall to Minos, the mythical king of Crete, because "the true translation of Minos is 'thy Nose.' The Head of the Court is seated in the Middle; He is the Gnomon of the Face—not only, as the prominent Feature, but to bear the Brunt. Especially in Cases, where in the other Members; though not led by, yet follow their Nose").

   A vulgar example came in a letter to Washington that began: "I interrupt your agreeable Law Engagements with a Bagatelle." Letter from Richard Peters to Bushrod

Washington, Feb. 10, 1810, Historical Society of Pennsylvania. Peters then proceeded to describe a maritime case that he heard in district court that he called "the case of 'Splitting Hairs,'" which involved a seaman disabled by venereal disease who claimed lost wages from the vessel. Judge Peters said that defense counsel remarked that "it may be doubtful whether your Honor has had competent knowledge. . . . Sailors, in the Course of their Voyages, have many *hard rules*. . . . But we must *enter* into *the Subject alleged to have produced the Disability*, by Proof of *Capacity*—and not *for Duty*." After more cringeworthy innuendo of this sort, Peters said that the seaman's case "has been occasioned by *his* Fondness for the *Splitting of Hairs*" and awarded him half his wages.

10. Horace Binney, *Bushrod Washington* (Philadelphia: C. Sherman & Son, 1858), 17.
11. See Eduardo C. Robreno, "Learning to Do Justice: An Essay on the Development of the Lower Federal Courts in the Early Years of the Republic," *Rutgers Law Journal* 29 (1998): 567; see also Jean Edward Smith, *John Marshall: Definer of a Nation* (New York: Henry Holt and Company, 1996), 374 (giving the example of Marshall's letter to Peters on Aaron Burr's treason trial).
12. See Brown, *The Forum*, 1:362 (stating that Peters "was a man of great honesty of purpose and infinite wit, but certainly not a profound lawyer"); cf. Binney, *Bushrod Washington*, 17 ("Beside [Washington] there sat, during nearly all of his life, a most pleasant District Judge, Richard Peters, many years his senior, a very good Admiralty Judge, but much disposed to leave the watch on deck in all weathers to his sleepless colleague").
13. Letter from Bushrod Washington to Richard Peters, Mar. 15, 1826, Historical Society of Pennsylvania ("I called upon Mr. Webster and had some conversations with him upon the subject to which you alluded"; describing Senator Webster's view that pending legislation would pass and raise district judge "salaries to an amount so liberal as to render the office an object worth being sought after by able men of the profession"; lamenting "the shameful inadequacy of compensation which you have hitherto received"; "I know very few members of Congress but shall speak to such of them I do know"). The legislation that the justice discussed with Webster was not enacted and Judge Peters did not receive a raise.
14. See, e.g., Richard Peters Jr., ed., *Reports of Cases Determined in the Circuit Court of the United States, for the Third Circuit*, 4 vols. (Philadelphia: Phillip Nicklin), 1826–30.
15. See letter from Richard Peters Jr. to Robert Trimble, Mar. 5, 1827, Historical Society of Pennsylvania (telling Justice Trimble that he was applying for the position of Supreme Court Reporter and that "my friend Judge Washington most kindly recommended me to the Members of the Court for this office"); see also Craig Joyce, "The Rise of the Supreme Court Reporter: An Institutional Perspective," *Michigan Law Review* 83 (1985): 1351.
16. See Binney, *Bushrod Washington*, 11–12 (stating that Washington's "practice in Virginia having been chiefly in Chancery . . . he had not been previously familiar with Commercial Law; and he had had no experience at all, either in the superintendence or the practice of jury trials at Nisi Prius, after that fashion which prevails in Pennsylvania").

17. For maritime examples, see, e.g., *Phillips v. McCall*, 19 F. Cas. 517 (C.C.D. Pa. 1821) (No. 11,104) (affirming the dismissal of a ship surgeon's claim for salvage); *Caze v. Reilly*, 5 F. Cas. 332 (C.C.D. Pa. 1814) (No. 2,538) (assessing a general average claim); *Dederer v. Delaware Ins. Co.*, 7 F. Cas. 341 (C.C.D. Pa. 1807) (No. 3,733) (charging a jury in a barratry [embezzlement by a captain] case); see also *The Columbian Ins. Co. v. Ashby & Stribling*, 38 U.S. (13 Pet.) 331, 343 (1839) (citing Washington's maritime circuit opinion in *Caze* and praising "our late brother Mr. Justice Washington, than whom few judges had a clearer judgment, or more patient spirit of inquiry"). For commercial law, see Binney, *Bushrod Washington*, 12 (stating that Washington was "eminent" in commercial law notwithstanding his lack of background); see also *United States v. Hall*, 26 F. Cas. 84, 85 (C.C.D. Pa. 1809) (No. 15,285) ("In mercantile transactions, particularly, it has often become necessary, in order to arrive at the real intention of the parties, to inquire into the meaning of certain phrases, used in commercial instruments, perfectly well understood by those who use them, but which are otherwise ambiguous, and sometimes unintelligible. When the meaning of those terms is once ascertained, public convenience requires that they should receive a legal definition and be considered as immutable. Infinite confusion and uncertainty would prevail in legal proceedings, if the construction of commercial any more than of other instruments, should be confided to the jury, who might in one case decide one way, and vary it in some other, so as in truth to afford in none a rule by which men should govern themselves").
18. See, e.g., *Treadwell v. Bladen*, 24 F. Cas. 144, 156 (C.C.E.D. Pa. 1827) (No. 14,154) ("What constitutes form, and what principle, is often a nice [in other words, not obvious] question to decide; and upon none, are the witnesses who are examined in patent causes, even those who are skilled in the particular art, more apt to disagree"); *Ewer v. Coxe*, 8 F. Cas. 917 (C.C.E.D. Pa. 1824) (No. 4,584) (holding that a copyright infringement claim for a book could not be maintained because no copyright existed); *Isaacs v. Cooper*, 13 F. Cas. 153 (C.C.D. Pa. 1821) (No. 7,096) (invalidating a patent for lack of specificity); *Dixon v. Moyer*, 7 F. Cas. 758 (C.C.D. Pa. 1821) (No. 3,931) (rejecting a patent infringement claim on the ground that the patent did not adequately describe an advance over the prior art); *Evans v. Hettick*, 8 F. Cas. 861 (C.C.E.D. Pa. 1818) (No. 4.562) (canvassing the law on patent infringement).
19. See *Gray v. James*, 10 F. Cas. 1015, 1017 (C.C.D. Pa. 1817) (No. 5,718) ("What constitutes a difference in principle between two machines, is frequently a question of difficulty more especially if the difference in form is considerable, and the machinery complicated. But we think it may safely be laid down as a general rule, that where the machines are substantially the same, and operate in the same manner, to produce the same result, they must be in principle the same").
20. See *Binns v. Woodruff*, 3 F. Cas. 421, 423 (C.C.D. Pa. 1821) (No. 1,424) (rejecting a copyright claim for an engraving of the Declaration of Independence and stating that a person cannot "claim a copyright for a mere invention, the work of his imagination locked up in his own mind, or existing in a form not visible to others. Neither is he so entitled, unless he has not only invented, but also designed or represented the subject in some visible form").

21. In rare high-profile cases, an observer in the courtroom produced something closer to a verbatim transcript of a trial. See *The Trial of John H. Jones: First Lieutenant of the Privateer Schooner* Revenge, *on a Charge of Piracy, Including the Arguments of Counsel and Charge of Judge Washington* (Philadelphia: John Binns, 1813).
22. Letter from Bushrod Washington to Richard Peters Jr., Nov. 30, 1814, Historical Society of Pennsylvania; see Binney, *Bushrod Washington*, 27 (stating that Washington's reports "were for the most part written out in his note-books, *calamo currente* [that is, in a hasty way], as they are now written").
23. One example where Washington did use his reports to erase the past was *United States v. Passmore*. In *Passmore*, the defendant was tried for perjury even though there was no federal perjury statute. See *United States v. Passmore*, 4 U.S. (4 Dall.) 372, 372 (C.C.D. Pa. 1804) (No. 16,005). Consistent with his broader view, the justice apparently told the jury that federal courts had criminal common-law jurisdiction over perjury. See *United States v. McGill*, 4 U.S. (4 Dall.) 426, 429 (C.C.D. Pa. 1806) (No. 15,676) ("I have often decided that the federal courts have a common law jurisdiction in criminal cases"). When he prepared his report of the case years later, however, Washington told Peters: "Omit the argument to show that the common law supports a rule of decision in criminal cases in the federal courts, because it is irrelevant to the case and unnecessarily prolongs the opinion." Letter from Bushrod Washington to Richard Peters Jr., Dec. 24, 1816, Historical Society of Pennsylvania. Another motivation for omitting the argument was that the Supreme Court had held in 1812 (with Washington absent due to illness) that federal courts did not have criminal common-law jurisdiction. See *United States v. Hudson & Goodwin*, 11 U.S. (7 Cranch.) 32 (1812). Justice Washington told Peters, "I hoped that by not abandoning the doctrine, it might again become popular and maintain its just ground. In this I have been disappointed, and of course have no wish to disturb the subsequent decision of the Supreme Court"). Letter from Bushrod Washington to Richard Peters Jr., Dec. 24, 1816, Historical Society of Pennsylvania; see Bruce Ackerman, *The Failure of the Founding Fathers: Jefferson, Marshall, and the Rise of Presidential Democracy* (Cambridge, MA: Harvard University Press, 2005), 240 (quoting Washington's comment during an oral argument that he had wanted to revisit *Hudson & Goodwin* earlier in 1816, the failure of which probably convinced him that the issue was settled).

    Passmore is a curious case. In the brief report that the justice let Peters publish, he told the jury that Passmore could not be convicted of perjury because the federal bankruptcy statute that led to his alleged perjury was subsequently repealed. See *Passmore*, 4 U.S. (4 Dall.) at 373. This makes no sense. Perjury is a crime that is independent of any other related law. One scholar suggests that Passmore was a popular Republican in Pennsylvania and that Washington concocted an excuse to obtain an acquittal to avoid a possible impeachment by the House of Representatives. See David A. Faber, "Justice Bushrod Washington and the Age of Discovery in American Law," *West Virginia Law Review* 102 (2000): 757; see also Henry Adams, *History of the United States During the First Administration of Thomas Jefferson* (New York: Charles Scribner & Sons, Inc., 1903), 2:161 (quoting a letter stating that someone named Passmore was accused of contempt in state court and that this might lead to the impeachment of judges in

Pennsylvania). Perhaps Washington was trying to cover his tracks by deleting the portion of *Passmore* that discussed common-law crimes. There is no way to know for sure.

24. Letter from Bushrod Washington to Richard Peters Jr., Dec. 24, 1816, Historical Society of Pennsylvania ("I have read over all of the cases in my notebooks to the end of the fall term of 1809, with some attention, and now enclose you some observations upon some of the cases as seemed to merit attention"). For an example of how Justice Washington worked on publishing reports of Supreme Court opinions, see letter from Bushrod Washington to Henry Wheaton, May 24, 1817, J. P. Morgan Library.
25. General information about the Chicago History Museum, which houses the collection of the Chicago Historical Society, can be found at www.chicagohistory.org.
26. See *Le Tigre*, 15 F. Cas. 404 (C.C.D. N.J. 1820) (No. 8,281); see also *Ogden v. Saunders*, 25 U.S. (12 Wheat.) 213 (1827) (opinion of Washington, J.).
27. The information about Gunther and his items that are now in the Chicago History Museum comes from the museum's exhibits and from an email from Leslie Martin, a reference librarian at the museum, to the author dated September 12, 2018.
28. Brown, *The Forum*, 2:194; see Binney, *Bushrod Washington*, 28–29; cf. Joseph Hopkinson, *Eulogium in Commemoration of the Hon. Bushrod Washington, Late One of the Justices of the Supreme Court of the United States* (Philadelphia: T. S. Manning, 1830), 15 (telling members of the bar: "He loved you—he respected you—he was proud of you—but he yielded not a jot of his independence; he gave not a line of his duty, to any of you").
29. See, e.g., Robert J. Lukens, "Jarod Ingersoll's Rejection of Appointment as One of the 'Midnight Judges' of 1801: Foolhardy or Farsighted?," *Temple Law Review* 70 (1997): 202–4. Ingersoll's son, Charles Jared Ingersoll, also practiced in the circuit.
30. Letter from Bushrod Washington to Richard Peters Jr., Sept. 6, 1828, Historical Society of Pennsylvania; see John T. Nockleby, "Two Theories of Competition in the Early 19th Century Labor Cases," *American Journal of Legal History* 38 (1994): 465; cf. letter from Bushrod Washington to Joseph Hopkinson, Jan. 7, 1817, Harvard Law Library (writing to Hopkinson when he was in Congress: "I trust also that the Judicial bill which I believe was introduced at the last Session (the same which we read over in my room) will be pressed forward").
31. *Montana v. Kennedy*, 366 U.S. 308, 311 (1961). Binney was a founding member of the Hasty Pudding Club at Harvard when he was an undergraduate. See *Catalogue of the Members and Library of the Hasty-Pudding Club of Harvard University* (Cambridge, MA: Cambridge Press, Metcalf, Torry, and Ballou, 1841), 3.
32. See, e.g., Daniel Farbman, "Resistance Lawyering," *California Law Review* 107 (2019): 1913 and n. 271.
33. *McFadden v. The Exchange*, 16 F. Cas. 85, 87 (C.C.D. Pa. 1811) (No. 8,786), reversed by 11 U.S. (7 Cranch.) 116 (1812).
34. See Binney, *Bushrod Washington*, 23 ("For more than twenty-five years the Circuit Court was a model for judicial administration"). For an example of the justice's eye for detail in court administration, see letter from Bushrod Washington to William Tilghman, Apr. 21, 1814, in "Letters of Bushrod Washington," 167 (asking the Chief

Justice of the Pennsylvania Supreme Court a question about when judgments became final so that the federal practice could be made consistent with the Pennsylvania rule).

35. Binney, *Bushrod Washington*, 7–8.
36. Ibid., 8.
37. Brown, *The Forum*, 1:357.
38. Binney, *Bushrod Washington*, 8–9.
39. Ibid., 10.
40. Ibid., 11. For another strong endorsement of Bushrod's judicial ability, see Lucius Q. C. Elmer, *The Constitution and Government of the Province and State of New Jersey* (Newark, NJ: Martin R. Dennis & Company, 1872), 281–93 (giving an account by a lawyer who then served on the New Jersey Supreme Court), 293 ("If I was asked, Who of all the judges you have known do you consider to have been the best fitted for that high office, taking into account integrity of character, learning, deportment, balance of mind, natural temper and disposition, and ability to ascertain and regard the true merits of a cause . . . I should say Bushrod Washington").
41. See Binney, *Bushrod Washington*, 12.
42. Ibid., 12–13, 13 ("A trial by jury is a battle. With the Judge, as well as with the Counsel, it is, for the most part, now or never. It is folly to be wise after the defeat, and it is therefore stultifying and criminal to be torpid or volatile during the combat—as criminal in the Judge as in the Counsel; for although the Judge is not to fight the battle, he is in a great degree to award the victory to the better cause").
43. Ibid., 16.
44. Ibid., 17.
45. Ibid., 21.
46. See, e.g., Brown, *The Forum*, 1:374.
47. Binney, *Bushrod Washington*, 18–20; cf. Hopkinson, *Commemoration of Bushrod Washington*, 16 ("There was a frankness, sometimes a playfulness, in his manners, which, nevertheless, detracted nothing from the respect due to his station").
48. Brown, *The Forum*, 1:357.
49. Ibid., 1:359.
50. Ibid., 1:360.
51. Ibid., 1:361.
52. Ibid., 1:373. Another of Brown's anecdotes was about a prominent lawyer who entered the courtroom during a trial and gave a rambling statement about "the attempted overthrow of the American Republic, by the influence of foreign governments and domestic traitors, through their emissaries amongst us." After the man left, Washington simply directed the case "to proceed, as though nothing extraordinary had happened" (1:371).
53. Ibid., 1:373.
54. In the modern era, Learned Hand may be the best example of a judge who was highly regarded when he was a district judge and when he was a circuit judge. Chief Justice Marshall was also a strong trial judge, most notably during the Burr treason trial, though I do not know enough about his record on circuit to evaluate his ability there.

55. Nowadays jury instructions are more standardized so that judges do not have to reinvent the wheel for each trial. No such "pattern instructions" existed in the nineteenth century.
56. See, e.g., Renee Lettow Lerner, "The Transformation of the American Civil Trial: The Silent Judge," *William and Mary Law Review* 42 (2000): 195–264 (discussing the early prevalence of judicial commentary on evidence and the practice's decline by the twentieth century); see also Binney, *Bushrod Washington*, 20 ("His arrangement of the evidence in his charge, and of the reciprocal bearing of the parts, was, of itself, an argument for the side he favored, and he would sometimes manifest his leaning rather more clearly, by his emphasis on certain parts; but he never expressed a direct opinion upon the evidence, to rule, still less to overrule, the fair judgment of the Jury upon the whole evidence").
57. *Harrison v. Rowan*, 11 F. Cas. 663, 664 (C.C.D. N.J. 1820) (No. 6,142), 665 ("It would be a most pernicious practice, and in its consequences dangerous to this much valued mode of trial, to permit a verdict, openly and solemnly declared in court, to be subverted by going behind it and inquiring into the secrets of the jury room, to find out from some of the members of that body, what was the process by which they or others had come to the result declared by their verdict").
58. *Willis v. Burcher*, 30 F. Cas. 63, 67 (C.C.D. Pa. 1818) (No. 17,769) ("It is not on the ground of dissatisfaction at the conduct of the jury, who are respectable men, and no doubt thought they were doing right, that the court will set this verdict aside. It is important that the law should be adhered to, and that the rights of courts should be preserved. We should sit here for a very poor purpose indeed, and should disregard our duty and our oath, if we should submit to verdicts against law. The safety, and happiness, and prosperity of every one, are deeply interested, that if a jury undertake to decide, and does decide against the law of the land, their verdict should be corrected; for if they err, and the court has no control over their decision, where is the remedy for any injury or wrong an individual may sustain by their verdict?"). Binney was the lawyer who won the motion to set the verdict aside, and a newspaper article on the case quoted Washington as saying, "If juries should find a verdict *one hundred times* in opposition to the charge of the court, he would grant a new trial." "Trial by Jury," *Niles' Weekly Register*, July 18, 1818, 14:360; Binney, *Bushrod Washington*, 21–22 (describing the case); see also *Willis*, 30 F. Cas. at 66–67. When the hustice read the article, he reportedly said: "I would set it aside a thousand times." Binney, *Bushrod Washington*, 22 (adding that he said this "with an expletive that he never used in later days").
59. *United States v. Wiltberger*, 28 F. Cas. 727, 729 (C.C.E.D. Pa. 1819) (No. 16,738). For a related example in a charge to a grand jury, see "Law Intelligence," *Niles' Weekly Register*, Nov. 7, 1817, 13: 169–71 (explaining the law of murder and other subjects).
60. *Collings v. Hope*, 6 F. Cas. 111, 111 (C.C.D. Pa. 1812) (No. 3,003).
61. Binney, *Bushrod Washington*, 16.
62. Brown, *The Forum*, 1:372–73.
63. Hopkinson, *Commemoration of Bushrod Washington*, 15; see Binney, *Bushrod Washington*, 28 (quoting Washington's view in one case that "this reasoning will carry

me to a conclusion directly opposite to that which my mind had before arrived at; nevertheless I shall follow it").

64. *Letters of Joseph Story*, 2:30.
65. See Chief Justice John Roberts, "2014 Year-End Report on the Federal Judiciary," https://www.supremecourt.gov/publicinfo/year-end/2014year-endreport.pdf, 11–12 ("Perhaps to remind us which animal won that famous race, Cass Gilbert places at the bases of the Court's exterior lampposts sturdy bronze tortoises, symbolizing the judiciary's commitment to constant but deliberate progress in the cause of justice").
66. See *Le Tigre*, 15 F. Cas. 404 (C.C.D. N.J. 1820) (No. 8,281); Bushrod Washington Journal, Chicago History Museum, 6–9, 12, 14, 16–17, 24–34. Washington's notes and draft opinion on *Le Tigre* are interrupted by some blank pages and by one page that contains the draft of an unrelated letter on the personnel of the American Colonization Society.
67. See *Le Tigre*, 15 F. Cas. at 408–9. Washington's draft opinion uses the singular "I," whereas the published opinion uses the plural "we." Presumably this means that the district judge concurred in the final opinion, but the justice did not presume that he would join when he wrote the draft. Chapter 9 uses the journal to show that a similar norm seems to have applied in the Supreme Court.
68. See Lynch, *Role of the Circuit Courts*, 56–64 (making this criticism of Washington's circuit opinions). I say "excessive" because on occasion the justice did clutter his analysis with discussions of case law that were akin to beating a dead horse. On the other hand, Chief Justice Marshall and Justice Story are subject to the opposite criticism that they sometimes did not cite enough (or any) precedent in their opinions, which created a different set of problems.
69. Hopkinson, *Commemoration of Bushrod Washington*, 16.
70. *Hurst v. Wickerly*, 12 F. Cas. 1046, 1046 (C.C.D. Pa. 1805) (No. 6,940).
71. *Pryor v. Dunkle*, 20 F. Cas. 29, 30 (C.C.D. Pa. 1809) (No. 11,548) (construing a will). Judge Peters did not participate in this case.
72. *Goodwin v. United States*, 10 F. Cas. 625, 626 (C.C.D. Pa. 1811) (No. 5,554) (construing two provisions of a customs statute), affirmed by *United States v. Goodwin*, 11 U.S. (7 Cranch) 108 (1812).
73. *McFadden v. The Exchange*, 16 F. Cas. 85, 88 (C.C.D. Pa. 1811) (No. 8,786) (holding that maritime jurisdiction existed over a French warship sued in Philadelphia), reversed by *The Schooner Exchange v. McFadden*, 11 U.S. (7 Cranch.) 116 (1812); see also Herbert A. Johnson, "Bushrod Washington," *Vanderbilt Law Review* 62 (2009): 480–82 (providing additional background on the case).
74. *Sperry v. Delaware Ins. Co.*, 22 F. Cas. 923, 925 (C.C.D. Pa. 1808) (No. 13,236) (charging the jury in a maritime insurance case).
75. See *Odlin v. Insurance Co. of Pennsylvania*, 18 F. Cas. 583 (C.C.D. Pa. 1813) (No. 10,433) (analyzing whether a domestic embargo constituted a restraint of princes under maritime contract law).
76. Put another way, Washington might not have made some of these comments if he had been writing the Supreme Court's opinion in the case.

77. David Lynch argues that Washington's public expressions of doubt betrayed a lack of confidence, but I think that conclusion is mistaken. See Lynch, *Role of the Circuit Courts*, 84.
78. Today this sort of communication might be deemed improper, in that another justice was not part of the circuit court that heard the arguments.
79. Letter from John Marshall to Bushrod Washington, May 31, 1824, in *The Papers of John Marshall Digital Edition*, ed. Charles Hobson (Charlottesville: University of Virginia Press, 2014); see letter from John Marshall to Bushrod Washington, May 25, 1813, in *Papers of John Marshall Digital Edition* ("Having much less of Admiralty business in my circuit on the Atlantic I am always inclined when an admiralty question of some intricacy occurs to consult my brethren upon it").
80. Letter from John Marshall to Bushrod Washington, June 15, 1821, in *Papers of John Marshall Digital Edition*; see letter from John Marshall to Bushrod Washington, May 31, 1819, in *Papers of John Marshall Digital Edition* ("I have a case before me which depends entirely on the question whether the master of a vessel belonging to one port can hypothecate [in other words, pledge] her in the port of a different state. Is the port of one state a foreign port with respect to the vessel of a citizen of another state? Will you give me your opinion on this point?").
81. See letter from Joseph Story to Bushrod Washington, July 4, 1827, Massachusetts Historical Society; letter from Joseph Story to Bushrod Washington, Apr. 11, 1816, Mount Vernon Library; see also letter from John Marshall to Bushrod Washington, July 12, 1823, in *Papers of John Marshall Digital Edition* ("I received your letter expressing your wish to know the principle decided in the case of the Bank of the United States v. Dandridge's securities"). Once Washington asked Marshall for his understanding of a Supreme Court opinion that reversed and remanded one of Washington's circuit opinions. See letter from John Marshall to Bushrod Washington, Oct. 28, 1818, in *Papers of John Marshall Digital Edition* (responding to the unknown question and stating that he did not think that the published report of the Supreme Court opinion was erroneous, though he was uncertain). A second trial was held, and this time the judgment was upheld on appeal. See *Evans v. Eaton*, 8 F. Cas. 856 (C.C.D. Pa. 1818) (No. 4,560), affirmed by 20 U.S. (7 Wheat.) 356 (1822).
82. Letter from John Marshall to Bushrod Washington, July 13, 1821, in *Papers of John Marshall Digital Edition* ("I thank you for the opinion you have been so good as to give me in the case on which I consulted you. I have from the first thought it doubtful but shall decide it in conformity with your opinion"). This process is similar to the way that some modern circuits operate when judges seek revisions to panel opinions rather than calling for an en banc hearing of the full circuit court.
83. See letter from Joseph Story to Bushrod Washington, Aug. 13, 1829, Massachusetts Historical Society; letter from Bushrod Washington to Joseph Story, Dec. 21, 1825, University of Michigan, William L. Clements Library; letter from Bushrod Washington to Joseph Story, Jun. 8, 1825, University of Michigan, William L. Clements Library; letter from Bushrod Washington to Joseph Story, June 27, 1823, Massachusetts Historical Society; letter from Bushrod Washington to Joseph

Story, Dec. 22, 1823, University of Michigan, William L. Clements Library; letter from Bushrod Washington to Joseph Story, Nov. 18, 1822, Massachusetts Historical Society; letter from Joseph Story to Bushrod Washington, Dec. 21, 1821, Mount Vernon Library; letter from Bushrod Washington to Joseph Story, Dec. 4, 1821, Massachusetts Historical Society; letter from Bushrod Washington to Joseph Story, June 19, 1821, Massachusetts Historical Society.

84. Letter from Bushrod Washington to Smith Thompson, May 24, 1827, Huntington Library.
85. Letter from Bushrod Washington to Joseph Story, Dec. 22, 1823, University of Michigan, William L. Clements Library. In this report, Washington refrained from saying anything about his cases that might be heard by the Supreme Court.
86. See letter from Bushrod Washington to Joseph Story, Oct. 1, 1825, Massachusetts Historical Society; letter from Bushrod Washington to Joseph Story, Aug. 9, 1821, Massachusetts Historical Society. In one letter Justice Story apparently criticized one of Washington's opinions, to which Washington responded: "Your reasons for condemning my opinion . . . are so satisfactory, that I write heartily in the condemnation." Letter from Bushrod Washington to Joseph Story, Sept. 11, 1823, Massachusetts Historical Society.

    The justice's response to a similar circuit report sent to him by Justice Thompson, who joined the Court in 1823, was somewhat different. See letter from Bushrod Washington to Smith Thompson, May 25, 1825, Mount Vernon Library. Washington instead gave detailed comments to Thompson that have a "break in the new guy" feel to them (stating at one point that he "would suggest a doubt" about one of Thompson's circuit opinions).
87. Letter from John Marshall to Bushrod Washington, May 28, 1822, in *Papers of John Marshall Digital Edition*; see letter from John Marshall to Bushrod Washington, June 25, 1823, in *Papers of John Marshall Digital Edition* ("The court which has just terminated has furnished some business for your Honors at Washington. I have had some new and intricate questions on one of which, that goes up to the Supreme Court, I decided on reflection differently from my first impression. That judgment will probably be reversed").
88. See, e.g., *Smith v. Delaware Ins. Co.*, 22 F. Cas. 509 (C.C.D. Pa. 1811) (No. 13,035), reversed by 11 U.S. (7 Cranch.) 434 (1813) (noting that Washington was absent from the Supreme Court decision); *Coxe v. Pennington*, 6 F. Cas. 692 (C.C.D. Pa. 1803) (No. 3,311), reversed by 6 U.S. (2 Cranch.) 33 (1804). The justices also sometimes wrote and affirmed their own circuit opinions. See *United States v. Ortega*, 27 F. Cas. 359 (C.C.E.D. Pa. 1825) (No. 15,971), affirmed by 24 U.S. (11 Wheat.) 468 (1826). The recusal customs of the Marshall Court with respect to the review of circuit decisions were haphazard. Sometimes a justice would recuse himself when his circuit opinion was heard. Sometimes not. Sometimes a justice would recuse but (much as Justice Washington did in *Fisher*) still write a statement about the Supreme Court's ruling in the case. There was no general practice that a justice sitting in review of his own decision was wrong, in part because that would almost always leave the Court a man down in circuit appeals. See Ackerman, *Failure of the*

Founding Fathers, 348n63 (pointing out that English judges in this period also regularly heard appeals of their own rulings).

89. See *United States v. Lowry*, 26 F. Cas. 1008 (C.C.D. Pa. 1808) (No. 15,636).
90. Ibid. at 1010.
91. *United States v. Bright*, 24 F. Cas. 1232, 1232–34 (C.C.D. Pa. 1809) (No. 14,647).
92. Hopkinson, *Commemoration of Bushrod Washington*, 22–23.
93. Ibid., 27.
94. The facts of *Bright* as stated in the text are drawn from *Bright*, 24 F. Cas. at 1232–34; *United States v. Judge Peters*, 9 U.S. (5 Cranch) 115, 116–134 (1809); Barry Friedman, *The Will of the People: How Public Opinion Has Influenced the Supreme Court and Shaped the Meaning of the Constitution* (New York: Farrar, Straus, and Giroux, 2009), 84–85; and Hopkinson, *Commemoration of Bushrod Washington*, 23–27. A transcript of the trial proceedings can be found in *A Report of the Whole Trial of Gen. Michael Bright, and Others, Before Washington & Peters in the Circuit Court of the United States in and for the District of Pennsylvania in the Third Circuit, on an Indictment for Obstructing, Resisting, and Opposing the Execution of the Writ of Arrest, Issued out of the District Court of Pennsylvania, in the case of Gideon Olmstead and Others Against the Surviving Executrices of David Rittenhouse, Deceased* (Philadelphia: Thomas Lloyd, 1809); see also M. Ruth Kelly, *The Olmstead Case: Privateers, Property, and Politics in Pennsylvania* (Selinsgrove, PA: Susquehanna University Press, 2005) (providing an overview of this saga).
95. *Peters*, 9 U.S. (5 Cranch) at 115; see Hopkinson, *Commemoration of Bushrod Washington*, 25 ("The District Court hesitated to proceed. The question was one of great difficulty and delicacy; the anticipated conflict, terrible in the extreme"). The district court decision was made in 1803, but nothing happened for years afterward. Why? Probably because Judge Peters and the justices did not want a high-profile fight with a state while Jefferson was president. Once Madison was the president-elect, there may have been more confidence that the federal courts would receive political support.
96. *Peters*, 9 U.S. (5 Cranch) at 136. The Court rejected Pennsylvania's argument that the Eleventh Amendment left federal courts with no jurisdiction over the case (at 139–41).
97. One could argue there was something inappropriate about Judge Peters participating in the trial of someone who tried to obstruct the judge's own order.
98. Brown, *The Forum*, 1:377–78.
99. Letter from Bushrod Washington to Julia Blackburn Washington, Apr. 24, 1809, Mount Vernon Library. The letter stated that Washington was working on other cases as well, but he specifically mention Olmstead's case.
100. Ibid., 1:378. I removed Brown's unnecessary italics and all-caps from the quote.
101. *Bright*, 24 F. Cas. at 1235; see also at 1232–35.
102. See ibid. at 1235. Washington also construed the Eleventh Amendment to apply only when a state was a party to a lawsuit rather than simply interested in the outcome. See ibid. (stating that if "the mere claim of interest by a state in the subject in dispute between two citizens can have the magic effect of suspending all the functions of a

court of justice over that subject, and of annihilating its decrees when pronounced, this effective and necessary branch of our government, and of all free governments, may be rendered useless at any moment, at the pleasure of a state"); ibid. at 1236 (stating that to hold otherwise would "convert this amendment, this sacrifice made to state pride, into an engine to demolish altogether one of the essential branches of the general government").

103. See U.S. Const., amend. XI ("The Judicial power of the United States shall not be construed to extend to any suit in law or equity, commenced or prosecuted against one of the United States by Citizens of another State, or by Citizens or Subjects of any Foreign States").
104. *Bright*, 24 F. Cas. at 1236.
105. Over a century later, the Supreme Court held that the Eleventh Amendment applied to maritime cases. See In Re *State of New York*, 256 U.S. 490 (1921). The holding rested in large part on a dubious precedent in which the Court said that the text of the amendment should not be read literally. See *Hans v. Louisiana*, 134 U.S. 1 (1890); William Baude and Stephen Sachs, "The Misunderstood Eleventh Amendment," *University of Pennsylvania Law Review* 169 (2021): 635 (criticizing the Court's extension of the Eleventh Amendment to admiralty jurisdiction and praising Washington's contrary reasoning).
106. *Bright*, 24 F. Cas. at 1237.
107. Ibid. (going on to explain the specifics of Section 25). Justice Washington also made the weaker claim that federal judges would not go beyond their proper authority because that would give them more work.
108. See, e.g., Patricia M. Wald, "Foreword: War Tales and War Trials," *Michigan Law Review* 106 (2008): 911–12.
109. *Bright*, 24 F. Cas. at 1237–38.
110. Ibid. at 1238.
111. See ibid.
112. *Golden v. Prince*, 10 F. Cas. 542 (C.C.D. Pa. 1814) (No. 5,509). *Prince* was unusual in that the opinion was published in contemporary newspapers and not just years later in the reports prepared by Richard Peters Jr. See letter from Bushrod Washington to Richard Peters Jr., Nov. 30, 1814, Historical Society of Pennsylvania ("The case of the constitutionality of the Bankrupt Law was published in the U.S. Gazette").
113. Act of Apr. 4, 1800, ch. 19, 2 Stat. 19 (repealed 1803).
114. See U.S. Const., art. I, § 10, cl. 1 ("No State shall . . . pass any . . . Law impairing the Obligation of Contracts"). One of Washington's most influential comments as a circuit judge came in *Evans v. Easton*, a patent case, in which he told a jury that "there is nothing in the constitution of the United States which forbids congress to pass a law violating the obligations of contracts, although such a power is denied to the states individually." *Evans v. Eaton*, 8 F. Cas. 846, 849 (C.C.D. Pa. 1816) (No. 4.559), reversed on other grounds, 16 U.S. (3 Wheat.) 454 (1818). The Supreme Court ultimately sustained this view in upholding the constitutionality of federal paper money as legal tender, though not without dissent. See *Legal Tender Cases*, 79 U.S. (12 Wall.) 457, 671–72 (1870) (Field, J., dissenting) (stating that Washington's

dictum was a minority view "without significance"); cf. at 501–2 (argument of Mr. Potter) (dismissing the dictum as "a singular instance of a casual observation, passing for years unaffirmed and unchallenged by all the great commentators upon the Constitution").

115. See *Prince*, 10 F. Cas. at 543–44.
116. Letter from Joseph Story to Bushrod Washington, Apr. 21, 1814, New-York Historical Society.
117. Letter from John Marshall to Bushrod Washington, Apr. 19, 1814, in *Papers of John Marshall Digital Edition*.
118. See *Prince*, 10 F. Cas. at 544.
119. See *Ogden v. Saunders*, 25 U.S. (12 Wheat.) 213 (1827).
120. On this issue, *Prince* relied heavily on the text of the Bankruptcy Clause in Article One, Section Eight, which gave Congress the power "to establish a uniform Rule of Naturalization, and uniform Laws on the subject of Bankruptcies throughout the United States." U.S. Const., art. I, § 8, cl. 4; see *Prince*, 10 F. Cas. at 545–46. The crucial word for the justice was "uniform." How could bankruptcy law be uniform if each state could enact its own law? "That the exercise of the power to pass bankrupt and naturalization laws by the state governments, is incompatible with the grant of a power to congress to pass uniform laws on the same subjects, is obvious," he stated, "from the consideration that the former would be dissimilar and frequently contradictory; whereas the systems are directed to be uniform, which can only be rendered so by the exclusive power in one body to form them." "The inconvenience of dissimilar and discordant rules upon the subjects of bankruptcy and of naturalization, no doubt, suggested to the framers of the constitution," the justice said, "the remedy which that body adopted, of vesting the right to legislate in those cases in the general government; that some uniform system might prevail throughout the United States, if congress should think that any regulations upon those subjects ought at all to be made." *Prince*, 10 F. Cas. at 546. Put another way, Congress could create a uniform bankruptcy system either by doing something or by doing nothing, but the states could never create a uniform system as the Constitution required.
121. *Prince*, 10 F. Cas. at 543.
122. Ibid. at 543–44; see also at 544 ("Thus, for example, if the laws of a state, which regulated the distribution or transmission of property in the year 1789, should be totally varied by a subsequent law, the latter only would be the rule by which property could be distributed or transmitted from the time the law came into operation; and it can never be seriously contended, that a person interested in this property, and from the adventitious circumstance of his residence in another state, entitled to make his claim, either in the federal or state court, should recover more by resorting to the former, than he would have recovered had he applied to the latter court").
123. Ibid. at 544 ("It is in reference to this principle, that the 17th section of the same judicial act authorizes the courts of the United States to make all necessary rules for the orderly conducting business in the said courts, provided the same are not repugnant

to the laws of the United States; and under this power, the different circuit courts, at their first sessions, adopted the state practice as it then existed, which continues to this day, we believe, in all the states, except so far as the courts have thought proper, from time to time, to alter and amend it").

124. *Swift v. Tyson*, 41 U.S. (16 Pet.) 1 (1842), overruled by *Erie R.R. Co. v. Tompkins*, 304 U.S. 64 (1938). *Swift* can be understood as a partial vindication of Justice Story's view that the federal courts possessed broad common-law authority, though he was never able to convince his colleagues that this should extend to criminal law.
125. Robert H. Jackson, *The Struggle for Judicial Supremacy: A Study of a Crisis in American Power Politics* (New York: Alfred A. Knopf, 1941), 275.
126. The literature on *Swift* and *Erie* is immense, and thus I will not attempt to summarize those materials here. For the classic discussion, see Henry J. Friendly, "In Praise of *Erie*—And of the New Federal Common Law," *New York University Law Review* 39 (1964): 383–422.
127. See *Erie R.R. Co. v. Tompkins*, 304 U.S. 64 (1938). *Erie* held that *Swift v. Tyson* was not just wrong but unconstitutional, though the basis for that holding was vague (see at 77–80).

Chapter 9

1. See Joel Richard Paul, *Without Precedent: John Marshall and His Times* (New York: Riverhead Books, 2018), 298; Jean Edward Smith, *John Marshall: Definer of a Nation* (New York: Henry Holt and Company, 1996), 350–51. Livingston killed a man in a duel before he became a judge (Smith, *Marshall*, 350).
2. 8 U.S. (4 Cranch) 75 (1807). Bollman was one of Burr's alleged accomplices. For more on *Bollman* and the murky circumstances surrounding Burr's treason trial, see Amanda L. Tyler, *Habeas Corpus in Wartime: From the Tower of London to Guantanamo Bay* (New York: Oxford University Press, 2017), 152–55.

   All the cases during the 1807 term were decided unanimously, with Marshall writing all but one of the signed opinions and Justice Johnson authoring the other, in a case where the chief justice recused himself. Justice Johnson's opinion for the Court marked the first time during the Marshall Court where the justices did not issue seriatim opinions in the chief justice's absence. See *Marshall v. Currie*, 8 U.S. (4 Cranch) 172 (1807).
3. See R. Kent Newmyer, *John Marshall and the Heroic Age of the Supreme Court* (Baton Rouge: Louisiana State University Press, 2001), 189–201 (discussing Marshall's actions during the Burr trial); see also Jon Meacham, *Thomas Jefferson and the Art of Power* (New York: Random House, 2012), 422–23 (describing Jefferson's hostile attitude).
4. See Smith, *Marshall*, 373; cf. *Vance v. Trump*, 140 S. Ct. 2412 (2020) (discussing the Burr trial and the competing perspectives of President Jefferson and Chief Justice Marshall).

5. See letter from Caesar Augustus Rodney to Thomas Jefferson, Oct. 31, 1808, https://founders.archives.gov/?q=%20Author%3A%22Rodney%2C%20Caesar%20Augustus%22%20Recipient%3A%22Jefferson%2C%20Thomas%22&s=1111311111&r=49.
6. See Bruce Ackerman, *The Failure of the Founding Fathers: Jefferson, Marshall, and the Rise of Presidential Democracy* (Cambridge, MA: Harvard University Press, 2005), 230; Paul, *Without Precedent*, 298.
7. See John W. Wayland, *The Washingtons and Their Homes* (Staunton, VA: McClure Printing Company, 1944), 335 (noting that Lucy Washington was the widow of George Steptoe Washington and the sister of Dolley Madison). Lucy Washington and Justice Todd were married at the White House.
8. See Smith, *Marshall*, 351; see also Paul, *Without Precedent*, 299 (noting that Justice Todd dissented publicly from Marshall only once in two decades). Justice Todd missed five of the nineteen terms in which he served. Sometimes this was due to illness, though sometimes the fact that he had to travel from Kentucky was simply too much for him.
9. See, e.g., *United States v. Gurney*, 8 U.S. (4 Cranch) 333 (1808) (referring repeatedly to the agreement of a majority but expressing itself formally as unanimous).
10. *Croudson v. Leonard*, 8 U.S. (4 Cranch.) 434, 442–43 (1808) (Washington, J., concurring); see ibid. at 443n* (noting that Justices Chase and Livingston dissented without opinion). The rule of law that Washington was referring to was that "the sentence of a foreign court of competent jurisdiction condemning the property upon the ground that it was not neutral, is so entirely conclusive of the fact so decided, that it can never be controverted, directly or collaterally, in any other court having concurrent jurisdiction." Ibid. at 436. *Croudson* was the only Supreme Court case in 1808 in which the chief justice participated but did not author the Court's decision. Justice Johnson wrote the opinion instead.
11. Letter from Joseph Story to Samuel Fay, Feb. 25, 1808, in *Life and Letters of Joseph Story*, ed. William Wetmore Story (Boston: Little & Brown, 1851), 1:167.
12. See Embargo Act of 1807, ch. 5, 2 Stat. 451 (1807); Gerald Leonard and Saul Cornell, *The Partisan Republic: Democracy, Exclusion, and the Fall of the Founders Constitution, 1780s–1830s* (New York: Cambridge University Press, 2019), 124–25.
13. See David McCullough, *John Adams* (New York: Simon and Schuster, 2001), 599; David O. Stewart, *Madison's Gift: Five Partnerships That Built America* (New York: Simon and Schuster, 2015), 219–21.
14. 10 U.S. (6 Cranch) 87 (1810); see James Traub, *John Quincy Adams: Militant Spirit* (New York: Basic Books, 2016), 159 (noting that John Quincy Adams argued *Fletcher* at that time).
15. See *Fletcher*, 10 U.S. (6 Cranch) at 129; Leonard and Cornell, *The Partisan Republic*, 105–6.
16. See Paul, *Without Precedent*, 301–2 (explaining that Alexander Hamilton and Marshall both supported relief from Congress for the third-party purchasers); see also Ackerman, *Failure of the Founding Fathers*, 212 (noting that John Randolph strongly opposed relief and broke with Jefferson on this issue).
17. See *Pierce v. Turner*, 9 U.S. (5 Cranch.) 154 (1809); ibid. at 168 (Johnson, J., dissenting).

18. See *Fletcher*, 10 U.S. (6 Cranch) at 115; Paul, *Without Precedent*, 303–4.
19. *Fletcher*, 10 U.S. (6 Cranch) at 139; see ibid. at 136–39. Justice Johnson wrote a concurring opinion. See ibid. at 143–48. A theme that runs through many of the Marshall Court's cases is that Republican state legislatures (and state courts) tended to see contract or property rights in more utilitarian terms and thought that they could be modified when necessary to serve the public interest. The Supreme Court (and Federalists more generally) tended to view contract and property rights as more fundamental and entitled to protection from the states by the federal government.
20. Ibid. at 130.
21. Ibid. at 138.
22. See *Campbell v. Gordon*, 10 U.S. (6 Cranch) 176 (1810); *Smith v. Maryland*, 10 U.S. (6 Cranch) 286 (1810). *Smith* was decided by only four justices, as the chief justice recused himself and Cushing and Chase were absent. See *Smith*, 10 U.S. (6 Cranch) at 304n*.
23. See Paul, *Without Precedent*, 297; Smith, *Marshall*, 397.
24. See letter from Bushrod Washington to John Marshall, May 2, 1810, in *The Papers of John Marshall Digital Edition*, ed. Charles Hobson (Charlottesville: University of Virginia Press, 2014) ("Willing and Francis consent to receive the eldest of the boys into their counting house. . . . [I]n about 4 years John will be ready to commence his professional studies with these gentlemen"). A few years later he would do the same for Marshall's son James. See letter from Bushrod Washington to Willing and Francis, Apr. 11, 1815 (Historical Society of Pennsylvania); letter from John Marshall to Bushrod Washington, Mar. 16, 1815, in *Papers of John Marshall Digital Edition* (thanking Washington for his assistance).
25. See Smith, *Marshall*, 400. I have been unable to determine why Justice Johnson and Justice Todd were absent that year.
26. See Ackerman, *Failure of the Founding Fathers*, 233; Smith, *Marshall*, 401.
27. Circuit assignments and the practices surrounding Supreme Court appointments were more fluid when Washington was appointed in 1798. Starting with Justice Johnson's selection in 1804, though, the expectation was that a new justice would be someone familiar with the state law of a state within the circuit assigned to the vacant Supreme Court seat.
28. See Ackerman, *Failure of the Founding Fathers*, 232; Smith, *Marshall*, 399.
29. See letter from Levi Lincoln to James Madison, Nov. 27, 1810, in *The Papers of James Madison: Presidential Series*, ed. J. C. A. Stagg, Jeanne Kerr Cross, and Susan Holbrook Perdue (Charlottesville: University of Virginia Press, 1996), 3:29–30; letter from James Madison to Levi Lincoln, Jan. 2, 1811, in *Papers of James Madison: Presidential Series*, 3:91; Smith, *Marshall*, 399. The notion that the president would nominate someone for an important position without first obtaining his consent is hard to understand, but in the early years of the Republic this occurred more often, mainly because of the time required to communicate these requests and to receive an answer.
30. See Ackerman, *Failure of the Founding Fathers*, 232; Smith, *Marshall*, 400.
31. See Smith, *Marshall*, 400; Traub, *John Quincy Adams*, 172.

32. See letter from John Quincy Adams to James Madison, June 3, 1811, in *Papers of James Madison: Presidential Series*, 3:324–27; Traub, *John Quincy Adams*, 173.
33. See Ackerman, *Failure of the Founding Fathers*, 233;
34. For the best twentieth-century biography of Story, see R. Kent Newmyer, *Supreme Court Justice Joseph Story: Statesman of the Old Republic* (Chapel Hill: University of North Carolina Press, 1985). The basic facts about Story relayed in the text come primarily from that source.
35. See Joseph Story, *Commentaries on the Constitution of the United States*, 3 vols. (Boston: Hillard, Gray, 1833).
36. See, e.g., David Herbert Donald, *Charles Sumner* (New York: Da Capo Press, 1996), 22–28 (describing Justice Story's mentorship of Sumner at Harvard).
37. See, e.g., *Mayor of New York v. Miln*, 36 U.S. (11 Pet.) 102, 153–61 (1837) (Story, J., dissenting) (rejecting a conclusion that a New York statute was consistent with the Commerce Clause); see ibid. at 161 (stating that Chief Justice Marshall agreed with his view when the case was initially argued prior to Marshall's death).
38. See Paul, *Without Precedent*, 297–98; Smith, *Marshall*, 396–97.
39. Charles J. Ingersoll, *Inchiquin: The Jesuit's Letters* (New York: Riley, 1810), 52. The book was written anonymously but is now commonly attributed to Ingersoll.
40. See Smith, *Marshall*, 406–7.
41. See *Fitzsimmons v. Ogden*, 11 U.S. (7 Cranch) 2 (1812) (resolving a trust dispute); see ibid. at 1 (noting Marshall and Justice Johnson's absence); *The James Wells*, 11 U.S. (7 Cranch) 22 (1812) (upholding the condemnation of a vessel for violating the embargo laws) (noting Marshall's absence). The chief justice also missed one case written by Justice Johnson, *Maryland Ins. Co. v. LeRoy*, 11 U.S. (7 Cranch) 26 (1812), and one in which Washington issued a brief order, *Hudson & Smith v. Guestier*, 11 U.S. (7 Cranch) 1 (1812).
42. Washington's unknown illness explains why he did not participate in *United States v. Hudson & Goodwin*, the case that held the federal courts did not possess criminal common-law jurisdiction. See *United States v. Hudson & Goodwin*, 11 U.S. (7 Cranch) 32, 32 (1812) (noting Washington's absence); see also *Shirras v. Caig*, 11 U.S. (7 Cranch) 34, 46 (1812) (stating that Washington was indisposed and could not attend five days of the Court's session in February). Justice Story did not dissent in *Hudson & Goodwin* but soon concluded that the decision was erroneous. He then drafted legislation (with the aid of Marshall and Washington) to expressly grant criminal common-law jurisdiction to the federal courts. See *Letters of Joseph Story*, 1:300. The bill did not pass. This may have been the same bill that Justice Washington discussed with Joseph Hopkinson, but I am not certain if they were the same.
43. See letter from Joseph Story to Nathanial Williams, Feb. 16, 1812, in *Letters of Joseph Story*, 1:213; Smith, *Marshall*, 377–78.
44. A contrary view is that the chief justice lost control of the Court in 1812 due to the influx of Republican Justices. See Ackerman, *Failure of the Founding Fathers*, 234. The proof offered for this claim is the result of *Hudson & Goodwin*, which flatly contradicted Federalist doctrine on the existence of federal criminal common law.

See ibid. at 234–38; see generally Gary D. Rowe, "The Sound of Silence: *United States v. Hudson & Goodwin*, the Jeffersonian Ascendancy, and the Abolition of Federal Common Law Crimes," *Yale Law Journal* 101 (1992): 919–48 (providing a fine overview of the case). But the fact that Marshall exerted less control over the Court in that case does not support the conclusion that the wider distribution of opinions during the 1812 term was caused by his reduced control. A better (though duller) explanation is that Marshall wrote a lower percentage of opinions because he missed some cases, his shoulder was aching, and there were more cases to decide due to the cancellation of the 1811 term.

45. In addition to the two opinions Washington wrote as the acting chief justice, he authored *United States v. Goodwin*, 11 U.S. (7 Cranch) 108 (1812) (holding that district court decisions in civil cases could not be reviewed by the Supreme Court under the applicable statutes) and *Barton v. Petit*, 11 U.S. (7 Cranch) 194 (1812) (explaining how a return of process against a defendant in a joint civil action relates to a plaintiff's right to enforce a judgment against the other defendant).
46. There were also no changes in the membership of the Court from 1994 to 2005, a period of stability even more impressive given that there were nine justices during that span.
47. One explanation for this is that Marshall simply lost some of his control due to Jefferson and Madison's appointments. But Marshall was also older and his newer colleagues were young and more able than people such as Chase, Cushing, and Patterson were at the end of their lives.
48. James D. Richardson, ed., *A Compilation of the Messages and Papers of the Presidents* (New York: Bureau of National Literature, Inc., 1897), 2:484–90; see Leonard and Cornell, *The Partisan Republic*, 130.
49. See Stewart, *Madison's Gift*, 244–46, 248–49. For a lively account of the War of 1812 from Madison's vantage point, see Noah F. Feldman, *The Three Lives of James Madison: Genius, Partisan, President* (New York: Random House, 2017), 547–609.
50. See Feldman, *Madison*, 545; Stewart, *Madison's Gift*, 243–44.
51. See McCullough, *Adams*, 606.
52. See Smith, *Marshall*, 414; see also *The Schooner Jane v. United States*, 11 U.S. (7 Cranch) 363 (1813) (upholding the condemnation of a vessel for violating the embargo); *Otis v. Bacon*, 11 U.S. (7 Cranch) 589 (1813) (affirming a judgment of liability against a customs inspector who exceeded his authority in enforcing the embargo); cf. *Barton v. Petit*, 11 U.S. (7 Cranch) 288 (1813) (resolving a procedural issue created after a circuit court's response to the Supreme Court's opinion from the previous term); *Thornton v. Carson*, 11 U.S. (7 Cranch) 596 (1813) (upholding an award in a debt action).
53. See *The Grotius*, 12 U.S. (8 Cranch) 456 (1814) (remanding a prize case for further fact-finding); *The Hiram*, 12 U.S. (8 Cranch) 444 (1814) (reversing a judgment denying a prize); *The Joseph*, 12 U.S. (8 Cranch) 451 (1814) (affirming a judgment of condemnation for trading with the enemy); cf. *The Frances*, 12 U.S. (8 Cranch) 418 (1814) (affirming a condemnation by a prize court), 420 (Livingston, J., dissenting)

(rejecting unqualified condemnation of the property). Washington also wrote one opinion in 1814 in an ordinary civil case. See *Smith v. Edrington*, 12 U.S. (8 Cranch) 66 (1814) (affirming a decree involving an estate).

54. 12 U.S. (8 Cranch) 253 (1814).
55. See McCullough, *Adams*, 606 (giving the date of the war declaration as June 19, 1812); see also *The Venus*, 12 U.S. (8 Cranch) at 253 (stating that the vessel left Liverpool on July 4, 1812).
56. See *The Venus*, 12 U.S. (8 Cranch) at 287 (noting Johnson's absence) (providing a brief statement from Justice Story stating that he recused himself but expressing "his entire concurrence in the opinion of Judge Washington").
57. See ibid. at 280 ("Although he cannot be considered an enemy, in the strict sense of the word, yet he is deemed such, with reference to the seizure of so much of his property concerned in the trade of the enemy, as is connected with his residence").
58. Ibid. at 281.
59. See ibid. at 284–86. The chief justice spent most of his opinion trying to distinguish these cases, which all came from Great Britain. See ibid. at 298–315. His lengthy effort reads like a brief written by a lawyer swimming against the cases, though this does not necessarily mean that Marshall's dissenting conclusion was wrong.
60. See ibid. at 288 (Marshall, C.J., dissenting). The chief justice also suggested that the Court treated the owners of *The Venus* harshly because they were naturalized citizens and would not have done the same to citizens by birth. See ibid. at 316–17 (Marshall, C.J., dissenting). The Court's opinion, though, made no distinction between types of citizens.
61. Ibid. at 297. (Marshall, C.J., dissenting).
62. Ibid. at 298 (Marshall, C.J., dissenting).
63. Ibid. at 283.
64. See *Brown v. United States*, 12 U.S. (8 Cranch) 110, 121 (1814).
65. Ibid. at 125. The chief justice and Justice Story discussed executive power in *Brown*, but neither asserted that the president could on his own seize enemy property.
66. See ibid. at 126 (pointing out that the power to declare war is immediately followed by the power to "grant letters of marque and reprisal, and make rules concerning captures on land and water").
67. Ibid. at 150 (Story, J., dissenting). Most of Story's published dissent was a reprint of his circuit opinion. See ibid. at 129 (Story, J., dissenting) (explaining that he would first restate his circuit opinion before addressing the Supreme Court's decision reversing him).
68. Ibid. at 150–51 (Story, J., dissenting).
69. Ibid. at 154 (Story, J., dissenting).
70. Smith, *Marshall*, 653n5; see ibid. at 418.
71. See *United States v. 1,960 Bags of Coffee*, 12 U.S. (8 Cranch) 398, 405–6 (1814) (Story, J., dissenting) (stating that "two of my brethren concur" in his dissent without naming them). By contrast, Marshall's *Venus* dissent stated that Justice Livingston joined his opinion. See *The Venus*, 12 U.S. (8 Cranch) at 317 (Marshall, C.J., dissenting).

72. *The Merrimack*, 12 U.S. (8 Cranch) 317, 334 (1814) (Story, J., dissenting in part). Chief Justice Marshall delivered a unanimous opinion for part of *The Merrimack*, but Justice Johnson wrote a separate majority opinion for the other portion of the case.
73. See ibid. at 334n*.
74. Justice Todd joined Washington's opinion in *The Venus* and Story's dissent in *The Merrimack*, so he could have been the other dissenter in *Brown*.
75. See McCullough, *Adams*, 616; Paul, *Without Precedent*, 321.
76. See Smith, *Marshall*, 420; Stewart, *Madison's Gift*, 254–56.
77. See Paul, *Without Precedent*, 322, 326–27; Smith, *Marshall*, 421. Over the next two decades, the justices moved at different points to other boarding houses, such as Davis's Hotel and Brown's Hotel. See Smith, *Marshall*, 434, 471.
78. Letter from John Marshall to Bushrod Washington, Dec. 29, 1814, in *Papers of John Marshall Digital Edition*.
79. See Paul, *Without Precedent*, 327; Smith, *Marshall*, 421.
80. Letter from Bushrod Washington to Chancellor Henry DeSaussure, Nov. 29, 1814, New York Public Library.
81. See Feldman, *Madison*, 600; Stewart, *Madison's Gift*, 263.
82. See Feldman, *Madison*, 601; Traub, *John Quincy Adams*, 194.
83. See, e.g., Daniel Walker Howe, *What Hath God Wrought: The Transformation of America, 1815–1848* (New York: Oxford University Press, 2007), 8–15.
84. See Barry Friedman, *The Will of the People: How Public Opinion Has Influenced the Supreme Court and Shaped the Meaning of the Constitution* (New York: Farrar, Straus, and Giroux, 2009), 78–79; Traub, *John Quincy Adams*, 195.
85. See David S. Schwartz, *The Spirit of the Constitution: John Marshall and the 200-Year Odyssey of McCulloch v. Maryland* (New York: Oxford University Press, 2019), 42–46; see Leonard and Cornell, *The Partisan Republic*, 132–33.
86. An enduring puzzle of the Marshall Court is how the chief justice and Washington kept advancing Federalist doctrines when most of the justices were Republicans. Part of the answer is that Justice Story (though picked by Madison) was broadly sympathetic to Federalist ideas about national power and property rights. Another answer is that public opinion moved in a nationalist direction due to the War of 1812, at least until the mid-1820s.
87. See *The Alerta*, 13 U.S. (9 Cranch) 199 (1815) (affirming circuit court jurisdiction to restore neutral property illegally seized); *The Grotius*, 13 U.S. (9 Cranch) 368 (1815) (holding that a ship was a prize); *Drummond's Adm'rs v. Magruder & Co's Trustees*, 13 U.S. (9 Cranch) 122 (1815) (reversing and remanding a judgment on a deed assignment for want of evidence); *Evans v. Jordan & Morehead*, 13 U.S. (9 Cranch) 199 (1815) (construing a private act of Congress on a patent). Only four justices participated in *Drummond's Administrators*, and only three of them agreed with Washington's conclusion that the case should be remanded for further fact-finding. See *Drummond's Adm'rs*, 13 U.S. (9 Cranch) at 122, 125.
88. 13 U.S. (9 Cranch) 43 (1815). *Terrett* was unanimous, though Justices Johnson and Todd did not participate. Justice Story indicated, though, that only a majority of the other five justices agreed with his sweeping analysis. See ibid. at 55.

89. *Turpin v. Locket*, 10 Va. 113 (1804); see ibid. at 186–87 (opinion of Carrington & Lyons, JJ.) (stating that the chancellor's decree in favor of the state was affirmed because the Supreme Court of Appeals was equally divided). The reporter of the decision claimed that "Mr. Pendleton, then president of the court, and who sat in the cause, prepared his opinion in writing . . . that the glebes belonged to the protestant episcopal church; and that the act of 1802 was unconstitutional. But the opinion was not delivered, as he died the night before it was to have been pronounced." Ibid. at 187.
90. *Terrett*, 13 U.S. (9 Cranch) at 44–45.
91. Ibid. at 52. Story did not cite any specific provisions of the Constitution or cases as authority for this sweeping statement, although he could have cited the Contracts Clause or *Fletcher v. Peck*. At this time, the First Amendment's religion clauses did not apply to the states.
92. Ibid. at 51; see Va. Decl. of Rights, § 16.
93. Opinion of Bushrod Washington, Esq. on the Subject of the Glebes and Churches, Dec. 27, 1797, Special Collections, University of Virginia Library, 1–2.
94. *Terrett*, 13 U.S. (9 Cranch) at 51.
95. Opinion of Bushrod Washington, 3.
96. *Terrett*, 13 U.S. (9 Cranch) at 50.
97. There is an argument, of course, that Washington should have recused himself from *Terrett* given his past experience and his membership in Virginia's Episcopal Church.
98. The case was *Osborn v. Bank of the United States*, 22 U.S. (9 Wheat.) 738 (1824). The written argument was printed in a book. See Charles Hammond, *State of the Case and Argument from the Appellants, in the Case of the Bank of the United States, Versus the Auditor and Treasurer of the State of Ohio, in the Supreme Court of the United States* (Cincinnati, OH: Morgan and Lodge, 1823). The letter from Hammond to Marshall is lost.
99. See letter from John Marshall to Charles Hammond, Dec. 23, 1823, in *Papers of John Marshall Digital Edition*.
100. See *Morean v. United States Ins. Co.*, 14 U.S. (1 Wheat.) 219 (1816) (affirming his own circuit opinion in a maritime insurance case); *The Edward*, 14 U.S. (1 Wheat.) 261 (1816) (affirming, over Justice Livingston's dissent, the forfeiture of a vessel for violating the embargo against Britain prior to the War of 1812); *Hepburn & Dundas Heirs v. Dunlop & Co.*, 14 U.S. (1 Wheat.) 179 (1816) (resolving several issues in a complex chancery case involving a request for specific performance).
101. See *Fairfax's Devisee v. Hunter's Lessee*, 11 U.S. (6 Cranch) 603 (1812).
102. See *Hunter v. Martin*, 18 Va. 1 (1815), reversed by *Martin v. Hunter's Lessee*, 14 U.S. (1 Wheat.) 304 (1816); Smith, *Marshall*, 427–28.
103. *Hunter*, 18 Va. at 26 (opinion of Roane, J). Judge Roane also rejected the authority of *The Federalist* as "a mere newspaper publication, written in the heat and hurry of the battle." Ibid. at 27 (explaining why he would not follow what *The Federalist* said about the Supreme Court's authority to review state court judgments). Ironically,

Roane was Marshall's neighbor in Richmond, though they did not socialize. See Smith, *Marshall*, 447.

104. See *Hunter*, 14 U.S. (1 Wheat.) at 323–62. Justice Johnson concurred separately in *Martin*. See ibid. at 362–82 (Johnson, J., concurring).
105. Ibid. at 324. In *Bright*, Washington discussed the importance of Section 25 of the Judiciary Act of 1789; see United States v. Bright, 24 F. Cas. 1232, 1237 (C.C.D. Pa. 1809) (No. 14,647). However, the passage was dictum given that the case involved a conflict between federal courts and state officials who were not judges. The Supreme Court did not remand *Martin* to the Virginia Supreme Court of Appeals. Instead, the justices exercised their power under Section 25 to execute the judgment themselves and thus avoid further conflict. See Leonard and Cornell, *Partisan Republic*, 180; Smith, *Marshall*, 430.
106. See Howe, *What Hath God Wrought*, 123; Smith, *Marshall*, 428.
107. See G. Edward White, "The Working Life of the Marshall Court, 1815–1835," *Virginia Law Review* 70, no. 1 (1984): 15 (laying out the evidence for this chain of events).
108. See ibid. The *Martin* petition is in the National Archives and includes Washington's note in the margin accepting the application. The justice probably assigned the opinion to Justice Story to allow him to vindicate his prior opinion, though perhaps there was some political calculation involved in having someone not from Virginia write the Supreme Court's opinion.
109. See Act of March 3, 1817, ch. 63, 3 Stat. 376; Smith, *Marshall*, 431n*.
110. See Paul, *Without Precedent*, 332; Smith, *Marshall*, 430–31. All the justices attended President Adams's inaugural (see McCullough, *Adams*, 467), though that may have been out of respect for George Washington's retirement. There is no indication that Washington or many of his colleagues went to the ceremonies for Madison or for Jefferson, though the chief justice did go to all of them to administer the oath of office.
111. See Paul, *Without Precedent*, 331; Smith, *Marshall*, 35.
112. See, e,g., Howe, *What Hath God Wrought*, 93 (explaining how the term was coined). Monroe is the only president other than Washington to run unopposed for reelection.
113. See *Colson v. Lewis*, 15 U.S. (2 Wheat.) 377 (1817) (holding that federal jurisdiction was present when land grants were made by Virginia and Kentucky even though they were first made when they were not separate states); *United States v. Sheldon*, 15 U.S. (2 Wheat.) 119 (1817) (holding that the transport of oxen by foot to Canada during the War of 1812 was not covered by the laws prohibiting the transportation of goods to the enemy); *The Ariadne*, 15 U.S. (2 Wheat.) 143 (1817) (affirming a prize confiscation); *Leeds v. Marine Ins. Co. of Alexandria*, 15 U.S. (2 Wheat.) 380 (1817) (reversing and remanding a chancery case due to the "irregular and equivocal" record); *Colson v. Thompson*, 15 U.S. (2 Wheat.) 336 (1817) (rejecting a contract breach claim); *Patterson v. United States*, 15 U.S. (2 Wheat.) 221 (1817) (reversing a jury verdict for finding facts that were not at issue); *The San Pedro*, 15 U.S. (2 Wheat.) 132 (1817) (holding that a writ of error was not the proper means to appeal

an admiralty case to the Supreme Court); *Thelusson v. Smith*, 15 U.S. (2 Wheat.) 396 (1817) (affirming his own circuit opinion in a federal bankruptcy case).

114. See *Dunlop v. Hepburn*, 16 U.S. (3 Wheat.) 231 (1818) (affirming the circuit court's implementation of a prior Supreme Court opinion in a property case); *Craig v. Radford*, 16 U.S. (3 Wheat.) 594 (1818) (holding that an alien's land title was not divested by Virginia); *Craig v. Leslie*, 16 U.S. (3 Wheat.) 563 (1818) (holding that an alien was entitled to a bequest from an estate as personal property).
115. To be more precise, Story wrote the second-greatest number of opinions in each term from 1813 to 1820, though in some of those years he tied with Washington or another justice. Washington wrote the second-greatest number of opinions in 1812. Justice Johnson often wrote separately, of course, and thus his overall opinion count was quite high.
116. See Paul, *Without Precedent*, 377–78; Smith, *Marshall*, 433. Washington wrote two unanimous opinions in 1819. See *Eliason v. Henshaw*, 17 U.S. (4 Wheat.) 225 (1819) (holding that a contract offer was not accepted); *Sergeant's Lessee v. Biddle*, 17 U.S. (4 Wheat.) 508 (1819) (concluding that certain depositions in the case were admissible evidence for a jury). All the cases decided in the 1819 term were unanimous except for *Dartmouth College*.
117. 17 U.S. (4 Wheat.) 518 (1819).
118. See Merrill D. Peterson, *The Great Triumvirate: Webster, Clay, and Calhoun* (New York: Oxford University Press, 1987), 100. There is no evidence that Webster said this, and the first claim that he did came decades later after he died (100–101).
119. See *Dartmouth College*, 17 U.S. (4 Wheat.) at 521 (noting that Webster's argument occurred in March 1818).
120. See *Dartmouth College*, 17 U.S. (4 Wheat.) at 624–54. Justice Duvall dissented without opinion. See ibid. at 713. Justice Johnson concurred with Chief Justice Marshall's opinion, while Justice Livingston concurred with the opinions of Marshall, Washington, and Story. See ibid. at 666. Justice Todd did not participate in *Dartmouth College*.
121. Ibid. at 626.
122. See ibid. at 656–57 (Washington, J., concurring).
123. See ibid. at 663–64 (Washington, J., concurring).
124. See ibid. at 600–601 (argument of Mr. Holmes).
125. See ibid. at 629.
126. Ibid. at 696–97 (Story, J., concurring).
127. I cannot say that divorce was the stumbling block to a unanimous opinion in *Dartmouth College*, but that issue represents the most striking difference among the three opinions.
128. *McCulloch v. Maryland*, 17 U.S. (4 Wheat.) 319 (1819).
129. See ibid. at 402–21; Schwartz, *Spirit of the Constitution*, 17–19. To be sure, Marshall included limiting language in *McCulloch* to create a unanimous Court, most notably by stressing the fact that the bank was a corporation and that a corporation was always a means to an end rather than end in itself. See *McCulloch*, 17 U.S. (4 Wheat.) at 411, 422; Schwartz, *Spirit of the Constitution*, 54–58.

130. See *McCulloch*, 17 U.S. (4 Wheat.) at 421.
131. Ibid. at 415.
132. Ibid. at 431; see John Hart Ely, *Democracy and Distrust: A Theory of Judicial Review* (Cambridge, MA: Harvard University Press, 1980), 85–86.
133. Letter from John Marshall to Bushrod Washington, Mar. 27, 1819, in *Papers of John Marshall Digital Edition*. None of Washington's letters about the *McCulloch* essays survive.
134. See Smith, *Marshall*, 448; see also letter from John Marshall to Bushrod Washington, Aug. 3, 1819, in *Papers of John Marshall Digital Edition* (stating that "Amphyction is Judge Brockenbrough").
135. See Gerald Gunther, "John Marshall, 'A Friend of the Constitution': In Defense and Elaboration of *McCulloch v. Maryland*," *Stanford Law Review* 21 (1969): 451. Professor Gunther revealed the backstory of the Marshall essays in the 1960s.
136. Letter from John Marshall to Bushrod Washington, May 6, 1819, in *Papers of John Marshall Digital Edition*.
137. See letter from John Marshall to Bushrod Washington, Aug. 3, 1819, in *Papers of John Marshall Digital Edition* ("Hampden is Judge Roane"); Smith, *Marshall*, 451.
138. Letter from John Marshall to Bushrod Washington, May 6, 1819, in *Papers of John Marshall Digital Edition*; see letter from John Marshall to Bushrod Washington, May 31, 1819, in *Papers of John Marshall Digital Edition* ("I received a few days past your letter inquiring whether the defense of the opinion had been correctly republished in the Alexandria paper. I went to the coffee house for the purpose of reading it but the papers had been mislaid and I was disappointed").
139. Letter from John Marshall to Bushrod Washington, June 17, 1819, in *Papers of John Marshall Digital Edition*.
140. Letter from John Marshall to Bushrod Washington, June 28, 1819, in *Papers of John Marshall Digital Edition*.
141. Letter from John Marshall to Bushrod Washington, Aug. 3, 1819, in *Papers of John Marshall Digital Edition*.
142. Justice Story was informed of these essays only after their publication began. See letter from John Marshall to Joseph Story, May 27, 1819, in *Papers of John Marshall Digital Edition*.
143. See Newmyer, *Heroic Age*, 299–300; Schwartz, *Spirit of the Constitution*, 44.
144. 18 U.S. (5 Wheat.) 1 (1820); see *United States v. Holmes*, 18 U.S. (5 Wheat.) 412 (1820) holding that the circuit court had jurisdiction in a case involving murder on the high seas and clarifying the burden of proof for determining whether a murder had been committed against a pirate or a foreign national); *Stevenson's Heirs v. Sullivant*, 18 U.S. (5 Wheat.) 207 (1820) (rejecting an estate claim by illegitimate children).
145. See *Houston*, 18 U.S. (5 Wheat.) at 3–4.
146. Pennsylvania enacted a law during the War of 1812 that just piggybacked on the federal law regulating the national militia and provided that identical penalties be imposed for desertion. See ibid. at 2.
147. Ibid. at 12, 32 (opinion of Washington, J.). Justice Johnson wrote a concurring opinion. See ibid. at 32–47.

148. See ibid. at 67–76 (Story, J., dissenting).
149. Letter from John Marshall to Joseph Story, July 13, 1819, in *Papers of John Marshall Digital Edition*. Marshall referred to *Houston* as "the militia case," but there was no militia case argued in the 1819 term other than *Houston*.
150. See *Houston*, 18 U.S. (5 Wheat.) at 16–17 (opinion of Washington, J.); see also U.S. Const., art. I, § 8, cl. 16 (stating that Congress was granted the power "for governing such Part of them [the militia] as may be employed in the service of the United States").
151. Ibid. at 18 (opinion of Washington, J.). A premise of Washington's analysis was that "the laws which I have referred to, amount to a full execution of the powers conferred upon Congress by the constitution." Ibid. at 15 (opinion of Washington, J.) In other words, he thought that there was no difference between the constitutional meaning of "in the service of the United States" and the meaning that Congress gave to that phrase in its militia statutes.
152. Ibid. at 20 (opinion of Washington, J.)
153. See ibid. at 24 (opinion of Washington, J.) ("Admit that the legislature of Pennsylvania could not constitutionally legislate in respect in respect to delinquent militia men, and to prescribe the punishment to which they should be subject, had the State Court Martial jurisdiction over the subject, so as to enforce the laws of Congress against these delinquents?").
154. See ibid. at 25, 28–29 (opinion of Washington, J.); ibid. at 29 (opinion of Washington, J.) ("The act of 1795 merely declares, that this offence shall be tried by a Court Martial. This was clearly not exclusive; but, on the contrary, it would seem to import, that such Court might be held under national, or State authority"). One confusing aspect of *Houston* for modern lawyers is that the opinions characterized a state law that conflicted with federal law as unconstitutional under the Supremacy Clause. Today lawyers would instead say that state law was "preempted" by federal law. Indeed, *Houston* can be read as the Court's first significant encounter with preemption. Speaking just for himself, Justice Washington rejected the claim that only a direct collision between state and federal law rendered a state law invalid. See ibid. at 22 (opinion of Washington, J.) ("From this doctrine, I must, for one, be permitted to dissent"). Washington instead suggested something like the modern idea of implied preemption, which is that the scope of state authority depends on the intent of Congress, which "is to be discovered as well by what the legislature has not declared, as by what they have expressed." Ibid.
155. See ibid. at 67–70 (Story, J., dissenting). Washington's reply to Justice Story was that Congress made clear when federal courts had exclusive jurisdiction. See ibid. at 26–29 (opinion of Washington, J.). The absence of such a statement in the militia acts was, therefore, telling in his view. See ibid. at 29 (opinion of Washington, J.).
156. Ibid. at 31 (opinion of Washington, J.); Justice Story pointed out that his reading of the act of Congress as vesting exclusive federal authority for courts martial eliminated this issue, which was against "the principles of the common law, and the genius of our free government." Ibid. at 72 (Story, J., dissenting).
157. Ibid. at 23 (opinion of Washington, J.).

158. See *Bartkus v. Illinois*, 359 U.S. 121, 130 (1959) (stating that the"language by Mr. Justice Washington reflected his belief that the state statute imposed state sanctions for violation of a federal criminal law. As he viewed the matter, the two trials would not be of similar crimes arising out of the same conduct; they would be of the same crime. . . . Thus *Houston v. Moore* can be cited only for the presence of a bar in a case in which the second trial is for a violation of the very statute whose violation by the same conduct has already been tried in the courts of another government empowered to try that question" [citations omitted]).

159. 131 S. Ct. 1960, 1977 (2019) (quoting *Bartkus* and explaining: "In other words, Justice Washington taught only that law prohibits two sovereigns (in that case, Pennsylvania and the United States) from both trying an offense against one of them (the United States)"); see ibid. at 1992 (Ginsburg, J., dissenting) (stating that the "distinction is thin, given the encompassing language in Justice Washington's opinion"); ibid. at 2004 (Gorsuch, J., dissenting) (stating that in *Houston* both Washington and Story "acknowledged that a second prosecution for the same underlying offense would be prohibited even if brought by a separate government").

The Court's effort to limit Justice Washington's skeptical language on successive state and federal prosecutions is rather tendentious. A more straightforward answer is that the justice was not writing for the Court in *Houston*—his opinion announced the judgment only. Thus, his views were not binding in subsequent cases and could be disregarded. The wisdom of doing that, though, is another matter.

160. See letter from Bushrod Washington to Richard Peters, Sept. 27, 1820, Historical Society of Pennsylvania.

161. Letter from Bushrod Washington to Richard Peters, Oct. 3, 1820, Historical Society of Pennsylvania; see letter from Bushrod Washington to Richard Peters, Oct. 17, 1820, Historical Society of Pennsylvania (saying much the same).

162. Letter from Joseph Story to Bushrod Washington, Jan. 13, 1821, New-York Historical Society; see letter from Bushrod Washington to Joseph Story, Mar. 19, 1822, Massachusetts Historical Society (reciprocating by telling Story to "take care of your health—Neither the Judiciary, nor your Country, can spare you").

163. Letter from John Marshall to Bushrod Washington, Feb. 8, 1821, in *Papers of John Marshall Digital Edition*.

164. The most important decision in 1821 was *Cohens v. Virginia*, a unanimous opinion by Chief Justice Marshall that upheld the constitutionality of the Court's appellate jurisdiction in certain criminal cases. See *Cohens v. Virginia*, 19 U.S. (6 Wheat.) 264 (1821). Judge Roane resumed his anonymous essays attacking the Marshall Court. See Paul, *Without Precedent*, 346; Smith, *Marshall*, 464; letter from John Marshall to Bushrod Washington, June 15, 1821, in *Papers of John Marshall Digital Edition* (commenting on the essays). Roane's death in 1822 was a blow to states' rights advocates. See Smith, *Marshall*, 468.

165. Letter from Joseph Story to Sarah Wetmore Story, (Feb. 27, 1821), in *Letters of Joseph Story* 2:398.

166. Letter from Bushrod Washington to Joseph Story, June 19, 1821, Massachusetts Historical Society.

167. See *Macker's Heirs v. Thomas*, 20 U.S. (7 Wheat.) 530 (1822) (reversing a circuit court judgment on the ground that an action did not survive a party's death); see also letter from Bushrod Washington to Joseph Story, Nov. 18, 1822, Massachusetts Historical Society (indicating that Washington thought that he might die in 1822). One opinion was the lowest number for Washington in any year between 1810 and 1829.
168. *Green v. Biddle*, 21 U.S. (8 Wheat.) 1, 11 (1823) (quoting from Justice Story's first opinion in the case). For additional background on *Green*, see Newmyer, *Heroic Age*, 240–43; David A. Faber, "Justice Bushrod Washington and the Age of Discovery in American Law," *West Virginia Law Review* 102 (2000): 795–98; Herbert A. Johnson, "Bushrod Washington," *Vanderbilt Law Review* 62 (2009): 473–76.
169. See *Green v. Biddle*, 21 U.S. (8 Wheat.) at 11–12 (quoting Justice Story's initial opinion).
170. See ibid. at 17–18 (motion of Mr. Clay as *amicus curiae*); ibid. at 38–58 (argument of Mr. Clay).
171. See ibid. at 69; ibid. at 18 (noting that the case was argued for the second time in 1822); see also ibid. at 94–107 (opinion of Johnson, J.). I cannot explain why Justice Johnson concurred with the first opinion in *Green* but dissented from the second one.
172. See Bushrod Washington Journal, Chicago History Museum, 71–94 (arranged under the heading "Green v. Biddle"). There is no way to know if the differences between Washington's draft and the final version of *Green* were (except for one example described in the text) the result of his edits or the suggestions of other justices. My comparison of the two texts does not reveal any dramatic distinctions.
173. Ibid., 94.
174. *Biddle*, 23 U.S. (8 Wheat.) at 39.
175. Bushrod Washington Journal, 90. Before addressing the constitutional question, he described the state laws and gave an overview of Virginia property law at the time that the interstate agreement was reached to show that the Kentucky statutes were inconsistent with Virginia law (69–85).
176. See ibid., 85; see also U.S. Const., art. I, § 10, cl. 3 ("No State shall, without the consent of Congress . . . enter into an Agreement or Compact with another State").
177. See *Green*, 23 U.S. (8 Wheat.) at 86–87.
178. See ibid. at 89.
179. Ibid. at 92.
180. Ibid. at 93. In his draft opinion, Washington made the deference point more forcefully. See Bushrad Washington Journal, 94 (praising "the validity of the laws, which ought never to be questioned but where the objections to them are fairly and clearly made out. In my apprehension this is precisely such a case").
181. Justice Todd's absence was costly because he was from Kentucky. And Marshall's recusal is curious given that he had joined Justice Story's opinion in *Green*. See *Green*, 23 U.S. (8 Wheat.) at 17n(a) (stating that the chief justice was part of the

Court in *Green*). He may have discovered afterward that his family owned land in Kentucky.

182. See Theodore W. Ruger, "'A Question Which Convulses the Nation': The Early Republic's Greatest Debate About the Judicial Review Power," *Harvard Law Review* 117 (2004): 886; see also *Bodley v. Gaither*, 19 Ky. (3 T.B. Mon.) 57, 58 (1825) (rejecting *Green* as binding because only three of the seven justices joined the decision). In 1831, the Court largely retreated from *Green* in an opinion by Justice Johnson that the chief justice and Justice Story joined. See *Hawkins v. Joshua Barney's Lessee*, 30 U.S. (5 Pet.) 457 (1831) (upholding a new Kentucky law as consistent with the compact).

 Washington probably agreed with the Court's initial conclusion in *Green*. But even if he did not, the justice may have felt constrained to affirm what the Court had done. An immediate about-face under political pressure from a state would have undermined the Court's authority in a manner at odds with Washington's broader institutional project.

183. See letter from Joseph Story to Bushrod Washington, Dec. 12, 1821, Mount Vernon Library.

184. See, e.g., Gerald Gunther, *Learned Hand: The Man and the Judge* (New York, Oxford University Press, 2011), 558.

185. A reasonable argument can be made that Justice Story's judgment became more of a problem once Washington and the chief justice were no longer on the Court to provide wise counsel. Story's misguided pro-slavery opinion in *Prigg v. Pennsylvania* might be an example. See *Prigg v. Pennsylvania*, 41 U.S. (16 Pet.) 539 (1842) (upholding the constitutionality of the Fugitive Slave Act of 1793); Paul Finkelman, *Supreme Injustice: Slavery in the Nation's Highest Court* (Cambridge, MA: Harvard University Press, 2018), 140–68.

186. See *Sneed v. Wister*, 21 U.S. (8 Wheat.) 690 (1823) (affirming a judgment in a debt action); *Society for the Propagation of the Gospel in Foreign Parts v. New Haven*, 21 U.S. (8 Wheat.) 464 (1823) (holding that a British corporation was not divested of its property in Vermont by the American Revolution or by the Treaty of Ghent); *Daly's Lessee v. James*, 21 U.S. (8 Wheat.) 495 (1823) (affirming his circuit decision involving a disputed will).

 New Haven was argued (on the losing side) by Daniel Webster and is worth noting because Washington articulated the view that corporations and individuals held equal rights to own property. See *New Haven*, 21 U.S. (8 Wheat.) at 475–80 (including Webster's argument). He cited both *Terrett* and *Dartmouth College* as authority for rejecting the claim that the Revolution wiped out royal charters. See ibid. at 481. He then stated: "It is very obvious, from the course of reasoning adopted in the last two cases that the Court was not impressed by any circumstance peculiar to such corporations, which distinguished them, in this respect, from natural persons; on the contrary, they were placed upon precisely the same ground." Ibid. at 481–82.

187. See Smith, *Marshall*, 469; Charles Warren, *The Supreme Court in United States History* (Boston: Little, Brown, and Company, 1926), 2:47.

Chapter 10

1. The phrasing in this sentence is deliberate. Washington died in Philadelphia and (as far as I can determine) had no enslaved people with him on the day that he died.
2. 4 F. Cas. 904 (C.C.D. Pa. 1806) (No. 2,241). The cases reviewed in this section are those in which Washington wrote an opinion about slavery. There are other cases, of course, in which enslaved people were involved but slavery was not an issue in the trial or appeal (for instance, an estate dispute where the estate included enslaved people). For a thorough review of those cases in the Supreme Court, see Paul Finkelman, *Supreme Injustice: Slavery in the Nation's Highest Court* (Cambridge, MA: Harvard University Press, 2018), 54–69, 78–89.
3. See *Butler*, 4 F. Cas. at 904; Ron Chernow, *Washington: A Life* (New York: Penguin Books, 2004), 536–37.
4. See *Butler*, 4 F. Cas. at 905.
5. See ibid.; see also U.S. Const., art. IV, § 2, cl. 3 ("No Person held to Service or Labor in one State, under the Laws thereof, escaping into another, shall, in Consequence of any Law or regulation therein, be discharged from such service or Labor, but shall be delivered up on Claim of the Party to whom such Service or Labor may be due").
6. *Butler*, 4 F. Cas. at 905. Butler was a member of Congress at one time, but not when Ben claimed his freedom.
7. 22 F. Cas. 151 (C.C.E.D. Pa. 1823) (No. 12,863). *Simmons* involved a petition for relief under the Fugitive Slave Act of 1793, so Washington's ruling simply denied the owner's request for federal intervention—apparently no other proceeding had occurred. See Fugitive Slave Act of 1793, 1 Stat. 302.
8. See *Simmons*, 22 F. Cas. at 151.
9. See ibid. at 152.
10. See Chernow, *Washington*, 637–39; Mary V. Thompson, "*The Only Unavoidable Subject of Regret*": *George Washington, Slavery, and the Enslaved Community at Mount Vernon* (Charlottesville: University of Virginia Press, 2019), 59–60.
11. Chernow, *Washington*, 761; see more generally 759–63.
12. 12 F. Cas. 172 (C.C.E.D. Pa. 1822) (No. 6,494).
13. It is not stated in the opinion that Ezekial escaped again, although that is the most logical reading of the jury's damage award.
14. See 12 F. Cas. 172 (C.C.E.D. Pa. 1822) (No. 6,494) at 172–73.
15. See ibid. at 173.
16. Ibid.
17. See ibid. at 173–74 (going through a series of hypotheticals to illustrate the point).
18. 30 F. Cas. 645, 646 (C.C.E.D. Pa. 1824) (No. 18,055). *Worthington* directed a jury to reject a negligence suit brought by a slave owner alleging that someone holding Tom, a fugitive who allegedly belonged to the owner, negligently permitted him to escape. The instruction said that negligence was not established. See ibid at 646–47.
19. See ibid. at 646.

20. Bushrod Washington Journal, Chicago History Museum, 68. The entry was a draft letter to someone, though I do not know to whom or whether the letter was, in fact, sent.
21. Ibid. at 69. Washington appears to be referring to a Pennsylvania law enacted in 1826. See *Prigg v. Pennsylvania*, 41 U.S. (16 Pet.) 539, 554–55 (1842) (quoting § 9 of the 1826 statute, which barred state magistrates from exercising jurisdiction under the Fugitive Slave Act). The journal entry was probably written in 1826, as he mentions "the legislation of Pennsylvania, lately passed." Bushrod Washington Journal, 69.
22. Bushrod Washington Journal, 70.
23. See *Worthington,* 30 F. Cas. at 645 ("An attempt has been made in Congress to correct these glaring defects in the act, without which correction the act is found to be practically of little avail, but the attempt has not as yet succeeded").
24. Letter from Bushrod Washington to Richard Peters, Mar. 15, 1826, Historical Society of Pennsylvania; cf. letter from Bushrod Washington to C. P. Wayne, Aug. 24, 1806, Historical Society of Pennsylvania (stating that "Francis Jackson, my manager, who goes to Philadelphia in order to apprehend a runaway slave of his own, who, he understands, is now in [Philadelphia]").
25. *Tryphenia v. Harrison*, 24 F. Cas. 252, 253 (C.C.D. Pa. 1806) (No. 14,209). *Tryphenia* was an appeal of a judgment that a vessel had illegally carried enslaved people from the United States to Cuba. The circuit court reversed on the ground that the enslaved people were the property of two passengers, and the relevant act of Congress applied only if enslaved people were transported for sale. Over a decade later, in *United States v. Kennedy*, Justice Washington reiterated that interpretation and charged the jury that if they "be satisfied that this negro boy was a slave in St. Thomas, and was carried to the island of Cuba for the purposes of sale, then it is the opinion of the court that you should find [the defendant] guilty . . . As to the credit to be given to the witness examined in support of the prosecution, you must judge." *United States v. Kennedy*, 26 F. Cas. 762 (C.C.D. Pa. 1821) (No. 15,525). The jury returned a verdict of not guilty.

    In the manifesto of the American Colonization Society, Washington referred to the slave trade abroad as "inhuman and abominable traffic, in the guilt and disgrace of which most of the civilized nations of the world were partakers." See *A View of Exertions Lately Made for the Purpose of Colonizing the Free People of Colour in the United States, in Africa or Elsewhere* (Washington, DC: Jonathan Elliot, 1817), 15.
26. 22 U.S. (9 Wheat.) 391 (1824).
27. See ibid. at 391–94.
28. Ibid. at 404. Prior to addressing the merits, the justice brushed aside three procedural and jurisdictional objections to the forfeitures. See ibid. at 400–403.
29. Ibid. at 404.
30. See ibid. at 405–8. The technical error was that the two vessels were accused of "holding them as slaves" rather than as transporting them "for the purpose of their being held to service." Ibid. at 405–6. The Court indicated that amending the libel would validate the forfeiture.
31. See Robert Cover, *Justice Accused: Antislavery and the Judicial Process* (New Haven, CT: Yale University Press, 1975).

32. See *Colonizing the Free People of Colour*, 4; see also Daniel Walker Howe, *What Hath God Wrought: The Transformation of America, 1815–1848* (New York: Oxford University Press, 2007), 261–66 (providing additional background on the ACS).
33. See letter from John Marshall to Bushrod Washington, Jun. 17, 1819, in *The Papers of John Marshall Digital Edition*, ed. Charles Hobson (Charlottesville: University of Virginia Press, 2014) ("I send you a check for $30 on account of my subscription to your society for colonization"); see *Colonizing the Free People of Colour*, 13 (listing all the officers, including Francis Scott Key, treasury secretary William Crawford, John Taylor of Caroline, and Elias Caldwell (the Supreme Court's clerk)); Finkelman, *Supreme Injustice*, 179–80 (noting Taney's membership); David O. Stewart, *Madison's Gift: Five Partnerships That Built America* (New York: Simon and Schuster, 2015), 323 (noting Madison's membership).
34. See R. Kent Newmyer, *John Marshall and the Heroic Age of the Supreme Court* (Baton Rouge: Louisiana State University Press, 2001), 419; see also *Colonizing the Free People of Colour*, 15 (stating that a free colony in Africa would might lift the continent to "the sublime morality and humanizing discipline of the Gospel").
35. Scott E. Casper, *Sarah Johnson's Mount Vernon: The Forgotten Memory of An American Shrine* (New York: Hill and Wang, 2008), 14.
36. *Colonizing the Free People of Colour*, 14.
37. Ibid., 15.
38. See, e.g., Doris Kearns Goodwin, *Team of Rivals: The Political Genius of Abraham Lincoln* (New York: Simon & Schuster, 2003), 406–7.
39. James Traub, *John Quincy Adams: Militant Spirit* (New York: Basic Books, 2016), 242 (quoting Adams's diary).
40. Newmyer, *Heroic Age*, 423.
41. See Kate Masur, *Until Justice Be Done: America's First Civil Rights Movement, from the Revolution to Reconstruction* (New York: W. W. Norton & Co., 2021), 33–34, 78–80.
42. I am unable to find a published version of this address, which could mean that the remarks were informal and unpublished. Or the address may not have occurred. My best guess is that the notes were written in 1821 or 1822, as the justice says at one point, "Cut off as I have been this year by indisposition," which would seem to refer to the illness that he suffered in the latter half of 1820 and the first half of 1821.
43. Bushrod Washington Journal, 65–66.
44. Ibid., 66.
45. See letter from Bushrod Washington to unknown recipient, undated, Mount Vernon Library. The justice refers to the colonization society in the letter, thus he must have drafted the document between 1816 and 1829. I could not determine if the letter was ever sent, so the thoughts expressed there must be viewed as tentative.
46. See ibid. (stating that the proposals "are exposed to difficulties which I have not been able to surmount . . . [H]as the national government the power under the Constitution to adopt the proposed measure[?] It is certainly not to be found amongst the defined powers, and I do not perceive that it can fairly be implied from any part of that instrument. If Congress possesses the power, then the difficulty occurs—is it likely that the Northern states would concur to pay their proportion of any general tax"

that would go to only states with slaves). I could not identify the essay that prompted Washington's draft letter or the essay's author.

47. One visitor to Mount Vernon said that Bushrod tried to attract free whites to farm the estate but there was no interest. See Sir Augustus John Foster, *Jeffersonian America: Notes on the United States of America* (San Marino, CA: Huntington Library, 1954), 144.
48. See Finkelman, *Supreme Injustice*, 50; see also Newmyer, *Heroic Age*, 420 (giving the figure as 12,000).
49. Washington, like many of the Founding Fathers, worried that slavery could split the Union. See letter from Bushrod Washington to Richard Peters, May 29, 1820, Historical Society of Pennsylvania ("No man can feel more regret or alarm than I do at attempts to create parties in our Country partaking of a sectional character, or marked by any of those Circumstances which are connected unavoidably with the different status of society within those sections"; "[M]y prayer is 'let the Union be preserved, whatever other evil may befall us' ").
50. Some secondary sources say that Justice Washington did send some of his enslaved people to Liberia, but I am unable to find any evidence to support that claim. Bushrod's niece Jane did free some of her slaves and let them emigrate to Liberia.
51. The initial account appeared in the *Genius of Liberty*, a newspaper published in Leesburg. See "Judge Washington," *Niles' Weekly Register*, Sept. 29, 1821, 21:70; Casper, *Sarah Johnson's Mount Vernon*, 16. Recent research at Mount Vernon (shared with me by Jason Burroughs) indicates that the enslaved people who were sold came primarily from Union Farm, which was farther away from the mansion.
52. *Morning Chronicle and Baltimore Advertiser*, Aug. 24, 1821, 2.
53. See Casper, *Sarah Johnson's Mount Vernon*, 15. This conclusion rests on the fact that these enslaved people were absent from the estate when Washington died in 1829. See ibid., 233n15. It is possible that some of them died before that, but it is doubtful that all of them did before 1830.
54. *Morning Chronicle and Baltimore Advertiser*, Aug. 24, 1821, 2. The author also explained: "The reader ought to know that GEORGE WASHINGTON set all his slaves free upon his death, and that Judge Washington is his nephew."
55. Washington does seem to have become more thin-skinned with age, as he also felt compelled (as Chapter 7 explained) to answer press criticism of his alleged rudeness to the members of Congress who visited Mount Vernon by steamboat.
56. "Judge Washington," *Niles' Weekly Register*, Sept. 29, 1821, 21:70.
57. See David W. Maxey, *A Portrait of Elizabeth Willing Powel, 1743–1830* (Philadelphia: American Philosophical Society, 2006), 54.
58. Ibid.
59. "Judge Washington," *Niles' Weekly Register*, Sept. 29, 1821, 21:70. His reply was reprinted in newspapers across the country, though I am citing to the version reprinted in *Niles' Weekly Register*.
60. There are examples in Mount Vernon's archives of the justice's slave transactions. In one document entitled "Valuation of Negroes" that dates from 1813, there is a list of their names and estimated worth, with an entry for one named Moses that says

"$75 sold." And given the number of enslaved people that he inherited as compared to those whom the justice recorded when he made an inventory in 1815, there is a high likelihood that others were sold before 1821. See Casper, *Sarah Johnson's Mount Vernon*, 233n15.

61. "Judge Washington," *Niles' Weekly Register*, Sept. 29, 1821, 21:71.
62. Washington said that one reason some families were separated was that some of their members were his property while others were not. He claimed that he tried to buy these other family members so that he could then sell the whole family together, but that did not work out in some cases. Ibid.
63. See ibid., 72.
64. Ibid., 71.
65. See ibid., 71.
66. See Casper, *Sarah Johnson's Mount Vernon*, 18–19; cf. "Judge Washington," *Niles' Weekly Register*, Sept. 29, 1821, 21:72 (stating that Seal was Washington's estate manager). Hannah was found guilty following a trial in which she was represented by a lawyer, though there were doubts about her guilt. See Casper, *Sarah Johnson's Mount Vernon*, 20. She died in prison a year later. See ibid. at 22–23. Seal lived at Union Farm, which was where most of the enslaved people who were sold lived and worked.
67. "Judge Washington," *Niles' Weekly Register*, Sept. 29, 1821, 21:72.
68. See ibid; Casper, *Sarah Johnson's Mount Vernon*, 15.
69. See Casper, *Sarah Johnson's Mount Vernon*, 15. Enslaved people continued to flee Mount Vernon when they could get away. See letter from Bushrod Corbin Washington to Bushrod Washington, Apr. 12, 1823, Mount Vernon Library (telling the justice that he was trying to track down George and Nathan, two enslaved people who had escaped).

    Oliver Smith's son Phil became the gardener at Mount Vernon, but George and Ned were given by Bushrod's will to other relatives, shattering what was left of the Smith family. See Casper, *Sarah Johnson's Mount Vernon*, 28–29; Matthew R. Costello, *Property of the Nation: George Washington's Tomb, Mount Vernon, and the Memory of the First President* (Lawrence: University Press of Kansas, 2018), 95.
70. Letter from "Urbain Babier" to Bushrod Washington, Aug. 12, 1822, Mount Vernon Library.
71. See Newmyer, *Heroic Age*, 420; see generally Benjamin Lundy, *A Plan for the Gradual Abolition of Slavery in the United States, Without Danger or Loss to the Citizens of the South* (Baltimore: Benjamin Lundy, 1825).
72. "Judge Washington," *Genius of Universal Emancipation*, Oct. 1821, 52.
73. See ibid. Lawrence Augustine Washington was the son of George's younger brother Samuel. See Chernow, *Washington*, 464; see also Justin Glenn, *The Washingtons: A Family History, Volume One: Seven Generations of the Presidential Branch* (El Dorado Hills, CA: Savas Beatie, 2015), 72–76 (providing more information on Lawrence Washington's decision to emancipate his enslaved people).
74. "Judge Washington," *Genius of Universal Emancipation*, Oct. 1821, 52. After the justice's death, William Lloyd Garrison's abolitionist newspaper, *The Liberator*, recounted the controversy and was harshly critical of Washington. See "Judge

Washington, or a Specimen of the Conduct of the First President of the American Colonization Society," *Liberator*, Mar. 22, 1834, 45.

75. "Judge Washington," *Niles' Weekly Register*, Sept. 29, 1821, 21:70.

Chapter 11

1. See *Corfield v. Coryell*, 6 F. Cas. 546 (C.C.E.D. Pa. 1825) (No. 3,230). There is some confusion about the proper way to cite *Corfield*. Many cases and sources use 1823 as the date, because the case was formally from the circuit court's April 1823 term. The final opinion, though, was not issued until 1825, as the case report explains (see ibid. at 550), and the most recent Supreme Court opinion citing *Corfield* gives 1825 as the date. See *McBurney v. Young*, 569 U.S. 221, 229 (2013). I therefore use 1825.
2. See *Corfield*, 6 F. Cas. at 550.
3. None of the crew were New Jersey residents, which might have cured the problem. There was a dispute over whether the oyster harvesting had occurred in New Jersey waters. See ibid. at 553. *Corfield* examined the royal charters setting the state's boundaries and some colonial compacts before ruling that New Jersey did have jurisdiction over plaintiff's vessel. See ibid. at 553–55. The court also rejected the argument that the state proceeding was invalid for being held in the wrong county. See ibid. at 555.
4. See ibid. at 549. Two other constitutional claims were advanced. The first was that the state statute violated "the second section of the third article, which extends the judicial authority to all cases of admiralty and maritime jurisdiction." Ibid. at 549. This claim was rejected on the ground that "the power to regulate the fisheries belonging to the several states, and to punish those who should transgress those regulations, was exclusively vested in the states, respectively, at the time when the present constitution was adopted, and that it was not surrendered to the United States, by the mere grant of admiralty and maritime jurisdiction to the judicial branch." Ibid. at 553. The plaintiff also said the state proceedings "were contrary to the fourth article of the amendments to the constitution; the seizure having been made without a warrant," ibid. at 549, but this argument was evidently abandoned, as the Court never addressed the point.

   Corfield said that the plaintiff could not maintain a trespass action because the vessel was operating under a charter at the time of seizure. See ibid. at 555. Plaintiff's "only remedy is an action on the case for consequential damages," though the point was moot once the New Jersey statute was upheld as constitutional.
5. Ibid. at 549.
6. Ibid. at 549–50.
7. Ibid. at 550. Judge Peters probably participated in *Corfield*, but there is no evidence that his views carried any weight.
8. U.S. Const., art. I, § 8, cl. 3. The fact that Washington's *Corfield* notes do not mention *Gibbons v. Ogden* allows us to conclude with confidence that the notes were written before the Supreme Court decided that case in 1824.

9. Wolcott's Veto Message can be found in the *Columbian Register* (New Haven) of June 1, 1822 (hereinafter Wolcott Veto). The veto was overridden. See also *Gibbons v. Ogden*, 22 U.S. (9 Wheat.) 1, 6 (1824) (argument of Daniel Webster) (mentioning the Connecticut law). Washington and Wolcott had known each other since the Adams administration, though there is no indication that they corresponded about the veto. The Wolcott Veto is not a famous text, and I do not know why the justice found the message useful.
10. See *Gibbons*, 22 U.S. (9 Wheat.) at 1; Wolcott Veto ("The Bill is professedly retaliatory. . . . The object of this Bill is, not to create a right in our citizens to the use of the waters of New-York, but to prohibit the use of our waters, until that right is surrendered to us"). Washington was well versed in Fulton's invention of the steamboat, as he had upheld the validity of Fulton's patent in a separate case. See *Cutting v. Myers*, 6 F. Cas. 1081 (C.C.D. Pa. 1818) (No. 3,520).
11. See Wolcott Veto ("If our citizens are unlawfully excluded from the waters of the State of New-York, by the operation of their acts, it creates no right in us to deprive their citizens of the use of our waters"). Wolcott also discussed the Privileges and Immunities Clause in his veto, but Justice Washington referred only to the Commerce Clause discussion in his notes.
12. See ibid. ("I cannot believe that our National Constitution is so defective, that the questions cannot be fairly and speedily presented, or that the enlightened tribunal created to decide them, either has refused or would refuse, or delay a decision, upon a case regularly presented for their adjudication").
13. Bushrod Washington Journal, Chicago History Museum, 100.
14. Ibid., 100–101.
15. *Corfield*, 6 F. Cas. at 551.
16. U.S. Const., art. IV, § 2, cl. 1.
17. See *Livingston v. Van Ingen*, 9 Johns. 507 (N.Y. 1812).
18. Bushrod Washington Journal, 102–3; see *Livingston*, 9 Johns. at 561 (opinion of Yates, J.) ("The Constitution of the *United States* intends that the same immunities and privileges shall be extended to all the citizens equally, for the wise purpose of preventing local jealousies, which discriminations (always deemed odious) might otherwise produce"); ibid. at 577 (opinion of Kent, C.J.) (stating that the Privileges and Immunities Clause "means only that citizens of other states shall have equal rights with our own citizens, and not that they shall have different or greater rights").
19. Bushrod Washington Journal, 102.
20. Letter from Bushrod Washington to Joseph Story, June 27, 1823, Massachusetts Historical Society.
21. See Jean Edward Smith, *John Marshall: Definer of a Nation* (New York: Henry Holt and Company, 1996), 470; Charles Warren, *The Supreme Court in United States History* (Boston: Little, Brown, and Company, 1926), 2: 54.
22. Letter from John Marshall to Bushrod Washington, Aug. 6, 1823, in *The Papers of John Marshall Digital Edition*, ed. Charles Hobson (Charlottesville: University of Virginia Press, 2014).

23. *Gibbons v. Ogden*, 22 U.S. (9 Wheat.) 1 (1824); see Smith, *Marshall*, 475–76. The main steamboat captain for Gibbons was Cornelius Vanderbilt, who later became America's leading shipping and railroad mogul. See T. J. Stiles, *The First Tycoon: The Epic Life of Cornelius Vanderbilt* (New York: Alfred A. Knopf, 2009), 36–64 (describing Vanderbilt's employment under Gibbons and the run-up to *Gibbons v. Ogden*).
24. See *Gibbons*, 22 U.S. (9 Wheat.) at 3–33 (argument of Mr. Webster); ibid. at 159–86 (argument of Attorney General Wirt).
25. See Joel Richard Paul, *Without Precedent: John Marshall and His Times* (New York: Riverhead Books, 2018), 368; Smith, *Marshall*, 476. An example of Washington presiding was *Stewart v. Ingle*, where he stated for the Court that a return of a record by a circuit court clerk was sufficient for certiorari. See *Stewart v. Ingle*, 22 U.S. (9 Wheat.) 526, 526 (1824) ("Mr. Justice Washington, after consultation with the Judges, stated, that according to the rules and practice of the Court, a return made by the Clerk was a sufficient return").
26. Letter from Bushrod Washington to Richard Peters, Mar. 18, 1824, Historical Society of Pennsylvania.
27. See Paul, *Without Precedent*, 368; Smith, *Marshall*, 477. Justice Johnson concurred separately in *Gibbons* and argued that the Commerce Clause vested Congress with exclusive power over that subject. See *Gibbons*, 22 U.S. (9 Wheat.) at 222–39 (Johnson, J., concurring).
28. See ibid. at 211–21.
29. Ibid. at 189.
30. Ibid. at 193.
31. Ibid. at 196.
32. Ibid. at 197.
33. Ibid. at 203.
34. Letter from Bushrod Washington to Richard Peters, Mar. 18, 1824, Historical Society of Pennsylvania.
35. See *Kerr v. Devisees of A. Moon*, 22 U.S. (9 Wheat.) 541 (1824) (reversing a circuit judgment in an estate dispute); *Hughes v. Edwards*, 22 U.S. (9 Wheat.) 489 (1824) (affirming a circuit court decree involving an unpaid debt); *The Fanny*, 22 U.S. (9 Wheat.) 659 (1824) (resolving a maritime case in which an American privateer illegally captured cargo from a Portuguese vessel); *Den* ex dem *Walker v. Turner*, 22 U.S. (9 Wheat.) 541 (1824) (reversing a circuit court for erroneously instructing a jury on the application of a statute of limitations in an ejectment case). *The Merino*, which was discussed in Chapter 10, was also decided in 1824. See 22 U.S. (9 Wheat.) 391 (1824).
36. See Wolcott Veto ("It may be assumed as an axiom, that all regulations by the states, which relate either to ferries, bridges, or roads, or other public improvements, which facilitate the intercourse between different parts of our Country, are clearly constitutional"; referring to "free and unconstrained commercial intercourse"). Wolcott also said (as Washington recorded) that the steamboat monopoly was invalid on statutory grounds even if Congress lacked the exclusive authority to regulate commerce or if commerce were defined more narrowly ("If it were admitted, that the powers

are *concurrent*, it may be observed, that Congress have already passed numerous acts relating to the commercial intercourse between the different States, all of which are necessarily founded on the admitted principle, that such intercourse may be carried on *freely and without interruption, by all the citizens of the United States*").

37. Webster's argument in *Gibbons* frequently referred to commerce or its equivalents as intercourse. See *Gibbons*, 22 U.S. (9 Wheat.) at 4.
38. *Corfield*, 6 F. Cas. at 550. I lack an airtight explanation for the timing of the events in *Corfield*. For instance, why were the plaintiff's legal arguments not heard until October 1824? I think the answer is that the spring 1824 circuit was cut short when Washington fell ill. And they were probably not heard in 1823 because *Gibbons* was pending in the Supreme Court, though I am unsure about that conclusion.
39. See letter from Bushrod Washington to Joseph Story, Jun. 8, 1825, University of Michigan, William L. Clements Library ("I send you the report of the case of Corfield v. Coryellas you perused the opinion at large during the last session of the Supreme Court"). He also sent Justice Thompson a summary of *Corfield* in his circuit report. See letter from Bushrod Washington to Smith Thompson, May 30, 1825, Huntington Library ("It would be difficult to abridge the case so as to lay before you the course of reasoning that was pursued, nor is it necessary as the points decided were deemed of sufficient importance by some of the bar to be published which it was I presume [in a newspaper]").
40. *Corfield*, 6 F. Cas. at 550–51.
41. Ibid. at 551.
42. Ibid. (quoting *Gibbons*, 22 U.S. (9 Wheat.) at 78).
43. *Corfield*, 6 F. Cas. at 552. *Gibbons* did make a brief reference to the Privileges and Immunities Clause, stating that the Constitution "only protects the personal rights of the citizens of one State, when within the jurisdiction of another, by securing to them 'all the privileges and immunities of a citizen' of that other, which they hold subject to the laws of the State as its own citizen." *Gibbons*, 22 U.S. (9 Wheat.) at 69. Washington did not, though, quote *Gibbons* in the privileges and immunities portion of *Corfield*.
44. See ibid. at 555. The rest of the opinion disposed of the other issues raised, none of which was deemed consequential in Washington's notes on the case.
45. Ibid. at 551–52; see Articles of Confederation of 1781, art. IV, para. 1.
46. See, e.g., Jack M. Balkin, *Living Originalism* (New York: Cambridge University Press, 2011), 406n84 ("Washington's statement that these rights 'have at all times been enjoyed' must be taken as aspirational rather than as an accurate account of history; the comity [or Privileges and Immunities] clause was necessary precisely because the state had not always respected these rights and might not in the future").
47. Va. Declaration of Rights of 1776, art. I.
48. See Akhil Reed Amar, *The Bill of Rights: Creation and Reconstruction* (New Haven, CT: Yale University Press, 1998), 177 ("Washington seemed to be following a quintessentially common-law approach in deducing 'fundamental' rights"); William Blackstone, *Commentaries on the Laws of England* (Chicago: University of Chicago Press, 1979), 1:134–42 (discussing the basic liberties of English subjects). The right against unequal taxation is more complex, but there was precedent concluding that

this was a privilege and immunity of citizens. See *Campbell v. Morris*, 3 H. & McH. 535, 554 (Md. 1797); David R. Upham, "*Corfield v. Coryell* and the Privileges and Immunities of American Citizenship," *Texas Law Review* 83 (2005): 1499–502.

49. Letter from Bushrod Washington to Edward S. Burd, Jan. 7, 1805, in "The Letters of Bushrod Washington (1762–1829) in the Hampton L. Carson Collection of the Free Library of Philadelphia," ed. Howell J. Heaney, *American Journal of Legal History* 2 (1958): 165 ("Another question before our *wise* Congress is—whether every free man in the Town of Alex[andria] shall be allowed the right of suffrage. If I am not mistaken a right like this would be attended with innumerable ill consequences").

50. See, e.g., Kurt Lash, *The Fourteenth Amendment and the Privileges and Immunities of American Citizenship* (New York: Cambridge University Press, 2014), 29–37 (discussing these antebellum cases).

51. See, e.g., Jack M. Balkin, *Living Originalism* (Cambridge, MA: Harvard University Press, 2011), 196–97, 208–9. A critical exception was Congressman John A. Bingham, who drafted the Privileges or Immunities Clause and never referred to *Corfield* during the Thirty-Ninth Congress. See Gerard N. Magliocca, *American Founding Son: John Bingham and the Invention of the Fourteenth Amendment* (New York: New York University Press, 2013), 117–18.

52. This conclusion rests on several observations. First, no court before 1866 cited *Corfield* to mean what many Reconstruction Republicans articulated. Second, Washington's notes referred to *Livingston*'s definition of the Privileges and Immunities Clause, which was about out-of-state discrimination only. He could have changed his mind about the meaning of the clause, just as he changed his mind about the application of that clause to oyster harvesting laws. But there is no indication that he did change his view of the principle underlying the clause.

53. See, e.g., John Harrison, "Reconstructing the Privileges and Immunities Clause," *Yale Law Journal* 101 (1992): 1416; *McDonald v. Chicago*, 561 U.S. 742, 821 (2010) (Thomas, J., concurring) ("Justice Washington did not indicate whether Article IV, § 2 *required* States to recognize these fundamental rights in their own citizens and thus in sojourning citizens alike, or whether the Clause simply prohibited the States from discriminating against sojourning citizens with respect to whatever fundamental rights state law happened to recognize"); *Hague v. CIO*, 307 U.S. 496, 511 (1939) (opinion of Roberts, J.) ("At one time it was thought that [the Privileges and Immunities Clause] recognized a group of rights which, according to the jurisprudence of the day, were classed as 'natural rights'; and that the purpose of the section was to create rights of citizens of the United States by guaranteeing the citizens of every State the recognition of this group of rights by every other State. Such was the view of Justice Washington").

54. *Congressional Globe*, 39th Cong., 1st Sess. (1866), 475 (statement of Sen. Trumbull), 1835–36 (statement of Rep. Lawrence).

55. Ibid., 1117–18 (statement of Representative Wilson).

56. Ibid., 1269 (statement of Rep. Kerr).

57. See ibid., 1121 (statement of Rep. Rogers).

58. Ibid., 475 (statement of Sen. Trumbull).

59. Civil Rights Act of 1866, § 1, ch. 31, 14 Stat. 27; see Magliocca, *American Founding Son*, 120.
60. *Congressional Globe*, 39th Cong., 1st Sess. (1866), 2765 (statement of Sen. Howard); see U.S. Const., amend XIV, § 1. Likewise, when Congress enforced Section One of the Fourteenth Amendment against the Ku Klux Klan, Republicans continued to invoke *Corfield* as their best case. Senator Arthur Boreman quoted *Corfield* in 1871 and then told his colleagues: "The rights, immunities, and privileges described by Judge Washington have, in numerous instances . . . been invaded and trampled upon and outraged." *Congressional Globe*, 42nd Cong., 1st Sess. (1871), app. 228 (statement of Sen. Boreman), app. 69 (statement of Rep. Shellabarger).
61. See U.S. Const., amend. XIV, § 2 (defining the potential voter pool as "any of the male inhabitants" of a state "being twenty-one years of age, and citizens of the United States" except those who participated "in rebellion, or other crime").
62. See Victoria C. Woodhull, "Address to the Judiciary Committee of the House of Representatives," in *History of Women's Suffrage, 1861–1876*, ed. Elizabeth Cady Stanton, Susan B. Anthony, and Mathilda Joslyn Gage (Rochester, NY: Charles Mann Printing Co., 1881), 2:444–48; Stiles, *The First Tycoon*, 502. The irony of Woodhull's petition and its reliance on *Corfield* is that New Jersey, which was within Washington's circuit, was the only state before the Civil War that permitted some women to vote. See Jan Ellis Lewis, "Rethinking Women's Suffrage in New Jersey, 1776–1807," *Rutgers Law Review* 63 (2011): 1017–35. Washington may have had this in mind when he wrote the line about voting rights in *Corfield*, though there is no way to know.
63. A. G. Riddle, "Speech in Support of the Woodhull Memorial, Before the Judiciary Committee of the House of Representatives," in *History of Women's Suffrage, 1861–1876*, ed. Elizabeth Cady Stanton, Susan B. Anthony, and Mathilda Joslyn Gage (Rochester, NY: Charles Mann Printing Co., 1881), 2:453; see Lash, *Privileges and Immunities*, 235 (describing Riddle's speech). Riddle repeated this argument in a losing effort to invalidate the District of Columbia's bar on women voting. See Elizabeth Cady Stanton, Susan B. Anthony, and Mathilda Joslyn Gage, eds., *History of Women's Suffrage, 1861–1876* (Rochester, NY: Charles Mann Printing Co., 1881), 2:235n13.
64. See "Women's Suffrage," *New York Times*, Jan. 31, 1871, 1 (reproducing the House Judiciary Committee Report written by John A. Bingham). The Supreme Court reached the same conclusion three years later in *Minor v. Happersett*, 88 U.S. (21 Wall.) 162 (1874), but the Court did not refer to *Corfield* in its opinion. The plaintiff in *Minor* challenging the exclusion of women from voting in Missouri did cite *Corfield*. See Stanton, Anthony, and Gage, *Women's Suffrage*, 2:725–26.
65. See William Loughridge and Benjamin Butler, "Minority Report of the House Committee on the Judiciary on the Subject of the Woodhull Memorial, H.R. Rep. No. 41-5, Pt. 2," in *History of Women's Suffrage, 1861–1876*, ed. Elizabeth Cady Stanton, Susan B. Anthony, and Mathilda Joslyn Gage (Rochester, NY: Charles Mann Printing Co., 1881), 2:464–82. Benjamin Butler, one of the dissenters, was a radical Republican and a controversial figure during the Civil War and Reconstruction. See, e.g., Ron

Chernow, *Grant* (New York: Penguin Books, 2017), 371–72; Magliocca, *American Founding Son*, 103–6.

66. See Loughridge and Butler, “Minority Report,” 2:470.
67. Ibid., 2:470–71.
68. Ibid., 2:471. But cf. *Congressional Globe*, 40th Cong., 2d Sess. (1868), 2054 (statement of Rep. Woodward) (citing *Corfield* for the proposition that “suffrage is one of the reserved rights of the States and that the Federal Government has no power to confer or take it away”).
69. See U.S. Const., art. I, § 4, cl. 1 (“The Times, Places, and Manner of holding Elections for Senators and Representatives, shall be prescribed in each State by the Legislature thereof; but the Congress may at any time by Law make or alter such Regulations”); see also U.S. Const., amend. XXVI (prohibiting age discrimination); amend. XXIV (prohibiting poll taxes); amend. XIX (prohibiting sex discrimination); amend. XV (barring race discrimination).
70. 83 U.S. (16 Wall.) 36, 76–77 (1873). *Slaughter-House* rejected a Fourteenth Amendment claim by some white butchers in Louisiana that a state law granting a monopoly on butchering to a New Orleans corporation was unconstitutional. See ibid. at 57–59.
71. Nonetheless, the Court said that the Privileges or Immunities Clause of the Fourteenth Amendment protected “the privilege of the writ of *habeas corpus*,” which was one of the rights listed in *Corfield*. See ibid. at 79; *Corfield*, 6 F. Cas. at 552.
72. *Slaughter-House*, 83 U.S. (16 Wall.) at 97 (Field, J., dissenting).
73. See ibid. at 117–18 (Bradley, J., dissenting) (“It is pertinent to observe that both the clause of the Constitution referred to, and Justice Washington in his comment on it, speak of the privileges and immunities of citizens in a State; not of citizens of a State. It is the privileges and immunities of citizens, that is, of citizens as such, that are to be accorded to citizens of other States when they are found in any State; or, as Justice Washington says, ‘privileges and immunities which are, in their nature, fundamental; which belong, of right, to the citizens of all free governments’ ”).
74. See *Blake v. McClung*, 172 U.S. 239, 248–49 (1898).
75. *Mason v. Missouri*, 179 U.S. 328, 335 (1900); see ibid. at 328–30.
76. See, e.g., *Poe v. Ullman*, 367 U.S. 497, 541 (1961) (Harlan, J., dissenting) (defending a constitutional right of privacy in certain contexts). The same is true for those who are critical of unwritten constitutional rights (or their scope) and hence seek to discredit *Corfield*. See Robert H. Bork, *The Tempting of America: The Political Seduction of the Law* (New York: The Free Press, 1990), 181 (describing *Corfield* as “a singularly confused opinion in 1823 by a single Justice of the Supreme Court”).

Chapter 12

1. Charles Warren, *The Supreme Court in United States History* (Boston: Little, Brown, and Company, 1926), 1:467.

2. Letter from Bushrod Washington to Joseph Story, June 18, 1824, Massachusetts Historical Society.
3. See letter from John Marshall to Bushrod Washington, Jun. 12, 1825, in *The Papers of John Marshall Digital Edition*, ed. Charles Hobson (Charlottesville: University of Virginia Press, 2014).
4. See letter from Bushrod Washington to Joseph Hopkinson, Apr. 22, 1826, Historical Society of Pennsylvania ("All my endeavors to find a pamphlet published many years ago, for Chief Justice Marshall have failed. It is entitled 'Calm Observer,' published during a period when the two great parties in the United States were highly excited; Farmer Giles, the supposed, or perhaps acknowledged author"); see also John Marshall to Bushrod Washington, May 31, 1826, in *Papers of John Marshall Digital Edition* (stating that he was "much obliged by your kind enquiries for 'The Calm Observer.' I now believe that those papers were never in the pamphlet form, or, if ever so published, are no longer to be found").
5. See James Traub, *John Quincy Adams: Militant Spirit* (New York: Basic Books, 2016), 302–3. The four candidates were Andrew Jackson (Tennessee), John Quincy Adams (Massachusetts), Henry Clay (Kentucky), and William Crawford (Georgia). See David McCullough, *John Adams* (New York: Simon and Schuster, 2001), 637.
6. See U.S. Const., amend XII (requiring the House to choose from among the top three candidates); McCullough, *Adams*, 639.
7. See Traub, *John Quincy Adams*, 306–11. There was no proof of a quid pro quo between Adams and Clay, though the sequence of events looked suspicious. The secretary of state was, during that era, the heir apparent to the president. Madison, Monroe, and Adams each served as secretary of state prior to his election.
8. See Jean Edward Smith, *John Marshall: Definer of a Nation* (New York: Henry Holt and Company, 1996), 485–86.
9. See *Thomas v. Brockenbrough*, 23 U.S. (10 Wheat.) 146 (1825) (affirming an equitable judgment as free of error); *McCormick v. Sullivant*, 23 U.S. (10 Wheat.) 192 (1825) (affirming a judgment concerning a disputed estate); *Keplinger v. De Young*, 23 U.S. (10 Wheat.) 358 (1825) (affirming a jury verdict rejecting a patent infringement claim).
10. See U.S. Const., art III, § 1.
11. *McCormick*, 23 U.S. (10 Wheat.) at 199. One party argued that a prior circuit court judgment that acted as a form of collateral estoppel should be considered null and void because diversity jurisdiction was not established in that prior case. See ibid. The Court's response was that a circuit court judgment was valid unless reversed or vacated, which had not happened in this case. See ibid. at 199–200.
12. See, e.g., *Chicot County Drainage District v. Baxter State Bank*, 308 U.S. 371, 376 (1940); *Cutler v. Huston*, 158 U.S. 423, 430–31 (1895).
13. See Smith, *Marshall*, 492.
14. See *United States v. Vanzandt*, 24 U.S. (11 Wheat.) 184 (1826) (reversing a judgment involving a surety bond for an army paymaster); *Perkins v. Hart*, 24 U.S. (11 Wheat.) 237 (1826) (holding that "the points reserved, upon which the Judges of that [Circuit] Court were opposed, are too imperfectly stated to enable this Court to pronounce

any opinion upon them"); *United States v. Kelly*, 24 U.S. (11 Wheat.) 417 (1826) (defining the federal offense of "endeavoring to make a revolt" on a vessel); *United States v. Ortega*, 24 U.S. (11 Wheat.) 467 (1826) (holding that a criminal prosecution against a private individual for assaulting a foreign diplomat did not fall with the Supreme Court's original jurisdiction).

15. See Smith, *Marshall*, 492; Warren, *Supreme Court*, 2:144.
16. See McCullough, *Adams*, 646–47.
17. See Last Will and Testament of Bushrod Washington, Mount Vernon Library (including a codicil dated July 10, 1826).
18. In 1826, Congress extended the Supreme Court's term by a month to give the justices more time to deal with their docket. See act of May 4, 1826, ch. 37, 4 Stat. 160. Washington delivered two unanimous opinions for the Court in 1827. See *Thornton v. Wynn*, 25 U.S. (12 Wheat.) 183 (1827) (reversing a judgment on a promissory note); *United States v. 350 Chests of Tea*, 25 U.S. (12 Wheat.) 486 (1827) (affirming a judgment rejecting the forfeiture of imported tea for failure to pay the tariffs).
19. See *Adams v. Storey*, 1 F. Cas. 141 (C.C.D. N.Y. 1817) (No. 66); Smith, *Marshall*, 439, 658n118 (stating that Justice Johnson's opinion was unpublished).
20. 17 U.S. (4 Wheat.) 122 (1819).
21. See *Sturges*, 17 U.S. (4 Wheat.) at 208.
22. *Crowninshield*, 17 U.S. (4 Wheat.) at 196.
23. *Ogden v. Saunders*, 25 U.S. (6 Pet.) 213, 272–73 (1827) (Johnson, J., concurring).
24. See ibid. at 263–64 (opinion of Washington, J.).
25. See ibid. at 213–14.
26. Letter from Bushrod Washington to Richard Peters, Mar. 18, 1824, Historical Society of Pennsylvania.
27. For a comprehensive tabulation of the Court's decisions by one vote up until the 1930s, see "Judgments of the Supreme Court Rendered by a Majority of One Vote," *Georgetown Law Journal* 24 (1936): 984–1002.
28. See *Ogden v. Saunders*, 25 U.S. (6 Pet.) at 254–70 (opinion of Washington, J.). Washington's opinion was not an opinion for the Court. Justices Johnson, Trimble, and Thompson each wrote concurring opinions in *Ogden*. See ibid. at 271–92 (opinion of Johnson, J.); ibid. at 292–313 (opinion of Thompson, J.,); ibid. at 313–32 (opinion of Trimble, J.). I describe Washington's opinion as the lead one because most of the subsequent citations by the Court treat his reasoning in that way.
29. See ibid. at 332–56 (Marshall, C.J., dissenting); ibid. at 332 ("Three Judges, Mr. Justice DUVALL, Mr. Justice STORY, and myself, do not concur in the judgment which has been pronounced"). A third argument in *Ogden* was held on the question whether New York's bankruptcy statute must be applied by a circuit court in Louisiana. On this question, the Court again divided 4–3, but Justice Johnson switched sides. See ibid. at 357–69 (opinion of Johnson, J.). What this leaves unclear is why Justice Johnson opined on the constitutional issue at all, given that he was able to resolve the case on another ground. Nor do I have a good explanation for why the chief justice dissented so vehemently when he usually strived for consensus.
30. Ibid. at 256 (opinion of Washington, J.).

31. Ibid. at 268 (opinion of Washington, J.).
32. Bushrod Washington Journal, Chicago History Museum, 114 ("Notes on the Cases Respecting State Bankruptcy Laws"), 116 (stating that *Sturges* decided that "the states are not prohibited from passing them provided they do not impair the obligation of contracts. They therefore cannot pass such laws as to prior contracts; and if they cannot pass them as to subsequent contracts, they cannot pass them at all").

    Washington's notes for *Ogden* look no different from his notes for other cases in the journal. It is hard to imagine, though, that he did not put some extra effort into his preparation given that he probably knew that Chief Justice Marshall was strongly opposed to his views.
33. *Ogden*, 25 U.S. (12 Wheat.) at 264 (opinion of Washington, J.); cf. ibid. at 267 (opinion of Washington, J.) ("Thinking, as I have always done, that that the power to pass bankrupt laws was intended by the authors of the constitution to be exclusive in Congress, or, at least, that they expected the power vested in that body would be exercised, so as effectually to prevent its exercise by the States, it is the more probable that, in reference to all other interferences of the State legislatures upon the subject of contracts, retrospective laws were alone in the contemplation of the Convention").
34. Bushrod Washington Journal, 114.
35. Ibid., 115.
36. *Ogden*, 25 U.S. (12 Wheat.) at 256 (opinion of Washington, J.).
37. Ibid. at 257 (opinion of Washington, J.).
38. Ibid. at 257–58 (opinion of Washington, J.). Here Washington made a fascinating (though probably unintentional) callback to one of his first separate opinions, in *Bas v. Tingy*, in which he described the military conflict between France and the United States as an "imperfect war."
39. Ibid. at 258 (opinion of Washington, J.). Counsel brought up *Green v. Biddle* to point out that contractual obligations could be created between sovereigns where no municipal law applied. See ibid. at 223 (argument of Mr. Wheaton) (referring to the interstate compact between Virginia and Kentucky). Washington agreed with that observation but said that it was irrelevant in *Ogden* when state law was available to regulate. See ibid. at 258 (opinion of Washington, J.).
40. Ibid. at 258–59 (opinion of Washington, J.).
41. Ibid. at 259 (opinion of Washington, J.) (also listing "laws of registration, and those which affect landlord and tenant, [and] sales at auction"); see ibid. at 261–63 (opinion of Washington, J.). Statutes of frauds hold that certain kinds of contracts must be put into writing.
42. Bushrod Washington Journal, 116.
43. *Ogden*, 25 U.S. (12 Wheat.) at 261 (opinion of Washington, J.).
44. Ibid. at 263 (opinion of Washington, J.).
45. Ibid. at 345 (Marshall, C.J., dissenting); see R. Kent Newmyer, *John Marshall and the Heroic Age of the Supreme Court* (Baton Rouge: Louisiana State University Press, 2001), 262–64 (explaining how Marshall's dissent in *Ogden* tracked John Locke's natural law reasoning).

46. *Ogden*, 25 U.S. (12 Wheat.) at 353–54 (Marshall, C.J., dissenting).
47. See ibid. at 348–49 (Marshall, C.J., dissenting).
48. See ibid. at 349 (Marshall, C.J., dissenting). On this point, Marshall was almost certainly wrong. Modern lawyers do not understand a statute of limitations as a rule of evidence, and there is no indication that a different opinion prevailed in 1827.
49. See ibid. at 261–62 (opinion of Washington, J.) (stating that usury laws did not just "annihilate a contract at its birth . . . since it may legitimately void all contracts afterward entered into, which reserve to the lender a higher rate of interest than this law permits").
50. See ibid. at 262 (opinion of Washington, J.).
51. Bushrod Washington Journal, 115.
52. See *Allgeyer v. Louisiana*, 165 U.S. 578, 589–90 (1897) (establishing the "liberty of contract" and quoting Justice Bradley's cite to the Declaration of Independence from his dissent in *Slaughter-House*); see generally David E. Bernstein, *Rehabilitating* Lochner: *Defending Individual Rights Against Progressive Reform* (Chicago: University of Chicago Press, 2011) (presenting a rich overview of the liberty of contract).
53. See *Adkins v. Children's Hospital*, 261 U.S. 525, 568 (1923) (Holmes, J., dissenting); see also *Lochner v. New York*, 198 U.S. 45, 75 (1905) (Holmes, J., dissenting) (invoking usury).
54. Justice Washington's support for federal criminal common law cuts against his positivism, but we lack his justification for that doctrine due to his decision (as a long note in Chapter 8 explained) to delete that passage from his report of *United States v. Passmore*. It is possible, of course, that his thinking moved away from natural law reasoning over time.
55. *Ogden*, 25 U.S. (12 Wheat.) at 265 (opinion of Washington, J.).
56. Ibid. (opinion of Washington, J.); see U.S. Const., art. I, § 10, cl. 1. The first part of Section Ten bars states from entering into treaties or granting letters of marque and reprisal, which relate to foreign policy.
57. *Ogden*, 25 U.S. (12 Wheat.) at 266 (opinion of Washington, J.).
58. Ibid. at 267 (opinion of Washington, J.).
59. Ibid. at 268 (opinion of Washington, J.).
60. Ibid. at 335 (Marshall, C.J., dissenting).
61. Ibid. at 336 (Marshall, C.J., dissenting.).
62. Ibid. at 269 (opinion of Washington, J.).
63. Ibid. at 270.
64. See *Ashwander v. Tennessee Valley Auth.*, 297 U.S. 288, 355 (1936) (Brandeis, J., concurring); *Untermyer v. Anderson*, 276 U.S. 440, 453 (1928) (Brandeis, J., dissenting); *Eisner v. Macomber*, 252 U.S. 189, 238 (1920) (Brandeis, J., dissenting); see also *Heiner v. Donnan*, 285 U.S. 312, 341 (1932) (Stone J., dissenting) (quoting Washington's maxim on deference). In some of these cases, Justice Brandeis was complaining about the Court's lack of deference to Congress rather than to state legislatures.
65. See, e.g., James B. Thayer, "The Origin and Scope of the American Doctrine of Constitutional Law," *Harvard Law Review* 7 (1893): 142n1; see Melvin I. Urofsky,

Louis D. Brandeis: A Life (New York: Pantheon Books, 2009), 37, 78–79, 477 (describing Brandeis's relationship with Thayer).

66. For some basic background on the Court-packing struggle, see, e.g. Jeff Shesol, *Supreme Power: Franklin Roosevelt v. the Supreme Court* (New York: W. W. Norton, 2010).
67. *FDR's Fireside Chats*, ed. Russell D. Buhite and David W. Levy (Rockville, MD: Arc Manor, 2009), 63 (providing the quote from the speech of March 9, 1937).
68. See "Mr. Justice Washington a Nephew of the President," *New York Times*, March 10, 1937, at 15.
69. See *Mason v. Haile*, 25 U.S. (12 Wheat.) 370 (1827).
70. See ibid. at 377. The split in *Haile* between the majority and the dissent was largely about what notice the Contracts Clause required for the creditor. In effect, the Court concluded that in Rhode Island constructive notice was given (according to the debtor's argument) by "unwritten law" consisting of the "established usage" of legislative petitions through private bills. See ibid. at 373. Washington, on the other hand, insisted that practice was not enough. Instead, he thought that the Contracts Clause required a general statute with a formal process for insolvency relief.
71. Ibid. at 379 (Washington, J., dissenting); see ibid. at 382–83 ("My object in declaring my dissent from that which has been delivered, being not so much to prove that opinion to be wrong, as to vindicate my own consistency"). Bushrod's dissent in *Haile* was oral, and he stated, "I have prepared no written opinion." See ibid. at 382 (Washington, J., dissenting). The court reporter must have taken notes on the oral dissent or obtained the justice's notes to publish the dissent.
72. Ibid. at 382 (Washington, J., dissenting); see ibid. at 381 (Washington., J., dissenting) (making the point about retroactivity).
73. Ibid. at 380 (Washington, J., dissenting).
74. 26 U.S. (1 Pet.) 351.
75. Letter from Bushrod Washington to Joseph Story, Feb. 15, 1828, Massachusetts Historical Society. I do not know why in this instance Washington wrote to Story rather than just speaking with him. The justice referred to the case as "Bell v. Wilkins, etc.," as Wilkins was one of the defendants.
76. See *Bell*, 26 U.S. (1 Pet.) at 359–60.
77. Ibid. at 375. Read in conjunction with Justice Washington's letter, the implication is that Chief Justice Marshall was a silent dissenter in *Bell*.
78. Washington wrote for the Court twice in 1828. See *Hunt v. Rhodes*, 26 U.S. (1 Pet.) 1 (1828) (affirming an equitable decree); *Greenleaf v. Queen*, 26 U.S. (1 Pet.) 138 (1828) (reversing a judgment involving a land sale by a trustee).
79. See letter from Bushrod Washington to Richard Peters Jr., July 21, 1828, Historical Society of Pennsylvania ("I am just recovering from a severe bilious attack").
80. Letter from Bushrod Washington to Richard Peters Jr., Sept. 7, 1828, Historical Society of Pennsylvania.
81. The Federal Judicial Center website (www.fjc.gov) contains the relevant information about Hopkinson's appointment to the bench.

82. See Joel Richard Paul, *Without Precedent: John Marshall and His Times* (New York: Riverhead Books, 2018), 384; Smith, *Marshall*, 501. Justice Trimble's tenure on the Court was one of the shortest ever—just two years.
83. See Daniel Walker Howe, *What Hath God Wrought: The Transformation of America, 1815–1848* (New York: Oxford University Press, 2007); Traub, *John Quincy Adams*, 363–75.
84. Letter from Joseph Story to Bushrod Washington, Dec. 22, 1828, New-York Historical Society. Washington may have shared Story's low opinion of Jackson, but I was unable to find any references to Jackson in Washington's letters.
85. See Paul, *Without Precedent*, 388; Smith, *Marshall*, 501–02.
86. See *Williams v. Bank of the United States*, 27 U.S. (2 Pet.) 96 (1829) (affirming a judgment for nonpayment of notes); *Bank of the United States v. Corcoran*, 27 U.S. (2 Pet.) 121 (1829) (affirming a judgment in a promissory note dispute); *LeRoy, Bayard & Co. v. Johnson*, 27 U.S. (2 Pet.) 186 (1829) (affirming a judgment in a partnership case); *The American Fur Co. v. United States*, 27 U.S. (2 Pet.) 357 (1829) (reversing a forfeiture of goods to the United States); *Satterlee v. Matthewson*, 27 U.S. (2 Pet.) 380 (1829); *Buckner v. Finley & Van Lear*, 27 U.S. (2 Pet.) 586 (1829) (holding that the commercial paper at issue was a foreign bill of exchange).
87. *Satterlee*, 27 U.S. (2 Pet.) at 411. Justice Johnson concurred separately in *Satterlee*. See ibid. at 414–16 (Johnson, J., concurring).
88. Ibid. at 412; see ibid. at 413 ("Retrospective laws which do not impair the obligation of contracts, or partake of the character of *ex post facto* laws, are not condemned or forbidden").
89. Ibid. at 413.
90. Ibid. at 413–14 (quoting *Fletcher*, 10 U.S. (6 Pet.) at 135–36). *Fletcher*'s unwillingness to rely exclusively on natural law grounds may reflect Washington's resistance to that idea, though other members of the Court may have shared his skepticism.
91. Joseph Hopkinson, *Eulogium in Commemoration of the Hon. Bushrod Washington, Late One of the Justices of the Supreme Court of the United States* (Philadelphia: T. S. Manning, 1830), 31–32; see Horace Binney, *Bushrod Washington* (Philadelphia: C. Sherman & Son, 1858), at 3 (noting that Hopkinson was the district judge at the time that he delivered his eulogy for Washington).
92. Hopkinson, *Bushrod Washington*, 32.
93. See ibid. (noting the date of Justice Washington's death); see also Binney, *Bushrod Washington*, 24 ("When his death occurred, in Philadelphia, it broke her heart; and, though she attempted to get home, when his remains were attended to Mount Vernon, she died upon the road"). The dates of Bushrod and Nancy's deaths are recorded on their respective markers at Mount Vernon's tomb.

    The Journal of Law, a short-lived publication by the Philadelphia bar, published an unsigned deathbed account of the justice. See "Judge Washington," *Journal of Law* 1 (Sept. 15, 1830): 88–91. As the account is unsigned, I cannot evaluate the credibility of what the justice allegedly told that author. Thus, I decided not to use that source.
94. "Obituary," 28 U.S. (3 Pet.) i, x (1830).

95. *Life and Letters of Joseph Story*, ed. William Wetmore Story (Boston: Little & Brown, 1851), 2:31; see more generally 29–33. Justice Story's tribute appeared in the *Boston Daily Advertiser* of December 10, 1829. See ibid., 2:29. Story told Richard Peters Jr. that "I wrote it without rising from my table. It is my sincere estimate of his character." Ibid.
96. Ibid., 2:31.
97. See letter from John Marshall to James Madison, Nov. 30, 1829, https://founders.archives.gov/?q=%20Author%3A%22Marshall%2C%20John%22%20Recipient%3A%22Madison%2C%20James%22&s=1111311111&r=3.
98. See letter from John Marshall to Joseph Hopkinson, Dec. 17, 1830, in *Papers of John Marshall Digital Edition*.
99. See letter from John Marshall to Joseph Story, May 15, 1833, in *Papers of John Marshall Digital Edition*.
100. See "Obituary," 28 U.S. (3 Pet.) v–x (1830). Marshall was serving as a delegate to Virginia's Constitutional Convention when Bushrod died and his return for the Court's 1830 session was delayed. See Paul, *Without Precedent*, 410–11; Smith, *Marshall*, 504–6.

    An understated salute to Justice Washington came in a garden-variety case about a bill of lading that he tried in circuit court. In *Conrad v. Nicoll*, the Supreme Court reporter stated: "By direction of the court, the whole of the charge delivered by Mr. Justice Washington is inserted, as follows." *Conrad v. Nicoll*, 29 U.S. (4 Pet.) 291, 291 (1830). After that unusual request, Justice Henry Baldwin—Washington's successor on the Court—wrote a two-paragraph opinion stating that the case was governed by a prior decision and "we do not think it necessary to enter into an examination of the principles on which the judge submitted the cause to the jury." Ibid. at 310; see Smith, *Marshall*, 507 (discussing the nomination of Baldwin to replace Washington). The inclusion of the charge in *Conrad*, the brief endorsement of its soundness, and the assignment of the opinion to Baldwin read like a collective sign of respect for Washington's legacy.
101. See Paul, *Without Precedent*, 411; Smith, *Marshall*, 507.

Epilogue

1. See Last Will and Testament of Bushrod Washington, July 19, 1828, Mount Vernon Library; Scott E. Casper, *Sarah Johnson's Mount Vernon: The Forgotten Memory of An American Shrine* (New York: Hill and Wang, 2008), 27.
2. For example, this was arguably how Jane Austen used "condescending" in one of her best novels. See, e.g., Jane Austen, *Pride and Prejudice* (London: T. Egerton, 1813), 163 (describing Lady Catherine de Bourgh this way: "You will be delighted with her. She is all affability and condescension"). I say arguably because there could be a double meaning in Austen's use of "condescending" that depends on the character's perspective.

3. See Last Will and Testament of Bushrod Washington, July 19, 1828, Mount Vernon Library; Casper, *Sarah Johnson's Mount Vernon*, 27, 59–60.
4. See letter from West Ford to John Augustine Washington III, Sept. 6, 1844, Mount Vernon Library (describing ongoing work at Mount Vernon); Casper, *Sarah Johnson's Mount Vernon*, 56–58, 76, 85.
5. The history of the purchase and the subsequent renovations at Mount Vernon is well documented at the museum itself.
6. See Benson J. Lossing, "Mount Vernon as It Is," *Harper's New Monthly Magazine* 18 (March 1859): 443–45; Casper, *Sarah Johnson's Mount Vernon*, 76.
7. Lossing, "Mount Vernon," 445.
8. See Casper, *Sarah Johnson's Mount Vernon*, 95. It appears that Ford was at Mount Vernon for about a month before he died.

Bibliography

Manuscript Collections

American Bible Society
American Philosophical Society Library
Chicago History Museum
Cincinnati History Museum and Library
Duke University Library
George Washington Masonic National Memorial Association
Harvard University Library
Historical Society of Pennsylvania
Huntington Library
Indiana University, Ruth M. Lilly Library
J. P. Morgan Library
Library of Congress
Library of Virginia
Massachusetts Historical Society
Morristown National Historical Park Library
Mount Vernon Library

National Archives

New York Historical Society
New York Public Library
Tulane University
University of Michigan, William L. Clements Library
University of Virginia, Special Collections

Books, Articles, and Miscellaneous Sources

Ackerman, Bruce. *The Failure of the Founding Fathers: Jefferson, Marshall, and the Rise of Presidential Democracy*. Cambridge, MA: Harvard University Press, 2005.
Adams, Henry. *History of the United States During the First Administration of Thomas Jefferson*. 2 vols. New York: Charles Scribner & Sons, Inc., 1903.
Amar, Akhil Reed. *America's Constitution: A Biography*. New York: Random House, 2005.
Amar, Akhil Reed. *The Bill of Rights: Creation and Reconstruction*. New Haven, CT: Yale University Press, 1998.
Annis, David Leslie. "Mr. Bushrod Washington, Supreme Court Justice on the Marshall Court." PhD dissertation, Notre Dame University, 1974.

Armes, Ethel, ed. *Nancy Shippen Her Journal Book: The International Romance of A Young Lady of Fashion of Colonial Philadelphia with Letters to Her and About Her.* Philadelphia: J. B. Lippincott Co., 1935.
Auricchio, Laura. *The Marquis: Lafayette Reconsidered.* New York: Alfred A. Knopf, 2014.
Austen, Jane. *Pride and Prejudice.* London: T. Egerton, 1813.
Avlon, John. *Washington's Farewell: The Founding Father's Warning to Future Generations.* New York: Simon & Schuster, 2018.
Balkin, Jack M. *Living Originalism.* Cambridge, MA: Harvard University Press, 2011.
Barnett, Randy. *Restoring the Lost Constitution: The Presumption of Liberty.* Princeton, NJ: Princeton University Press, 2004.
Baude, William, and Stephen Sachs. "The Misunderstood Eleventh Amendment." *University of Pennsylvania Law Review* 169 (2021): 609–63.
Bernstein, David. E. *Rehabilitating Lochner: Defending Individual Rights Against Progressive Reform.* Chicago: University of Chicago Press, 2011.
Beveridge, Albert J. *The Life of John Marshall.* 4 vols. Boston: Houghton & Mifflin, 1919.
Bilder, Mary Sarah. *Madison's Hand: Revising the Constitutional* Convention. Cambridge, MA: Harvard University Press, 2015.
Binney, Horace. *Bushrod Washington.* Philadelphia: C. Sherman & Son, 1858.
Bird, Wendell. "New Light on the Sedition Act of 1798: The Missing Half of the Prosecutions." *Law and History Review* 34 (2016): 541–610.
Bird, Wendell. *Press and Speech Under Assault: The Early Supreme Court Justices, the Sedition Act of 1798, and the Campaign Against Dissent.* New York: Oxford University Press, 2016.
Blackstone, William. *Commentaries on the Laws of England.* 4 vols. 1765. Reprint, Chicago: University of Chicago Press, 1979.
Blumberg, Phillip I. *Repressive Jurisprudence in the Early American Republic: The First Amendment and the Legacy of English Law.* New York: Cambridge University Press, 2010.
Bork, Robert H. *The Tempting of America: The Political Seduction of the Law.* New York: The Free Press, 1990.
Bowman, Frank O., III. *High Crimes and Misdemeanors: A History of Impeachment for the Age of Trump.* New York: Cambridge University Press, 2019.
Brooke, St. George Tucker. "The Brooke Family." *Virginia Historical Magazine* 19 (1911): 100–104.
Brown, David Paul. *The Forum: Or, Forty Years Full Practice at the Philadelphia Bar.* 2 vols. Philadelphia: Robert H. Small, Law Bookseller, 1856.
Campbell, Jud. "The Invention of First Amendment Federalism." *Texas Law Review* 97 (2019): 517–70.
Carpenter, Stanley D. M. *Southern Gambit: Cornwallis and the British March to Yorktown.* Norman: University of Oklahoma Press, 2019.
Casper, Scott E. *Sarah Johnson's Mount Vernon: The Forgotten History of An American Shrine.* New York: Hill and Wang, 2008.
Catalogue of the Members and Library of the Hasty-Pudding Club of Harvard University. Cambridge, MA: Cambridge Press, Metcalf, Torry, and Ballou, 1841.
Chernow, Ron. *Alexander Hamilton.* New York: Penguin Books, 2004.
Chernow, Ron. *Grant.* New York: Penguin Books, 2017.
Chernow, Ron. *Washington: A Life.* New York: Penguin Books, 2010.

Coe, Alexis. *You Never Forget Your First: A Biography of George Washington*. New York: Viking Press, 2020.
Cooke, Jacob, ed. *The Federalist*. Hanover, NH: Wesleyan University Press, 1961.
Costello, Matthew R. *Property of the Nation: George Washington's Tomb, Mount Vernon, and the Memory of the First President*. Lawrence: University Press of Kansas, 2018.
Cover, Robert. *Justice Accused: Antislavery and the Judicial Process*. New Haven, CT: Yale University Press, 1975.
Craughwell, Thomas J. *Stealing Lincoln's Body*. Cambridge, MA: Belknap Press, 2007.
Custer, Lawrence B. "Bushrod Washington and John Marshall: A Preliminary Inquiry." *Journal of American Legal History* 4 (1960): 34–48.
Dalzell, Robert F., Jr., and Lee Baldwin Dalzwell. *George Washington's Mount Vernon: At Home in Revolutionary America*. New York: Oxford University Press, 1998.
Donald, David Herbert. *Charles Sumner*. New York: Da Capo Press, 1996.
Douglas, M. Davison. "The Jeffersonian Vision of Legal Education." *Journal of Legal Education* 51 (2001): 185–211.
Elliot, Jonathan, ed. *The Debates in the Several State Conventions on the Adoption of the Federal Constitution as Recommended by the General Convention at Philadelphia in 1787*. Philadelphia: J. B. Lippincott, 1891.
Ellis, Joseph J. *His Excellency: George Washington*. New York: Vintage, 2004.
Elmer, Lucius Q. C. *The Constitution and Government of the Province and State of New Jersey* Newark, NJ: Martin R. Dennis & Company, 1872.
Ely, John Hart. *Democracy and Distrust: A Theory of Judicial Review*. Cambridge, MA: Harvard University Press, 1980.
Emmons, William Robert. "Mr. Justice Bushrod Washington and the American Constitution." Unpublished manuscript, 1991. Mount Vernon Library.
Ewald, William. "James Wilson and the Drafting of the Constitution." *University of Pennsylvania Journal of Constitutional Law* 10 (2008): 901–1009.
Faber, David A. "Justice Bushrod Washington and the Age of Discovery in American Law." *West Virginia Law Review* 102 (2000): 735–807.
Farber, Daniel A. "The Fourteenth Amendment and the Unconstitutionality of Secession." *Akron Law Review* 45 (2012): 488–512.
Farbman, Daniel. "Resistance Lawyering." *California Law Review* 107 (2019): 1877–953.
Feldman, Noah F. *The Three Lives of James Madison: Genius, Partisan, President*. New York: Random House, 2017.
Finkelman, Paul. *Supreme Injustice: Slavery in the Nation's Highest Court*. Cambridge, MA: Harvard University Press, 2018.
Fithian, Philip Vickers. *Journal and Letters of Philip Vickers Fithian, 1773–1774: A Plantation Tutor of the Old Dominion*. Edited by Hunter Dickson Farish. Williamsburg, VA: Colonial Williamsburg, 1943.
Fleming, Thomas J. *Beat the Last Drum: The Siege of Yorktown, 1781*. New York: St. Martin's Press, 1963.
Foster, Sir Augustus John. *Jeffersonian America: Notes on the United States of America*. San Marino, CA: Huntington Library, 1954.
Friedman, Barry. *The Will of the People: How Public Opinion Has Influenced the Supreme Court and Shaped the Meaning of the Constitution*. New York: Farrar, Straus, and Giroux, 2009.
Friendly, Henry J. "In Praise of *Erie*—And of the New Federal Common Law." *New York University Law Review* 39 (1964): 383–422.

Gienapp, Jonathan. *The Second Creation: Fixing the American Constitution in the Founding Era*. Cambridge, MA: Harvard University Press, 2018.

Glenn, Justin. *The Washingtons: A Family History, Volume One: Seven Generations of the Presidential Branch*. El Dorado Hills, CA: Savas Beatie, 2015.

Glick, Joshua. "On the Road: The Supreme Court and the History of Circuit Riding." *Cardozo Law Review* 24 (2003): 1753–843.

Glickstein, Jed. "After Midnight: The Circuit Judges and the Repeal of the Judiciary Act of 1801." *Yale Journal of Law and the Humanities* 24 (2012): 543–78.

Goodwin, Doris Kearns. *Team of Rivals: The Political Genius of Abraham* Lincoln. New York: Simon & Schuster, 2003.

Gordon-Reed, Annette. *The Hemingses of Monticello*. New York: W. W. Norton & Company, 2008.

Gottschalk, Louis. *Lafayette and the Close of the American Revolution*. Chicago: University of Chicago Press, 1942.

Gunther, Gerald. "John Marshall, 'A Friend of the Constitution': In Defense and Elaboration of *McCullough v. Maryland*." *Stanford Law Review* 21 (1969): 449–55.

Gunther, Gerald. *Learned Hand: The Man and the Judge*. New York: Oxford University Press, 2011.

Hamilton, Alexander. Edited by Harold C. Syrett. *The Papers of Alexander Hamilton*. 27 vols. New York: Columbia University Press, 1974.

Hammond, Charles. *State of the Case and Argument from the Appellants, in the Case of the Bank of the United States, Versus the Auditor and Treasurer of the State of Ohio, in the Supreme Court of the United States*. Cincinnati, OH: Morgan and Lodge, 1823.

Harrison, John. "Reconstructing the Privileges and Immunities Clause." *Yale Law Journal* 101 (1992): 1385–474.

Heintze, James R. "Music of the Washington Family." *Music Quarterly* 56 (1970): 288–93.

Henderson, Todd M. "From Seriatim to Consensus and Back Again: A Theory of Dissent." *Supreme Court Review* 2007 (2007): 283–344.

Hofstedt, Matthew. "The Switch to Black: Revisiting Early Supreme Court Robes." *Supreme Court Historical Journal* 46, no. 1 (2001): 13–41.

Hopkinson, Joseph. *Eulogium in Commemoration of the Hon. Bushrod Washington, Late One of the Justices of the Supreme Court of the United States*. Philadelphia: T. S. Manning, 1830.

Howe, Daniel Walker. *What Hath God Wrought: The Transformation of America, 1815–1848*. New York: Oxford University Press, 2007.

Ingersoll, Charles. *Inchiquin: The Jesuit's Letters*. New York: Riley, 1810.

Isaacson, Walter. *Benjamin Franklin: An American Life*. New York: Simon and Schuster, 2003.

Jackson, Robert H. *The Struggle for Judicial Supremacy: A Study of a Crisis in American Law*. New York: Alfred A. Knopf, 1941.

Jefferson, Thomas. *The Life and Selected Writings of Thomas Jefferson*. Edited by Adrienne Koch and William Peden. New York: The Modern Library, 1993.

Jefferson, Thomas. *The Papers of Thomas Jefferson*. 45 vols. Edited by Julian P. Boyd. Princeton, NJ: Princeton University Press, 1958.

Johnson, Herbert A. "Bushrod Washington." *Vanderbilt Law Review* 62 (2009): 447–90.

Johnson, William. *Sketches of the Life and Correspondence of Nathanael Greene, Major General of the Armies of the United States in the* Revolution. 2 vols. Charleston: A. E. Miller, 1822.

Joyce, Craig. "The Rise of the Supreme Court Reporter: An Institutional Perspective." *Michigan Law Review* 83 (1985): 1291–391.

"Judge Washington." *Journal of Law* 1 (1830): 88–91.

"Judgments of the Supreme Court Rendered by a Majority of One Vote." *Georgetown Law Journal* 24 (1936): 984–1002.

Kaminski, John P., and Gaspare J. Saladino, eds. *The Documentary History of the Ratification of the Constitution*. 32 vols. Madison: State Historical Society of Wisconsin, 1988.

Kelly, M. Ruth. *The Olmstead Case: Privateers, Property, and Politics in Pennsylvania*. Selinsgrove, PA: Susquehanna University Press, 2005.

Kent, James. *Commentaries on American Law*. 4 vols. New York: O. Halsted. 1826.

Ketcham, Ralph. *James Madison: A Biography*. Charlottesville: University Press of Virginia, 1990.

Ketchum, Richard M. *Victory at Yorktown: The Campaign that Won the Revolution*. New York: Henry Holt and Company, 2004.

Klarman, Michael J. *The Framers' Coup: The Making of the United States Constitution*. New York: Oxford University Press, 2016.

Kukla, Jon. *Patrick Henry, Champion of Liberty*. New York: Simon & Schuster, 2017.

LaCroix, Alison. *The Ideological Origins of American Federalism*. Cambridge, MA: Harvard University Press, 2010.

Langbein, John, Renee Lettow Lerner, and Bruce P. Smith, eds. *History of the Common Law: The Development of Anglo-American Legal Institutions*. New York: Aspen, 2009.

Larson, Carlton F. W. *The Trials of Allegiance: Treason, Juries, and the American Revolution*. New York: Oxford University Press, 2019.

Lash, Kurt. *The Fourteenth Amendment and the Privileges and Immunities of American Citizenship*. New York: Cambridge University Press, 2014.

Lash, Kurt, and Alicia Harrison. "Minority Report: John Marshall and the Defense of the Alien and Sedition Acts." *Ohio State Law Journal* 68 (2007): 435–516.

Latrobe, Benjamin Henry. *The Papers of Benjamin Henry Latrobe: Correspondence and Miscellaneous Papers*. Edited by Edward C. Carter II. New Haven, CT: Yale University Press, 1984.

Latrobe, Benjamin Henry. *The Virginia Journals of Benjamin Henry Latrobe, 1795–1798*. Edited by Edward C. Carter II. New Haven, CT: Yale University Press, 1977.

Lee, Jean B., ed. *Experiencing Mount Vernon: Eyewitness Accounts, 1784–1865*. Charlottesville: University of Virginia Press, 2006.

Leonard, Gerald, and Saul Cornell, *The Partisan Republic: Democracy, Exclusion, and the Fall of the Founders Constitution, 1780s–1830s*. New York: Cambridge University Press, 2019.

Lerner, Renee Lettow. "The Transformation of the American Civil Trial: The Silent Judge." *William and Mary Law Review* 42 (2000): 195–264.

Lewis, Jan Ellis. "Rethinking Women's Suffrage in New Jersey, 1776–1807." *Rutgers Law Review* 63 (2011): 1017–35.

Lukens, Robert J. "Jared Ingersoll's Rejection of Appointment as One of the 'Midnight Judges' of 1801: Foolhardy or Farsighted?" *Temple Law Review* 70 (1997): 189–231.

Lundy, Benjamin. *A Plan for the Gradual Abolition of Slavery in the United States, Without Danger or Loss to the Citizens of the* South. Baltimore: Benjamin Lundy, 1825.

Lynch, David. *The Role of the Circuit Courts in the Shaping of United States Law in the Early Republic: Supreme Court Justices Washington, Livingston, Story and Thompson on Circuit and on the Court*. Portland, OR: Hart Publishing, 2018.

Madison, James. *The Papers of James Madison*. Edited by Robert A. Rutland and Charles F. Hobson. Charlottesville: University Press of Virginia, 1977.

Madison, James. *The Papers of James Madison: Presidential Series*. Edited by J. C. A. Stagg, Jeanne Kerr Cross, and Susan Holbrook Perdue. Charlottesville: University of Virginia Press, 1996.

Madison, James. *The Papers of James Madison: Retirement Series*. Edited by David Mattern, J. C. A. Stagg, Mary Parke Johnson, and Anne Mandeville Colony. Charlottesville: University of Virginia Press, 2009.

Madison, James. *The Papers of James Madison: Secretary of State Series*. Edited by Mary Hackett, J. C. A. Stagg, Jeanne Kerr Cross, Susan Holbrook Perdue, and Ellen J. Barber. Charlottesville: University Press of Virginia, 1998.

Magliocca, Gerard N. *American Founding Son: John Bingham and the Invention of the Fourteenth Amendment*. New York: New York University Press, 2013.

Magliocca, Gerard N. *The Heart of the Constitution: How the Bill of Rights Became the Bill of Rights*. New York: Oxford University Press, 2018.

Maier, Pauline. *Ratification: The People Debate the Constitution, 1787–1788*. New York: Simon and Schuster, 2010.

Marcus, Maeva, and Robert Teir. "Hayburn's Case: A Misinterpretation of Precedent." *Wisconsin Law Review* 1988, no. 3 (1988): 527–46.

Marshall, John. *The Life of George Washington*. 5 vols. Philadelphia: C. P. Wayne, 1804–7.

Marshall, John. *The Papers of John Marshall Digital Edition*. Edited by Charles Hobson. Charlottesville: University of Virginia Press, 2014.

Masur, Kate. *Until Justice Be Done: America's First Civil Rights Movement, from the Revolution to Reconstruction*. New York: W. W. Norton & Co., 2021.

Maxey, David W. *A Portrait of Elizabeth Willing Powel, 1743–1830*. Philadelphia: American Philosophical Society, 2006.

McCullough, David. *John Adams*. New York: Simon and Schuster, 2001.

McRee, Griffith J. *Life and Correspondence of James Iredell: One of the Associate Justices of the Supreme Court of the United States*. 2 vols. New York: D. Appleton & Co., 1858.

Meacham, Jon. *Thomas Jefferson and the Art of Power*. New York: Random House, 2012.

Minor, Benjamin Blake. *"Memoir of the Author" from Decisions in Virginia by the High Court of Chancery*. Richmond, VA: J. W. Randolph, 1852.

Newmyer, R. Kent. *John Marshall and the Heroic Age of the Supreme Court*. Baton Rouge: Louisiana State University Press, 2001.

Newmyer, R. Kent. *Supreme Court Justice Joseph Story: Statesman of the Old Republic*. Chapel Hill: University of North Carolina Press, 1985.

Nockleby, John T. "Two Theories of Competition in the Early 19th Century Labor Cases." *American Journal of Legal History* 38 (1994): 452–81.

Norton, Mary Beth. *Liberty's Daughters: The Revolutionary Experiences of America's Women, 1750–1800*. Ithaca, NY: Cornell University Press, 1980.

"Original Records of the Phi Beta Society." *William and Mary Law Quarterly* 4 (1896): 215–41.

Patrick, Stephen A. "'I Have at Length Determined to Have My Picture Taken': An Eighteenth-Century Young Man's Thoughts About His Portrait by Henry Benbridge." *American Art Journal* 22 (1990): 68–81.

Paul, Richard Joel. *Without Precedent: John Marshall and His Times*. New York: Riverhead Books, 2018.

Paulsen, Michael Stokes. "The Most Dangerous Branch: Executive Branch to Say What the Law Is." *Georgetown Law Journal* 83 (1994): 217–345.

Peters, Richard, Jr., ed. *Reports of Cases Determined in the Circuit Court of the United States, for the Third Circuit.* 4 vols. Philadelphia: Phillip Nicklin, 1826–30.

Peterson, Merrill D. *The Great Triumvirate: Webster, Clay, and Calhoun.* New York: Oxford University Press, 1987.

Rehnquist, William H. *Grand Inquests: The Historic Impeachments of Justice Samuel Chase and President Andrew Johnson.* New York: William Morrow, 1992.

A Report of the Whole Trial of Gen. Michael Bright, and Others, Before Washington & Peters in the Circuit Court of the United States in and for the District of Pennsylvania in the Third Circuit, on an Indictment for Obstructing, Resisting, and Opposing the Execution of the Writ of Arrest, Issued out of the District Court of Pennsylvania, in the Case of Gideon Olmstead and Others Against the Surviving Executrices of David Rittenhouse, Deceased. Philadelphia: Thomas Lloyd, 1809.

Rhodehamel, John. *George Washington: The Wonder of the Age.* New Haven, CT: Yale University Press, 2017.

Richardson, James D., ed. *A Compilation of the Messages and Papers of the Presidents.* 10 vols. New York: Bureau of National Literature, Inc., 1897.

Robreno, Eduardo C. "Learning to Do Justice: An Essay on the Development of the Lower Federal Courts in the Early Years of the Republic." *Rutgers Law Journal* 29 (1998): 555–78.

Roosevelt, Franklin Delano. *FDR's Fireside Chats.* Edited by Russell D. Buhite and David W. Levy. Rockville, MD: Arc Manor, 2009.

Rowe, Gary D. "The Sound of Silence: *United States v. Hudson & Goodwin*, the Jeffersonian Ascendancy, and the Abolition of Federal Common Law Crimes." *Yale Law Journal* 101 (1992): 919–48.

Ruger, Theodore W. "'A Question Which Convulses the Nation': The Early Republic's Greatest Debate About the Judicial Review Power." *Harvard Law Review* 117 (2004): 826–97.

Saxton, Martha. *The Widow Washington: The Life of Mary Washington.* New York: Farrar, Straus, and Giroux, 2017.

Schwartz, David S. *The Spirit of the Constitution: John Marshall and the 200-Year Odyssey of* McCullough v. Maryland. New York: Oxford University Press, 2019.

Shakespeare, William. *The Complete Works of William Shakespeare.* Edited by David Bevington. New York: Harper Collins Publishers, 1980.

Shesol, Jeff. *Supreme Power: Franklin Roosevelt v. the Supreme Court.* New York: W. W. Norton, 2010.

Skowronek, Stephen. *The Politics Presidents Make: Leadership from John Adams to Bill Clinton.* Cambridge, MA: Harvard University Press, 1997.

Smith, Jean Edward. *John Marshall: Definer of a Nation.* New York: Henry Holt and Company, 1996.

Stanton, Elizabeth Cady, Susan B. Anthony, and Matilda Joslyn Gage, eds. *History of Women's Suffrage, 1861–1876.* Rochester, NY: Charles Mann Printing Co, 1881.

Stewart, David O. *George Washington: The Political Rise of America's Founding Father.* New York: Dutton, 2021.

Stewart, David O. *Madison's Gift: Five Partnerships That Built* America. New York: Simon and Schuster, 2015.

Stiles, T. J. *The First Tycoon: The Epic Life of Cornelius Vanderbilt*. New York: Alfred A. Knopf, 2009.

Stoner, James R., Jr. "Heir Apparent: Bushrod Washington and Federal Justice in the Early Republic." In *Seriatim: The Supreme Court Before John Marshall*, edited by Scott Douglas Gerber, 322–50. New York: New York University Press, 1998.

Story, Joseph. *Commentaries on the Constitution of the United States*. 3 vols. Boston: Hillard, Gray, 1833.

Story, Joseph. *Life and Letters of Joseph Story*. Edited by William Wetmore Story. 2 vols. Boston: Little & Brown, 1851.

Tarter, Brent, ed. *Revolutionary Virginia: The Road to Independence*. 7 vols. Charlottesville: University Press of Virginia, 1983.

Taylor, John. *An Inquiry into the Principles and Policy of the Government of the United States*. Fredericksburg, VA: Green and Cady, 1814.

Thayer, James B. "The Origin and Scope of the American Doctrine of Constitutional Law." *Harvard Law Review* 7 (1893): 129–56.

The Trial of John H. Jones: First Lieutenant of the Privateer Schooner Revenge, on a Charge of Piracy, Including the Arguments of Counsel and Charge of Judge Washington. Philadelphia: John Binns, 1813.

Thompson, Mary V. *"The Only Unavoidable Subject of Regret": George Washington, Slavery, and the Enslaved Community at Mount Vernon*. Charlottesville: University of Virginia Press, 2019.

Thwaites, Reuben Gold, ed. *Early Western Travels, 1748–1846*. 32 vols. Cleveland: Arthur H. Clark Co., 1905.

Traub, James. *John Quincy Adams: Militant Spirit*. New York: Basic Books, 2016.

Tyler, Amanda L. *Habeas Corpus in Wartime: From the Tower of London to Guantanamo Bay*. New York: Oxford University Press, 2017.

Upham, David R. "*Corfield v. Coryell* and the Privileges and Immunities of American Citizenship." *Texas Law Review* 83 (2005): 1483–534.

Urofsky, Melvin I. *Louis D. Brandeis: A Life*. New York: Pantheon Books, 2009.

Van Buren, Martin. *The Autobiography of Martin Van Buren*. 2 vols. Edited by John C. Fitzpatrick. Washington, DC: Government Press Office, 1920.

A View of Exertions Lately Made for the Purpose of Colonizing the Free People of Colour in the United States, in Africa or Elsewhere. Washington, DC: Jonathan Elliot, 1817.

Wald, Patricia M. "Foreword: War Tales and War Trials." *Michigan Law Review* 106 (2008): 901–22.

Warren, Charles. *A History of the American Bar*. Boston: Little, Brown, and Company, 1911.

Warren, Charles. *The Supreme Court in United States History*. 3 vols. Boston: Little, Brown, and Company, 1926.

Washington, Bushrod. *Cases Argued and Determined in the Court of Appeals of Virginia*. 2 vols. Richmond, VA: Thomas Nicolson, 1798.

Washington, Bushrod. "The Letters of Bushrod Washington (1762–1829) in the Hampton L. Carson Collection of the Free Library of Philadelphia." Edited by Howell J. Heaney. *American Journal of Legal History* 2 (1958): 161–71.

Washington, George. *The Papers of George Washington: Colonial Series*. Edited by W. W. Abbot, Dorothy Twohig, and Philander Chase. 10 vols. Charlottesville: University Press of Virginia, 1983.

Washington, George. *The Papers of George Washington: Confederation Series*. Edited by W. W. Abbot and Dorothy Twohig. 6 vols. Charlottesville: University Press of Virginia, 1997.

Washington, George. *The Papers of George Washington: Presidential Series*. Edited by W. W. Abbot, Dorothy Twohig, Philander D. Chase, David R. Hoth, Christine Sternberg Patrick, and Theodore J. Crackel. 15 vols. Charlottesville: University Press of Virginia, 1987–.

Washington, George. *The Papers of George Washington: Retirement Series*. Edited by W. W. Abbot and Dorothy Twohig. 4 vols. Charlottesville: University Press of Virginia, 1998–99.

Washington, George. *The Papers of George Washington: Revolutionary War Series*. Edited by W. W. Abbot, Dorothy Twohig, Philander Chase, Edward G. Lengel, Theodore J. Crackel, and David R. Roth. 18 vols. Charlottesville: University Press of Virginia, 1985-.

Washington, George. *The Writings of George Washington*. Edited by Jared Sparks. 12 vols. Boston: Ferdinand Andrews, 1839.

Wayland, John W. *The Washingtons and Their Homes*. Staunton, VA: McClure Printing Company, 1944.

White, G. Edward. *The Marshall Court and Cultural Change, 1815–1835*. New York: Macmillan Publishing Company, 1988.

White, G. Edward. "The Working Life of the Marshall Court, 1815–1835." *Virginia Law Review* 70 (1984): 1–52.

Wiencek, Henry. *An Imperfect God: George Washington, His Slaves and the Creation of America*. New York: Farrar, Straus, and Giroux, 2003.

Wilson, James. *Collected Works of James Wilson*. Edited by Kermit L. Hall and Mark David Hall. 2 vols. Indianapolis, IN: Liberty Fund, 2007.

Yearbook of the Association for the Preservation of Virginia Antiquities for 1898 and 1899. Richmond, VA: Wm. Ellis Jones, 1900.

Cases and Statutes

Act of Apr. 4, 1800, ch. 19, 2 Stat. 19 (repealed 1803).

Act of March 3, 1817, ch. 63, 3 Stat. 376.

Act of May 4, 1826, ch. 37, 4 Stat. 160.

Act to Establish the Judicial Courts of the United States, ch. 20, 1 Stat. 85 (1789).

Adams v. Storey, 1 F. Cas. 141 (C.C.D. N.Y. 1817) (No. 66).

Allgeyer v. Louisiana, 165 U.S. 578 (1897).

Anderson v. Carter, 802 F.3d 4 (D.C. Cir. 2015).

Armroyd v. Williams, 1 F.Cas. 1132 (C.C.D. Pa. 1811).

Ashwander v. Tennessee Valley Auth., 297 U.S. 288 (1936).

Bank of the United States v. Corcoran, 27 U.S. (2 Pet.) 121 (1829).

Bank of the United States v. Northumberland Bank, 2 F. Cas. 726 (C.C.E.D. Pa. 1824) (No. 931).

Banks v. Greenleaf, 2 F. Cas 756 (C.C.D. Va. 1799) (No. 959).

Barnett v. Watson, 1 Va. 372 (1794).

Barron v. Baltimore, 32 U.S. (7 Pet.) 243 (1833).
Bartkus v. Illinois, 359 U.S. 121 (1959).
Barton v. Petit, 11 U.S. (7 Cranch) 194 (1812).
Barton v. Petit, 11 U.S. (7 Cranch) 288 (1813).
Bas v. Tingy, 4 U.S. (4 Dall.) 37 (1800).
Bell v. Morrison, 26 U.S. (1 Pet.) 351 (1828).
Berk v. Laird, 317 F. Supp. 715 (S.D.N.Y. 1970).
Binns v. Woodruff, 3 F. Cas. 421 (C.C.D. Pa. 1821) (No. 1,424).
Blake v. McClung, 172 U.S. 239 (1898).
Bodley v. Gaither, 19 Ky. (3 T.B. Mon.) 57 (1825).
Brock v. Phillips, 2 Va. 68 (1795).
Brown v. United States, 12 U.S. (8 Cranch) 253 (1814).
Brown's Adm'x v. Garland, 1 Va. 221 (1793).
Buckner v. Finley & Van Lear, 27 U.S. (2 Pet.) 586 (1829).
Burnley v. Lambert, 1 Va. 308 (1794).
Butler v. Farnsworth, 4 F. Cas. 902 (C.C.E.D. Pa. 1821).
Butler v. Hopper, 4 F. Cas. 904 (C.C.D. Pa. 1806) (No. 2,241).
Campbell v. Gordon, 10 U.S. (6 Cranch) 176 (1810).
Campbell v. Morris, 3 H. & McH. 535, 554 (Md. 1797).
Carr v. Gooch, 1 Va. 260 (1794).
Carter v. Tyler, 5 Va. 165 (1797).
Caze v. Reilly, 5 F. Cas. 332 (C.C.D. Pa. 1814) (No. 2,538).
Chapman v. Turner, 5 Va. 280 (1798).
Chichester v. Vass, 5 Va. 83 (1797).
Chicot County Drainage District v. Baxter State Bank, 308 U.S. 371 (1940).
Civil Rights Act of 1866, ch. 31, 14 Stat. 27.
Clarke v. Russel, 3 U.S. (3 Dall.) 415 (1799).
Collings v. Hope, 6 F. Cas. 111 (C.C.D. Pa. 1812) (No. 3,003).
Colson v. Lewis, 15 U.S. (2 Wheat.) 377 (1817).
Colson v. Thompson, 15 U.S. (2 Wheat.) 336 (1817).
Columbian Ins. Co. v. Ashby & Stribling, 38 U.S. (13 Pet.) 331 (1839).
Commonwealth v. Banks, 8 Va. 338 (1798).
Conard v. Nicoll, 29 U.S. (4 Pet.) 291 (1830).
Cooper v. Telfair, 4 U.S. (4 Dall.) 14 (1800).
Corfield v. Coryell, 6 F. Cas. 546 (C.C.E.D. Pa. 1825) (No. 3,230).
Coxe v. Pennington, 6 F. Cas. 692 (C.C.D. Pa. 1803) (No. 3,311), reversed by 6 U.S. (2 Cranch) 33 (1804).
Craig v. Leslie, 16 U.S. (3 Wheat.) 563 (1818).
Craig v. Radford, 16 U.S. (3 Wheat.) 594 (1818).
Croudson v. Leonard, 8 U.S. (4 Cranch) 434 (1808).
Currie v. Donald, 2 Va. 58 (1795).
Cutler v. Huston, 158 U.S. 423 (1895).
Cutting v. Myers, 6 F. Cas. 1081 (C.C.D. Pa. 1818) (No. 3,520).
Daly's Lessee v. James, 21 U.S. (8 Wheat.) 495 (1823).

Dartmouth College v. Woodward, 17 U.S. (4 Wheat.) 518 (1819).
Davi v. Laird, 318 F. Supp. 478 (W.D. Va. 1970).
Dederer v. Delaware Ins. Co., 7 F. Cas. 341 (C.C.D. Pa. 1807) (No. 3,733).
Den *ex dem* Walker v. Turner, 22 U.S. (9 Wheat.) 541 (1824).
Dixon v. Moyer, 7 F. Cas. 758 (C.C.D. Pa. 1821) (No. 3,931).
Doe v. Northern, 1 Va. 282 (1794).
Dred Scott v. Sandford, 60 U.S. (19 How.) 393 (1857).
Drummond's Adm'rs v. Magruder & Co's Trustees, 13 U.S. (9 Cranch) 122 (1815).
Dunlop v. Hepburn, 16 U.S. (3 Wheat.) 231 (1818).
Eisner v. Macomber, 252 U.S. 189 (1920).
Eliason v. Henshaw, 17 U.S. (4 Wheat.) 225 (1819).
Evans v. Eaton, 8 F. Cas. 846 (C.C.D. Pa. 1816) (No. 4.559), *reversed on other grounds*, 16 U.S. (3 Wheat.) 454 (1818).
Evans v. Eaton, 8 F. Cas. 856 (C.C.D. Pa. 1818) (No. 4,560), *aff'd*, 20 U.S. (7 Wheat.) 356 (1822).
Ex Parte Bollman, 8 U.S. (4 Cranch) 75 (1807).
Ex Parte Cabrera, 4 F. Cas. 964 (C.C.D. Pa. 1805) (No. 2,278).
Ex Parte Simmons, 22 F. Cas. 151 (C.C.E.D. Pa. 1823) (No. 12,863).
Eustace v. Gaskins, 1 Va. 188 (1793).
Evans v. Jordan & Morehead, 13 U.S. (9 Cranch) 199 (1815).
Fairfax's Devisee v. Hunter's Lessee, 11 U.S. (6 Cranch) 603 (1812).
Fitzsimmons v. Ogden, 11 U.S. (7 Cranch) 2 (1812).
Fowler v. Lindsey, 3 U.S. (3 Dall.) 411 (1799).
Fugitive Slave Act of 1793, 1 Stat. 302.
Gamble v. United States, 139 S. Ct. 1960 (2019).
Gibbons v. Ogden, 22 U.S. (9 Wheat.) 1 (1824).
Gibson v. Fristoe, 5 Va. 62 (1797).
Golden v. Prince, 10 F. Cas. 542 (C.C.D. Pa. 1814) (No. 5,509).
Goodwin v. United States, 10 F. Cas. 625 (C.C.D. Pa. 1811) (No. 5,554).
Gray v. James, 10 F. Cas. 1015, 1017 (C.C.D. Pa. 1817) (No. 5,718).
Green v. Biddle, 21 U.S. (8 Wheat.) 1 (1823).
Greenleaf v. Queen, 26 U.S. (1 Pet.) 138 (1828).
Hague v. CIO, 307 U.S. 496 (1939).
Hans v. Louisiana, 134 U.S. 1 (1890).
Harrison v. Rowan, 11 F. Cas. 66 (C.C.D. N.J. 1820) (No. 6,142).
Hawkins v. Joshua Barney's Lessee, 30 U.S. (5 Pet.) 457 (1831).
Hayburn's Case, 2 U.S. (2 Dall.) 409 (1792).
Heiner v. Donnan, 285 U.S. 312, 341 (1932).
Hepburn & Dundas Heirs v. Dunlop & Co., 14 U.S. (1 Wheat.) 179 (1816).
Hill v. Low, 12 F. Cas. 172 (C.C.E.D. Pa. 1822) (No 6,494).
Hooe v. Marquess, 8 Va. 416 (1798).
Houston v. Moore, 18 U.S. (5 Wheat.) 1 (1820).
Hudson & Smith v. Guestier, 11 U.S. (7 Cranch) 1 (1812).
Hughes v. Edwards, 22 U.S. (9 Wheat.) 489 (1824).

Hunt v. Rhodes, 26 U.S. (1 Pet.) 1 (1828).
Hunter's Ex'rs v. Spotswood, 1 Va. 145 (1792).
Hurst v. Wickerly, 12 F. Cas. 1046 (C.C.D. Pa. 1805) (No. 6,940).
In Re State of New York, 256 U.S. 490 (1921).
Issacs v. Cooper, 13 F. Cas. 153 (C.C.D. Pa. 1821) (No. 7,096).
Judiciary Act of 1801, ch. 4; 2 Stat. 89 (repealed 1802).
Judiciary Act of 1802, ch. 31; 2 Stat. 256.
Keplinger v. De Young, 23 U.S. (10 Wheat.) 358 (1825).
Kerr v. Devisees of A. Moon, 22 U.S. (9 Wheat.) 541 (1824).
Kirkpatrick v. White, 14 F. Cas. 685 (C.C.D. Pa. 1826) (No. 7,850).
Lambert's Lessee v. Paine, 7 U.S. (3 Cranch) 97 (1805).
Lee v. Tuberville, 2 Va. 162 (1795).
Leeds v. Marine Ins. Co. of Alexandria, 15 U.S. (2 Wheat.) 380 (1817).
Legal Tender Cases, 79 U.S. (12 Wall.) 457 (1870).
LeRoy, Bayard & Co. v. Johnson, 27 U.S. (2 Pet.) 186 (1829).
Le Tigre, 15 F. Cas. 404 (C.C.D. N.J. 1820) (No. 8,281).
Livingston v. Van Ingen, 9 Johns. 507 (N.Y. 1812).
Lochner v. New York, 198 U.S. 45 (1905).
Mackie's Ex'r v. Davis, 2 Va. 219 (1796).
Macker's Heirs v. Thomas, 20 U.S. (7 Wheat.) 530 (1822).
Marbury v. Madison, 5 U.S. (1 Cranch) 137 (1803).
Marine Ins. Co. v. Wilson, 7 U.S. (3 Cranch) 187 (1805).
Marshall v. Currie, 8 U.S. (4 Cranch) 172 (1807).
Martin v. Hunters Lessee, 14 U.S. 304 (1 Wheat.) 304 (1816).
Maryland Ins. Co. v. LeRoy, 11 U.S. (7 Cranch) 26 (1812).
Mason v. Haile, 25 U.S. (12 Wheat.) 370 (1827).
Mason v. Missouri, 179 U.S. 328 (1900).
Mayor of New York v. Miln, 36 U.S. (11 Pet.) 102 (1837).
M'Call v. Peachy, 5 Va. 55 (1797).
McBurney v. Young, 569 U.S. 221 (2013).
McCormick v. Sullivant, 23 U.S. (10 Wheat.) 192 (1825).
McCulloch v. Maryland, 17 U.S. (4 Wheat.) 319 (1819).
McDonald v. Chicago, 561 U.S. 742 (2010).
McFadden v. The Exchange, 16 F. Cas. 85 (C.C.D. Pa. 1811) (No. 8,786), *reversed by* 11 U.S. (7 Cranch) 116 (1812).
McWilliams v. Willis, 1 Va. 199 (1793).
Montana v. Kennedy, 366 U.S. 308 (1961).
Montoya v. United States, 180 U.S. 261 (1901).
Morean v. United States Ins. Co., 14 U.S. (1 Wheat.) 219 (1816).
New York Times v. Sullivan, 376 U.S. 254 (1964).
Norton v. Rose, 2 Va. 233 (1796).
Odlin v. Insurance Co. of Pennsylvania, 18 F. Cas. 583 (C.C.D. Pa. 1813) (No. 10,433).
Ogden v. Blackledge, 6 U.S. (2 Cranch) 272 (1804).
Ogden v. Saunders, 25 U.S. (12 Wheat.) 213 (1827).

Osborn v. Bank of the United States, 22 U.S. (9 Wheat.) 738 (1824).
Otis v. Bacon, 11 U.S. (7 Cranch) 589 (1813).
Patterson v. United States, 15 U.S. (2 Wheat.) 221 (1817).
Pendleton v. Vandevier, 1 Va. 381 (1794).
Perkins v. Hart, 24 U.S. (11 Wheat.) 237 (1826).
Phillips v. McCall, 19 F. Cas. 517 (C.C.D. Pa. 1821) (No. 11,104).
Pierce v. Turner, 9 U.S. (5 Cranch) 154 (1809).
Poe v. Ullman, 367 U.S. 497 (1961).
Prigg v. Pennsylvania, 41 U.S. (16 Pet.) 539 (1842).
Pryor v. Dunkle, 20 F. Cas. 29 (C.C.D. Pa. 1809) (No. 11,548).
Randolph v. Ware, 7 U.S. (3 Cranch) 503 (1806).
Roy v. Garnett, 2 Va. 9 (1794).
Satterlee v. Matthewson, 27 U.S. (2 Pet.) 380 (1829).
Sedition Act, ch. 74, 1 Stat. 596 (1798).
Sergeant's Lessee v. Biddle, 17 U.S. (4 Wheat.) 508 (1819).
Shelton v. Barbour, 2 Va. 64 (1795).
Shermer v. Shermer's Ex'rs, 1 Va. 266 (1794).
Shirras v. Caig, 11 U.S. (7 Cranch) 34 (1812).
Simms v. Slacum, 7 U.S. (3 Cranch) 300 (1806).
Sims' Lessee v. Irvine, 3 U.S. (3 Dall.) 425 (1799).
Slaughter-House Cases, 83 U.S. (16 Wall.) 36 (1873).
Smith v. Delaware Ins. Co., 22 F. Cas. 509 (C.C.D. Pa. 1811) (No. 13,035), *reversed by* 11 U.S. (7 Cranch) 434 (1813).
Smith v. Edrington, 12 U.S. (8 Cranch) 66 (1814).
Smith v. Maryland, 10 U.S. (6 Cranch) 286 (1810).
Sneed v. Wister, 21 U.S. (8 Wheat.) 690 (1823).
Society for the Propagation of the Gospel in Foreign Parts v. The Town of New Haven, 21 U.S. (8 Wheat.) 464 (1823).
Spencer v. Moore, 8 Va. 423 (1798).
Sperry v. Delaware Ins. Co., 22 F. Cas. 923 (C.C.D. Pa. 1808) (No. 13,236).
Stephens v. White, 2 Va. 203 (1796).
Stevens v. Taliaferro, 1 Va. 155 (1793).
Stevens v. Vancleve, 23 F. Cas. 35 (C.C.D. N.J. 1822) (No. 13,412).
Stevenson's Heirs v. Sullivant, 18 U.S. (5 Wheat.) 207 (1820).
Stewart v. Ingle, 22 U.S. (9 Wheat.) 526, 526 (1824).
Stuart v. Laird, 5 U.S. (1 Cranch) 299 (1803).
Sturges v. Crowninshield, 17 U.S. (4 Wheat.) 122 (1819).
Swift v. Tyson, 41 U.S. (16 Pet.) 1 (1842), *overruled by* Erie R.R. Co. v. Tompkins, 304 U.S. 64 (1938).
Talbot v. Seeman, 5 U.S. (1 Cranch) 1 (1801).
Tate v. Tally, 7 Va. 354 (1802).
Taylor's Adm'x v. Peyton's Adm'x, 1 Va. 252 (1794).
Terrett v. Taylor, 13 U.S. (9 Cranch) 43 (1815).
The Alerta, 13 U.S. (9 Cranch) 199 (1815).

The Amelia, 4 U.S. (4 Dall.) 34 (1800).
The American Fur Co. v. United States, 27 U.S. (2 Pet.) 357 (1829).
The Antelope, 23 U.S. (10 Wheat.) 66 (1825).
The Ariadne, 15 U.S. (2 Wheat.) 143 (1817).
The Edward, 14 U.S. (1 Wheat.) 261 (1816).
The Fanny, 22 U.S. (9 Wheat.) 659 (1824).
The Frances, 12 U.S. (8 Cranch) 418 (1814).
The Grotius, 13 U.S. (9 Cranch) 368 (1815).
The Hiram, 12 U.S. (8 Cranch) 444 (1814).
The James Wells, 11 U.S. (7 Cranch) 22 (1812).
The Joseph, 12 U.S. (8 Cranch) 451 (1814).
The Marine Ins. Co. of Alexandria v. Tucker, 7 U.S. (3 Cranch) 357 (1806).
The Merino, 22 U.S. (9 Wheat.) 391 (1824).
The Merrimack, 12 U.S. (8 Cranch) 317 (1814).
Thelusson v. Smith, 15 U.S. (2 Wheat.) 396 (1817).
The San Pedro, 15 U.S. (2 Wheat.) 132 (1817).
The Schooner Jane v. United States, 11 U.S. (7 Cranch) 363 (1813).
The Venus, 12 U.S. (8 Cranch) 253 (1814).
Thomas v. Brockenbrough, 23 U.S. (10 Wheat.) 146 (1825).
Thomas v. Perry, 23 F. Cas. 964 (C.C.D. N.J. 1811) (No. 13,908).
Thornton v. Carson, 11 U.S. (7 Cranch) 596 (1813).
Thornton v. Spotswood, 1 Va. 142 (1792).
Thornton v. Wynn, 25 U.S. (12 Wheat.) 183 (1827).
Treadwell v. Bladen, 24 F. Cas. 144 (C.C.E.D. Pa. 1827) (No. 14,154).
Trustees of Dartmouth College v. Woodward, 17 U.S. (4 Wheat.) 518 (1819).
Tryphenia v. Harrison, 24 F. Cas. 252 (C.C.D. Pa. 1806) (No. 14,209).
Tuberville v. Self, 2 Va. 71 (1795).
Tuberville v. Self, 8 Va. 580 (1795).
Turner v. Moffett, 2 Va. 70 (1795).
Turpin v. Locket, 10 Va. 113 (1804).
United States v. Bright, 24 F. Cas. 1232 (C.C.D. Pa. 1809) (No. 14,647).
United States v. Fisher, 25 F. Cas. 1087 (C.C.D. Pa 1803) (No. 15,103), *reversed by* 6 U.S. (2 Cranch) 358 (1805).
United States v. Goodwin, 11 U.S. (7 Cranch) 108 (1812).
United States v. Gurney, 8 U.S. (4 Cranch) 333 (1808).
United States v. Hall, 26 F. Cas. 84 (C.C.D. Pa. 1809) (No. 15,285).
United States v. Heth, 7 U.S. (3 Cranch) 399 (1806).
United States v. Holmes, 18 U.S. (5 Wheat.) 412 (1820).
United States v. Hudson & Goodwin, 11 U.S. (7 Cranch) 32 (1812).
United States v. Kelly, 24 U.S. (11 Wheat.) 417 (1826).
United States v. Kennedy, 26 F. Cas. 762 (C.C.D. Pa. 1821) (No. 15,525).
United States v. Lowry, 26 F. Cas. 1008 (C.C.D. Pa. 1808) (No. 15,636).
United States v. McGill, 4 U.S. (4 Dall.) 426 (C.C.D. Pa. 1806) (No. 15,676).
United States v. 1,960 Bags of Coffee, 12 U.S. (8 Cranch) 398 (1814).

United States v. Ortega, 27 F. Cas. 359 (C.C.E.D. Pa. 1825) (No. 15,971), *aff'd* 24 U.S. (11 Wheat.) 468 (1826).
United States v. Passmore, 4 U.S. (4 Dall.) 372 (C.C.D. Pa. 1804) (No. 16,005).
United States v. Peters, 9 U.S. (5 Cranch) 115 (1809).
United States v. Sheldon, 15 U.S. (2 Wheat.) 119 (1817).
United States v. 350 Chests of Tea, 25 U.S. (12 Wheat.) 486 (1827).
United States v. Vanzandt, 24 U.S. (11 Wheat.) 184 (1826).
Untermyer v. Anderson, 276 U.S. 440 (1928).
Vance v. Trump, 140 S. Ct. 2412 (2020).
Warder v. Arell, 2 Va. 282 (1796).
Watson v. Alexander, 1 Va. 340 (1794).
Williams v. Bank of the United States, 27 U.S. (2 Pet.) 96 (1829).
Williamson v. Kincaid, 4 U.S. (4 Dall.) 20 (1800).
Willis v. Bucher, 30 F. Cas. 63 (C.C.D. Pa. 1818) (No. 17,769).
Wood v. Baughan, 5 Va. 329 (1798).
Worthington v. Preston, 30 F. Cas. 645 (C.C.E.D. Pa. 1824) (No. 18,055).
Wroe v. Washington, 1 Va. 357 (1794).

Index

For the benefit of digital users, indexed terms that span two pages (e.g., 52–53) may, on occasion, appear on only one of those pages.

Note: Figures are indicated by *f* following the page number.

Adams, Abigail, 47–48
Adams, John, 41*f*
  appointment of "midnight" circuit judges, 52–53
  death of, 144
  presidential election of 1800, 50
Adams, John Quincy, 99
  candidacy for president in 1824, 143
  candidacy for president in 1828, 153–54
Alexander, Francis, 110*f*
Alexandria, Virginia, move to, 28
Ambler, Polly, 21–22
American Colonization Society, 118, 121–24
  and Bushrod Washington's mindset regarding slavery, 124
  manifesto, 122
  membership certificate, 123*f*
  ultimate failure of, 124
  understanding of colonization, 123–24
  viewpoints regarding, 122–23
Anglican Church, and proposed property confiscation, 33–35
Appalachia, trek with George Washington through, 16–17
Arnold, Benedict, 8
Articles of Confederation, 22

bankruptcy laws, federal *vs.* state, 144–52
Bas v. Tingy, 49–50, 53–54
Bell v. Morrison, 152–53
Benbridge, Henry, 13–14, 15*f*
Binney, Horace, 30, 43–44, 47–48, 82*f*
  visit to Mount Vernon, 73
  on Washington's work as circuit judge, 81–84
Blackburn, Julia Ann "Nancy," 19–22, 20*f*, 157
Blackstone, William, 6
Brandeis, Louis, 150
Bright, Michael, *United States v. Bright*, 89–93
Brown, David Paul, 81–83, 84, 90
Brown, Mather, 59*f*
Brown v. United States, 103–4
Bushfield plantation, 4–5
  See also Washington, West Ford
Bushrod, Hannah, 4, 34–35
Butler, Pierce, 118–19
Butler v. Hopper, 118–19

career
  legal apprentice, 12–16
  local political activities, 22–24
  Virginia constitutional ratifying convention, 26–27
  Virginia House of Delegates, election to, 24
  See also circuit judge, work as; Supreme Court
Chase, Samuel, 44, 60–62
childhood and youth, 5–6
circuit judge, work as, 78, 85
  Butler v. Hopper, 118–19
  colleagues, 81–82
  colleagues, descriptions by, 82–84
  Corfield v. Coryell, 130–34
  Ex Parte Simmons, 118–19
  Golden v. Prince, 93–95
  Hill v. Low, 119–20
  journals and notebooks kept, 80–82
  and Philadelphia, 79–80
  structure of circuit courts, 78–79, 84–85
  temperament and characteristics, 85–89
  United States v. Bright, 89–93
  Worthington v. Preston, 119–20
  See also Supreme Court
Civil Rights Act of 1866, 139–40
Clay, Henry, 115
  candidacy for president in 1824, 143
  membership in American Colonization Society, 121
Commentaries on the Law of England (Blackstone), 6
Commerce Clause, 130–33

Congress, candidacy for, 39–40, 42–43
Constitutional Convention, 25–27
constitutionality, presumption of, 48–49
Contracts Clause, 109–10, 146–52
Cooper v. Telfair, 48–49
Corfield v. Coryell, 130, 132*f*, 135–39, 158–59
  Civil Rights Act of 1866, 139–40
  Commerce Clause, 130–33
  elements of case, 130–34
  Privileges and Immunities Clause, 133–34
  privileges and immunities of citizens, 137–39
  and Reconstruction, 139–42
  and women's suffrage movement, 140–42, 141*f*
Cover, Robert, 121
Crittenden, John, 153–54
Cushing, William, 44

Dartmouth College v. Woodward, 109–10
debtors' prison, and *Mason v. Haile*, 151–52
description of Bushrod Washington, 13–14, 16
domestic life, at Mount Vernon, 76–77
Double Jeopardy Clause, 113–14
Durrell, William, 49

education
  law school at William and Mary, 6–8
  school at Fredericksburg, 6
Ellsworth, Oliver, 44
Episcopal Church, and proposed property confiscation, 33–35
Erie Railroad Company v. Tompkins, 94–95
Ex Parte Bollman, 96
Ex Parte Simmons, 118–19
Eyerman, Jacob, 46
eyesight, deterioration of, 35–36

family life
  death of brother Augustine Washington, 16
  father's death, 24–25
  at Mount Vernon, 76–77
Federalists
  and Constitutional Convention, 25–26
  and Hartford Convention of 1814, 104–5
  and presidential election of 1796, 37
federal judiciary, and repeal of Judiciary Act of 1801, 55–58
Ferry Farm, 3–4
Field, Stephen, 142
Fifth Virginia Convention, 5–6
financial needs and issues, 10
Finley, Robert, 121
Fletcher v. Peck, 97–99
Fowler v. Lindsay, 44–45
France, U. S. relationship with, 37–38, 49–50
  seizure of merchant ship, 53–55
Fugitive Slave Act, 119–20, 121

Gamble v. United States, 113–14
Genius of Universal Emancipation, The, 129
Gibbons v. Ogden, 134–35
Ginsburg, Ruth Bader, 113–14
Golden v. Prince, 93–95, 158–59
Gorsuch, Neil, 113–14
Green Spring, Battle of, 8
Green v. Biddle, 115–17
Gum Springs, Virginia, 17–18

Hamilton, Alexander, 50, 69–70
Hamilton, Eliza Schuyler, 70
Harding, Chester, 98*f*, 100*f*, 153*f*
Hartford Convention, 105
health concerns
  and absence from 1821 term, 114
  final illness and death, 154–56
  in mid-1820s, 143
Henry, Patrick, 26–27, 29–30
Hill v. Low, 119–20
Holmes, Oliver Wendell, 148–49
Holt, Charles, 49
Hopkinson, Joseph, 81–82, 85–86, 87*f*, 89, 153–55
House of Burgesses, 3–4, 24
Houston v. Moore, 112–14
Howard, Jacob, 140

Ingersoll, Charles, 100–1
Ingersoll, Jarod, 81–82
Iredell, James, 40–41, 44, 46–47

Jackson, Andrew
  candidacy for president in 1824, 143
  candidacy for president in 1828, 153–54
  membership in American Colonization Society, 121
Jackson, Robert H., 94–95
Jefferson, Thomas, 59*f*
  on biography of George Washington, 68
  death of, 144
  1808 embargo on exports, 97
  legal representation by Bushrod Washington, 33
  and *Marbury v. Madison*, 58–60
  presidential election of 1800, 50
Johnson, Andrew, 139–40
Johnson, William, 54, 63, 64*f*

journals, of work as circuit judge, 80–82
Judiciary Act of 1789, 59–60
Judiciary Act of 1801, 52–53, 55–58
Justice Accused (Cover), 121

Kentucky, and property law in *Green v. Biddle*, 115
King, Rufus, 70

Latrobe, Benjamin, 29–30
law, skill at practicing, 30
Lee, Henry "Light-Horse Harry," 45
Leedstown Resolves, 4–5
legal apprenticeship, 12–16
legal practice
  skill at practicing law, 30
  Virginia Court of Appeals, 30–33
Le Tigre, 86
Liberia, resettlement of freed slaves in, 118, 121, 124
Life of George Washington (Marshall), 67–69
Lincoln, Levi, 99
Livingston, Henry, 96
Longacre, James Barton, 7*f*
Lossing, Benson, 158*f*, 159
Lundy, Benjamin, 129

Madison, James, 26–27, 97–105, 98*f*
  membership in American Colonization Society, 121, 123*f*
Marbury v. Madison, 58–60
marriage, to Nancy Blackburn, 19–22
Marshall, John, 32*f*
  appointment to Supreme Court, 40–42, 52–53
  as Chief Justice, 1
  and civic life in Richmond, Virginia, 31
  correspondence on *Golden v. Prince*, 93
  and *Dartmouth College v. Woodward*, 109–10
  dissent on *Ogden v. Saunders*, 148–50
  dissent on *The Venus*, 103
  as envoy to France, 37–38
  Fletcher v. Peck, 98–99
  illness of wife, Polly Ambler, 21–22
  law school at William and Mary, 7–8
  Life of George Washington, 67–69, 71
  and *Martin v. Hunter's Lessee*, 108
  membership in American Colonization Society, 121
  as "one judge" with Bushrod Washington, 63–65, 112
  opinion on *Gibbons v. Ogden*, 134–35
  practice in Richmond, Virginia, 29–30, 31–33
  on reaction to *McCulloch v. Maryland*, 111–12
  role of Bushrod Washington on Supreme Court, 107
  as Secretary of State, 49–50
  slave ownership, 33
  tribute to Bushrod Washington, 155–56
  at Virginia ratifying convention, 26
Martin v. Hunter's Lessee, 107–8
Mason, George, 26
Mason v. Haile, 151–52
McCormick v. Sullivant, 143–44
McCulloch v. Maryland, 110–12
memorial service, 156
Mercer, John, 8
military service, 8
Monroe, James, 108, 143
Moore, Alfred, 46–47
Mount Vernon, 67*f*, 72*f*
  description of, 66
  dilapidation of, 73–75
  domestic life at, 76–77
  freeing of enslaved people at, 1, 125, 127–28
  Martha Washington, death of, 66–67
  public pilgrimages to, 72–73
  sale of, 159
  slavery and daily life at, 77, 159
  and War of 1812, 74–75
  Washington tomb, 74, 75*f*

Newsam, Albert, 82*f*

Ogden v. Saunders, 144–52, 157–58

Paterson, William, 44, 96
Patriotic Society, 22–23
Pendleton, Edmund, 26, 29–31
Peters, Richard, 46, 74, 79, 80*f*, 153–54
Philadelphia
  life as legal apprentice in, 12–16
  life as Supreme Court justice in, 43–44
Pickering, John, 58
Pickering, Timothy, 35, 40–41
Pinckney, Charles Cotesworth, 50–51
political life
  activism and campaigning, 49–50
  and candidacy for Congress, 39–40, 42–43
  1800 presidential campaign, 50–51
Powel, Elizabeth "Eliza" Willing, 13–16, 14*f*, 66–67
Pratt, Matthew, 14*f*
Privileges and Immunities Clause, 133–34

Randolph, Edmund, 29–30, 31
religious faith, and membership in Episcopal Church, 34–35
Richmond, Virginia
  civic life in, 31
  move to, 29–36
Riddle, Albert, 140
Roane, Spencer, 7–8, 107–8
  reaction to *McCulloch v. Maryland*, 111
  Virginia Court of Appeals, 30–31
Rogers, Andrew, 139–40
Roosevelt, Franklin D., 150–51

Sartain, John, 87*f*
Satterlee v. Mathewson, 154
Sedition Act of 1798, 45–47, 49
Shelton v. Barbour, 32–33
Shermer v. Shermer's Executors, 31
Shippen, Anne Nancy, 16
Slaughter-House Cases, 142
slavery, 118
  and bequest from George Washington, 47–48
  Butler v. Hopper, 118–19
  comments on family separation, 126–27
  and daily life at Mount Vernon, 77, 159
  Ex Parte Simmons, 118–19
  freeing of slaves at Mount Vernon, 1, 125
  Fugitive Slave Act, 119–20, 121
  Hill v. Low, 119–20
  litigation involving human property, 32–33
  The Merino, 120–21
  mindset regarding, 124, 159
  sale of slaves at Mount Vernon, 125–29
  slaves brought to Mount Vernon, 66–67
  West Ford Washington and Bushfield plantation, 17–18
  Worthington v. Preston, 119–20
slave trade, court opinion on, 120–21
Smith, Jean Edward, 104
Smith, Oliver, 4–5
social relationships, as legal apprentice in Philadelphia, 13–16
Stamp Act of 1765, 4–5
Story, Joseph, 85–86, 93, 96–97, 98–99
  biography, 100
  dissent on *Brown v. United States*, 104
  on election of Andrew Jackson to presidency, 153–54
  opinion on *Bell v. Morrison*, 152–53
  opinion on *Green v. Biddle*, 115, 116–17
  opinion on *Houston v. Moore*, 113
  opinion on *Martin v. Hunter's Lessee*, 107–8
  opinion on *Terrett v. Taylor*, 106
  portrait, 100*f*
  tribute to Bushrod Washington, 155
  volume of opinions written by, 108
Sturges v. Crowninshield, 144–45
Supreme Court, 96–97
  absence from 1821 term, 114
  1811 adjournment, 99
  appointment to, 40–45
  Bell v. Morrison, 152–53
  boarding house in Washington, DC, 53, 156
  Brown v. United States, 103–4
  circuit riding for, 43
  Corfield v. Coryell, 158–59
  correspondence among members, 88–89
  Dartmouth College v. Woodward, 109–10
  Era of Good Feelings, 108, 117
  Fletcher v. Peck, 97–99
  Golden v. Prince, 158–59
  Green v. Biddle, 115–17
  Houston v. Moore, 112–14
  Martin v. Hunter's Lessee, 107–8
  Mason v. Haile, 151–52
  McCormick v. Sullivant, 143–44
  McCulloch v. Maryland, 110–12
  The Merino, 120–21
  Ogden v. Saunders, 144–52, 157–58
  and "presumption of constitutionality," 48–49
  and repeal of Judiciary Act of 1801, 55–58
  role on, 2
  Satterlee v. Mathewson, 154
  Sturges v. Crowninshield, 144–45
  Terrett v. Taylor, 106–7
  unanimity of opinions, 53–55, 60
  United States v. Bright, 158–59
  The Venus, court case of 1814, 102–3
  vs. "inferior" courts, 143–44
  war, perfect *vs.* imperfect, 49–50
  and War of 1812, 97, 101–5
  See also circuit judge, work as

Talbot v. Seeman, 53–55
Taney, Roger, membership in American Colonization Society, 121
Terrett v. Taylor, 106–7
Thayer, James Bradley, 150
The Merino, 120–21
The Venus, Supreme Court case of 1814, 102–3
Thompson, Cephas, 32*f*
Thompson, Smith, 134
Todd, Thomas, 96
Trimble, Robert, 144, 153–54
Trumbull, John, 41*f*
Trumbull, Lyman, 139–40

United States v. Bright, 89–93, 158–59
United States v. Fisher, 63–65

Van Buren, Martin, 21–22, 71–72
Virginia
  consideration for appointment as United States attorney, 28–29
  constitutional ratifying convention of 1788, 26–27
  Court of Appeals, 30–33, 106, 107–8
  and property law in *Green v. Biddle*, 115
  reaction to *McCulloch v. Maryland*, 111
  Revolutionary War in, 8
Virginia Declaration of Rights, 5–6
Virginia House of Delegates, election to, 24

Wallace, Ph. B., 80*f*
war, perfect *vs.* imperfect, 49–50
War of 1812, 74–75, 97, 101–5
Washington, Augustine, 16
Washington, Bushrod
  burial of, 157
  childhood and youth, 5–6
  description, 13–14, 16
  final illness and death of, 154–56
  health concerns in 1820s, 114, 143
  official memorial service for, 156
  portrait, 15*f*, 153*f*
  roles inherited by, 1–2
Washington, George, 11*f*
  advice from, 10–12
  Appalachian trek with Bushrod, 16–17
  archives of, 69–71
  bequests from, 1–2, 47–48
  on brother John Augustine, 3
  burial at Mount Vernon, 74, 75*f*
  correspondence with, 22–24, 28–29, 42–43
  death of, 47–48
  on escaped slaves, 119
  as lieutenant general of new national army, 38–39
  Life of George Washington (Marshall), 67–69
  on political societies, 22–24
  relationship with, 9–12, 38
  retirement, 37, 38
Washington, John Augustine "Jack"
  death of, 24–25
  life of, 3–4
  revolutionary governance, roles in, 5–6
Washington, Lawrence Augustine, 129
Washington, Martha, 47–48
  burial at Mount Vernon, 74, 75*f*
  death of, 66–67
Washington, Mary Ball, 3–4, 9–10
Washington, West Ford, 158*f*, 159
  arrival at Mount Vernon, 1
  biography, 17–18
  portrait, 18*f*
Webster, Daniel, 109, 110*f*, 134
Wertmuller, Adolf Ulrik, 11*f*
Wilson, James, 9, 12–13, 40–41, 139–40
Wolcott, Alexander, 99
Wolcott, Oliver, 50–51
women's suffrage movement, and *Corfield v. Coryell*, 140–42, 141*f*
Woodhull, Victoria, 140, 141*f*
Worthington v. Preston, 119–20
Wythe, George, 6–8, 7*f*, 26

youth and childhood, 5–6

www.ingramcontent.com/pod-product-compliance
Ingram Content Group UK Ltd.
Pitfield, Milton Keynes, MK11 3LW, UK
UKHW041433160926
475595UK00019B/15

9 780190 947040